INSTITUTION BUILDING

Melvin G. Blase

INSTITUTION BUILDING
A Source Book
Revised Edition

University of Missouri Press
Columbia, 1986

Library of Congress Cataloging-in-Publication Data

Blase, Melvin G.
   Institution building,

   Includes index.
   1. Institution building—Abstracts.   I. Title.
HM101.B613 1985   016.306   85–50911
ISBN 0–8262–0479–1

∞™ This paper meets the minimum requirements of the American National Standard for Permanence of Paper for Printed Library Materials, Z39.48, 1984.

The revision of this book was financed under Contract No. DAN-0000-00-C-2075-00 between the Agency of International Development, U.S. Department of State and the author. The original writing of this book was financed jointly under Contract No. AID/csd-3392 between the Agency for International Development, U.S. Department of State, and the author and by a grant from MUCIA's Program for Advanced Study in Institution Development and Technical Assistance Methodology, which is funded by a 211d grant from U.S. AID. Contractors undertaking projects under government sponsorship are encouraged to express freely their professional judgment in the conduct of the project. Points of view or opinions stated do not, therefore, necessarily represent official AID position or policy.

To my wife Betty
  whose inspiration made the book conceivable
        and
to my son Larry
  whose untiring work made it a reality

Preface to the Revised Edition

Source Books become outdated and the first edition of this one was no exception. Hence, the Board for International Food and Agricultural Development (BIFAD) and USAID have financed this revision. In an effort to make it as current as possible, the approach used to prepare the first edition was duplicated. The result is two new chapters, one at the beginning and one at the end of the book. In addition, selected contributions have been added to Chapter 4.

Revisions such as this are possible only with the assistance of many people. The list of survey respondents, to each of whom I owe a debt of thanks, has grown too long to reproduce. The BIFAD staff, especially Dr. Jean Weideman, has been extremely helpful. But, as those of you who are authors know, most of the thanks have to be reserved for one's own family. In my case, the one to be singled out from that special group is my oldest son, Larry. He helped with the first edition as an early teenager by running the photocopy machine. But as a recent college graduate, his contribution to this edition warrants co-authorship if that were possible. I hope the institution builders who read this edition receive as much satisfaction seeing institutions grow and develop as I have from seeing that happen to my son.

M. G. B.
Columbia, Missouri
1985

Preface to the First Edition

In the slightly more than two decades since the phrase *institution building* was coined, a proliferation of literature has emerged bearing this nomenclature. Unfortunately, such literature is widely scattered and highly diffused. Hence, its impact has been reduced substantially.

The poor use of the institution building literature has many facets. Because it is so far flung, many practitioners engaged in institution building efforts are neither aware of much of its existence nor able to acquire readily copies of that with which they are acquainted. Likewise, academicians apparently are making inefficient use of the literature. Scholars tend to write in discipline-oriented journals and their reading habits generally are focused on their disciplines. They are thus unaware of and, consequently, do not make full use of relevant information found in disciplines outside their own. Finally, in light of the problems of acquainting both practitioners and academicians with the literature, the exchange of institution building literature between them hardly can be expected to be satisfactory. This source book is designed to overcome some of these problems.

Much of the institution building literature is in mimeographed form, which both restricts its circulation and increases the chances of its being lost. These unpublished manuscripts, in addition to those in journal or book form, were sought and are summarized in this book. Further, the MUCIA (Midwest Universities Consortium for International Activities, Inc.) project, of which this effort is a part, is making provisions for not only retaining but also duplicating and distributing all manuscripts reviewed herein as well as future additions to the literature. (To obtain such literature, see the reverse of the title page of this book.)

In the preparation of this book an effort has been made to glean significant, relevant concepts and research findings from psychology, anthropology, sociology, political science, economics, social psychology, management, agricultural economics, communications, rural sociology, business administration, and community development. No pretext is made that the works cited herein exhaust all of the insights

ix

that could be of value in building institutions. However, for the first time an effort has been made to identify and summarize in a systematic way the most important contributions in these disciplines to the institution building literature.

THE APPROACH

To assume that any one individual is capable of identifying all the components of the diverse literature on institution building would be naive indeed. Consequently, the methodology upon which this work is based is premised on the assumptions that the literature central to any discipline or subdiscipline is defined by the professionals actively engaged in that field and, then, that identifying the central institution building literature should be accomplished by contacting knowledgeable practitioners and academicians working in the area. Therefore, the professionals known to be engaged actively in the institution building field were mailed questionnaires along with lists of publications previously compiled from the two consortia projects completed in the field of institution building, i.e., the reports of the Inter-University Research Program in Institution Building (IRPIB) and the Committee on Institutional Cooperation-Agency for International Development (CIC-AID) Rural Development Research Project. The respondents were asked to do three things. First, they were asked to add to the list citations they felt were central to the institution building literature. Second, they were asked to designate works they felt had made significant contributions to the central literature, regardless of whether or not they had resulted from one of the consortia projects. Third, they were asked to provide names and addresses of other professionals actively working in the institution building field to whom they felt similar questionnaires should be sent. As a result, the list of respondents was expanded substantially beyond those whose active work was known to the author and representatives of the sponsoring agencies.

Many of the successful results of the survey are credited to the following individuals who contributed substantive suggestions and comments concerning the project: M. Ahmed, Bruce Anderson, Eric Ashby, G. S. Aurora, George H. Axinn, I. L. Baldwin, David E. Bell, Eduardo S. Bello, Gail Benjamin, Hans C. Blaise, Davis B. Bobrow, J. C. Caldwell, Harry L. Case, Harvey Choldin, Kamla Chowdhry, Nicolos J. Demerath, Joseph W. Eaton, Milton J. Esman, Herman Fel-

Contents

but also to partially related manuscripts.

This organization should facilitate the use of this part of the book by many types of readers. A few hypothetical uses will be mentioned for illustrative purposes. Practitioners interested in building an institution of a particular type are directed to the summaries classified as institutional-organizational in chapters 1 and 2, as well as those categorized according to their type of institution in the first section of chapter 3. Administrators interested in regional and worldwide cross-sectional analyses are urged to review the first chapters in their entirety and read carefully the second portion of chapter 3, dealing with cross-sectional studies. Academicians desirous of some knowledge of the institution building literature in its entirety—including partially related, supporting works—are encouraged to read Part I in its entirety. Suffice it to say, Part I has been designed to enable the reader to focus on selected sources, thereby justifying the title, Institution Building: A Source Book.

To further facilitate the acquisition of information by readers, summary statements have been constructed in a somewhat unusual manner. First, where individual authors have made multiple contributions of a highly similar nature, only the most complete statement has been summarized and citations to the other contributions have been cross-referenced to that manuscript. Second, the length of individual summary statements largely reflects the contributions made to the field of institution building. In chapters 1 and 2 sufficient details have been provided in the summaries to enable the reader to glean the most important, substantive aspects of the manuscript with regard to institution building. In chapter 3 important contributions relevant to institution building have also been summarized quite thoroughly. Justification for these procedures lies in the desire to make the source book perform the function its title suggests.

1
The Essential Core of the Literature, 1973–1983

One of the basic problems this Source Book is designed to solve is the scattered nature of the literature. The difficulty obtaining copies of some of the current literature undoubtedly results in it being underutilized. The problem is so severe that many practitioners are unaware that much of the valuable literature even exists. Efforts made during the past year to identify and obtain copies of important parts of the literature suggest that the problem has grown worse since the first edition was published. This may be due to the fact there are no longer any focal points as dominant as IRPIB and the CIC-AID project were in the decades of the 1950s and 1960s. Nevertheless, the recent literature is rich with insights, especially those works concerning micro aspects found in the first chapter of this book.

Although not as voluminous, the macro oriented literature summarized in the second part of the chapter is worthy of attention. Clearly, Ruttan's recent work is quite helpful in gaining a more complete understanding of the direction of development in developing countries. It, as well as many of the summaries in the micro section of the book, e.g., those by Korten, are commended to the reader.

MICRO-ORIENTED LITERATURE

[1] KORTEN, David C. "Community Organization and Rural Development: A Learning Process Approach." *Public Administration Review* (September/October 1980), 480–511.

The editor's note that prefaces this article states:

This study combines both extensive and intensive analysis of development assistance programs in Asia, and focuses specifically on five case
studies which provide the basis for the author's strong conviction that
Third World development assistance programs must be part of a holis-
tically perceived learning process as opposed to a bureaucratically mandated blueprint design . . . The real value of Korten's efforts, however,
may be found in his case studies which provide rich insights into just
what can be accomplished in the way of social development if the
development process can be viewed as a leaning experience for all
participants involved. (p. 480)

David Korten contends that insufficient attention has been given
to the difficult problems of how to involve the rural poor in their own
development, whether it be through local organizations or otherwise.
He examines past unsatisfactory experiences of cooperatives and
community development projects to involve and impact the rural
poor.

Current donor-funded projects present difficult problems.
Their solution is inhibited by programming procedures better suited
to large capital development projects than to people-centered rural
development. Lessons that continue to go unrecognized include:

(a) reliance for the planning and implementation of "participative"
    development on centralized bureaucratic organizations which have
    little capacity to respond to diverse community-defined needs or to
    build from community skills and values,

(b) inadequate investment in the difficult process of building commu-
    nity problem solving capacity,

(c) inadequate attention to dealing with social diversity and especially
    with highly stratified social structures, and,

(d) insufficient integration of the technical and social components of
    development action. (p. 483)

Accumulated experience seems to indicate that in dealing with
the poor, a redirection of funds to new categories of projects is only
part of the need. The other part is building the capacity in donor
organizations to provide assistance in ways that respond to local needs
while building local social and technical capacity. Most large donors
seem to be under substantial pressure not to follow the latter course.

Excessive pressures for immediate results, as measured by goods and services delivered, drive out attention to institution building and make it difficult to move beyond a relief and welfare approach to poverty; the distribution of food is a lot faster than teaching people how to grow it. A substantial bias toward *project* as contrasted to *program* funding compounds the problems. Projects by nature deal with time bounded start-up costs and emphasize facilities and equipment to the neglect of the development and funding of capacities for their sustained operation and maintenance. Their demands for detailed, up-front planning, coupled with rigourous adherence to fast-paced implementation schedules and pre-planned specifications, assumes task requirements are well understood when, in fact, even the nature of the problem is ill defined. Furthermore it virtually ensures that the real decisions will remain with professional technicians and government bureaucrats neither of whom are rewarded for being responsive to local conditions nor contributing toward the development of local institutional capacities. (p. 484)

Emphasis on meeting project disbursement schedules and on terminal project outcomes leads to an insistence on the creation of special project units, using special incentives to buy people away from more permanent organizations and, thus, undermining their potential for sustained long-term action. Pressures to move ever-larger amounts of money quickly without commensurate staff increases place a premium on large capital and technology intensive projects. As a consequence, heavy import components are best able to absorb such large sums of money on schedule, whereas effective work with the rural poor requires a high ratio of people to financial input; and it almost always takes longer than anticipated. When a large donor such as the World Bank operates with a few field offices, relying instead on the supervision of itinerate groups of experts with divergent views making quick judgments during short visits, there is little prospect of providing the consistent, informed, and sympathetic support required for effective institution building. (p. 484)

The author then examines five cases where participative approaches to rural development have not failed. These include the Indian National Dairy Development Board, the Sri Llankan Sarvodaya Shramadana Movement, the Bangladesh Rural Advancement Committee, the Thailand Community Based Family Planning Services, and the Philippine National Irrigation Administration Communal Irrigation Program. These five Asian cases share three characteristics in common: (1) each involves a rural development effort which seeks to engage rural people in their own advancement; (2) each is generally recognized as more successful than average development approaches; and (3) each depends on effective program action more than on a uniquely favorable setting.

After discussing the five case studies, Korten sums up:

> Each project was successful because it had worked out a program model responsive to the beneficiary needs at a particular time and place and each had built a strong organization capable of making the program work. (p. 496)

Examination of the Asian success cases suggests:

> These five programs were not designed and implemented—rather, they emerged out of a learning process in which villagers and program personnel shared their knolwedge and resources to create a program which achieved a fit between needs and capacities of the beneficiaries and those of the outsiders who were providing the assistance. Leadership, and teamwork, rather than blueprints, were the key elements. (p. 497)

Achieving a good fit between the institution and its environment through the learning process approach calls for organizations with a well-developed capacity for responsive and anticipatory adaptation—organizations that embrace error, plan with the people, and link knowledge building with action.

The learning process approach to program development consists of three stages: effectiveness, efficiency, and expansion.

> In Stage I—*learning to be effective*—the major concern is with developing a working program model in the setting of a village level learning laboratory that has a high degree of fit with beneficiary needs. Normally this phase will be resource intensive, particularly rich in its requirements for intellectual input, and will require substantial freedom from normal administrative constraints. It is a time of investment in knowledge and capacity building—learning what is required to achieve fit for a given time and setting. Not only does this stage involve basic learning about community dynamics, and even learning what are the relevant questions to be asked, but it also involves learning how to learn though an action research process. As in the beginning of any learning process it should be considered normal for error rates to be high, though on a downward trend, and efficiency low. The program begins to make the transition from Stage 1 to Stage 2 when it is found to be effective in responding to an identified need and it achieves an acceptable level of fit between beneficiaries, the working program model, and the capabilities of the action research team.
>
> In Stage 2—*learning to be efficient*—the major concern shifts to reducing the input requirements per unit of output. Through careful analysis of Stage 1 experience, extraneous activities not essential to effectiveness are gradually eliminated and the important activities routinized. While there may also be some continued gains in effectiveness with further experience, it is more likely that some loss of effectiveness will be a necessary price of increasing efficiency. In Stage 2, there should also be

serious attention paid to the problem of achieving fit between program requirements and realistically attainable organizational capacities, recognizing the organizational constraints that will have to be accepted in the course of program expansion. Modest program expansion during Stage 2 will increase the cadre of persons experienced in making the program work available to help build the expanded organizational capability required in Stage 3. Once acceptable levels of effectiveness and efficiency have been obtained, the program model reasonably stabilized, an expanded cadre trained, and basic management systems requirements worked out, then the way is prepared for transition to Stage 3.

In Stage 3—*learning to expand*—the central concern is with an orderly phased expansion of the program. The emphasis will be on expansion of organizational capacity, though continued refinements may also be required in the program to respond to the demands of larger scale operation. But constant attention must be given to ensuring that an acceptable level of fit is maintained even though expansion will mean some inevitable sacrifice in effectiveness and efficiency. The rate of expansion will be governed largely by how fast the necessary organizational capabilities can be developed to support it. By the end of Stage 3 the program should have matured to the point of a relatively stable, large-scale operation.

Once Stage 3 has been completed the organization may turn to the solution of new problems, as several of the organizations studied had started to do. Or, if by this time the beneficiary population has made such progress as to upset the fit previously attained, there may be need to repeat the learning cycle to redefine the program and realign organizational capabilities accordingly. (pp. 499–501)

The author concludes:

The concepts and methods of the blueprint approach may be more of a hindrance than an aid in the programming of effective rural development action where the need is for an adaptive, bottom-up process of program and organizational development through which an adequate fit may be achieved between beneficiary needs, program outputs, and organizational competence. (p. 502)

[2] KORTEN, David C., and Alfonso, Felipe B., eds. *Bureaucracy and the Poor: Closing the Gap.* West Hartford: Kumarian Press, 1983. 258 pages.

In 1977 an informal collegial association, the Management Institutes Working Group of Social Development, was formed. The group was composed of professionals from the Asian Institute of Management in Manila (AIM), the Indian Institute of Management at

Ahmedabad (IIMA), the Instituto Centroamericano de Administracion de Emprisas in Managua (INCAE), and the Instituto de Estudios Superiores de Administracion in Caracas (IESA).

> In early 1979 AIM hosted a meeting of the Working Group in Manila. At the earlier meeting in Caracas there had been substantial discussion of the limitations of the conventional management concepts and methods of either enterprise or public management in addressing the needs of social development. Thus it was decided that the Manila meeting should concentrate on gleaning insights from the action research efforts of the member schools toward more adequate conceptual frameworks. This was the mandate to which the contributors to this volume were responding. Each prepared a paper which was discussed in Manila and then subjected to extensive revision for this volume. (p. xvi)

This book examines development management based on the central theme of the need to develop the capacities of development bureaucracies. Korten emphasizes using social learning approaches to empower people and communities as the prime movers of development process. The editors state:

> Recognition is growing rapidly that broadly based people-centered development will not be achieved without the significant reorientation of development bureaucracies, and the emergence of a new development management attended to this need. (preface)

This publication consists of seven parts. Part 1 relates the results of a study of five Central American countries. In the early 1970s they embarked on holistic rural development strategies intended to simultaneously achieve growth, well being, equity, and participation. This study shows a number of ways in which the structures of organizations, through which the new strategies were implemented, largely defeated the intentions of the planners.

Part 2 discusses the structural and managerial role requirements of programs that depend on collaborative inputs from a number of individual agencies.

The need for reform of the "meta-structures" that provide the framework for rural development policy and action is considered in Part 4. This is done by contrasting the requirements for flexible location specific interdisciplinary action with the Indian government's existing planning and implementing structures and by pointing out a number of needed reforms. The need for reform of the meta-structures is also demonstrated in the case of Tanzania, which embarked on a radical reform of its political and administrative structures to address problems similar to those in India.

Part 5 examines the biases of policy analysts, demonstrating how planners might benefit from being more sensitive to the behavior of the poor as consumers.

In Part 6 two authors each develop a theme that cuts across the earlier chapters, "one providing a managerial perspective on the problems of community participation, and the other examining advances being made toward development of more people centered development programming methodologies" (p. xvii).

Finally, Part 7 refocuses on the Third World management initiatives that have produced the studies reported in this volume. Korten suggests that their longer term success in contributing to the development of new management technologies for social development may require important changes in their own internal structures. Many times these changes may be as difficult as those the institutes call for in the governments they are advising.

In Chapter 1, Ickis discusses the performance of an organization as a function of the fit between strategy and its structure. In the absence of appropriate supporting reforms in the structure of the implementing institutions, policy changes should be introduced by the central planners, Ickis feels that more attention needs to be given to the reform of government structures. He goes on to suggest that such reforms should be an "integral part of efforts to introduce basic reorientations in development strategies toward more holistic outcomes and that effective leadership at both institutional and supra-institutional levels is crucial to the accomplishment of those reforms" (p. 3).

Ickis concludes that there is a need to build the capacity of action agencies to work in a supportive interactive mode with their client populations, rather than relying on the application of more sophisticated methods for pre-planning of development action or on conventional management training to build implementation skills. The key input to this capacity-building process is effective leadership by individuals who understand the nature of the problems and who are willing to make strong personal commitments to problem resolution. Planners and management specialists have the responsibility to facilitate the emergence of such leadership.

> The next two chapters report experiences involving attempts to develop within a single agency a new competence in responding to the needs

of rural populations. The first report, by Rushikesh Maru, deals with the Community Health Worker (CHW) scheme in India; the second, by Felipe Alfonso, with assistance to farmer run communal irrigation associations in the Philippines. Both illustrate in detail the problem encountered when the task requirements of programs addressed to the rural poor are at odds with the culture and structure of the organizations assigned to implement them; and point to the need for sustained investment in the development of organizations with cultures and structures supportive of the new definition of the task.

In both of the cases examined there was early recognition of the problem, but the ways in which the two agencies studied chose to address it were quite different. The leaders of the Indian health system hoped that by making the newly appointed CHWs responsible to local village councils they would create an intentional conflict within the health system, forcing a change in the values and operating styles of its personnel toward greater response to community health needs, particularly in the area of preventive health. But community leaders also defined local health priorities in terms of curative rather than preventive services. Furthermore the balance of power clearly rested with the clinic personnel who in most cases quickly co-opted the new CHWs and turned them into extensions of the clinic system to assist in meeting the clinic's centrally defined performance targets. The CHWs did contribute to increases in clinic performance as a result of the insights they provided other health personnel into community response to available services. But in terms of mobilizing community participation to deal with community health issues, especially those involving prevention and health education, the effort seemed to have little prospect of success. Maru proposes a number of structural reforms intended to limit the control exercised over the CHW program by medical personnel, but he concludes that needed attention to preventive health promotion cannot come through structural innovations alone and that a massive educational effort is required, directed not only to local leaders, but also to the personnel of the health system itself.

The leaders of the Philippines National Irrigation Administration (NIA) chose a learning process model of organizational change over the conflict model chosen by the Indian Health Ministry. Their first step was to try out participative methods of assistance to farmer-irrigator groups on two pilot sites to gain experience and an initial understanding of unanticipated problems. This provided a basis for identifying needed refinements in field methods and in the agency's supporting systems prior to large-scale implementation. Looking at this initial experience Alfonso suggests that the changes which will be required to support the new participative methods are quite comprehensive—touching every level and function of the organization—but the prospective returns from the improved capacity of farmer controlled organizations to provide their members with reliable irrigation service are equally substantial. (pp. 33–34)

Part 3, entitled "Managing Multi-Agency Programs," contains four chapters. In the first and second chapters the reader is provided with an insight into the nature of the system manager's job and the strong parallels between the roles of top- and middle-level system managers.

In the third chapter of this section Staia reports that in India middle managers perform mainly a post-office function; in other words, they merely pass information back and forth from their superiors to their subordinates. The author goes on to recommend a re-definition of the role of middle management. In his new role the middle manager would concentrate on identifying and analyzing the needs of defined populations, and on developing lateral linkages with other district level agencies as required to carry out coordinated efforts to address them. His job would become one of managing population changes.

In the fourth chapter of this section the authors examine the use of a convenience center to offer a wide range of government services to residents of urban squatter communities. The authors feel that when properly used these centers have the opportunity to make each of the service agencies more responsive to their clientele, to revitalize local government, and to facilitate local residents taking a more active role in improving the conditions of life within their community. "The key to this in their view is to upgrade the role of the module administrator to make him an effective development systems manager committed to building both the horizontal and vertical linkages required for more effective support of local initiatives" (p. 55).

Part 4, entitled "Managing Meta-Structures and Processes," consists of two chapters that discuss the important contributions toward advancing understanding of the relationship between meta-structures and development strategies. Both chapters point out a distinction between two contrasting ways to approach planning for poverty-focused rural development. The first approach concentrates on determining what types of development projects should receive priority in development funding. The second concentrates on reforming the structures governing the process by which such project choices are made.

Part 5 is entitled "The Need for New Planning Frameworks."

The following chapter by Labdhi Bhandari takes these frameworks as its central concern, illustrating how poverty focused planning might benefit from the methods of consumer analysis. He begins with the

observation that efforts in India to improve the well being of the poor
have been demonstrable failures, with the proportions of the rural
population living below the line of absolute poverty in fact growing
from 1960 to 1974. He examines specific government policies on food
distribution and the production of basic commodities to demonstrate
how they have been ineffective and in some instances even counter-
productive in responding to the needs of the poor.

Searching for an explanation, Bhandari points out three implicit planning biases which have limited the effectiveness of government policies.

(1) A greater concern for the individual as producer than as consumer.

(2) A faith that increased purchasing power will automatically translate
    into improved living conditions.

(3) An assumed preference for urban or Western values. He suggests
    that a more effective attack on poverty must proceed from a well-
    developed understanding of how the poor—appropriately disag-
    gregated by demographic, socio-economic and cultural charac-
    teristics—in fact fulfill the spectrum of their human needs. He
    argues that such understanding will increase substantially prospects
    for designing policy interventions which recognize the poor as
    whole persons, reflect their true value preferences, address actual
    needs, and place a greater range of choice within their means. (pp.
    163–64)

Part 6, entitled "Helping the Poor Help Themselves," contains
two chapters. In the first chapter Frances Korten "reviews the inherent limitations of centralized, service-delivery approaches to benefit-
ing rural and urban poor; inventories the obstacles to more participatory approaches posed by the institutional frameworks of the
individual implementing agency, the community, and the broader
society; and suggests guidelines for actions appropriate to each obstacle" (pp. 179–80).

In the second chapter Korten examines the argument that social development calls for new methods of development programming that build from an understanding of the real needs and resources of the poor, as well as for a special type of development
manager.

Part 7 is entitled "Postscript: Knowledge Building Institutions
for Social Development":

The need to re-examine structures in the light of new strategies does
not apply alone to the public and private agencies directly engaged in
holistic social development field operations. Institutions engaged in
research and training in management and in the social and physical
sciences which chose to assume effective roles in support of such agen-

cies may find as well that they are in effect embarking on new strategies which call for re-examination of their internal structures. Specifically they may find that their past roles have consisted mainly of the transfer of existing technologies, including routine application in the name of research of standardized research methodologies, whereas the new strategy calls for them to create new knowledge, even new research methodologies more appropriate to the task at hand. Successful transition from technology transfer to true knowledge building may require substantial re-orientation in their own internal structures and reward systems. (p. 223)

[3] DUNCAN, Richard L. *Institution Building Incidents, Ideas, and Applications. An Experimental Guidebook in Scholar-Practitioner Communication.* Washington, D.C.: U.S. Agency for International Development, U.S. Department of State. Final Report Contract No. AID/ta-c-1069, March 25, 1975. 79 pages.

Duncan summarizes the publication as follows:

Essentially the Guidebook is composed of incidents drawn from actual cases of development put together in the form of composite cases: institution building perspectives on those cases; and checklists of items that you might want to consider in institution building situations. Appendix I contains short statements about some of the important things that we have learned from institution building research conducted over the past 10 years. These are divided according to the different variables in the model. Finally, Appendix II has a short bibliography which contains some basic references. (p. 1)

The author uses the term *organization* as the intermediate criteria from which measurements may be devised for each case.

An organization is considered to be institutionalized when there is reasonable evidence that:

(a) it has survived over a period of time, i.e., it continues to do what it was designed to do;

(b) it has achieved a degree of autonomy in determining its program via budgetary means or through the influence of its leadership;

(c) it is accepted and valued by its clientele, by the public and by its cooperators and competitors as a part of the environment;

(d) it has some impact on the environment, i.e., the changes it sponsors are tolerated, if not applauded and possibly even copied. (p. 5)

The author goes on to make some comments concerning culture.

> The doctrine factor of the internal variables and the normative linkages
> variable are particularly influenced by the cultural factors of each situa-
> tion. For that reason, there are no easy formulas about how new ideas
> which imply different doctrines can be introduced into developing
> countries. (p. 5)

The practitioner has to be alert to cultural elements that underlie the
rational arguments presented by those involved in the institution
building process. For example, this publication emphasizes common
elements in the culture of bureaucracy which cut across culture. Illustrations include the closeness of family, school, or tribal ties; the
significance of political relationships to development decisions; and
resentment, open or covert, to outside interference in the bureaucratic process. A second common element is the development culture that
has evolved in developing countires. This development culture has
an interest and a stake in change and modernization processes.

> It is extremely important, however, to distinguish between what we
> might call the symbolic modernist . . . who believes that every change,
> or every tool of developed society should be incorporated—and the
> development professional. The latter understands the need for change,
> but also the need for its careful adaptation to the cultural value of his
> own environment. This is not always an easy distinction. (p. 6)

The institution building process has been divided into four
stages: initiation, consolidation of early gains, maturity, and rejuvenation. For each stage, there is a composite case illustrating the institution building process. Each is followed by one way an analyst using the
Institution Building (I.B.) model developed by Esman, et al., might
look at that case. Finally, there is a checklist of items that may need to
be considered in that stage of the process.

The first composite case is entitled "Phase I Starting Out In
Tantla." This case examines discontinuous leadership, bureaucratic
maneuvering, and the trials and tribulations of getting a planning
board established. This case leads to some perspectives and questions
about the problems of introducing complex new ideas into equally
complex governmental structures.

The second case is entitled "Phase II Consolidating Early Gains
in Carlovingia." This case examines the difficulties of expanding
small programs. It emphasizes how important time and patience can
be in building resources and linkages. Institution building should not
be viewed as a political quick fix; rather it is people committed to
innovative doctrines. But it takes much more than people committed
to doctrine if failure is to be averted and small successes are to be

expanded on a national scale.

The third case is entitled "Phase III Maturity In Longoria." This case considers how years of struggle, crisis, war, politics, and administrative change can lead to a situation that looks like success. Closer examination, however, reveals new problems and expectations that offer challenges for the future.

The fourth case is entitled "Phase IV Rejuvenation in Kashvar." In this case, evidence is provided that new organizations do not always succeed. Further, it illustrates that major changes in old organizations can take place if the circumstances warrant and the institution building skills are applied to the problems. In this case, the struggles of a hypothetical Ministry of Education bring the problem into focus. The point emerges that the age of the institution is not as important as whether the analytical tools developed by institution builders help organizations deal with problems of the society.

After each of the above cases, there are questions (checklist) concerning the major components of the I.B. model: leadership, doctrine, program, resources, internal structure, enabling linkages, functional linkages, normative linkages, and diffuse linkages. These questions are designed to help the practitioner grasp the perspectives of I. B. that are illustrated in the composite cases.

After discussing the composite cases, the author provides an extensive examination of the internal variables of the I. B. model in Appendix 1(a). The following list summarizes his perspectives for each of the five internal variables.

Leadership:

(1) Leadership delivers resources.

(2) Leadership promotes the doctrine internally and externally.

(3) Leadership keeps the internal structure functioning.

(4) Leadership mobilizes the organization to accomplish the program.

(5) Leadership establishes and cements linkages with external groups.

(6) Leadership is alert to opportunities to incorporate new groups for support, output, and acceptance. (p. 57)

Doctrine:

(1) Doctrine dramatizes the new idea as well as innovation and change.

(2) Doctrine helps to sell a program and organization with it.

(3) Doctrine defines the goals.

(4) Doctrine can generate support.

(5) Doctrine helps define and limit internal and external conflict.

(6) Doctrine absorbs ideas and needs and combines them with new ones to make the organization acceptable in the society. (p. 60)

Program:

(1) Program provides impact in the environment.

(2) Program provides visibility.

(3) Program provides vital contact with the environment.

(4) Program is the ultimate testing ground for output.

(5) Program promotes support by the environment of the organization.

(6) Program provides a specific focus for change-oriented activities.

(7) Program provides an identity for clientele and staff and ultimately for the society. (p. 63)

Resources

(1) Resource mobilization involves using old and new sources.

(2) Resource mobilization involves a wide variety of elements, money, people, technology, etc.

(3) Resources hold the organization together until it can become accepted.

(4) Resources provide internal strength and cohesion in the organization.

(5) Resources contribute to autonomy. (p. 66)

Internal Structure:

(1) Internal structure is a key to converting resources to program.

(2) Internal structure is a base for organization mobilization.

(3) Internal structure is a device for demonstrating innovative capacity.

(4) Internal structure is a means for reflecting goals and doctrine.

(5) Internal structure provides a means for resolving internal conflict. (p. 68)

In Appendix 1(b), the author explores the concept of institutional linkages. The following summarizes the author's findings for each of the four institutional linkages.

Enabling Linkages:

(1) Enabling Linkages provide power to act.

(2) Enabling Linkages provide protection.

(3) Enabling Linkages provide initial resources.

(4) Enabling Linkages support a new public image. (p. 71)

Normative Linkages:

(1) Normative Linkages show what values must be observed.

(2) Normative Linkages define relationships with other organizations.

(3) Normative Linkages can help legitimized activities.

(4) Normative Linkages can provide support in making new ideas fit present values.

(5) Normative Linkages provide the framework for defining objectives in the national institutional structure. (p. 73)

Functional Linkages:

(1) Functional Linkages provide inputs the organization needs to function.

(2) Functional Linkages promote the use of what the organization does.

(3) Functional Linkages help define program boundaries.

(4) Functional Linkages reinforce the effect on organizational clientele.

(5) Functional Linkages provide opportunities for mutually beneficial support in the environment. (p. 75)

Diffuse Linkages:

(1) Diffuse Linkages broaden the base of support.

(2) Diffuse Linkages strengthen the public image of the organization.

(3) Diffuse Linkages help reinforce acceptance by the society.

(4) Diffuse Linkages provide alliances with other change-oriented groups.

(5) Diffuse Linkages promote an understanding in the society of the goals of the organization. (p. 77)

Appendix 2 consists of a short bibliography that contains basic references.

This publication is an excellent guide for the novice practitioner. It is written in straightforward, easy-to-understand language that eliminates much of the ambiguity found in some of the institution building literature.

[4] UNITED Nations, Department of Technical Co-operation for Development. *Elements of Institution-Building for Institutes of Public Administration and Management.* (ST/ESA/SER.E/25), 1982. 41 pages.

This publication is comprised of papers taken from two conferences attended by two United Nations Expert Groups. The first conference took place in December 1977 to discuss institution building for planned development. The follow-up conference took place in June 1979 and focused on the issue of institution building for organizations involved in management development. "While there was concern for the internal efficiency of such organizations, the main emphasis was on their capability and effectiveness for development purposes" (p. 1).

Planned development efforts seem to require at least a minimum amount of administrative support, including the capability to collect, synthesize, and analyse information as a basis for planning. Information requirements for planning concern (1) the task environment, (2) target areas of planned interventions, and (3) possible methods of action and evaluation. Effective development planning also requires an ability to relate needed information about the environment and the potentialities for intervention. The conferences stressed that institution building for planned development begins with efforts to create the necessary mechanisms for effective planning and synthesizing of information.

> Specifically, this study attempts to abridge and amalgamate the two expert group discussions in such a way as to present conceptual knowledge and point out workable strategies that might assist practitioners to deal with organizational and environmental problems in their institution-building efforts. It also points out functions, objectives, and programmes of management development organizations and indicates ways and means of ensuring their effectiveness for development purposes. (p. 1)

In Chapter 1, entitled "A Conception of Organization and Institution," the authors suggest that governments in developing countries aim to make organizations effective instruments for societal change and development. "Institution-building is therefore tacitly accepted as a major effort for promoting consistent accelerated economic, social and political progress" (p. 3).

The purposes of institution building are to introduce, foster, and guide more efficient social changes and new patterns of individual and group relations in government agencies and in industry. Institution builders face two tasks: to simultaneously build a viable organization and to manage the linkages with other organizations on which the institution must depend for resources and support.

> The main goal in achieving developmental targets is the accomplishment of institutionality, measured by steady growth of organizational capability, penetration of the relevant environment (producing and protecting desired changes, philosophies, systems, and behavior in governmental and national organizations), by maintaining their innovative thrust. (p. 3)

Institution builders are responsible for making things happen and not merely for responding to pressures. To avoid this tendency to respond to pressure, the institution builder must choose deliberate strategies of action and tactics and to implement them as he learns from experience. But institution builders must be prepared to revise their strategies and even their goals in order to cope with unexpected problems or to take advantage of fresh opportunities.

Institution building is the possible consequence or effect of deliberate action.

> The word *institution* is sometimes used as a synonym for *organization*. This is acceptable, if we recognize that an institution includes more than formal structure and process. Institutions may be regarded as regulative principles which organize most of the activities of individuals in a system or society into some definite organizational patterns from the point of view of some of the perennial, basic problems of any society or ordered social life. (p. 4)

> A significant body of writing on the subject agrees generally with the following dimensions of the problem of institution-building: to build or change an institution is to establish a stable set of desired behaviours in a particular place and time. To do this, it is necessary to get people to accept certain norms or standards and to pattern their behaviours to fit these norms which must be grounded in some underlying regulative principles. The hub of the task of building (or changing) institutions is to establish a combination of behaviours—norms—regulative principles which will serve developmental aims. Institution-building is indirect because it involves changing or creating values as well as behaviour. It may involve undermining and replacing existing norms which may have proved inimical, or a liability, to development and societal well-being. If institution-building is not simple to understand, it is often even harder to do. (p. 5)

An institution's activities are justified and ordered by norms linked to basic principles of the social system. Norms have two values:

> (1) They guide behavior which is useful in the system because they are functional or practical; (2) They are also proper; they are justified because they reflect more basic values or principles. (p. 5)

The strength of norms stems from two sources, *practical workability* and *merit*.

> Leaders (who are change agents) in institution-building begin by identifying the need for improved conditions in a social system. They then try to find a way to meet this need, by creating new conditions or outcomes in society, through effective patterns of action. In such efforts two related value problems are involved. One is to get the values produced by the intervention accepted within the system. The other is to design an intervention whose internal norms are acceptable as well as effective. Leaders often assume that (1) the aims and effects they propose are good and will be valued within the social system; therefore (2) that the means they propose will likewise be valued as instruments of a desirable end; and therefore (3) that the rules or norms included in the means will tend to be accepted without serious resistance.

> Hence the process of institutionalization is not a simple, linear function. There are interruptions, retreats, accommodations, regroupings, divisions, and emergence of secondary goals, amended objectives and even altered doctrines. Be that as it may, an institution must embody changes in values, functions, physical and/or social technology; it should establish, foster and protect normative relationships and action patterns and it should attain support and complementarity in the environment. It should survive the vicissitudes of time and emerge as a vibrant innovative "institution," capable of withstanding the stresses of turbulent periods, and as an instrument for accelerated development. (p. 6)

In Chapter 3, the authors turn their attention to the topic of power: "In a normative approach to institution building, the primacy of articulated and internalized values of the 'powerful' is an inescapable reality" (p. 9).

If institutional change is induced, the types of power that may be brought to bear on an objective can range from stark coercion to education that changes the awareness and value orientations of its clients. Some instruments of power include strong leadership, control of resources, positive and negative sanctions, promotion of such latent regulative principles as progress and prestige, and various incentives. When the objective is to change the institutional patterns of a target group, one important source of power is the ability to reduce the risk associated with changes in behavior patterns.

> Coercion can be used to eliminate an institutionalized interest, but not as the primary mechanism for creating a new one. Education may be used as an instrument of power, not only to create technical efficacy but to change the sense of identity and the value orientations of participants. Trustworthy appeals to self-interest are powerful ways to induce the acceptance of new norms. (pp. 9–10)

In Chapter 4, entitled "Whole System or Step-by-Step Change," the authors state:

> When the scope of an action extends across the line between a bureaucracy and its environment, institutionalization can be quite difficult. For example, an agricultural development progamme may combine efforts from a number of parts of the bureaucracy, in the ministries of agriculture and finance and elsewhere, to provide information, credit, and materials. This public sector activity must be mated with the behaviours of farmers, marketing organizations, and perhaps, local community leaders. The bureaucratic aspect of the programme may require, along with careful planning, co-ordination and funds, some important changes in values. Bureaucrats, who may be accustomed to acting on the basis of authority and inclined to be ignorant of the problems and realities of the peasantry, will have to adopt new norms, a desire to understand the farmers and a willingness to promote their well-being. None of this will make much difference unless the programme appeals to, perhaps even changes the norms and behaviours of, the target population and other important people such as farmers or merchants. The family itself may be institutionalized around a farming tradition. Certain work may be proper for the men or for the women. The community structure may be arranged in terms of traditional rights and obligations, and the programme may threaten that tradition. (p. 12)

In Chapter 5, entitled "Some Pertinent Environmental Constraints and Issues," the authors explain:

> Public institutions can be differentiated into those forming the public bureaucracy and those others functioning under public sponsorship or support to achieve other economic and social goals. The public bureaucracy is a necessary institutional device required for progress and survival. The institutional role of governments is preponderant but not absolute. The bureaucratic institution exists not on the sufferance of governments but in partnership with governments. The situation varies, however, from one country to another, and constitutes a national specificity of institutional modes peculiar to each country. Yet another dynamic aspect lies in the institutional task system itself. For example,

PART I
A Descriptive Bibliography of the
Central Literature on Institution Building

GUIDE TO PART I

A special effort has been made in this book to facilitate the acquisition of information by widely differing classes of readers. Thus, the book is divided first into parts, and the parts into chapters. Part I contains chapters 1, 2, 3, and 4. The first chapter contains the essential core of the literature published in the last decade. Chapter 2 contains the essential core literature published prior to 1973. All readers are urged to give these chapters their attention. However, those readers who have very clearly defined interests and do not want to read the entire chapters can choose between the summaries concerning the micro (institutional-organizational) aspects of institution building and those dealing with the macro (interinstitutional) aspects, e.g., the role of institutions in the process of economic development.

The remaining central literature is classified in chapter 3 first on the basis of date publication. Second, it is categorized on the basis of whether the focus of analysis was an individual institution (case study), a cross section of institutions, or some other focus. Readers concerned with building a specific type of institution may want to review the summaries of analyses of that type only and skip the remainder of the chapter. Regardless, the summaries in this chapter emphasize concepts of special interest to institution builders rather than constitue all-inclusive reviews of the works cited.

Finally, chapter 4 contains citations to supporting literature. These may be of interest especially to academicians seeking an inclusive set of citations not only to the central literature presented in the earlier chapters

1

in the field of rural development, at a particular stage of development, production and productivity may acquire primacy over other considerations. The institutions concerned can, in the process, acquire "growth" values as their key impetus. At another stage of development, distributive justice may come to be of crucial relevance. However, it is often the experience that the "growth" values do not transcend into "developmental" values. There arises in this context a dilemma: whether new institutions are to be created or whether situational imperatives are to be brought to bear upon older institutions to respond to the needs. It seems that there are no either-or options. (p. 14)

In Chapter 6, entitled "Institutional Change and Demands on Institutional Leadership," the authors examine some of the characteristics a leader must possess in order to continually motivate an organization. It is continuity of effective leadership that affects staff performance and overall organizational effectiveness. It is the leader's responsibility to develop incentives for the motivation of staff personnel. The word *incentive* here refers to the full set of factors that shape human behavior within organizations, including norms, standards, and motivational and material rewards.

The authors go on to discuss the problem of inducing desired behavior to create and design organizations compatible with existing potentiality. One part of this problem is that the internalization of new value systems and the establishment of technological norms and standards of performance take time. This length of time affects the willingness of politicians to initiate or support a reform scheme. "Strong and persistent political support is necessary if institutionalization is to be successful" (p. 17). Organizational inertia is also an important incentive factor that relates to time.

> Any organization, once established, resists change. A new institution requires time to become stable. Yet administrative reform institutions are expected to be both change-inducing and viable. This often creates a conflict and may preclude the prospect of long-standing developmental institutions. (p. 17)

In Chapter 8, entitled "Issues of Institutional Support and its Effects," the authors examine the need for external support for the institution.

> Support for an organization may be divided into two categories, namely: the kind of support which essentially accords recognition of an organization and acceptance of its right to exist; and the kind which might be labeled material and which consists of a flow of resources which the organization uses to carry on its existence. (p. 21)

> For purposes of institution-building, this distinction between acceptance and material support is particularly useful in thinking about the long-term existence and effectiveness of an administrative reform agency or a public administration institute. Legitimation as a basis for securing support is essentially a rational-legal approach to the issue, and may consist simply of the statutory enactments by the legislative authority. There is, simultaneously, an emotive aspect to the support base. With special historical heritage, cultural uniqueness, and other social ties and ramifications in the developing countries, the support base for institution-building will involve, equally forcefully, the emotional components. (p. 21)

There are two problems with attempting to obtain initial legitimation or "foundational" support. One problem is determining how much to promise, i.e., how much to represent in the way of the future results, in order to gain the necessary initial support. The other problem is the status and behavior of a leader seeking to establish or reform an existing institution. This status and behavior may differ strikingly from later requirements for the sort of leadership that can influence the flow of material support.

> Management is a two-phased activity. One phase is directed internally, to shape, guide, direct and assess the inside workings of an organization. The other phase of management is concerned with maximizing the relations between the organization and its environment. This is sometimes referred to as working at the "institutional" level of the organization. The essential task of institutional management is to influence, as much as possible, the interaction of the organization and its environment, to promote both the survival and the effectiveness of that agency. This task requires, first of all, the ability to perceive and interpret the environment. The absence of this competence is like flying blind, without map or instruments. In the real world of action, however, knowledge alone does not suffice. Institutional management includes the ability to act, taking a pro-active stance with respect to environmental elements. Or, it may be more a matter of making internal adjustments to inexorable external realities. (p. 23)

Conclusions and Recommendations

The two Groups of Experts that met in 1977 and 1979 on institution-building for development decided to highlight several specific conclusions and recommendations which had featured most prominently in their discussions. These are summarized below:

(1) Although a number of developing countries have made substantial progress in increasing their supply of competent managers by establishing a variety of management development institutions, some of these institutions have failed to play decisive roles in the over-all

national development process. In view of the importance of management in national development, all institutions concerned with
management development should be made to play a strategic role
in the national development scene.

In particular, instead of isolating themselves from the public systems
that they seek to influence, they should actively promote a view of
public management to be shared effectively by the political leadership,
development planners and public managers.

(2) Management development comprises more than the mere organization of training courses. It involves intensive and extensive ac-
culturization of managers so that they may better serve the needs of
the common man. There is need to improve access to public services by all members of the society, particularly the weak and the
deprived. The time has thus come for management development
institutions to reflect on their accomplishments and environments,
with a view to defining more realistic roles and policies which will
enhance their impact on strategic problem areas of public management, and to influencing their environment rather than being dom-
inated by it.

(3) In order to reduce intellectual dependence on exogenous management theories and enhance their own credibility, management development institutions must develop, through meaningful research,
a management philosophy, models and approaches which reflect
their cultural environments and needs.

Correspondingly, national policies and objectives should be defined by
the national leadership in such a way as to ensure that the management
development institutions' contributions reflect the assessed realities and
priorities.

(4) Management development institutions should promote collaboration and communication at the national, regional and global levels.
For this purpose, networks of institutions should be established at
those levels for exchange of information and experiences. At the
national level, there should be greater debate and discussion of
major management trends and development involving the participation of all sectors of the society.

(5) Developing countries as well as the regional and international organizations concerned with management development should pay
greater attention to the task of institution-building and devote
larger resources to management development institutions, co-ordi-
nate their efforts and periodically evaluate the impacts of their
outputs. (p. 37)

[5] AXINN, George H. *New Strategies for Rural Development.* East Lansing,
Mich.: Rural Life Associates, 1978. 194 pages.

This book is a collection of papers written between 1968 and 1977 by one of the leaders in institution building thinking. Some of the papers are presented in other parts of the *Source Book* [117]. Only new material will be reviewed in this annotation. Part 1 suggests a conceptual framework for understanding rural social systems in their dynamic form and calls for a rural renaissance. Part 2 presents papers focusing on communication and education. Finally, Part 3 deals with strategic concepts for rural development. Four of the sixteen chapters are of particular interest to the institution building practitioner.

The first of these four chapters, Chapter 13, is entitled "Institution Building Concepts." This paper was originally presented at the Conference on Institution Building in Agriculture, Center for Agricultural Technology, San Salvador, El Salvador, July 27, 1971. The concepts presented in this chapter draw heavily on the work of institution building analysts who have conducted field research, but most of all this chapter draws on the work of Esman. The major concepts presented in this chapter include a definition of criteria of institutionality, institutional variables, and institutional linkages. These are followed by a brief discussion on how to use the I.B. model developed by Esman, et al.

Another chapter of interest to institution building practitioners, Chapter 14, is entitled "Linkages and Components in a Typical Rural Social System." This paper was originally presented at the Annual Meeting of the Rural Sociological Society, Denver, Colorado, August 27–29, 1971. Topics include a discussion of the agricultural extension education function, a look at a typical system of agricultural education and extension in a composite of rural societies, and, finally, an examination of six education/extension components, including the different combinations and permutations these components can take.

A third chapter of interest, Chapter 15, is entitled "A System of Services to Support Agricultural Development." This is the second half of a paper presented at the Conference on Institution Building in Agriculture, Center of Agricultural Technology, San Salvador, El Salvador, July 27, 1971. This chapter primarily examines the seven components of a rural social system. "The rate of agricultural development is said to be dependent on the degree of effectiveness of the various components in the rural social system and on the degree to which they function as an integrated system" (p. 177). These components are education, production, research, education extension, supply, governance, and marketing. This chapter concludes by emphasizing that every component is important; hence, changing any one component or any one linkage will affect the entire system. The system's impacts will depend on the uniqueness of each environment.

The last chapter of interest, Chapter 5, is entitled "Developing Needed Institutional Infrastructure to Sustain Agricultural Development Technology." This paper was presented as part of a panel discussion on "The Problem of the Food Crisis in our Expanding World Population," at the Annual Meeting of Rural Sociological Society, August 27, 1975, San Francisco, California. The emphasis of this paper is on five problems associated with the development of appropriate institutional infrastructure. The first problem entails the wide array of institutions involved. A second problem is the role of rural development acquisition systems (institutions owned and controlled by rural people themselves and designed to help facilitate desired change). A third problem is rural development stimulation systems (agencies and organizations that supply rural needs, those that market rural products, the educational and research institutions, the government and regulating institutions, health care delivery, and multipurpose institutions). A fourth problem is intersystem interactions common to most interfacing systems. The final problem is inadequate conceptualization of change in rural social systems as a process. These problems of conceptualization are the rationale behind attempts to develop the needed institutional infrastructure to sustain agricultural development and technology.

[6] GANESH, S. R. "From Thin Air To Firm Ground: Empirical Guidelines For A General Processual Model of Institution Building." *Human Relations*, 32, 9 (September 1979), 751–79.

This article promotes the development of institution building as a management theory with emphasis on praxis rather than as an organization theory.

> This paper reports one set of data from an exploratory study of management education institutions in India, with the purposes of establishing some empirical basis for Institution Building theory and of developing a general processual model of institution building that may be applied to planned change in organizational and social change settings. The paper attempts to do this by placing the study in the wider perspective of organization theory, outlining the methodological aspects, then focuses on the various process mechanisms that contribute to institution building and which emerge empirically; finally a general processual

model of institution building and the directions for further inquiry are proposed. (p. 753)

Ganesh (1976) identifies the limitations of the I.B. model: in the model's present form, the I.B. perspective is rooted in organizational theory, and I.B. has limited usefulness with its origins in the context of international aid. These limitations are attributed to a lack of sharp analytical tools to find suitable answers for policymakers. With this in mind, the author feels that a case can be made for developing I.B. as a management theory with emphasis on praxis rather than as an organizational theory.

In developing a management theory, Ganesh states that the first step is to strengthen the I.B. model in its explanatory and predictive powers. This means that the model first has to develop into a stronger organizational theory before it can progress into a management theory. For this to occur, a strong empirical research base is needed. This base can be formulated only if one subjects the available experience to critical analysis in order to develop the model further.

This study was undertaken to examine the creation and development of various institutions of management education during the 1950s and 1960s in India. As a result of initial contact with all the institutions involved, and as a result of some preliminary analysis of the initial data, the objectives of the inquiry were formulated as follows:

(1) To identify the institutional performance variables.

(2) To chart the changes in the institutional performance over a period of time.

(3) To identify various processes which influence institutional performance.

(4) To discover whether the performance changes follow some pattern which could be characterized as phases of institutional development.

(5) To show how the processes are related to institutional development. (p. 758)

Thus, the problem definition led to a sharper focus on performance as a key to institutionalization and processor as important influences on institutional performance. From preliminary analysis, four categories of processes emerged as important in the life of an institution. These are: (1) Birth processes, (2) Development processes, (3) Renewal processes, (4) Institutionalization processes. (p. 758)

Ganesh subsequently examines these processes and process mechanisms in the light of the experience of six management education institutions in India. By category of process, he concludes the following are important:

(1) Birth processes
    (a) Idea origination and nurturance
    (b) Choice of institutional form
    (c) Location of the institution
    (d) Choice of model
    (e) Choice of early leadership
    (f) Resource mobilization
    (g) Support mobilization
(2) Development processes
    (a) Initial recruitment
    (b) Enculturation
    (c) Decision making
    (d) Structure
    (e) Leadership style
    (f) Boundary management
(3) Renewal processes
    (a) Change in leadership
    (b) Regeneration
    (c) Exit
    (d) Voice
    (e) Redefinition of mission
    (f) Integration
(4) Institutionalization processes
    (a) Research
    (b) Dialogue
    (c) Dissemination
    (d) Transfer

Analysis of these elements leads the author to postulate five concepts to develop a general processual model of institution building. These concepts are context, capability development, innovative thrust, penetration, and process mechanisms. Figure 1 graphically depicts this revised model.

We, then, have a revised model which has rectified the confusion between inputs and outputs. Thus, the context influences capability development mediated by process mechanisms of set 1; capability development, in turn, influences innovative thrust of the institution through a second set of process mechanisms; and innovative thrust, in turn, influences penetration through a third set of process mechanisms. It should

Figure 1 *A General Processual Model of Institution Building*

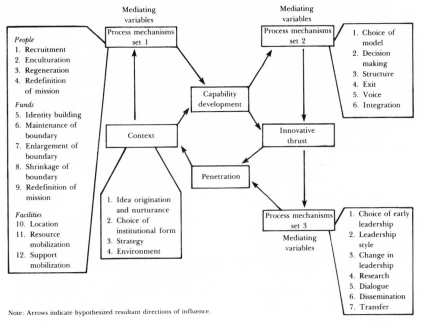

Note: Arrows indicate hypothesized resultant directions of influence.

be noted here that the capability development process mechanisms are primarily externally or contextually oriented; the innovative thrust process mechanisms are basically internally oriented; and the penetration mechanisms are externally oriented. Thus, we have contextual process mechanisms, internally oriented process mechanisms, and externally oriented process mechanisms. By isolating and identifying process mechanisms in the three sets and also postulating directions of influence (the arrows in Fig. 1), the revised model has made possible the development of the institution building model into a more practical model.

The revised model can answer questions about what the institution builder can do in order to develop the institution. The revised model provides both a diagnostic frame and an action frame. Institutional leaders need to know the current state of institutional development and probable future states to result from actions that they initiate. They also need guidance as to what action options are available to them. The revised model is a step in this direction and in this sense is neither complete nor comprehensive. Using the revised model, the institution builder can generate valid data from context, level of capability development in the institution, level of innovative thrust, and extent of penetration. He will also be able to compare these levels with similar institutions operating in the same context. Moreover, he will be able to generate valid data on the relative strengths of various process mechanisms which mediate capability development, innovative thrust, and penetration. Thus, knowing the state of the system and knowing the action options available to him with respect to strengthening, neutralizing, or reducing the weakness of appropriate process mechanisms, an institution builder is placed in a better position to act. This is not to imply that an institution builder can consciously engineer all the outcomes. Quite the contrary. The model points out that institutional leadership is precarious and uncertain. The contextual process mechanisms highlight the dependence of the institutional leadership on factors outside conscious control. The model only serves to sharply focus the attention of institution builders on identifiable sources of problems. Further, the internally oriented process mechanisms and the externally oriented process mechanisms which mediate institutionalization sequentially underscore the difficulties of conscious manipulation. It is no wonder that the easiest course of action for institutional leadership is to let the institution drift. Worse still, given the uncertainties of performance on innovative thrust and more so on penetration, the institutional leadership may focus wrongly on capability development. Capability development is important, but represents basically performance on input development. Innovative thrust and penetration concern themselves with input utilization and conversion. Institutionalization, in the final analysis, can take place and social change can occur only if penetration takes place. Given a context where the clientele are not demanding, it is easier to stop at capability development and innovative thrust. This is also evident from the relatively low attention paid to institutionalization mechanisms in the six institutions. This has resulted in a situation of penetration by default rather than by design. The impression one is left with is that management education institutions cannot be considered to be change agents in the sense of bringing about radically different values on their own. They react more than initiate. (pp. 772–73)

The author maintains that this study not only has isolated the various process mechanisms, but also has provided guidelines for their detailed operationalization. The study has also related performance to processes and in doing so has moved the I.B. model one step closer to becoming more practical and more useful to institution builders.

The most important contribution of the present study has been to integrate the "evolutionary" and "engineering" approaches to institutional development. Through a conception of institutions as social arenas and through an elaboration of process mechanisms related to performance in the arena, the study has made possible a longitudinal processual analysis. The study underscores the possibilities of engineering institutional development. All the process mechanisms are manipuable [sic] by the key actors in the situation, although the degree of difficulty of manipulation would vary widely among the mechanisms. (p. 776)

[7] GANESH, S. R. "Institution Building for Social and Organizational Change: An Appreciation." *Organization Studies* (December 1980), 209–28.

In this article Ganesh attempts to synthesize various streams of thought that relate to institution building. In doing so he attempts to develop a general processual model of institution building rooted in empirical work.

First, we will discuss the major features of both the "evolutionary" and the "engineering" models. We will examine an "engineering" model of institution building as developed by the consortium of American scholars—the different elements of the model, its assumptions, scope, and limitations. This will lead us to a consideration of four major perspectives of institution building which are important to its elaboration and refinement. These perspectives are: (a) the leadership / elite / entrepreneurial perspective; (b) the interorganization perspective; (c) the organizational design perspective; and (d) the diffusion of innovation perspective. In fact, attention will be focused on perspectives "b" and "d". With these perspectives we will turn to exploratory research on institution building. Finally, an attempt at synthesis will be made through a general processual model of institution building based on empirical guidelines. (p. 211)

Ganesh uses the term "evolutionary model" to describe the slow, incremental changes that take place as a result of social interaction.

The element of purposive induction of the change is minimal. In a historical framework, the development of institutions is viewed as the spontaneous crystallization of recurring interaction patterns around needs. Alternately, existing institutions are postulated as adapting to changing needs. In this sense it is an "adaptation" model. This model concerns itself with what might be considered as the "central" or "fundamental" needs of the society, e.g. the family. To the extent that this model emphasizes norms and behaviour it de-emphasizes structure and organization. (p. 211)

The "engineering model" differs from "evolutionary model" in a fundamental way.

> It is the rejection of the "natural selection" process and the acceptance of an "elitist" engineered adaptation or innovation that differentiates the "engineering" model of institution building from the "evolutionary" model. (pp. 212–13)

> Esman (1972) deals with . . . "institutionality" as the end-state of institution-building efforts. He posits two conditions (a) the establishment of a viable organization which incorporates innovations and (b) the acceptance and espousal of the organization and its innovations by relevant groups in the environment.

> Thus, the IB model as developed by Esman and others is an elitist model emphasizing changes from the top down, particularly by people who enjoy a degree of official authority of sanction. Although developed with specific reference to the modernizing countries, Esman and Bruhns visualize the possibility of applying this model to the developed countries also. Because of its marked "organizational" bias, this model provides greater potentialities for operationalization, and therefore, for research-based action strategies for the creation of new institutions in the society. In its most abstract form it conforms to Zollschan and Hirshch's (1964) conception of exigency—articulation—action—institutionalization. (pp. 213–14)

Ganesh goes on to give a brief discussion of the key elements of the I.B. model, after which he examines the scope and limitations of the I.B. model.

Four new directions for further development of the I.B. model are presented. The first of these new directions is the need for increased awareness of leadership emergence, leadership identification, and leadership development.

Another important direction for the development of the I.B. model is the design of organization.

> Explicit attention will have to be given to alternative designs as well as to an examination of the conditions under which various designs would bring about the desired results. That there are serious limitations to planned change should not deter development along this dimension. Such developments should also examine the three possibilities available to an institution builder and the consequence of adoption of one strategy in preference to another. These possible design options are:

> (1) alteration of an existing institution,

> (2) creation of a new institution with a specialized function hitherto not carried out in the society, and

(3) creation of new institutions to integrate existing specialized and fragmented institutions or functions.

Unless the IB model develops along this line it will not be in a position to provide guidance to the institution builder in the choice of an appropriate design not only initially but also continuously over time as the institution develops. (p. 219)

The third direction for development of the I.B. models deals with the dimensions of diffusion of innovations in society.

What must be remembered is that in insitution building the concern is with the spread of values and norms and their acceptance by the society. Further, the innovation in the IB model is the institution itself and the concern is with the adoption of the institution by the society. Rogers and Shoemaker (1971) provide a typology of social change as a prelude to discussing communication of innovations. Their typology rests on whether or not the origin of the innovation and the recognition of the need are internal or external to the society. Accordingly, they have developed four types, namely:

(1) Imminent change which occurs when people internal to the society primarily on their own create and develop the innovation.

(2) Induced imminent change in that the innovation could be catalysed by someone who is a "temporary" member of the society, though the primary burden of the creation rests with the members of the society.

(3) Selective contact change when members of one system adopt an innovation primarily as a result of their exposure to the innovation outside their own system or society.

(4) Directed contact change caused by actors external to the system who seek to induce change for achievement of goals defined by them.

The IB model, as is apparent, is concerned only with directed contact change. Viewed from an innovation perspective, the model has to develop capabilities of handling the other three types of changes and, therefore, for choosing appropriate models of diffusion. (pp. 219–20)

The final new direction for development of the I.B. model deals with the interorganizational dimension.

Van de Ven et al. (1974) define an "Interorganizational Collectivity (IC)" as a social-action system of two or more organizations which acts as a unit. They elaborate this by specifying the implications such as: (1) that occupants of one or more roles of the collectivity can make decisions that are binding for the collectivity as a whole; (2) that the participants in the collectivity can perform actions (i.e., pursue goals) in a manner similar to that of an individual participant; (3) that the participants in the collectivity are interdependent in terms of the unit's decision; and (4) that the collectivity can participate in, and must adapt to, other collectivities or other social systems more encompassing than itself, just as an individual participant does by being a member of the collectivity.

In the institutional context such collectivities would serve three ends, namely: (1) to promote areas of common interest; (2) to jointly obtain and allocate a greater amount of resources than would be possible when each institution acts independently; and (3) to protect areas of common interest. In the context of the collectivity one can examine the linkage relationship between organizations. In fact, out of the four linkages in the IB model, this would mean a detailed examination of one poorly understood linkage—the normative linkage. (p. 221)

[8] BUNKER, Douglas R. "Understanding and Practicing Institution Building: Concepts for a Theory of Practice." Chapter 2 in Bunker's forthcoming *Building New Social Institutions: The Case of National Health Planning.*

"Understanding and Practicing Institution Building Concepts for a Theory of Practice" is chapter two in a forthcoming book, *Building New Social Institutions: The Case of National Health Planning* by Douglas R. Bunker. The author considers the medical care and health service system from the perspective that in every society these services are provided by a social institution in a universalistic sense. Bunker states that "any effort to effect institutional change requires that one deal with both universalistic and particularistic aspects of societal structures relating to health care and with the linkage between them" (p. 2).

The author reviews the works of Janowitz (1969), Perlmutter (1965), and Esman (1972) and their emerging thoughts that institution building differs from evolutionary adjustment in its emphasis on deliberately designed change processes. These deal with both the substance of new institutional patterns and the processes by which they can be put into place.

After summarizing the I.B. model developed by Esman et al. the author develops a set of propositional statements representing first order generalizations from the I.B. approach. The author states, "I

Figure 2 *Universalistic and Particularistic Aspects of Social Institutions*

	Universalistic	Particularistic
Formal	Statutes Administrative policies, regulations, and programs Judicial decisions—Case Law	Charters and bylaws for focal organizations and networks Authority structures Organizational designs Job descriptions
Informal	Value orientations Customs of thought and practice External status systems	Internal status systems Informal roles Reciprocal expectations Group norms Emergent relationships Shared attitudes toward the organization and its purpose

present them for their heuristic value and as provisional and partial guides to action, rather than as explanatory assertions" (p. 15).

Proposition 1

Successful institutionalization of new or replacement social patterns requires coordinated and complementary efforts to build support for the new action pattern in four aspects of social systems: (a) universalistic-formal, (b) universalistic-informal, (c) particularistic-formal, and (d) particularistic-informal. (p. 16)

Proposition 2

In implementing programs of institution building the serial order of developmental tasks proceeds from (a) the establishment of minimum levels of legitimacy, to (b) the achievement of operational competence to produce expected benefits, to (c) the cultivation of active and continuous exchanges with the environment, to (d) the development of adaptive capacity. (p. 18)

Proposition 3

Successful IB projects require a variety of staff resources including specialists of at least the following three kinds: (1) those with skills in political liaison and in achieving normative representation, (2) those with technical-analytic expertise on the content of the institutional change sought, on the IB process, and on other relevant knowledge areas and analytic methods, and (3) administrative and program operations personnel who are competent in the application of the technologies selected, in project management, and in eliciting cooperation from those they encounter in operational situations. When any of these resource groups are not adequately represented or differentiated by unique competence and task orientations, the probability of the success of an IB project will be significantly reduced. (pp. 22–23)

Proposition 4

Success in IB requires that the innovation-carrying organization differentiates for itself a position in the organizational network which facilitates active exchange by defining its unique and limited functions and identifying the net gains to the system which accrue from its activities and from its interactions with other actors. (p. 25)

Proposition 5

Action orientations which comprehend both (a) the development and promulgation of explicit substantive positions, (relating to the content of change), and (b) the creation of new socio-political processes to broaden involvement or to enhance the quality or acceptability of decisions are more likely to lead to successful institutionalization of proposed innovations than approaches which emphasize either content or process without significant attention to the other. (p. 26)

Proposition 6

Successful IB projects will provide for complementary adjustments at each level of Federalistic hierarchies related to the area of activity in which the changed action patterns are designed to occur. (p. 27)

The author then elaborates and qualifies these six propositions through an examination of the particular task of building a national network of areawide health planning agencies. The subsequent chapters of the book are sequenced to fit the phase model depicted in Proposition 2.

[9] MORIS, Jon R. *Managing Induced Rural Development.* Bloomington, Ind.: International Development Institute, 1981. 184 pages.

In his foreword to the book, Siffin makes several important observations.

This book might have had a different title—*Fundamentals of Rural Development* would have been apt, for this is a fundamental book, probably the most comprehensive statement on the subject.

The bibliography contains more than a thousand items. It is supported by classifications which invite selective penetration of a vast body of material. In addition, each of ten chapters identifies the major sources which bear upon the topic under examination.

But Jon Moris's book is more than a survey or synthesis of the literature. It is a powerful source of lessons; it presents an argument; it proposes and recommends.

The thesis of this book is suggested in its actual title—the *management* of rural development. The word is used in its most comprehensive sense, and related to the total business of strategizing, designing, implementing, and evaluating. There is much in this book about experience, and about theories as well—their biases and their effects. The organizational formats common in rural development are analyzed. The problems of attempting to transfer technology are diagnosed. The aim of this book is to help people find out what is actually needed and what is possible and how things work. There is pungent opinionation, and recommendations which make this much more than a critical dissection of its subject. (p. ix)

Especially useful for the institution builder is the comparison of the blueprint approach with the learning process approach to rural development.

Thus the blueprint approach splits program planning and organization into three disconnected segments: an initial determination of resource requirements (often reached in advance of operational experience), a scheduling in time and space of anticipated implementation activities (generally the last phase of the planners' formal task), and the subsequent establishment or assignment of an operational field unit . . .

When applied to rural development projects, the major flaw in blueprint (or "top-down") planning is the strong assumptions which must be met before it will work. These are: (a) a clear specification of goals in advance of design, (b) a fully adequate organizational blueprint which anticipates all eventual needs, (c) firm control over the field units which can supply high quality monitoring information, (d) project staff which can realize targeted outputs on schedule, and (e) a stable environment where the ancillary linkages are already operative. And, of course, one assumes the planners are interested in their project and have direct access to the ears of decision-makers. (p. 20)

If we consider the situations that typify rural development administration, the superiority of the "learning" approach over "blueprint" planning is quite apparent. The administrative models on which LDC institutions have been based were imported. They often do not suit field requirements. The environment is in a constant state of flux— droughts, disease outbreaks, price changes, etc.—which necessitate that field units show reactive capability. Errors have been repeated time and time again; in some countries, we are now in the third cycle of the implementation of badly chosen policies. Communication to headquarters units is faulty, and the planners seem asleep. For these and many other reasons field experience in LDCs overwhelmingly supports the need for a "learning" approach to planning and implementation, one which puts intelligence back into the field organization . . .

Korten suggests (1980:499–501) that three learning cycles often characterize successful programs: (a) initial development of an effective program design, one that can potentially deliver the expected outputs; (b) learning how to make this design efficient within its local setting; and (c) finding ways to expand the model into other communities (replication). (p. 21)

Requirements for organizational learning are summarized:

Organizational learning requires the same capabilities as good planning, the capacity of a corporate group to act intelligently vis-a-vis group goals and activities. We can identify the properties that make learning possible by identifying what an individual needs in order to respond to changing circumstances:

(1) a grasp of objectives

(2) control over the resources being planned for

(3) reliable models of external reality

(4) information about past experience

(5) sufficient interest to get the necessary planning done

(6) familiarity with methods for making projections

(7) open communication with all the parties involved

(8) ability to get the principal doer committed to the plan

(9) enough stability in the situation so that past experience is relevant (p. 21)

This extraordinarily comprehensive work concludes with guidelines based on past experience for rural developers:

A colleague with long experience in rural development noted that the foregoing observations are not the kind of positive guidelines USAID and the World Bank want for use in their field programs. We anthropologists have a tendency to dwell in the minefields of culture conflict, while ignoring the safe ground in between. I close this chapter therefore with a rephrasing of these lessons in a positive idiom:

(1) Find the right people to lead a project and let them finalize its design if you want commitment and success.

(2) Keep supervision simple and the chain of command short.

(3) Build your project or program into the local administrative structure, even though this will seem initially to cause frictions and delay.

(4) If the program aims at achieving major impact, secure funding and commitment for a ten to fifteen year period.

(5) Put the project under the control of a single agency, and see that the agency can supply all necessary external inputs.

(6) Work through local officials when first approaching farmers.

(7) Attempt major projects only when the nation's top leadership is ready for change and willing to support the program.

(8) Find ways to utilize momentum already within the system to amplify project productivity.

(9) Get sufficient flexibility of goals and funding to deal with new problems as they arise without reformulation of the program.

(10) Make choices about projects and contractors based on records of past performance.

(11) Insure that the field team has somebody good in public relations during the early years before impact materializes.

(12) Be prepared to locate activities wherever politicians point.

(13) (But) as a rule try to locate agricultural projects in areas that have not been heavily influenced by prior urbanization.

(14) Treat political constraints as real if you wish to survive.

(15) Recruit the core staff from those who have already done at least one tour of duty in an area.

(16) Find ways to minimize the riskiness of participation for farmers who are joining a program for the first time.

(17) Choose innovations for farmers that give at least a 25 percent increase on present practice.

(18) Aim to establish a high value cash crop at an early stage if farmers do not already have such a source of income.

(19) Start small and aim at complete success at each step.

(20) Find a secure source of recurrent finance before expecting farmers to take over responsibility for their own production services.

(21) Be sure to include a revenue producing component in any package of activities to be sponsored through farmers' groups or villages.

(22) Concentrate efforts on only one or two innovations at a time.

(23) Make certain the contact staff in touch with farmers is adequately trained, supervised, motivated, and supported.

(24) Identify and use the folk management strategies which managers rely upon within the local system to get things done.

(25) Simplify scientific solutions to problems into decision rules that can be applied routinely without special expertise.

(26) Look for the larger effects of an item of technology on the entire system before deciding upon its adoption.

(27) Insure that experienced leaders have subordinates who do stand in for them on occasion, and that there is a pool from whom future leaders can be drawn. (p. 124–25)

[10] KORTEN, David C. "The Management of Social Transformation." *Public Administration Review* (November–December 1981), 609–18.

This article concerns social transformation from an administrative point of view. Korten begins by arguing that "the modernization of human society has been accompanied by a sharp dichotomization of the individual's public and private lives" (p. 609). He goes on to say, "One key to sustainable society is to reestablish the individual's lost sense of intimacy with and responsibility for his or her local community and its natural environment" (p. 610). The answer is to substantially reform society's megastructures, which include the modern state, the large economic conglomerates and both capitalist and socialist enterprise, big labor, and the governmental bureaucracies that administer major sectors of society's affairs. This can be done by loosening central control and strengthening feedback systems to increase self-direction.

The author develops open system economics versus closed system economics, followed by a discussion of scientific knowledge versus social knowledge. Korten then turns his attention to the capacity to manage social learning.

The key to its formation is to encourage a growing number of experiments in innovative social learning through facilitating the formation of what for the sake of convenience will be referred to as social learning clusters. Each such cluster would include the major public or private operating agency in which a learning process is centered and a group of supporting knowledge resource institutions.

Then to encourage the reflection, exchange, and documentation that is crucial to making social learning a fully conscious process and to speeding its advance it is desirable that knowledge resource institutions involved in a variety of social learning clusters be formed into social learning networks. While the primary purpose of such networks would be to facilitate the exchange of experience gained through the cluster involvements of their members, secondary outputs would include: (1) a continually growing understanding of the unique nature and requirements of the role of the knowledge resource institution in facilitating social learning; and (2) contributions to the building of a more formalized body of knowledge and method which, while no substitute for firsthand experience, would make the process of acquiring such experience easier for others. (p. 614)

The author concludes:

The proposed effort to facilitate the formation of social-learning clusters and networks is in part an effort to form a larger action coalition *within* the system, linking together such individuals in a collective commitment to appropriate action and providing them with an enlarged mutual support system able to lend legitimacy to their efforts and to facilitate the more rapid emergence of the operational concepts and methodologies needed to translate their good intentions into effective action. This proposal sketches the bare outlines of such an effort. The details can only emerge out of the social learning process itself, a product of an ever expanding circle of creative minds addressing a shared concern with the context of their individual local realities. (p. 617)

[11] BARNETT, Stanley A., and Engel, Nat. *Effective Institution Building: A Guide for Project Designers and Project Managers Based on Lessons Learned from the AID Portfolio.* A.I.D. Program Evaluation Discussion Paper No. 11, Office of Evaluation, Bureau for Program and Policy Coordination. Washington, D.C.: U.S. Agency for International Development, U.S. State Department, March 1982. 55 pages plus appendices.

The Guide was prepared based on an examination of Agency evaluations and audits. The focus of the majority of these documents is on the quality of project implementation efforts and the ways in which project development can positively or negatively affect the implementation process. Thus, the Guide itself tends to be oriented toward project development and project implementation concerns, as opposed to impact measurement and prediction. To understand fully the impact of institution building projects, as well as the optimum ways of designing and managing them, one needs to examine the Guide in conjunction with AID Impact Evaluations of projects in particular sectors and countries.

The analysis of the patterns in AID's portfolio of institution building projects presented in Part I of this volume will provide Agency managers with an overview of AID's investments in this important area over past decades. While we believe that the projects examined are representative of the Agency's experience, we are aware that some elements of this experience may not be fully reflected in the analysis. For example, during the 1970's, AID supported a number of integrated rural development projects that involved micro-level institution building efforts; these may not have been captured fully in the research because this component was simply not recognized as such or was inadequately defined in the documentation reviewed.

The checklist, in Part II of the Guide draws on the lessons of experience to remind project designers and project managers of particular factors they need to consider as projects are developed and implemented. As a "stand-alone" design and management aid, we anticipate that the checklist presented in Part II may prove to be a useful device for training development personnel and for those who review project proposals, particularly for their soundness. Over time, AID's Impact Evaluations will be able to provide additional information on the questions of the sustainability and impact of the institution building projects to supplement the evaluative materials reviewed by this volume. (Introductory Note, unnumbered)

Part II, the portion of the report of interest here, begins by analyzing the "lessons learned" from 302 "field" projects of the Bureaus for Near East, Asia, Latin America, the Caribbean, and Africa. These were active in September 1974 and since and were accessed from DS/DIU's collection with the key subject descriptor "Institution Building." The following is a summary of the key lessons learned in this study:

I. *Problems to Anticipate during Project Design*
(A) Lessons learned concerning program planning factors
    (1) Undertake indepth predesign studies.
    (2) Tailor the project to host-country capabilities.
    (3) Set realistic time frames.
    (4) Develop clear and attainable project designs.
    (5) Establish strong institutional linkages.
    (6) Formulate clear lines of authority and/or relationships among project participants and sponsors.
(B) Lessons learned concerning host country factors
    (1) Obtain government commitment to support the project (commitment is prerequisite to success).
    (2) Design project to further the government's development plan.

(3) Select a politically strong, technically competent counterpart agency.

(4) Investigate thoroughly the availability and experience of required local personnel.

(5) Identify and compensate for potential problems that may result from the host government's bureaucratic process.

(C) Lessons learned about project inputs

    (1) Investigate the financial viability of the target institution and its ability to retain personnel through payment of reasonable, but competitive, salary levels.

    (2) Provide in the design for adverse impacts of inflation.

    (3) Specify compatible project equipment.

    (4) Insist on duty-free import of project materials.

    (5) Specify realistic project staffing levels.

    (6) Insist on local-language fluency when required of contractor.

(D) Lessons learned with reference to training

    (1) Confirm that educational institutions will provide graduates with diplomas required for further advancement educationally or in the job market.

    (2) Allow adequate time for teaching the socially and economically disadvantaged (a longer-than-normal process).

    (3) Specify sufficient lead time for participant trainees.

    (4) Pave the way for reintegration of returned participant trainees into the institution.

(E) Lessons learned concerning the target institution

    (1) Anticipate potential management problems, especially in the case of new entities.

    (2) Provide for attraction of competent leaders.

    (3) Remember that indigenization is a key aim of institutionalization.

    (4) Obtain agreement that formal legal status will be accorded the target entity.

    (5) Follow certain procedures for private institutions:

        (a) Focus design attention on overcoming organization inexperience.

        (b) Investigate the entity's past operations and grass-roots support.

        (c) Avoid over-identification of the institution with the U.S.

II. *Problems Encountered During Program Delivery*

(A) Attributable to AID: lack of sustained backstopping support to contractor or granter; inconsistent project monitoring; inflexibility during implementation, including failure to update project design.

(B) Attributable to contractor: inadequate to improper staffing, project management, leadership, and/or communication with host-country personnel.

(C) Attributable to host government: Delays caused by the bureaucratic process and too-rapid transfer of government personnel from the target institution.

(D) Attributable to the target institution: weak management organization, and/or leadership.

After the summary of key lessons learned, Barnett and Engel turn their attention toward a comprehensive checklist that serves as a practical guide for project designers and managers in the field. The checklist details and particularizes key lessons and organizes them by subject and project-design, state and document, and implementation stage. The following is an abbreviated version of this checklist:

I. *Program Planning Factors*
(A) Pre-Design Studies
    (1) Collect sufficient baseline data.
    (2) Use latest available data.
    (3) Check demographics.
    (4) Explore cost/benefit aspects in depth.
    (5) Investigate the effects of pertinent government policies.
    (6) Base assumptions on country-specific practice and experience.
    (7) Country-specific experience should include historic, climatic, and physiographic patterns.
(B) Overall Design Guidelines
    (1) Review designs of consultants.
    (2) Tailor the project to have host-country capabilities.
    (3) Consider innovative approaches.
    (4) Specify relevant institutional linkages.
    (5) Use the Logical Framework design matrix.
    (6) Use the Logframe with precision.
    (7) PROAG (Project Agreement) between AID and host government should complement PP (Project Paper), an internal AID project document that follows the PID (Project Identification Document, initial formal document in the AID program design process).
(C) Realistic Time Frames
    (1) Tailor to host-country capability.
    (2) Consider logistics.
    (3) Consider culture.
    (4) Allow more time for new institutions.
    (5) Remember that new management techniques take 2 years before consultants can be used effectively.
(D) Lines of Authority
    (1) Establish clear lines of authority among host government agencies participating in the project.
    (2) Clarify status of personnel loaned to the institution.
    (3) Formalize the authority of a coordinating institution.
(E) Project Roles
    (1) Delineate the relationship between the contractor and host-country counterpart institutions.
    (2) Prepare the appropriate ministry for projected role of a subsidiary agency.
    (3) Clarify roles of contractor and counterpart personnel.

II. *Host Country Factors*
(A) Commitment of the Host Government
    (1) Obtain commitment of the host government, which is fundamental to success.
    (2) Involve the government in project design.
    (3) Favor projects that seek to further the government's development plan.
    (4) Seek community support.
(B) Host Country Counterpart Agency
    (1) Focus on the appropriate ministry or host-country entity.
    (2) Assess the agency's capabilities.
    (3) Consider the agency's role within government operations.
(C) Host Country Personnel
    (1) Check local availability of needed technicians.
    (2) Explore the limits of local expertise.
(D) Host Government Bureaucratic Process: identify areas where project progress can be delayed by host country bureaucratic problems.
III. *Project Inputs*
(A) Financial Inputs
    (1) Consider long-term financial viability.
    (2) Advocate reasonable salary levels.
    (3) Check on the financial resources of sub-national entities.
    (4) Provide for the effects of inflation.
    (5) Process the project quickly to ease financial problems.
(B) Commodity Inputs
    (1) Set commodity costs at realistic levels.
    (2) Ensure compatibiltiy of equipment.
    (3) Avoid specifying inappropriate machinery.
    (4) Specify duty-free import of project equipment.
(C) Personnel Inputs
    (1) Set realistic project staffing requirements.
    (2) Anticipate potential trouble in the contractor-counterpart relationship.
    (3) Closely monitor contractor team's proposed selections.
    (4) Insist on local language fluency of the contractor, when required.
IV. *Training, Including Participant Training*
(A) Provide extra time for teaching the socially disadvantaged.
(B) Avoid post-training job-placement difficulties.
(C) Confirm that government trainees obtain per diem.
(D) Ensure ample lead time for participant training.
(E) Anticipate delays in participant training due to lack of English ability.
(F) Check whether participant trainees will lose normal government benefits.
(G) Pave the way for reintegration of returned participant trainees.
V. *The Target Institution*
(A) Management
    (1) Anticipate management problems.

      (2) Focus on target-institution executives who exhibit leadership ability.
(B) Personnel Retention: seek competitive conditions of employment for target-institution personnel.
(C) Indigenization
      (1) Remember that indigenization is the aim of institution-building projects.
      (2) Specify linkages required to accomplish the transformation.
      (3) Provide for legal transformation, where necessary.
(D) Legal Status and Local Laws
      (1) Obtain agreement on legal status for target entity.
      (2) Obtain legal counsel to check the country's laws.
VI. *Special Situations*
(A) Private Entities
      (1) Focus design attention on helping overcome organizational inexperience.
      (2) Concentrate on long-term viability.
      (3) Investigate past operations of the target entity.
      (4) Pay special attention to credit programs of associations and cooperatives.
      (5) Stress the need for charging realistic interest rates.
      (6) Analyze the institution's grass-roots support.
      (7) Avoid over-identification of the institution with the U.S.
(B) Projects with Construction Elements
      (1) Insist on adequate pre-construction economic and environmental studies.
      (2) Investigate the applicability of the Fixed Amount Reimbursement (FAR) contracting concept.
(C) Isolated Project Sites: take difficult locational factors into account.
(D) Study-Oriented Projects: tailor design to encouarge use of project-produced studies.
VII. *Program Delivery*
(A) Implemented by AID
      (1) Sustain backstopping support to contractor to facilitate project management.
      (2) Monitor the project closely via the mission staff.
      (3) Anticipate delays on AID's part caused by the bureaucratic process.
      (4) Enhance project success by updating project designs.
      (5) Note that project replicability indicates good project design.
(B) Implementation by the Contractor
      (1) Ensure that staffing is timely with few turnovers.
      (2) Note that project management can be affected by contractor's failure to comply with contract obligations.
      (3) Note that leadership is attributable to the quality and turnover of contractor's chief-of-party.
      (4) Facilitate communication between contractor and host country personnel.

(C) Implementation by Target Institution
    (1) Assign definite lines of authority to management and organization.
    (2) Provide consistent leadership.
(D) Implementation by the Host Government
    (1) Obtain commitment by the host government to ensure project success, especially with regard to financial commitment and legislative action.
    (2) Avoid delays in project implementation due to bureaucratic process.
    (3) Discourage personnel transfers.
VIII. *Delivery of Inputs cited as causing poor project performance*
(A) Commodity Inputs
    (1) Avoid late procurement and arrival.
    (2) Pay close attention to customs duty on project material.
(B) Financial Inputs
    (1) Investigate financial obligations not met by host government.
    (2) Monitor host country disbursements by the Mission.
(C) Local Logistical Support
(D) Personnel Inputs
    (1) Avoid late arrival of contractor personnel.
    (2) Ensure the availability of host government personnel.

[12] BJUR, Wesley E. *Taking an Institution's "I.Q."* Los Angeles, Calif.: The Public Policy Institute of the Center for Public Affairs, University of Southern California, 1982–1983. 31 pages.

In this publication, Bjur develops an index of relative levels of institutionalization. First, he discusses a brief history of institution building beginning with the initial Ford Foundation grant in the early 1960s. Subsequently, he examines some shortcomings of the I.B. model developed by Esman et al., although he points out that it does offer some useful and important advantages over traditional sociological models.

During the mid-1960s, attempts were made to use the I.B. model as an analytical tool to evaluate the success of technical assistance projects employing I.B. theory. Practitioners commissioned to do such studies encountered considerable difficulty fitting empirical realities unambiguously into the I.B. categorical scheme, particularly the matter of linkages with sister institutions.

In response to the need to develop some measure of institutionalization, the author has developed seven general requirements for an adequate measuring tool:

(1) Institutions need to be studied as societal organisms, with life spans covering stages in some ways analogous to the human life span, and with longer cycles analogous to the generational cycle. This means that a temporal dimension lacking in the early IB model had to be incorporated into the conceptual scheme.

(2) Valuedness as a core variable needs to be measured both internally and externally by means of inferential, observable indicators rather than by attempts at opinion sampling.

(3) Autonomy, as the single most important indicator of institutionalization, must be measured as a function of the organization's legal or legitimacy status, its program activities, and its resource use rather than attempting to evaluate it as a separable quality.

(4) Leadership should be dealt with as more than "management" or "administration" of the organization under study.

(5) The instrument should yield a cumulative index level of institutionalization such that, over time, when applied to the same organization, it shows a higher number when it has become more successfully institutionalized, and a lower number if there have been setbacks. It can thus serve as a kind of institutionalizing thermometer for managers and/or consultants.

(6) It should be easy to use, not requiring sophisticated statistics nor expensive and laborious research techniques. It should codify some readily observable factors associated with institutionalization, weighting them realistically for incorporation in the index formula so that the interrelationship among factors bears some real-world relation to their importance as institutional indicators.

(7) The overall quotient should give a generally useful number as to relative level of institutionalization, and also, the different categorical factors should provide useful analytic insights, case by case, for remedying weaknesses or counter balancing sectorial emphases. In short, it should be useful as both a research and a diagnostic tool for managers, consultants, and planners. (pp. 4–5)

The I.Q. Index Formula.

The formula which evolved stems from the observation that in early and middle stages, institutionalization is analogous to, and correlated with, social legitimization. (There are known cases of old institutions having lost much of their societal support or "legitimacy" but which still exhibit many of the indications of strong institutionalization). Being valued in the social or institutional environment is part of, or the same as, being considered legitimate in one's institutional role and function(s).

Legitimacy is recognized as a cumulative phenomenon in two important senses: (1) an organization's legitimacy tends to improve or be increased with the passage of time as it comes to be accepted in its identity role, and (2) legitimacy is cumulative in the sense that it is always better to possess a half-dozen role-legitimating qualities than to be perceived as demonstrating only one or a few.

Thus the Institutionalization Index is oriented toward the display of a cumulation of factors generally associated with evidences of increasing legitimacy in its societal context. It differentiates category levels by adding or subtracting small-number increments, each of which is thought to be a partial indicator of an institutional status or condition.

The IQ instrument yields two related scores: a cumulated Q-score and an IQ Index number. The latter is an effort to provide an easily understood index number correlated with a relative level of institutionalization at any given age. It is derived by dividing the cumulated Q-score by an empirical mean of the scores earned by other institutions of a similar age. This yields an Institutionalization Quotient (IQ) for which a score greater than 1.0 indicates better than average and scores of less than 1.0 indicate less than average levels of institutionalization. (pp. 5–6)

The index consists of six categories scored on the basis of observed empirical correlations within, and external to, the organization under study.

$$Q(y) = (L + K + P + R + V)$$
and, $IQ(y) = Q/M$
when L = legal legitimacy status
K = charisma; leadership characteristics
P = program autonomy and success
R = resources and resource autonomy
V = valuedness, internal and external
Y = years-in-function of the organization
M = mean of Q-scores of similar institutions (pp. 6–7)

The author then goes into a more detailed empirical examination of each of the above categories, followed by a brief discussion of the IQ Index in use.

Step one for using the index is to

. . . select two or three points in time for which information about the organization is available which will enable reliable ratings for as many of the Index factors as possible. (p. 16)

The second step is to begin methodically to rate the organization according to the factors of the Index. (p. 16)

Subsequently, Bjur refers to four case studies to which the I.Q. index was applied. The first of these is DASP (Departamento d'Administração e Servicios do Personal), an agency of the Brazilian government. The second study examines the case of Radio-Quebec. The third study is an examination of the Malabar Branch Library, and, finally, the fourth is a look at the Regional Technological Institute of Tijuana.

Bjur concludes:

> . . . institutionalization is defined as an evolutionary process taking a decade or more to mature. Institutions seem to develop in a kind of life-cycle, analogous to life-cycles in organisms. Surviving is always an issue. If institutions survive to "mature" status, senescence becomes a problem for the organization, internally, and sometimes a problem for the supporting society as well.

> Evaluating this sub-category of organizations more appropriately called institutions is more complex and difficult than evaluating organizational efficiency or profitability. The author has presented a theory of institution building and an instrument, the I.Q. Index, for evaluating existing institutions according to qualities considered vital to institutional survival and growth. The I.Q. Index takes the institution's age into account in the evaluation process, thereby tracking it through its life-cycle. Other benefits from the use of the Index include:

> (1) Information about factors important to institutional success and/or failure is presented concisely.

> (2) Indices of strengths and weaknesses in certain vital areas of the organization are important to its survival as an institution. Recognizing them, a manager or leader can take steps to shore up the deficiencies.

> (3) There is a sense of change over time; the ups and downs are charted, thereby enabling the institution to "learn" from its own history.

> (4) The methodology permits, within certain constraints, cross-cultural comparisons of institution building successes and failures, thereby making possible a kind of science of institutions and of their life-cycles. (pp. 25–26)

[13] PRACTICAL Concepts Incorporated. *The P/C/I Model: Some Practical Concepts for Assessing Organizational Viability.* 3 vols. Washington, D.C.: Practical Concepts Incorporated, December 1974.

Practical Concepts Inc. (PCI) presents in three volumes the methodology, findings, recommendations, and guidelines for developing practical techniques for assessing the viability of health and family-planning organizations. The first volume of the report, annotated here, summarizes the study and presents PCI's recommendations to the Agency for International Development. The second volume of the report, submitted under separate cover, describes some of the study methods and concepts. The third and final volume of this report contains an "implementation package" to help AID managers assess the viability of organizations they have helped create.

PCI's model perceives an organization as comprising three basic resources or assets: P, C, and I—corresponding approximately to purchasables, connotation, and image. These are defined as follows:

(1) *Purchasables:* money and the things that have been and could be bought.

(2) *Connotation:* The affective dimensions of attitudes held about an organization: the assessment of those internal and external to the organization as to where they place the organization's image and operations in their structure of personal beliefs and priorities.

(3) *Image:* The cognitive dimension of what people think about an organization: knowledge, on the part of those internal as well as external to the organization, as to what the organization is and does, and why it exists. (p. II-4)

Those resources or assets are then used in developing three related and individually sufficient ways of assessing viability:

(1) *The Balance Sheet approach*—developing a statement similar to those used to characterize financial resources.

(2) *Observation of the individual transactions* in which the organization engages.

(3) *Direct observation* of the essential properties of viability—the organization's effect, *rate of change in effect,* and *feedback.* (p. I-2)

The above are alternative ways of assessing the dynamic equilibrium between the organization and its environment which are requirements for assessing viability. The balance sheet approach assesses the equilibrium itself. The micro-scale basis for that equilibrium is presented in the transaction analysis approach, and the macro-level equilibrium is presented in the observation of effect and feedback approach.

The balance sheet approach is favored by AID staff because of its simplicity and value. For this reason, it is the balance sheet approach that PCI has explained in its draft guidelines.

The authors define "organization" as:

The organization occupies some "space" in its environment and is *defined more by the dynamic interrelationship between its members and its societal
context than by its internal assets.* (p. II-1)

Thus, the defining *properties* of an organization are characterized in
terms of their *internal asset value* and their *external asset value.* The way in
which an organization is perceived by its clients, sponsors, competitors,
etc., and the place it occupies in their value systems, is perhaps the most
important asset of an organization. These "external assets" certainly
deserve consideration in addition to the internal assets, which include
staff values and perceptions—similar to the conventional concept of
"morale." This is consistent with the emphasis given "doctrine" in such
earlier organization models as that of Milton Esman. (p. II-1)

The conceptual basis of PCI's viability assessments rests on two
issues:

(1) Identifying the fundamental characteristics of an organization—
the properties of "organizationness" as contrasted to the conditions
necessary to achieve viability—in a way that directly addresses the
fact that these are mutual properties of the organization and its
environment;

(2) Defining viability as a homeostatic relationship between an organization and its environment so that these essential properties of the
organization are replenished. (p. II-3)

The authors then go on to examine each of the three essential
properties of an organization: image, connotation, and purchasables.

Image—"Image is the identification of what the organization is,
what it does, and why it does it. It includes two distinct components—
doctrine and program" (p. II-5).

The authors make the biological analogy to doctrine of genetic
coding—the information that limits, constrains, and defines what an
organization can do. PCI uses the term *doctrine* much as it is used by
Esman et al. In the P/C/I model, however, "doctrine is a measurable
and discrete quantity rather than simply an abstract" (p. II-5).

The biological analogy to program is the things an organism
does to survive. Within its genetic limits, an animal may develop particular functions to a highly specialized degree to adapt to the needs
of the environment. In other words, the program is changeable and
can be varied within limits that are fixed by doctrine. PCI uses the
term *program* compatibly both with general use and with the slightly
more specific use of the term by Esman et al.

Connotation—Connotation shows how the program and doctrine are valued.

> Internal to the organization, connotation equates well with the conventional use of the term *morale*. However, "connotation" is a more significant concept than morale because (a) of the distinction between the doctrinal and program concepts of image, and (b) connotation is concerned with views of those *external* to the organization as well as internal. (p. II-6)

> External to the organization, connotation is closely related to *value*, how much one's clientele is willing to pay for the service provided by the organization or, in the event that the doctrinal image is clear to its clientele, how much they would pay to perpetuate that doctrine. (p. II-7)

> "Program Connotation" may be reflected in such objective factors as the distances patients travel to obtain a given treatment. "Doctrinal connotation" might be reflected in such factors as how much the community will pay—in land, money, etc.—in order to have a hospital in the village. (p. II-7)

Doctrine comprises the basic organizational tenets from which program can be inferred.

Purchasables—Purchasables equate to financial and monetary concepts. The term *resources* is frequently used interchangeably with PCI's term *purchasables*. But in the P/C/I model *image* and *connotation* are resources in exactly the same way as monetary resources (otherwise known as purchasables).

> There is clearly a convertibility in the three elemental dimensions of the P/C/I model. Purchasables can be used to create or change image, connotation can and must be converted to purchasables, etc. This convertibility does not imply that these elements are non-orthogonal or statistically dependent. (p. II-8)

A section entitled "The P/C/I model, Origination Synergy, Effectiveness, and the Esman Model," is discussed next. Subsequently, PCI presents its recommendations. The most important of the latter is that the PCI model be field tested.

In appendix A, the authors turn their attention to the assessment techniques used in the P/C/I model. As mentioned earlier, there are three approaches to the measurement of organizational viability: (A) the Balance Sheet approach, (B) the "Effect/Feedback model," and (C) examining the individual transactions engaged in by the organization to determine the cumulative gain or loss of P, C, and I.

(A) *Balance Sheet Approach*—An institution is viable if it meets the following two conditions:

(1) P, C, and I are at or above certain norms;

(2) There is an appropriate gradient for both image and connotation—at the top of an organization, the greatest consensus and the greatest valuations of the doctrinal rather than the programmatic aspect of image. (pp. A-2 through A-3)

Meeting Basic Norms for P, C, and I

The balance sheet viability assessment quantitatively treats the basic three measurements of:

(1) *Image Strength*—the degree of consensus among those internal and external to the organization, as to what the organization is and does and why it does it.

(2) *Connotation Strength*—the extent to which individuals inside and outside the organization personally value the things that an organization does and is.

(3) *Purchasables*—the length of time that the organization can continue to operate without additional funding.

These factors are calculated as follows:

$$\text{Image Strength} = \frac{(\#\text{ of people giving each Image answer})^2}{(\#\text{ of people questioned})^2}$$

$$\text{Connotation Strength} = \frac{\#\text{ of answers in both "Do" and "Should" lists}}{\#\text{ of possible overlaps}}$$

$$\text{Endurance of Purchasables} = \frac{\text{Net Liquid Net Worth}}{\text{Operating Expenses per unit of Time}}$$
(p. A-3)

The viability criteria are then as tentatively established subject to further development of norms:

$I_s = 10$
$C_s = 0.5$
$P_b = $ time until next funding cycle (p. A-4)

(B) *Effect/Feedback Model*—This model recognizes that the real objective is to integrate the total "effectiveness curve," based on the fact that there is interest in viable institutions only because of the interest in the total cumulative effect.

Criteria for viability P/C/I Model and the effect/feedback approach requires that:

(1) The organization be synergistic—with total benefits exceeding total resource consumption. (Note that when PCI talks of resource consumption we consider image and connotation, as well as purchasables, to be resources.)

(2) The organization have feedback from the environment as to the results of its actions.

For analyzing the benefit of an organization we use conventional health impact assessments—tracer diseases, infant mortality figures, basic health statistics, etc. We then value this benefit in consistent terms—for example, productive man-years.

We then compare the benefit to the total cost—normalizing total cost again to the comparable benefit (e.g., total man-years). Here we consider total man-years consumed to include the man-years that individuals spend, man-year equivalents of dollars and equipment expended, man-years spent by patients and man-years represented by capitalized image and connotation.

If the man-years spent is much less than the man-years produced, the organization is synergistic. (p. A-5)

(C) *Analysis of Individual Transactions*—This method requires the use of a sophisticated evaluator, therefore this method has not been recommended as the first-line AID approach. The first step to be done when using this method is to define *all* of the interfaces between the organization and its environment—representative events and *all* key events by which P, C, and I are interchanged with the environment.

It was our basic hypothesis, deriving directly from our P/C/I Model, that an organization is viable if the sum of the transactions is positive in terms of P, C, and I. It is our measurement hypothesis that such an analysis can be based on three key types of transactions:

(1) Client Transactions;

(2) Sponsor Transactions;

(3) Internal or Housekeeping Transactions.

The first two types of transactions, involving "outsiders," generate P, C, and I. The organization itself generally consumes or transforms, but does not create resources. Only through interaction with the external environment can new resources be brought into the system. Any closed system is one of increasing entropy, and hence degenerative.

Internal or housekeeping transactions characterize the way in which organizational resources are distributed—replenishing image and restoring morale (internal connotation) to the "sites of" unsuccessful transactions, etc. (p. A-7)

A valid transaction is a transaction for which:

(1) The individuals involved in the transaction have the same expectations;

(2) Those expectations are met;

(3) The value of the transaction exceeds the cost. (p. A-8)

The PCI Model builds on, rather than simply replaces, the extensive "institution building" literature that pre-exists PCI's work . . . The correspondence between the Esman concepts (leadership, doctrine, programs, internal structure, linkages) and the PCI indicators of organizational viability reflects AID's evaluation doctrine that you cannot infer achievement of *Purpose* from completion of *Outputs*. (p. III-8)

MACRO-FOCUSED LITERATURE

Clearly, institutions do not exist in a vacuum. Much of the above literature views the environment within which a given institution operates from the vantage point of the institution itself. However, the macro-oriented literature summarized in the remainder of this chapter considers the broader perspective. That is, the vantage points are reversed so that, for example, the institutional infrastructure of a society can be viewed by those for which it is designed to serve. More important, with regard to why development occurs in the direction that it does, the forces that shape and redirect institutions are of interest to development scholars and practitioners alike. Both will find the following summaries worthy of their time and attention.

[14] RUSSELL, Clifford S., and Nicholson, Norman K., eds. *Public Choice and Rural Development*. Research paper R-21. Washington, D.C.: Resources for the Future, Inc., 1981. 299 pages.

This book contains proceedings of a conference held under the auspices of Resources for the Future with support from the U.S. Agency for International Development on September 18, 1979. Two chapters are of particular interest to institution builders, especially those in the field of rural development: "Applications of Public Choice Theory to Rural Development—A Statement of the Problem" by Norman Nicholson, and "Three Cases of Induced Institutional Innovation" by Vernon W. Ruttan.

Nicholson describes three political economy models: the induced innovation model, governance and technology, and collective choice theory. Of these, the first has the most implications for institution building. Hence, the chapter by Ruttan deserves attention. Before reviewing it, however, Nicholson's descriptions of all three models will be summarized.

Nicholson describes the induced innovation model by quoting Ruttan (1978). Ruttan stated the model was

> . . . a theory of institutional changes in which shifts in the demand for institutional change are induced by changes both in the relative prices of factors and products and in the technology associated with economic growth, and in which shifts in the supply of institutional change are induced by advances in knowledge in the social sciences. (p. 34)

With regard to the second model, Nicholson states:

> The second approach to the problem of integrating economic and political analysis can be found in the growing number of studies centering on the community governance of the production process at the local level . . . these approaches are certainly not deterministic and they currently may have better explanatory than predictive power, but they do demonstrate an intimate connection between the economic functions performed by an institution highly influenced by the technology and demography of production and the decision rules, scale, and organizational structure of local institutions. (p. 36)

Nicholson continues:

> The third approach to integrating political and economic analysis . . . builds on a growing body of literature on peasant behavior that argues that peasants' collective behavior can be modeled by microeconomic models because the assumptions about rational behavior built into such models are fundamentally valid. The weakness of the models to date, however, lies in assumptions made about the goals peasants pursue in collective economic activities. In particular, Popkin argues, peasants seek to achieve maximum security, not maximum profit, in their economic behavior. The social institutions which emerge, therefore, may be subject not only to changing factor prices, but also to changing survival strategies mandated by such changing factor prices. (p. 37)

In the other chapter of interest to institution builders, Chapter 9, Ruttan points out that the sources of demand for and supply of technical and institutional change are similar. He further states:

> The significance of the proposed theory of institutional change is that it suggests an economic theory of induced institutional change that is capable of generating testable hypotheses regarding (1) alternative paths of institutional change over time for a particular society, and (2)

divergent patterns of institutional change among countries at a particular time. It is possible to build on this model to develop a theory of induced institutional change that is not only explanatory, in the sense that the present is explained in terms of the past, but is capable of generating testable hypotheses regarding the future direction of institutional change, applicable in social science research to achieve more effective institutional performance and more rapid institutional innovation.

The induced institutional innovation hypothesis implies a strong demand for clarification of the conceptual relationships among resource endowments, cultural endowments, technological change and institutional change as they bear on the processes of development . . . It also calls for the careful testing of those relationships against both historic and contemporary experience. In the induced innovation literature, only the relationships among resource endowments, technical change and institutional change have received significant attention. (p. 247)

Ruttan then examines the induced institutional change hypothesis in three case studies. In the first case, he draws on the work of Kikuchi and Hayami (forthcoming) to examine the evolution of "efficient" crop-sharing institutions in spite of land reform legislation designed to provide greater equity between landlords and tenants. These occurred during a period of increasing rice yields and population pressure on land tenure and labor relationships in a Philippine village. Ruttan contends the study is unique in that it is based on a rigorous analysis of micro-economic data over a period of twenty years.

The increased rice yields were due to two technical innovations. The first was that the national irrigation system was extended to the village level. The second major technical change was the introduction of the modern high-yielding Green Revolution rice varieties.

The first institutional change, induced by the higher yields and the increase in population pressure, was the sharp increase in the number of plots farmed under subtenancy arrangements.

The number increased from one in 1956 to five in 1966, and sixteen in 1976. Subtenancy is illegal under the land reform code, and the subtenancy arrangements are usually made without the formal consent of the landowner. All cases of subtenancy was on land farmed under a leasehold arrangement. The most common subtenancy arrangement was fifty-fifty sharing of costs and output. (p. 250)

The second induced institutional change in the Philippine village study was the emergence of a new pattern of labor-employer relationships between farm operators and landless workers.

Traditionally, laborers who participated in the harvesting and thresh-
ing activity received a one-sixth share of the paddy (rough rice) harvest
(hunusan). By 1976, most of the farmers (83 percent) had adopted a
system in which participation in the harvesting operation was limited to
workers who performed the weeding operation without receiving
wages (*gama*). (p. 251)

Kikuchi and Hayami (forthcoming) interpret the emergence of the
gama system as an institutional innovation designed to reduce the wage
rate for harvesting to a level equal to the marginal productivity of labor.
In the 1950s, when the rice yield per hectare was low and labor was less
abundant, the one-sixth share may have approximated an equilibrium
wage level. They hypothesized that with the higher yields and the more
abundant supply of labor, a one-sixth share would undoubtedly be
larger than the marginal product of labor in the harvesting operation.
And they suggest that the *gama* innovation was introduced with less
social friction than a direct reduction in the harvest share . . .

The authors conclude that in the case of changes in rental and labor
relationships, the changes in institutional arrangements governing the
use of production factors were induced when disequilibria between the
marginal returns and the marginal costs of factor inputs occurred as a
result of changes in factor endowments and technical change. The
direction of institutional change was, therefore, toward resolution of a
new equilibria in factor markets. (p. 253)

In the second case, Ruttan considers the impact of changing
factor prices on property rights in Thailand. In the process, he draws
on work by Feeny (1970, p. 15), who summarizes his argument as
follows:

The appreciation of land prices led to demands for a more secure
property rights system and *the* . . . system was forthcoming because the
elite shared in the gains . . . The decline of property rights in man is
explained by the decline in real wages which made such ownership less
attractive and wage labor more attractive. Thus, declining real wages
lessened the opposition to the abolition of slavery and corvee. These
actions were in the interest of the monarch who had a clear political
incentive to abolish the control of manpower by his potential opposition. In sum, the changes in property rights in man and land contributed to labor mobility and security of land rights, both of which facilitated the expansion of paddy cultivation and rice exports. The (induced
innovation) model successfully explains the changes in Thai property
rights. (p. 258)

The third case analyzes the impact of institutional bias and the
direction of technical change in Argentina. More specifically the author examines the failure of the Argentine economy to undertake the

institutional innovations necessary to realize the relatively inexpensive sources of growth that were potentially available from the technical change in agricultural production. He cites work by de Janvry as follows:

> It has been argued by de Janvry (1973) that in Argentina, lack of economic incentive for the larger farmers to adopt yield-increasing technology has been a major factor in the lag in the development of agricultural research institutions capable of generating yield-increasing biological and chemical technologies suited to the factor endowments of the majority of small and medium farms. He also argues that choice of technology was biased more strongly in a labor-saving direction than it was consistent with factor endowments . . . (p. 259)

The significance of the de Janvry extension of the induced innovation model is that the gains from technical change can be captured by the owners of agricultural land in the form of rising land values rather than by consumers in the form of lower commodity prices. He refers to this as *land market treadmill,* in contrast to the *product market treadmill* described by Cochrane (1958). The land market treadmill operates with much longer lags than the product market treadmill in translating *latent* demand for technical change to *effective* demand. It initially affects only the asset position and opportunity costs of landowners rather than current costs or returns. The lag in translating the latent demand for a shift from, for example . . . one technology . . . to effective demand . . . for another technology is viewed by de Janvry as an important factor in explaining the low level of demand for yield-increasing agricultural technology by the landowning agricultural elite in Argentina. (p. 261)

A second major factor which, in de Janvry's view, contributes to the lag in translating latent into effective demand for land-substituting technology, is a combination of (1) elastic agricultural commodity demand and (2) duality in Argentine agrarian structure. He argues that the larger landowners have been able to capture a "discriminatory institutional rent" in the form of low fiscal burden, monopolization of institutional credit, and privileged access to public services. Thus large and small landowners face different relative factor costs. The lower costs of the large landowners become institutionalized in the price of land and drive down the return on land to the smaller and medium farmers. He then draws on farm management analysis to argue that intensive use of land-substituting biological and chemical technology is more profitable on small, rather than large, farms . . . (p. 261)

Thus, de Janvry concludes that in spite of a latent demand for yield-increasing seed-fertilizer technology in Argentine agriculture, institutional bias directed the limited research resources available for public sector research primarily in the direction of labor-saving rather than yield-increasing technical change. He argues that this explains the long delay in the evolution of a set of public sector institutions capable of inventing land-saving biological and chemical technologies and a strong set of private sector institutions capable of embodying land-saving technologies in low cost inputs. (p. 263)

Ruttan concludes:

The de Janvry rationale is only partially convincing. My own limited reading of Argentine economic and political history suggests that the answer, at least for the period following World War II, must not be found more in class-oriented urban-rural conflict than in interclass conflict within the rural sector. The large landowners have exercised much less control over the agricultural policy agenda, particularly since the revolution of 1943, than is suggested by de Janvry. (p. 263)

In reflecting on these cases, Ruttan states:

The three cases examined in this paper exhibit striking differences in the efficiency with which institutional innovations were induced in response to changes in relative factor endowments and prices. In the Philippine village studied by Kikuchi and Hayami (forthcoming) "efficient" crop-sharing institutions evolved rapidly in spite of land reform legislation designed to achieve greater equity between landlords and tenants. In Thailand, the system of property rights in land and man evolved gradually in association with changes in land-labor endowments. In Argentina, the development of agricultural research institutions capable of responding to the latent demand for yield-increasing agricultural technology suited to the needs of small and medium farmers was delayed by the rural elite. (p. 265)

The public choice literature, on which most of the chapters in this volume draw, has been concerned primarily with improving institutional performance through the design of more efficient institutions. The theory of institutional innovation complements this body of literature in that it is concerned with the forces which influence the direction of institutional innovation. It identifies changing resource endowments, interpreted through changing relative factor prices, as an important source directing both technical and institutional change. (p. 267)

[15] UPHOFF, Norman T., and Esman, Milton J. *Local Organization for Rural Development: Analysis of Asian Experience.* Special Series on Rural Local Government. Ithaca: Rural Development Committee, November 1979.

This monograph examines the role of rural local institutions and rural development as a process leading to improvements in agricultural productivity, income, and rural welfare. The authors base their findings on eighteen case studies of local institutions. Over an eighteen-month period strong empirical evidence is presented that a local organization is a necessary if not sufficient condition for accelerated rural development.

The authors extrapolate seven characteristics of a local organization which are necessary for it to be effectively contributing to rural development:

(1) Local institutions should have *more than one level of organization,* probably a two-tier pattern, in which the lower tier performs functions at the neighborhood or small group level, while the other undertakes more complex business and governmental activities that require relatively largescale operations . . .

(2) Local communities should be linked to higher level decision centers by *multiple channels,* both to achieve the benefits of specialization in communications and to enjoy alternative avenues of influence . . .

(3) As a rule, local institutions should be vested each with several functions to insure their viability and capacity to integrate diverse services, though not so many functions as to overload them or risk a monopoly of local power in a few hands . . .

(4) The more successful cases had engaged much more extensively in *decentralization* of operating decisions as well as local-level planning. Decentralization is usually more effective if it is *controlled* rather than complete . . .

(5) *Politics*—the competition and conflict among groups for influence and resources—must be accepted as unavoidable and legitimate in rural local organizations . . .

(6) *Leadership* is perhaps the most critical variable for establishing and maintaining local organizations . . .

(7) *Distribution of assets and income* poses a serious political issue whenever raised, but our studies indicate the importance of this issue . . . (pp. 99–103)

Finally, of major importance is the conclusion that linkage is a more significant variable than autonomy in promoting rural development.

[16] TECHNICAL Program Committee for Agriculture. "Occasional Paper No. 1." Washington, D.C.: Agency For International Development, undated. 26 pages. (Mimeographed.)

The purpose of this paper is to help Agency development officers to a better understanding of the concept "institution" and of how institutions can be utilized more effectively in agricultural and rural development projects and programs. It elaborates on one of the central concepts set forth in Occasional Paper One (OP/1) of the Technical Program Committee for Agriculture (TPCA). (p. 1)

The paper argues that the elimination of hunger requires both food production and income to buy food. These two needs can be met by focusing efforts on the development of a strong, small-scale, commercial agriculture. Recognizing that there is no short cut to agricultural development, the paper contends that a long-term planning horizon is necessary.

Initially, the concept of institutions is examined. Implications for AID operations are followed by an evaluation of what kinds of institutions are currently needed to support a small-scale, broadbased commercial agriculture. Finally, the paper examines selected institutional needs.

The authors use John R. Commons's definition of institutions as "Collective action in control of individual action."

Control, he says, can be in the form of *restraint* of the individual, *liberation* of the individual, or *expansion of the scope of action* of the individual. Restraint and liberation are self-evident. Expansion may not be. (p. 2)

Commons lists another criterion of an institution:

It must be stable and dependable providing for the individual a "security of expectations." (p. 3)

The authors state,

The "good" institution is one which causes the individual to act in such a way that in serving his own interests he serves the common good or the public or collective interest. (p. 3)

Institutions become visible, concrete, and tangible through organizations . . . These organizations nurture institutions and serve as the institution's means of expressing itself. Much of the work in institution building is dedicated to building organization, building up its facilities, developing linkages, and improving its financial support. All of this makes it easy to confuse *organization development* with *institutional development,* or even to equate the two. (pp. 4–5)

After examining the distinctions between an organization and an institution, the authors suggest that there is a relatively small group of individuals within each LDC who control the institutions. This group is accessible to AID personnel in most countries.

In agricultural and rural development, if we put our best foot forward, we must make institutions and the people who staff them the focus of our efforts, concentrating our great resource on this task. (p. 9)

The authors next suggest nine implications for AID operations if the agency is to make a full commitment to human and institutional resource development.

(1) AID will need to make adjustment in its thinking with respect to target group.

(2) Even with a full and frank commitment to human and institutional resource development (HIRD), AID will not abandon its capital transfer functions.

(3) An institutional approach leads AID in the direction of elitism, a direction which on its face does not seem to be in tune with an orientation to the small farmer.

(4) AID must discipline itself to develop projects on the basis of genuine needs of a country rather than by AID's own criteria, sometimes only for the need to move money, sometimes in desperation for high visibility or impact.

(5) Institutional development in the minds of many is equated with research, extension, and education . . . However, there are many other institutional arrangements essential to a viable, small scale, commercial agriculture.

(6) As AID makes institutional development its strong suit in development efforts, its personnel will need to learn some institutional technology.

(7) A human institutional resources development approach helps the Agency structure its work on policy.

(8) A program that emphasizes institutional development puts a heavy premium on collaboration among the USAID Mission, the Host Government, and the USAID contractor.

(9) The Linkage concept is critical in dealing with institutions. (pp. 10–17)

After developing each of the above in some detail the authors then examine the institutions needed to support small-scale, broad-based commercial agriculture. These can be put into eight categories.

(1) One of the most difficult institutional problems that AID confronts deals with access to land—land tenure, property rights, and the land market . . .

(2) One is the area of Technology and Generation and Diffusion (in some cases linked with education) . . .

(3) Resource conservation and management needs can be expected to increase greatly during the decade in importance to small-scale commercial agriculture . . .

(4) Local governance and taxation is another non-agricultural field that can be expected to play a key role in small-farm development . . .

(5) Agricultural commerce and industry is another area in which our LDC experience is relatively limited . . .

(6) Human resource development is a critical area . . .

(7) Infrastructure faces us on all directions, and each entails its own institutional needs . . .

(8) The field of public policy dealing with agriculture strikes at the very heart of the institutional problem. (pp. 19–22)

One way to categorize institutional characteristics is internal organizational requirements versus linkages between the institution and other organizations.

(1) An institutional organization needs the ability to define its role in the national family of institutions, i.e., its personnel must recognize their responsibility, role, and function, know what the institution is about.

(2) They need the ability to know the client, his problem, his resources, his motivation.

(3) They need the ability to provide what the client needs.

(4) They need the ability to deliver their product to their client.

(5) Finally, institutions need the ability to manage all of the above, including financing and personnel. (pp. 23–24)

2
The Essential Core
of the Literature Published
Prior to 1973

Outstanding contributions to the literature on institution building are summarized below in one of two categories: manuscripts with an institutional-organizational focus or works dealing with phenomena beyond this micro orientation.

The literature with an institutional-organizational orientation resulted largely, but not exclusively, from the Inter-University Research Program in Institution Building (IRPIB). This multidisciplinary program was undertaken by scholars from Michigan State University, Syracuse University, Indiana University, and the University of Pittsburgh, where the project's headquarters are located. This consortium program, financed largely by the Agency for International Development (AID) and the Ford Foundation, was the largest single source of the manuscripts reviewed in the preparation of this book.

Eight of the manuscripts nominated by professionals actively working in the field of institution building resulted directly from the IRPIB. In three others, the methodology developed in that program is used. Because these IRPIB contributions are consolidated in a recently published book of readings, that book is the source of most of the summaries of IRPIB contributions in this chapter. The one exception, however, is Milton Esman's manuscript, "The Institution Building Concepts—An Interim Appraisal." This manuscript is summarized in detail, rather than his shorter chapter in the book edited by Joseph Eaton, because it contains the important conceptual framework developed by him and others.

Although no one group of manuscripts dominates the macro oriented literature, a number of significant contributions have been made. Again, a recently published book—this one entitled *A Theory of Institutions* by John Powelson—is reviewed in detail. Likewise, the book of readings entitled *Modernization by Design* by Chandler Morse et al. is given considerable attention. An article by T. W. Schultz is reviewed in sufficient detail to indicate clearly its substantive contribution. Finally, attention is called to a bibliography that contains some references to macro oriented literature in the fields of technical assistance and institution building.

INSTITUTIONAL-ORGANIZATIONAL LITERATURE

[17] ESMAN, Milton J. "The Institution Building Concepts—An Interim Appraisal." Graduate School of Public and International Affairs, University of Pittsburgh, Pittsburgh, Pa., 1967. 66 pages. (Mimeographed. Part of Inter-University Research Program in Institution Building.)

Since much of the institution building literature refers to the framework conceptualized by Esman et al., it will be summarized first. Esman's manuscript contains not only basic concepts but also a partial evaluation of them on the basis of data obtained from the initial IRPIB case studies. These case studies were: the College of Education of the University of Nigeria, by John Hanson [28]; the Central University of Ecuador, by Hans C. Blaise and Luis A. Rodriguez [63]; the Institute of Public Administration of Thammasat, University of Thailand, by William Siffin [88]; and the Institute of Public Administration for Turkey and the Middle East, by Guthrie Birkhead [89].

Basic concepts

In the restatement of the basic concepts, Esman emphasizes that his approach has a pronounced bias toward social engineering that is based on the proposition that most significant, contemporary changes—especially in developing countries—are deliberately planned and guided. Further, the approach presupposes that the introduction of change takes place primarily in and through formal organizations. When these organizations are change-inducing, change-protecting, and formal, they are considered to be institutions. These organizations and the new patterns they foster become institutionalized, e.g., meaningful and valued in the societies in which they function. This involves a complex set of interactions between the institutions and the environment. The latter varies in its readiness or resistance to change both over time and from place to place.

Basic to Esman's approach is the assumption that the efficient assimilation of new physical and social technologies requires that the environment provide supporting values, norms, processes, and structures which usually are not present when the new technologies are introduced. Changing the environment to complement or accommodate the new technologies is an integral part of development. Since these new technologies are primarily introduced in and through organizations, the supportive values, norms, processes, and structures must be institutionalized in and through these organizations; that is, normative relationship and action patterns must be established in and through organizations which incorporate, foster, and protect normative relationship and action patterns and perform functions and services that are valued in the environment. The results of analyses of these institutionalized changes can serve as guides to social action. Hence, the assumption has been made that institution building is a generic social process, i.e., a set of elements and actions can be identified which is relevant to institution building in general.

The three analytical categories upon which Esman's analysis is built are depicted in the accompanying figure from citation [2]. Institution variables are those elements thought to be necessary and sufficient to explain the systemic behavior in an institution.

The Institution Building Universe

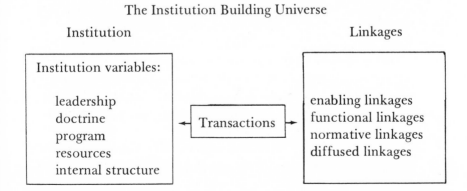

Leadership applies not only to people formally charged with the direction of an institution, but also to all others who participate in the planning, structuring, and the guidance of it. Within leadership, viewed as a unit, important factors include political viability, professional status, technical competence, organizational competence, role distribution, and continuity.

Doctrine, as the stable reference point of an institution to which all other variables relate, contains such characteristics as specificity, meaning the extent to which elements of doctrine supply the necessary foundation for action in a given situation; the extent to which the institutional doctrine conforms to the expected and sanctioned behavior of the society; and the degree to which the institution's doctrine conforms to the preferences, priorities, intermediate goals, and targets of the society.

Those actions related to the performance of functions and services constituting the output of the institution represent its program. Hence, important aspects of the program variable include its consistency with the institution's doctrine, stability of output, feasibility regarding resources, as well as complementary production of other organizations in the absorptive capacity of the society, and the contribution of the institution toward satisfying the specified needs of the society.

The inputs of an institution, here defined as resources, are important not only in quantitative terms, but also because of their sources. These sources and the ability to obtain resources through them affect decisions with regard to program, doctrine, and leadership. Hence, the two categories within this variable are availability and sources.

As both structure and process, the category of internal structure includes such things as the distribution of functions and authority, the processes of communication and decision making, and other relationship-action patterns. Consequently, it determines the efficiency and effectiveness of program performance. Components of this category include identification of participants within the institution, consistency of the structure with the institution's doctrine and program, and the structure's adaptability to shifts in program emphasis and other changes.

Every institution is dependent upon other organizations for its authority and resources; hence, its linkages with other entities are vitally important. These linkages also include an institution's dependency on complementary production of other institutions and on the ability of the environment to use its resources. Finally, linkages are also concerned with and subject to the norms of the society. Through these linkages the institution maintains exchange relationships with its environment, an interdependent complex of functionally related organizations. The four subcategories of linkages are discussed briefly below.

In the initial stages of an institution's life, its prime target is developing its relationship with other entities that control the allocation of authority and resources it needs; this category is called enabling linkages. Developing relationships with such entities is important not only for obtaining authority and resources, but also because these are the same entities through which the institution's opposition seeks to withhold needed inputs from it.

Functional linkages relate the institution to (1) organizations which are complementary in a productive sense—that is, which supply inputs and use the outputs of the institution; and (2) those organizations which constitute real or potential competition. Through functional linkages an institution attempts to spread its innovations as it embodies and promotes new patterns and technologies.

Both sociocultural norms and operating rules and regulations have important implications for institutions via normative linkages, through which the society places certain constraints on and establishes guidelines for institutions. The norms, rules, and regulations can either act as obstacles to or facilitate the process of institution building.

While these three categories of linkages refer to relationships of an institution with other specific institutions and organizations, diffused linkages refer to the relationship between the institution and public opinion and with the public in general. Thus, this category includes relationships established through news media and other channels for the crystallization and expression of individual and small-group opinion.

Through these four linkages, then, an institution carries on transactions with other segments of the society. These transactions involve not only physical inputs and outputs but also such social interactions as communication, support acquisition, and the trans-

fer of norms and values. More specifically, the purposes of transactions have been identified as (1) gaining support and overcoming
resistance, (2) exchanging resources, (3) structuring the environment, and (4) transferring norms and values.

Institution building is a time-consuming process. During its
initial phase certain values or goals are conceived by the change
agents, and a strategy is determined for their attainment. Also
during this period, support is sought for achieving goals and values,
an effort is made to overcome resistances, and an attempt is made
to acquire the necessary authority and resources for the establishment of the institution. Subsequently in the life cycle of the
institution, different strategies and actions are required for exe-
cuting the program, maintaining the institution, and facilitating
the transfer of norms and values to other elements of the society.

Case studies

In reflecting on the four case studies, Esman attempts to (1)
analyze and compare some of the researchers' most salient findings, (2) suggest implications for the program's general approach
to the institution building process and to the basic concepts which
were their common point of departure, and (3) indicate the future
development of theory, methodology, and practical application
toward which these studies point. Since these studies are summarized in [28], [63], [88], and [89], attention is now called to generalizations drawn from them rather than their individual findings.

Technical assistance in institution building

In all four of the cases studied, technical assistance staffs
made up of foreigners to the country in question provided the
main models for change and, in three cases, most of the impulse
for action. However, even in these three cases, the staff members
were unable to carry their local counterparts with them on significant issues. Although frequently disagreeing among themselves,
their counterparts were committed to only a few of the specific
changes that they endorsed. Local staff members frequently attached higher priority to protecting existing relationships than to

the changes proposed by technical assistance personnel, although they frequently agreed with the technical personnel about proposed goals.

In the instances studied, the technical assistance personnel were welcomed as suppliers of physical resources, as teachers, and, to some extent, as sources of technical ideas which would help the existing system do its old job better. But when viewed as a means of inducing new norms or action patterns within the institution itself or in transactions with linked cliental groups, they were threatening. These experiences suggest that congruence between the technical assistance personnel and indigenous institutional leaders over goals and tactics, as well as over the doctrine and the program of the subject institution, directly influences the effectiveness of foreign assistance. Without such congruence frustration is inevitable and even conflict may result.

On the basis of this admittedly small sample of four cases, several tendencies appeared to exist. One of these is that the doctrinal compatibility between the technical advisers and the institution's leadership cadre seemed to be more important than the formal positions of power that the technical assistance personnel occupied within the institution. Another is that technical assistance teams need to maintain a position that will enable them to capitalize upon changes in the external environment. A third is that technical assistance personnel tend to use mild and accommodating tactics rather than tension- or crisis-producing ones. Fourth, at the outset of a technical assistance project, leaders at the host institution are often uncertain of their goals, are more concerned with maintaining existing patterns and protecting their own interests within the present system than in fomenting changes, are unwilling to incur risks, and tend to be passive or inept in using the resources or the opportunities available. Fifth, in these situations institution builders must deploy a battery of survival and service tactics as well as change tactics. Sixth, the institution builder must be a manager par excellence, who can adjust to unplanned consequences of actions taken as well as to unanticipated contingencies, and who can attempt to create opportunities to facilitate his program goals. Finally, Esman concludes:

The most generalized proposition that seems to emerge at this stage of institution building research on the question of change tactics is that the institution building leadership should attempt in its transactions with each linked public to distribute or appear to be distributing a far greater volume of benefits than of costs. The margin of benefits over costs must be substantial because costs (dissatisfactions or threats) in status, respect, security, finance, or scope for action are usually perceived to be far more critical, triggering defensive action, than are anticipated benefits triggering supportive action. Where a wide margin of benefits over costs cannot be distributed, or where the organization appears to be under attack from a major linked institution, it must not hesitate to defer some of its activities which might be threatening to an external group. In such cases it must attempt to deal with a few negative situations at a time, must focus enough bargaining energy and resources on the potential conflict, and must be able to deploy enough power in that situation to be reasonably certain of a satisfactory outcome. This is simply the strategy of keeping one's opponents divided and dealing with them separately rather than allowing an effective coalition to mobilize. (p. 46)

Several strategies for institution building are suggested. One is that rather than creating an entirely new institution, an existing one should be strengthened, unless (1) important groups within the society perceive that the existing institution is discharging its functions inadequately or is neglecting activities which it should be performing, or (2) the original institution is not catering to emergent needs or demands within its field of jurisdiction. When the existing institution has a widely diffused internal power structure, the appropriate strategy would appear to be an attempt to create a new unit within the existing institution. In situations where both the leadership and environmental factors are favorable, a rational approach to timing is to give initial emphasis to building a solid and viable organization and then to construct reliable linkages within the environment. Only when these linkages have been established should the riskier and more difficult task of restructuring the environment and transferring norms to linked institutions be attempted. When the environment is especially receptive to change, a more apropos and certainly bolder strategy may be to foster changes within the environment before linkages have been firmly established and the basic organization built on a solid foundation.

Observations on methodology

The decision not to prescribe the detailed methodologies for the four case studies was quite deliberate. The researchers involved developed a number of instruments and used a variety of investigative methods based on standard social science research techniques. The latter included in-depth interviews, use of data from secondary sources and, where possible, internal records of the institution itself. However, the techniques of linkage mapping and blue-print mapping were not used.

Summary and conclusions

After briefly reviewing the primary findings and posing a number of hypotheses for future inquiry, Esman states:

> We have gained confidence in our basic approach to institution building. It has been found useful as an orientation to the process of organizationally induced and protected social change, though the approach needs to be relaxed to accommodate the variety of circumstances under which deliberate change is attempted. Our conceptual equipment has been tested and it too has been found useful, subject to more precise definition and refinement. The number of variables that enter into institution building analysis, the variety of environmental conditions, the dynamic context in which action occurs create such a multiplicity of possible combinations as to defy efforts at comprehensive theory building at this time. At a more modest and immediately useful level, we can study how single variables affect one another under limiting but important conditions and thus build knowledge incrementally and cumulatively. (p. 66)

For earlier statements of the institution building framework developed by Esman et al. see:

[18] ESMAN, Milton J., and Blaise, Hans C. "Institution Building Research: The Guiding Concepts." Graduate School of Public and International Affairs, University of Pittsburgh, Pittsburgh, Pa., 1966. 19 pages. (Mimeographed. Part of Inter-University Research Program in Institution Building.)

[19] ESMAN, Milton J., and Blaise, Hans C. "Inter-University Research Program in Institution Building." Graduate School of Public and International Affairs, University of

Pittsburgh, Pittsburgh, Pa., undated. 12 pages. (Mimeographed. Part of Inter-University Research Program in
Institution Building.)

[20] EATON, Joseph W., ed. *Institution Building and Development:
From Concepts to Application.* Beverly Hills, Calif.: Sage
Publications, 1972. 272 pages.*

On the basis of the basic concepts outlined above, the Inter-
University Research Program in Institution Building (IRPIB) conducted a number of inquiries, primarily in the 1960s. This recently
published book of readings contains some of the most important
manuscripts resulting from the IRPIB effort. Because it may be
regarded as the culmination of the consortium's activities, it has
special significance.

---

* Manuscripts similar to chapters 3, 4, 5, 8, and 9 of Eaton's book can be found
elsewhere:

[21]   NEHNEVAJSA, Jiri. "Institution-Building: Elements of a Research Orientation."
Paper prepared for the meetings of NSSTE at Chicago, Ill., February 1967. 14
pages. (Mimeographed, Part of Inter-University Research Program in Institution Building.)

[22]   NEHNEVAJSA, Jiri. "A Working Paper: Methodological Issues in Institution-
Building Research." Graduate School of Public and International Affairs,
University of Pittsburgh, Pittsburgh, Pa., 1964. (Mimeographed. Preliminary
work. Part of Inter-University Research Program in Institution Building.)

[23]   LANDAU, Martin. "Linkage, Coding, and Intermediacy: A Strategy for Institution Building." *Journal of Comparative Administration,* 2 (February 1971),
401–29.

[24]   UPHOFF, Norman T., and Ilchman, Warren F. "The Time Dimension in Institution Building." Graduate School of Public and International Affairs, University of Pittsburgh, Pittsburgh, Pa. 40 pages plus notes. (Mimeographed. Part of
Inter-University Research Program in Institution Building.)

[25]   THORSEN, Thomas W. "The Institution-Building Model in Program Operation
and Review." *Proceedings: Conference on Institution Building and Technical
Assistance.* Edited by D. Woods Thomas and Judith G. Fender. Washington,
D.C.: Agency for International Development and Committee on Institutional
Cooperation, December 4 and 5, 1969. Pp. 100-116.

[26]   DUNCAN, Richard L., and Pooler, William S. "Technical Assistance and Institution Building." Graduate School of Public and International Affairs, University of Pittsburgh, Pittsburgh, Pa., 1967. 111 pages. (Mimeographed. Part of
Inter-University Research Program in Institution Building.)

Chapter 1: The Elements of Institution Building
             by Milton J. Esman

In the opening chapter, Milton Esman presents many of the concepts summarized above and subsequently referred to in this source book as the institution building perspective of Esman et al. Rather than review them again, attention is turned to chapter 2.

Chapter 2: Institution Building as Vision and Venture: A Critique
             by William J. Siffin

The institution building approach already described argues that (1) technology is a key, if the not *the* key, to development; (2) the establishment of effective organizations is the essential instrumental problem of delivering technology; and (3) normative factors are the critical concern in building organizations to deliver technology and, hence, are an organization's developmental fruits. Therefore, William Siffin states that institution building means organization building, although the problem is specified in an unconventional way. Further, he contends that the problem of institution building can be reduced to one of relations between organizations and the environment.

According to Siffin,

> Institution building is not a theory (save in the loosest and most metaphorical sense of that much maligned word). One useful conventional conceptualization of a theory is that of "an empirical generalization"—a general statement of some regular, predictable relationships between two or more types of things. (p. 46)

Hence, he concludes that the institution building perspective of Esman et al. does not "explain" institutionality as a quality related to some other quality or qualities in a regular, determinate fashion that can be observed. Nor are the elements of Esman's perspective variables. Rather, they are broad, general labels of qualities, relationships, and categories of action.

> If institution building were an empirical theory, it would necessarily include indices of "institutionalization"—the discrete state or condition that is intended to be attained through a certain quality of intervention. But the IB literature is not clear and precise on this point. It offers a debatable set of stipulations, along with some latitude for choice. In the

absence of a clear and unequivocal index of the state to be achieved by
the appropriate interaction of the variables, it is rather obviously
impossible to subject the theory to the test of validation—or falsifica-
tion. (p. 47)

The institution building perspective of Esman et al. involves
too many possible kinds of interaction among too many complex
and illusive variables to be able to evolve into a relatively general
theory, i.e., one with explicit rules by which to operationalize its
variables to analyze a given problem. Consequently, any power of
the perspective must emanate from use of the approach by reasoning, analytical, and adroit individuals. Siffin contends, "The IB
perspective is explanatorily sterile—but this does not keep it from
being suggestive" (p. 48).

The perspective offers appeal as a promising model, a new
and better lens through which to see what needs to be seen. In
addition, it offers a certain amount of information about its
elements—some knowledge of such things as leadership, doctrine,
and linkages. But the perspective is static. It is a priori. It is
unoriented. Suffice it to say, the perspective has a number of
notable characteristics.

In spite of the fact that the perspective has been useful in
examining a wide range of experiences in institutional development and as a guide for training programs, there are important
difficulties embedded in the practical efforts to apply the perspective. First, empirical application of its linkage component demonstrates more explanatory appeal to analysts than explanatory
power in their analyses. If the model is to be used practically, it
must be by filling in the relatively empty boxes labeled linkages
with important knowledge about such things as strategies for
mapping and making linkages. Second, its gross prescriptive bias
needs to be refined. The conditions under which institution building efforts are likely to succeed must be determined. Third, the
perspective does not address the problem of validation, which
requires that: (1) the limitations of the perspective be realized, (2)
further knowledge about institution building processes and strategies be developed, and (3) strategically useful knowledge about
alternative interventions for social change be determined.

Siffin concludes his insightful critique by contending that
additional information is needed concerning (1) task environments

in which institution building efforts are likely to be successful and (2) strategies and tactics for effectively performing this aspect of the development process.

Chapter 3: Methodological Issues in
             Institution-Building Research
             by Jiri Nehnevajsa

The objective of this chapter is to begin mapping a type of research program in relation to which various particular studies could be located and acquire meaning greater than that which would result from uncoordinated endeavors. Its initial section provides a general frame of reference. The second part identifies the information required to satisfy this frame. The final portion identifies some of the methodological problems involved in the acquisition of data.

Assuming that an institution is falling short of its objectives, the purpose of analyzing it would be to identify the sources of discrepancy between intended and actual system outputs. Subsequently, the analysis should be designed to provide alternatives in the institution or in its relations with other elements of the system that would enhance the probability of its success in accomplishing its objectives. Finally, the institution should be monitored to determine whether the alterations did in fact improve its effectiveness.

Evaluation research identifies difficulties and reasons for them, when existing needs do not seem to be met adequately. In turn, the results of such evaluation lead to design, which identifies steps whereby the change will lead to the desired results. Further, evidence should be provided that the recommended solutions are better than alternative ones. Jiri Nehnevajsa describes the details of this analytical phase as components of an evaluation cycle. Likewise, he presents and discusses the components of the design cycle. Finally, he discusses the interaction of the cycles:

> The evaluation cycle is concerned with assessment of ongoing operations and their improvement, so that it blends into design problems when improvement is required and decided upon. The design cycle blends into the evaluation issue when a particular design is decided upon and implemented, so that a new institution is built to satisfy hitherto unmet social needs. (p. 77)

Later in the chapter, Nehnevajsa contends that research on institution building must deal with what men value, how they obtain it, and how this process can be improved. Thus, it is a search for betterment and not simply a search. However, it may involve a search for what constitutes betterment.

The first phase of this portion of the analysis involves blueprint mapping, i.e., determining what the institution ought to be like with regard to form and performance. The second portion, operations mapping, describes what actually goes on, i.e., the actual format and performance of the institution. Image mapping is involved in the third part of the analysis, and it focuses on what people think is going on with regard to the institution. More specifically, image mapping determines the images held by decision makers, leaders, personnel, clients, influentials, and the public.

The substantive aspects of these mapping activities focus on institutional doctrine, institutional themes, leadership, personnel, resources, the organization, enabling linkages, functional linkages, normative linkages, and diffuse linkages. These ten major clusters of issues then become the common axes of the blueprint, operations, and image maps.

After discussing the importance of time, Nehnevajsa deals with the implications for research of this reference frame.

1. There is a requirement to produce blueprint, operations and image maps of an institution at some given time zero, the present. . . .

2. There is a requirement to generate blueprint, operations, and image maps, insofar as possible, in the antecedent (historical) stages of the institution. . . .

3. There is a requirement to consider the kinds of circumstances or events which may account for either historical stability or change. . . .

4. There is a requirement to identify the kinds of futures which the institution may have as a whole and in the specific mapping dimensions, contingent upon persistence of already existing dynamics as well as upon deliberate introduction [of] innovative alternatives. . . .

5. Under ideal research conditions, the previous step presupposes a similar futuristic analysis of those institutions and agencies whose

actions and functioning is central to the institution under study, and whose behavior is thus a codeterminant of its future. . . .

6. There is a requirement to provide for the monitoring of the institution-building process along blueprint, operations, and image-mapping lines so that the process of actualization can be observed, and the time-zero maps can be updated in light of (a) secular changes, (b) changes specifically induced as an aspect of the institution-building effort, and (c) changes induced deliberately or accidentally by others. The descriptive aspect of this effort means that it is necessary to keep up to date with changes as they are occurring and when they are occurring, so that the institution-in-context maps [operations and image maps] do not become obsolete by the time they are actually produced. (pp. 85-87)

Chapter 4: Linkage, Coding and Intermediacy:
A Strategy for Institution Building
by Martin Landau

Martin Landau employs the concept of linkage as a point of departure in considering action strategy. In order for linkages to serve as points of exchanges (information or energy transfers), the exchanges must be properly coded so that messages will be transformed into sets of signs that capture the informational content of the message. These signs are constructs or events by which one entity affects the behavior of another.

Encoding is, therefore, crucial for it constitutes the process of making a set of signs intelligible. A code, thus, is a set of rules which provides the means by which this is done. At the linkage points (assuming effective coupling), these codes mesh—i.e., both the rules governing the institution and those which operate in its task environment are paired. It is on this basis that an exchange can be effected, as in the case of a seller and a buyer. Mapping linkages is, therefore, the *strategic consideration in the analysis of the institution-building process* and requires close analysis of the codes which both parties to the transaction bring to bear upon each other. (pp. 94-95)

If these codes become impaired, an ordered system becomes random and subject to the disorder and violence that have marked so many contemporary scenes.

Landau proposes a planning strategy relevant to the role of intermediate organizations in the process of development and institution building, i.e., between existent states and end states.

The distinctions to be made rest upon the quantity and type of linkage arrangements and their rates of change.

> The more simple the organizational stage, the less the number and variety of linkage points and the slower they change; the more complex, the larger the number and variety, and the greater the rate of change. What is to be classified as intermediate, of course, depends upon the particular concrete system with which we are dealing. (p. 97)

Critical features of modern, developed, urban societies are differentiation, specialization, and integration. Large-scale organizations (bureaucracies) assume prominence as institutional components of these societies. They represent the primary instruments for engineering social change in order to hasten development. These organizations tend to be achievement oriented, technical, rational, specific, effectively neutral, calculated, impersonal, and instrumental; use rules, means, matter-of-factness, and expertise to "dominate their being"; have structures that are deterministic (centralized), rules that are complete, operational codes that are specific and precise, formal channels, offices that are exact (jurisdiction); and have authority that is exercised without regard to persons. Formal organizations of this type displace actions which are based upon personal sympathy and favor, tradition, kinship, and the like.

In contrast to formal complex organizations, intermediate organizations tend to have the following properties: (1) they are, by design (intention), nondeterministic in structure, thus limiting the extent to which their internal processes are predictable and controllable; (2) they are much less differentiated structurally, and their degree of specialization is less pronounced; (3) their ethos is more reflective of *gemeinschaft* than *gesellschaft;* (4) further, they tend to be smaller in size, operate in terms of lesser magnitudes, and permit a larger social space to their members than do formal complex organizations. Intermediate organizations tend to be much closer to the "probability texture" of the task environment of the underdeveloped scene. The discrepancy between codes and linkages is not nearly as great between simple and intermediate institutions as it is between simple and complex systems. Hence, the former are much more easily reconciled than the latter. It is not surprising that the need for intermediate institutions is emphasized frequently.

Landau concludes by arguing for redundant intermediate organizations (systems), which would enhance the ability of the total system to achieve reliability of performance and attain considerable adaptability. Such a strategy is mandated by the enormous risks which attend development. Hence, redundancy increases reliability and decreases the risks of the development process.

Chapter 5: The Time Dimension in Institution Building
         by Norman T. Uphoff and Warren F. Ilchman

"Time is of the essence in institution building" is the general theme used in this chapter where the institution variables of resources, leadership, doctrine, program, and internal structure as well as the action strategies of leadership, doctrine, and program are reconsidered.

Rather than simply define the goal of institution building as social change, Norman Uphoff and Warren Ilchman maintain that the objective is better described as social control. Through institutions individuals are better able to control the course of change and bring about those changes desired within a shorter period of time than would be possible otherwise. In this sense, institutions enable individuals to have some control over time itself.

Most analyses within the social sciences neglect time. For example, both behavioral and structural analyses in organization theory treat time inadequately. Hence, organization theory hardly is prepared to contribute much toward the analysis of formal organizations as key instruments for social change in developing countries.

Time is not considered a resource per se. Rather, it is viewed as permitting the productive use of resources. Consequently, time is seen as a quality of resources. According to Uphoff and Ilchman, resources relevant to institution building include not only the financial, physical, human, technological, and informational inputs of the institution, but also economic resources, information, status, authority, force, legitimacy, and support. Institutions are marked by routine and relatively predictable flows of these resources over time. Through their possession and use, they determine the value of time. As a rule, the longer an institution has them, the greater output or value is accrued. Hence, the value of time is a proxy for the value of the resources possessed and used to produce valued outputs.

The leadership of an institution performs an entrepreneurial function, combining factors of organizational production in order to produce valued outputs. In turn, these outputs yield resources that may be used to further the process of organizational growth. In other words, the leadership seeks new sources of resources and support, attempts to find new, more productive combinations of these, and attempts to find new uses for the resulting output which has a greater value than previously. In the process, an organizational strategy may guide the use of existing resources over time in such a way as to obtain or maintain control over sufficient resources to achieve organizational objectives. This faculty for strategy to use resources over time is a distinguishing characteristic of leadership.

A basic element of doctrine is the time horizon. The importance of doctrine increases as the scarcity of available resources increases and the time available for achieving desired ends decreases.

An organization must invest certain of its available resources over time in order to maintain itself and achieve new or additional objectives. The resources invested have no immediate return but enable an organization to produce greater returns in the future than if no investment had been made. The result is an improvement in either its productive capacity or linkages with other organizations.

The program variable is more closely related to time than any other, because an organization's program consists of allocating resources over time. Three dimensions of timing—synchronization, sequence, and rate—are noted. The term *program* implies the first dimension—coordination—a concept intrinsically bound to time. Sequencing resource allocations is the essence of establishing program priorities. The rate of institutional production is important in that societal needs must be met in a timely manner—merely meeting them is not sufficient for institutionalization.

The significance and emphases of program are largely a function of time. The more rapidly desired the results, the more critical the content and implementation of program become. The fewer the resources, the more important is their efficient allocation through program strategy.

Internal structure involves the allocation of resources within an organization and represents flows of economic resources, information, status, authority, and coercion or other sanctions. Hence, internal structure is related intimately with time. The more ambitious the change goals of the institution builder and/or the less time in which he has to achieve these goals, the more critical is internal structure. Regardless, the aims of internal structure are to enhance the efficiency and productivity of the institution.

In turning to action strategies, Uphoff and Ilchman note that a concept of strategy implies the use of time or timing and that the formulation of action strategies requires a discerning analysis of the organization's environment. Those strategies aimed at institutionalization seek to increase over time the dependence of other organizations on the outputs of the institution in question. Regardless of the degree of dependency, exchange relationships (linkages) characterize the interrelationships among institutions.

The first of the five institutional variables related to action strategies in the context of time and timing is leadership. Rather than look at commitment and competence, the authors prefer to look at costs and benefits affecting different sectors of the environment and the leadership itself, not just in terms of economic resources, but in terms of their valued ends. By varying the timing and combination of resources according to doctrine and program, leadership may raise benefits relative to costs, thus contributing to institutionalization. Thus, formal and informal leaders of an organization are resource allocators. Resource allocation involves both time and strategy. Consequently, leadership can be referred to meaningfully in terms of its knowledge about the productive use of resources over time.

Doctrine is helpful in formulating action strategies by stating valued allocations of resources over time and leading organizations, which stand to benefit from proposed changes themselves, to make contributions toward achieving these goals. Doctrine may be self-fulfilling in that it may evoke the necessary resources in and of itself to achieve the goals. Thus, the skillful use or reformulation of doctrine, combined with the threats and offers implicit in program, may achieve results not possible within the initially existing resource constraints.

Action strategies must be integrated into programs for priorities to be established for the expenditure of resources and direction of activity. Given the scarcity of means to achieve an organization's ends, some sequenced pattern of expenditure and investment is necessary. In selecting among alternative action strategies, leaders need information on the expected consequences of these alternative sequences in order to choose the one that appears to be most efficient.

The authors conclude with comments on change tactics, technical assistance in institution building, and some propositions about institution building.

Chapter 6: Guideline to Development Theory Formulations
          by Joseph W. Eaton

Joseph Eaton views institution building concepts as guidelines for a systematic description of interactions within a macro system planned to facilitate development of innovative organizations. Comparative analysis of field study data gathered in accord with these concepts can lead to their refinement through deduction. Further, by relating two or more of the concepts, field analysts can formulate hypotheses such as the following: "Resident and entrenched leadership can more easily command resources for a new program and develop strong enabling linkages with other institutions in the society than absentee and changing leadership" (p. 144).

Another insight from institution building is identified as the sell-out syndrome, i.e., a tendency for leaders to purchase support from existing organizations by reducing their own institution's innovative thrust. Still another insight might be called the multiple-interest syndrome. William Siffin described this with respect to the Thai Institute of Public Administration: "Key professional personnel failed to perform their designated roles because their commitment to the new program conflicted with a pre-existing network of linkages to other institutions in the system who were already providing them with income, status and identity" (p. 145).

These inferences remain to be tested as hypotheses under a variety of rigorous field study conditions. "What could be done, but has not yet been attempted in any IB study, is a prospective field experiment," says Eaton. "Experimental controls would be introduced within certain limits, since every institution has compelling functions which cannot always be controlled in accordance with a detailed research design, no matter how meritorious the research may be, to test one or a few major hypotheses" (p. 145). Eaton speculates that perhaps because of the difficulty of finding a suitable laboratory such hypothesis testing has not been done, although every research director of IRPIB during its seven-year history recommended it.

Chapter 7: The Institution-Building Model: A Systems View
by Saul M. Katz

In taking a systems view of the institution building model, Saul Katz lists four starting premises.

> The first premise is that the guided societal change known as "development" is generally induced by the deliberate introduction of physical and social innovations. The famous economist Joseph Schumpeter considered innovation—the application of new techniques to production and distribution—to be the source of economic development. . . . A similar view may be identified in other social sciences. In fact, the cumulation of innovations may be seen as the core of societal change. . . .
>
> The second premise is that innovations, no matter how technical, affect and are affected by values, norms, and attitudes, as well as explicit behavior. These are not random occurrences. They have planned and anticipated interrelationships that can be expected. Any strategy of development must take this into account. . . .
>
> The third starting premise is that the deliberate propagation of innovations, by and large, takes place through formal organizations. Modern economic life puts particular emphasis on formal organizations that make possible specialization of tasks and exchange of goods and services. They make it feasible for large numbers of people to carry out complex tasks related to each other and to the deliberate establishing and achieving of common purposes. . . .
>
> The fourth premise is that a systems view of organizations is a useful frame for description and prescription. The use of "system" here, as an assemblage of elements that have ordered and recurrent patterns of interrelationships built around definable objectives or purposes, is not dissimilar to its usage by economists and sociologists. . . . The systems view may be used at different levels of aggregation and for various purposes. Organizations, and often, groups of organizations, interact as systems. (pp. 153-54)

The following three dimensions of analysis are suggested by a systems view of institution building: (1) identifiable purposes, (2) subsystems for carrying on essential organizational functions, and (3) linkages between the organization and its environment.

Within the systems framework Katz includes nine of the institution building concepts, albeit not grouped in the conventional way. Under purpose he includes doctrine and institutionality. Internal structure is discussed under functional subsystems. Environmental linkages include enabling, functional, normative, and diffuse linkages as well as resources and transactions. The concepts of leadership and program are omitted because of their ambiguity and redundancy for the purpose sought.

Katz concludes by stating, ". . . the model shows promise in three ways. If it can contribute to our understanding of the development process by generalizing from a variety of cases using a set of similar analytic concepts, it facilitates comparative study. Based on efforts at normative analysis, it assists in developing a framework for evaluation. . . . Finally, it contributes to guides for developmental action" (p. 160).

Chapter 8: The Institution-Building Model in
Program Operation and Review
by Thomas W. Thorsen

Thomas Thorsen states:

Effective institution development analysis requires careful rationalization of the entire process of institution building, identifying significant institutional characteristics and putting these into an analytical framework that can be understood and operationally applied. The institution-building matrix . . . is the end product of this process. The Esman institution-building model became the core of the matrix. I have considerably expanded the model in developing the matrix because I felt the institution-building model was not operationally complete. The matrix is a synthesis of concepts from a variety of sources . . . and has been used to analyze and evaluate a variety of institutions.

The matrix proved to be a very useful analytical as well as programming tool and contributed significantly both to the technicians' and host government institutional leaders' understanding of the institution-building process. It also confirmed my belief that an analytical and evaluative process could be developed upon which realistic institutional goals and strategies could be determined and initiated. (p. 167)

An analytical and an evaluative process compose this matrix. The former requires analysis of the most significant environmental factors of an institution, which are identified in checklist fashion. One of these is the donor of aid, which should be analyzed in terms of will, means, state of technology, constraints, project inputs, institution progress reporting, and influence. Environmental factors should also be analyzed for the host institution and its capacity for change should be evaluated.

The core of the matrix is the institution building profile, which consists of observations on (1) institutional leadership properties, (2) establishment of institutional doctrine, (3) capacity for program analysis, (4) institutional structures, (5) institutional linkages, and (6) capacity for institutional change. In turn, these 6 major categories are further divided into 37 subcategories in order to increase the number of intuitive and qualitative judgments about the institution. On the basis of subjective ratings of excellent, good, satisfactory, poor, and unsatisfactory, judgments can be made concerning each of these categories at several points in time, thus facilitating intertemporal comparisons. These comparisons are improved when narrative statements supporting the rationale used in each rating are recorded. Thorsen suggests that these ratings be undertaken every two years.

Similarly, combined administrative-managerial profiles are constructed. The former include such major staff services as planning, finance, budgeting, personnel, and procurement. Subdivisions of the management component include (1) management by objectives, (2) national capacity for attainment of objectives, (3) measurement and control of objectives, (4) political analysis for project implementation, and (5) project information dissemination.

> The objective of the entire analytical-evaluative process is to provide a rational framework upon which an institutional development strategy ... can be designed. The analytical-evaluative technique is intended to clearly identify major institutional strengths and weaknesses and permit improvement strategies and courses of action to be devised which will be instrumental in moving weak institutional factors from right to left on the profiles. ...

> The process gives the institutional leader good insight into the nature of his institution, permits the presentation of more critical and precise institutional goals or objectives, enables the institution to divert man-

power and resources to more clearly defined objectives and problem
areas, and charts a more orderly, well-balanced course for institutional
improvement and viability. (p. 175)

The institution building matrix, although still in the develop-
mental-experimental stage, has been used for five institutions.
Experience has demonstrated that leadership properties are the
most sensitive category to evaluate. Establishing institutional doctrine has proven to be the most difficult factor to understand. In
addition, the capacity for institutional change is proving trouble-
some to comprehend.

Chapter 9: Technical Assistance and Institution
            Building: An Empirical Test
            by William S. Pooler and Richard L. Duncan

The primary purpose of the research reported by William
Pooler and Richard Duncan was to examine the contributions
made by organized technical assistance teams in the building of
institutions. In their examination, Pooler and Duncan added the
dimensions of internal organization and environmental linkage to
the dimension of time, thereby creating a dynamic analytic
approach.

They used a definition of technical assistance that focuses on
several common elements. Technical assistance is purposive. It is
cooperative. It involves an international transfer of knowledge and
skill through individuals or agencies of a donor. It provides a
defined relationship between individuals and it involves recipient
groups or organizations in the accomplishment of mutually agreed
objectives.

Data from 46 institution building cases were analyzed. The
data were coded with the use of numerous specific criteria. Among
the more difficult to formulate were the criteria of success. Those
criteria used were (1) an institution's survival and continuity with
respect to performing functions for which it was designed; (2) an
institution's relatively greater autonomy in obtaining and determining the use of funds; (3) an institution's structural impact,
defined as evidence of societal structural change to accommodate
the emergence of the institution as a result of institutional output,
service, or other effects that it has on the environment; (4) the

degree to which institutional norms are recognized as being legitimate, i.e., desirability of services and methods of accomplishing them; and (5) degree to which institutional norms have been incorporated by other institutions in the society.

The dependent variable generated by adding the combined success scores calculated in the first two phases of each project were used to identify relationships among variables. The success score in phase two indicates the institutional potential of an organization at some point in its development. The score in phase three represents an evaluation of the degree to which the organization has been institutionalized, given that enough time has elapsed for the process to have taken place. In phase two, 52 percent of the cases were classified as highly successful, while in phase three 53 percent were so classified. Successful cases in the intermediate stages tended to maintain their development and become institutionalized.

Projects classified as successful tended to be assisted by direct-hire personnel, to be newly created organizations, to have initially involved technical assistance personnel in operational positions, to have switched technical assistance personnel from operational to advisory status later in the project, to have had technical assistance personnel involved in a variety of ways, to have had transition plans for leadership, to have included early emphasis on training indigenous leadership, to have had technical assistance efforts directed toward giving support to institutional leadership, to have had doctrine emphasized by the technical assistance personnel throughout the life of the project, to have shifted dependence for resource inputs from the technical assistance group to the host institution's environment at a relatively early stage, and to have had technical assistance with a wide rather than narrow focus.

The internal organization variables of leadership, internal structure, and resources were more clearly related to successful institution building than doctrine and program output, especially when emphasized in the early stages of the project. Other factors positively related to the success of projects included the effort that technical assistance makes to gain grants of authority from the recipient society's power structure; a relatively little effort on the part of technical assistance personnel and a relatively large amount of it on the part of indigenous leaders to encourage resource support, grants of authority, and resources by the recipient society; efforts by the technical assistance group and the recipient institution to develop functional linkages; efforts to control competition where competing institutions exist; efforts to encourage normative linkages; attempts to secure the support of the mass media; efforts to achieve a favorable image; joint efforts to build a clientele in the early stages; joint general commitment to the project; consistency of joint efforts in building and strengthening linkages; grants of authority by recipient enabling bodies; relatively available resource inputs; and consistent support for environmental linkages, especially by technical assistance personnel.

Other tentative conclusions include: (1) where consistent effort is expended by either the technical assistance group or the recipient society to build a favorable image for the organization, the project always proved successful; (2) those committed to the project must develop a conscious approach to forming enduring clientele relationships for there to be success; (3) as the organization matures and begins to become institutionalized, the technical assistance team should gradually decrease its initial heavy involvement in linkage formation and assume an advisory rather than an operational role; and (4) the greater the similarity between the project and other activities carried out in the recipient society, the greater the chance of success.

In concluding, Pooler and Duncan state, among other things, that there is an appropriate time sequence attached to the activities involved in a successful institutional development project.

Chapter 10: Field Application of Institution Building
            by Ralph H. Smuckler

In the final chapter, Ralph Smuckler first notes the limitations of the institution building concepts, then deals with their positive contributions. The latter include (1) a sharper insight into the process of strengthening institutions, (2) a more systematic nomenclature, (3) a way of viewing a major component of concerted modernization efforts, (4) a clearer understanding of the need for just as systematic and pointed an approach to institution building as to the technical side of any program, (5) greater insight into measures of success or failure, and (6) a useful means of comparing various institution building efforts in any country and among several of them.

In discussing application of the concepts, Smuckler states, "The institution-building concepts provide no help in estimating which institution should be strengthened or started. Once this policy decision has been made, they become distinctly useful in project planning. They provide an essential checklist of items to be carefully considered in evolving the strategy for a successful effort" (p. 234).

The following questions, which are based upon just one of the variables—doctrine—are suggestive of the types of questions that can be raised:

1. What philosophy . . . should prevail at the new institution?. . .
2. How can the institutional doctrine be made clear?
3. Can the doctrine become an asset in the building and operation of the institution?. . .
4. What relationships or linkages are suggested by the institutional doctrine? (pp. 234-35)

Clearly, during the planning phase, the institution building concepts in their present form have direct applicability by providing a checklist of significant questions to be considered, a better basis for discussion between local leaders and outside technical assistance planners, and a framework for suggesting data gaps and possible supporting research needs.

There are many implications of the concepts for such things as staffing, training, facilitating communications, evaluating projects, judging institutional maturity, and preparing future staff members for their assignments in the institution by means of training programs. These applications notwithstanding, Smuckler sees some shortcomings. The approach does not give specific guidance; it has a somewhat unique jargon, although minimal; and it falls short of providing a complete strategy.

Smuckler concludes:

Because the IB model is not designed to offer the full and final answer does not mean it cannot be highly useful within its domain. But even there, to the impatient, the institution-building model may be discouraging. Institution-building research will take time and some patience and those working in institution-building situations will receive only general, rather limited assistance from the model during the immediate years ahead. Had we started with this more systematic approach—and the research to support it—about twenty years ago when the main international assistance to institution building began, we might now be far along in attaining levels of certainty in prediction in these efforts. To those who are now impatient, we can offer the firm rejoinder— reinforced with the weight of experience—that the institution-building process is crucial, is far more complicated than one thinks, and requires a blend of patience and insight. The institution-building model offers a good approach to the latter. (p. 239)

[21–26] See page 76.

[27] BLAISE, Hans C. "The Process and Strategy of Institution Building in National Development: A Case Study in Cambodia." Unpublished Ph.D. dissertation, University of Pittsburgh, Pittsburgh, Pa., 1964. 260 pages.

Many of the concepts alluded to above were forged in a Ph.D. dissertation by Hans Blaise. This exploratory analysis was designed to identify and develop relevant concepts and formulate the design of a framework for analysis of the institution building process. More specifically, Blaise states:

> ... this study is concerned with institution building, defined as the planning, structuring, and guidance of new or reconstituted organizations which (a) embody changes in values, functions, physical and/or social technologies; (b) establish, foster, and protect normative relationship and action patterns; and (c) attain support and complementarity in the environment. (p. 4)

The specific purposes of Blaise's study are:

1. an analysis of the interdependence of values, norms, structure, process, and technology in a social action situation;

2. an examination of the role of institutional organizations in social action and their relevance to the introduction of change;

3. the identification of the major elements affecting the establishment of new or reconstituted organizations which (a) introduce changes in values, functions, or technologies; (b) develop an internally consistent set of action elements; (c) attain support and bring about complementarity in the environment; and (d) foster, protect, and spread normative relationship and action patterns. (p. 4)

In addition to using insights obtained from the social science literature, Blaise, in his effort to design a conceptual framework for institution building analyses, uses information about the creation and development of the Center for Teacher Preparation at Kompong Kantuot, Cambodia, where he undertook on-site field research.

After drawing heavily on the social science literature, especially sociology, political science, and economics, Blaise discusses and develops the definitions for key concepts that constitute the basis of the approach. A chronological review of the Cambodian Center for Teacher Preparation follows. Although many aspects of the development of the center may be of interest to social scientists, space permits reference to only two portions of Blaise's review, one specific and the other more general.

> The specific plans for the Center, its emphasis and program, meanwhile, were treated by the institution builders almost as a closely guarded secret. Although informal consultations and discussions took place with ministerial and other education officials, no memoranda or proposals on the actual plans were disseminated. No formal action was taken until all the details, including the question of financing the project, had been worked out in considerable detail. By using this strategy, the institution builders made it impossible for the potential and real forces of opposition to attack the plans directly and undermine the proposals and innovations in substance. (p. 122)

Blaise also provides a retrospective overview of the entire development process of the center.

> The short history of the Center at Kompong Kantuot indicates that it is well on the road toward becoming an institution. Over the years it has considerably expanded and strengthened its sources of support. It has effectively created its channels and instruments for the dissemination of its values and program in its task environment. It has thus far been able to protect the innovations it has introduced, without any serious attacks from the outside. . . . however, it is too early to judge whether in effect an institution has been established. In the final analysis this will depend to a considerable extent on the performance of the teachers who have graduated from the Center, on their continued identification with their alma mater and the extent to which these teachers have become imbued with the Center's educational values and approaches and spread them through the school system. (p. 170)

As indicated above, the objective of the analysis was to identify and develop relevant concepts as well as design a framework of analysis for the institution building process. In the course of concept development, Blaise justifies the identification of the process as institution building rather than organization building because of its focus on the valuative and normative exchange relationships between an institution and its environment rather than a focus on technical efficiency criteria applied to task performance. He summarizes the framework as follows:

> The three elements of our analysis, then, are (1) the change agents or leadership group which creates or innovates the organization; (2) the organization as the intermediate target system in which and through which new values and technologies are introduced; and (3) the task environment as the ultimate target to which new norms and values are spread to create a compatible and complementary environment for the institution to perform its functions and services. (p. 186)

Especially apropos of the last element are Blaise's tests of effectiveness of institution building, which are (1) the ability to survive, (2) the ability to establish intrinsic value as perceived by an institution's environment, and (3) the spreading of the institution's norms. Throughout, Blaise recognizes that institutionalization is a matter of degree.

Blaise relies on Esman's formulation of the institution building universe with its components of systems, variables, transactions, and linkages. The Cambodian center is analyzed with this approach. In turn, the concepts are perfected and conclusions drawn. Among the noteworthy conclusions are the following observations:

> Leadership is without doubt *the* critical variable in institution building. Even if all other variables are positive and all other conditions for institution building fulfilled, institution building will not be effective unless the value of the leadership variable and its component elements are positive. (p. 201)

The author's concluding paragraph states:

> In this study the concept institution building—as a systematic approach to the introduction of change—has been developed. We have analyzed the dimensions and elements of the process, suggested a framework for the analysis of institution building experiences, and submitted a number of variables which appear significant. . . . Ultimately, it is hoped that this will result not only in increased knowledge of interest to the social scientists, but also to meaningful guidelines for the innovators

who are actively engaged in the introduction of change in societies striving for modernization. (pp. 236-37)

[28] HANSON, John W. *Education, Nsukka: Study in Institution Building Among the Modern Ibo.* East Lansing, Mich.: African Studies Center and Institute for International Studies in Education, Michigan State University, 1968. 410 pages. (Part of Inter-University Research Program in Institution Building.)

In accord with Blaise's recommendations, a number of field studies were subsequently undertaken to test some of the hypotheses growing out of the concepts developed by him and Esman. One of the most thorough of these was conducted by John Hanson at the College of Education in the University of Nigeria at Nsukka.

In this analysis of how the College of Education in the University of Nigeria, a new university in the decade of the 1960s, came to be prized, the following broad search hypothesis is used:

> Institutionality will result if the leadership, doctrine, and program of an innovative organization realistically take account of (that is, adjust to, balance and reorganize) the significant elements in a related environment so these are marshalled in support of the organization and its innovations. (p. 7)

The initial focus in this hypothesized relationship is on leadership, especially the environment in which it was exercised. The author maintains that this active decision-making ingredient was able to establish and make clear to relevant publics both the normative linkages between university doctrine and emergent values in the environment and the functional linkages between university programs and the aspirations of individuals and social units. During its first six years, the university benefited because this leadership function was partially performed by its founder and the Nigerian leader, Azikiwe. Not only was he able to do this personally, but other university leaders used his charisma and authority to accomplish institutionalization during the initial, crucial years. Hence, the university was able to protect itself from opposition to innovation and to secure the support necessary to get programs initiated. Six years after the institution began operation, this shield, which was removed by a military coup, had performed its function of facilitating the acquisition of support both within the university and from outside of it. As a consequence, the following major innovations were institutionalized: (1) the general studies program; (2) priority and degree-granting status for vocationally oriented units of the university, including education; and (3) a flexible admissions policy making rapid expansion of the institution possible.

The primary focus of this analysis was the College of Education, which Hanson headed initially in a technical assistance capacity. From the outset, the personnel of this college shared a common set of educational values, including a commitment to pragmatic education, breadth in programs, cultural determination of curricular content, increased professionalization of teacher education, and the legitimacy of discarding educational patterns (albeit metropolitan and revered) that impeded the achievement of societal goals.

Not only was institutionality achieved as a consequence of the leadership within the university and college, but it was also influenced by the environment into which these organizations were born. The most important characteristic of the environment was that it was already a transitional one in which old and new values were competing. Hanson emphasizes that four features of this environment made it highly receptive to innovation: (1) The university was essentially an Ibo institution and was conceived of, executed by, and chiefly institutionalized among the Ibos—a people known for their receptivity to change, strong achievement motivation, an open social structure (permitting social mobility through education), and a willingness to employ alien institutions pragmatically to achieve utilitarian and other selfish purposes. (2) The university was conceived by the principal architect of Nigerian independence (Azikiwe), opened to coincide with independence, and was intended to stand as a monument to that political achievement. (3) The newly independent Nigerian federal and regional governments, and many of the educated elite, had, by 1960, already selected economic development as the prime national goal. (4) The Ibo's (and all southern Nigerians') adaptability and motivation toward achievement, the psychological release of political independence, and the zeal for economic development flowed together to produce a mind-set which, for lack of a better term, may be called *educationism*.

Both the high degree of common commitment among college leaders and the recognition of an external threat to the organization facilitated the early concentration on strategies for achieving institutionality of the college with outside publics. These strategies ultimately enabled the institution to become valued, via its services and products, by the public so that it could count upon mobilizing support from that public.

The initial strategy was to link doctrine explicitly and publicly to emergent values, slogans, and beliefs in the environment. By making its doctrine public the institution facilitated its institutionality. Rather than being presented in coherent, systematic fashion, this doctrine was regularly enunciated in slogans. Slogans such as "meeting the needs of Nigeria," "restoring the dignity of man," and "educating for an independent Nigeria" were specific enough to be relevant and yet ambiguous enough not to narrow their appeal to a limited few. In addition, the doctrine promised something tangible to most publics concerned with education. Furthermore, the doctrine was legitimized easily by other public pronouncements, many of which were forward-looking. Further import was added to this doctrine by virtue of its having been enunciated by effective spokesmen. Finally, the doctrine was not entirely new to the new nation.

The second strategy involved establishing partnership and supportive linkages. That is to say, the College of Education actively sought to develop mutually supportive linkages with other organizations. By developing reciprocal relationships with such institutions as the Ministry of Education, the college was able to gain initial acceptance of innovations by way of institutions that possessed a greater degree of legitimacy than did the university. This approach was closely related to the third strategy.

The third strategy provided for employing approved channels for legitimizing the programs of the college. After one unfortunate experience, the college deliberately avoided disrupting the complex network of organizations which comprised the Nigerian educational system. By working through this system, the institution ultimately was able to gain acceptance for its innovations.

Concentrating initial programs of the college in areas of greatest demand constituted the fourth strategy. Initially the college focused its efforts on producing an increased number of professionally trained teachers and educational specialists. Later, programs were devised to fulfill the high demand expressed by one or more of the power centers in the educational system.

The fifth strategy was stated as "deferring disruptive or threatening dimensions of the 'doctrine of educational reconstruction' until actual or potential support appeared to exist in the field." This strategy required that, during the first four years, programs were started only when based upon prior legitimization, e.g., from a widely known report or a clear external demand. However, when innovations were subsequently proposed, the privileged position of well-established, prestigious secondary schools was threatened in one instance and the educational power of the churches was threatened in another, before the innovations had been legitimized.

Hanson states:

> It was these five strategies, not always carefully conceived and . . . executed, which permitted College leaders to create and maintain a balance of forces which permitted institutionalization of the College without requiring the surrender of major innovations to which it was commited by doctrine. (p. 371)

Evidence of the fact that this institutionalization had occurred was gathered with the use of explicit criteria. These, which might be replicated in analyses of other institutions, are listed below under several aspects of institutionality.

> Institutionality as suggested by the use of services and products offered. . . .
>
> 1. Its graduates were employed in positions related to their training, that is, in education.
>
> 2. Its graduates were placed in positions from which they were able to exercise authority or influence, thus enhancing probability of norm diffusion.
>
> 3. Its graduates received salaries at least comparable to those accorded competing job candidates.
>
> 4. Its students were supported financially by units within government or the educational establishment which hoped to use their services.
>
> 5. Its leadership was called upon to serve in advisory or decision-making capacities within the educational establishment.

6. Its programs, physical facilities, and services were requested and/or used by a wide range of publics.

7. It conducted research, the results of which were requested or used by other units within the educational system.

8. It became a functional and articulated link in educational flow patterns. (pp. 307–8)

Institutionality as suggested by verbal approval. . . .

1. Respondents in the educational system stated explicitly their satisfaction with the University or the College.

2. Potential students indicated their preference for attending the University of Nigeria rather than other universities.

3. Respondents named the leaders of the College as being among the most competent Nigerian educators.

4. Graduates of the University or College were judged favorably by employers, principals, or colleagues.

5. University leaders outside of Education expressed their satisfaction with, or approval of, the College of Education, its leaders, and its programs. (pp. 317-19)

Institutionality as suggested by survival and growth. . . .

1. The innovations originally envisaged had been either implemented intact or modified into programs which still represented significant change in the environment.

2. Innovative programs or functions pioneered by the College have been transferred to other organizations which might more appropriately perform them.

3. The structure, programs and policies of the parent organization (the University) had developed in ways which supported, promoted, or exemplified the norms and values of the College.

4. Both programs which were derived from the original values of the College and the resources for implementing these programs have maintained a priority position within the University or have grown quantitatively.

5. The College has revealed innovative thrust, that is, the capacity to develop new and originally unforeseen programs and priorities. (pp. 324-26)

Institutionality as suggested by the support given an organization. . . .

1. The University provided the College with the resources the latter required to carry out its projected program.

2. Foundations, international organizations, and bilateral aid offices supported programs which were derived from College doctrine.

3. The Government or other Nigerian organizations undertook to support parts of the College program.

4. The University and relevant publics of the College exerted their influence in legitimizing College programs and mobilizing outside resources for putting them into effect. (pp. 334-35)

Institutionality as suggested by the criterion of autonomy. . . .

1. The spheres of freedom granted the College were equal to those granted comparable or competing organizations.

2. *De facto* limitations placed upon activities were made by expertly qualified bodies or by bodies with legal jurisdiction and responsibility.

3. Limitations on action were made by bodies on which the College was itself represented.

4. Such limitations on freedom as were imposed did not impede or preclude implementation of doctrine through program.

5. Restrictions on freedom were not discriminatory in the sense of singling out the particular organization (the College) for restraint. (pp. 340-41)

Institutionality as suggested by normative spread. . . .

1. Members of relevant publics came to approve the values the organization attempted to incorporate.

2. Official policy statements on education came to reflect the values and action patterns characteristic of the organization.

3. Values and action patterns which the organization pioneered became accepted to the point where they were no longer matters of public debate.

4. Other organizations came to incorporate these innovative patterns in their operations. (pp. 345-47)

In reflecting on the analysis, Hanson makes the following observation:

My more serious reservation is that, looking back on this study a year later, it appears less a study than a source book from which a scholar with a more varied background of experience might extract a significant study. (p. 16)

[29] JACOBSON, Eugene. "Research and Institution Building: Lessons from the Field." Paper presented at the Conference on Institution Building Overseas, French Lick, Indiana, August 1968. 25 pages. (Mimeographed. Part of Inter-University Research Program in Institution Building.)

The final manuscript resulting from the Inter-University Research Program in Institution Building (IRPIB) was written by Eugene Jacobson. In it he focuses on the role of research in the process of institution building. He describes the initial four field studies done under IRPIB auspices—[28], [63], [88], and [89]—sketches some of the generalizations about the institution building process suggested by these analyses, prescribes research implied by these findings, and concludes with three general recommendations about the role of research in the process of institution building.

The following generalizations illustrate some of the propositions implicit and explicit in the initial four institution building field studies:

1. The process of institutionalization of innovation is not a simple, linear function. There are interruptions, retreats, accommodations, regroupings, diversions, and emergence of secondary goals, amended objectives and altered doctrine. . . .

2. Technical assistance teams have unreliable means of estimating success or failure of specific actions they are taking. They have only partial and incomplete access to performance criteria. . . .

3. Performance criteria that are appropriate for assessing operations in one culture may not be available or appropriate in another. . . .

4. Prediction of response to innovation is difficult under any circumstances. In developing countries, prediction must be based on more careful and more inclusive data gathering operations. . . .

5. Innovation creates new situations which in turn demand innovative solutions. But original objectives and doctrine, which may become obsolete, will dominate program unless emergence of new demands is made apparent. . . .

6. As an institution emerges or changes, it has different impact on its environment at different phases of growth. The nucleus group, defining its objectives and functions, does not make the same demands or receive the same response from its environment as the relatively mature, relatively powerful, independently supported competitive institution. . . .

7. As an institution changes and matures, its opportunities for attracting and retaining different kinds of personnel change. . . .

8. The leadership of a new or reconstituted institution has different needs for being responsive to its environment than that of more mature institutions. . . .

9. A new institution in a developing country with an explicit program for selection, training and placement of staff, will, in many instances, be a unique resource for providing new cadres of leadership throughout the society. . . .

10. Changing domestic leadership and technical assistance staff make it difficult to achieve continuity in expressed doctrine. But situational demands and opportunities may, in fact, produce a relatively stable and continuous influence on doctrine as expressed through actual program and operations. . . .

11. Although new technologies and procedures may be introduced at a relatively rapid rate, there may not be corresponding complementary changes in relevant interpersonal relationships. The impact of traditional patterns of social relationships upon the implementation of innovation can be extensive. . . .

12. When an educational institution is being created or reconstituted, as contrasted, for instance, with an agricultural research institute, because of the flow of students through the institution, there is a relatively rapid and extensive dissemination of information about the institution. (pp. 16-19)

On the basis of these generalizations and field experience, Jacobson gives the following recommendations for institution building research:

1. Systematic research on institution building that has a comprehensive theoretical base can provide findings that have practical implications for increasing the effectiveness of institution building. Systematic applied studies should be an integral part of all phases of institution building, from the initial exploratory period through long term evaluation.

2. When possible, institution building research should be initiated by persons who will have responsibility for important aspects of the institution building process, including host country persons who introduce and administer change.

3. The use of applied research in institution building should be explicitly anticipated in planning and administering the project. Expert use of applied research requires training for the staff who will manage the change process. (p. 21)

[30] JORNS, William James. "Operational Analysis of Case Studies in Institution Building Theory." Unpublished Ph.D. dissertation, North Carolina State University at Raleigh, N.C., 1971. 177 pages.

A number of inquiries have been spawned as a consequence of the efforts of the Inter-University Research Program in Institution Building. Most of them deal in one way or another with the institution building framework conceptualized by Esman et al. William Jorns' investigation, which was selected from this group, was no exception. In it, Jorns makes an effort to further develop and evaluate this approach.

In this study, an analytical matrix is used to obtain data on problems of institution building. Four questions formed the basis for the study: (1) Does empirical evidence support the contention that institution building theory is a generic model of induced change? (2) What data can be obtained through research that suggests information for decision-making and action strategies useful in operationalizing the theory? (3) Are there key elements or factors in a guided change situation that are more critical to the institutionalization process than others? (4) Is the matrix developed for this study useful as a method for extracting the organizing data from institution building situations for comparative and analytical purposes? (Abstract)

The analytic matrix consists of the institution variables of leadership, doctrine, program, resources, and internal structure on one axis. The other axis consists of (1) a ranking of negative, adequate, or positive effects of these variables on the process of institutionalization, and (2) an indication of whether the effect was internal or on the linkages of the institution. The cells of the matrix are filled with the numbers of years during the life cycle of the projects examined.

Much of the analytical strength of the matrix results from the disaggregation of the institution variables. Leadership is subdivided into technical competence, administrative competence, political competence, commitment to doctrine, continuity and succession, and depth of leadership. The following are subdivisions of doctrine: its source; its realism in terms of needs and resources; its specificity, consistency, and articulation; its sensitivity to societal norms; its official legitimization; its provision for conflict management; and its degree of innovativeness. Program consists of these subdivisions: consistency with doctrine, consistency with resources, staff commitment, program visibility, program stability, and management of opposition. The resources variable is subdivided into indigenous financial support, staff training and development, physical facilities, information on new technologies, and access to feedback. Internal structure is disaggregated to include adequate structure, resource allocation, conflict regulation, and centralization versus decentralization.

Jorns assesses the effects that these 28 sectors of activity exert on the process of institutionalization. As suggested above, the assessments involve three dimensions: (1) the effect on the institutional or internal aspect of institutionalization, (2) the effect on the organization's relationships with its external environment, and (3) the changes in the effects during the life of the organization covered by the study.

Evidence from a comparative analysis of the three case studies supported the contention that the theory is generic. Although firm guidelines were not established for operationalizing the theory, information was suggested for decision-making and action strategies to be used by practitioners in institution building situations. (Abstract)

With regard to operationalizing the concept of institution building, Jorns states:

1. Early emphasis on the development of technical competence within leadership provides a strong base for subsequent planning and implementation of programs that are capable of making an impact on the external environment.

2. Doctrine must be sufficiently specific to obtain authority to operate. Specificity in excess of this minimum, however, may place undue restrictions on program development.

3. Legal or official legitimization is necessary for ultimate institutionality. However, the primary effort should be in developing an innovative program that makes an impact on and is valued in the environment.

4. Planning and implementing a program that makes an impact on the relevant elements of the external environment early in the life of the organization is one of the more critical aspects of institutionalization.

5. Adequate resources must be available to sustain the organization. However, emphasis on complete indigenous financial support can be delayed until after a demand has been established within the external environment for the products and services of the innovative organization.

6. An indigenous staff capable of implementing the innovative aspects of programs is a critical resource. One of the first requirements is the training and development of just such an indigenous staff. (pp. 168-69)

Jorns identifies the following key elements as critical in the process of an organization moving toward institutionality:

1. A technically competent presence in indigenous leadership.

2. Leadership that is committed to the doctrine of the organization.

3. The visibility and stability of program output that is accorded value by the relevant external environment.

4. The development and training of an indigenous staff competent in implementing the innovative aspects of the program.

5. An adequate internal structure of the organization coupled with the competence of leadership to administer it properly. (pp. 169-70)

[31] DERGE, David R.; Souder, Donald L.; et al. "Institution Building and Rural Development: A Study of United States Technical Assistance Projects." Indiana University, Bloomington, Ind., 1968. 170 pages. (Mimeographed. Part of Committee on Institutional Cooperation and Agency for International Development Rural Development Research Project.)

Another significant study relied heavily on the framework formulated by Esman et al. and was published as part of the CIC-AID Rural Development Research Project. This analysis, undertaken by David Derge et al., focused on factors influencing types of institutions best suited to the needs of developing countries. Data were gathered from a variety of sources, including the 68 rural development AID-university contract projects around the world that were included in the overall research project. Of those 68, 18 met the criteria established for the Indiana portion of the analysis and were used as a source of inputs for this study.

With the use of these data, 49 hypotheses were tested. These hypotheses were formulated in terms of the interrelationships of variables in the framework formulated by Esman et al. The hypotheses also reflected the decision to emphasize the institutionality, or lack of it, for each institution rather than to work from descriptions of countries' needs in trying to determine the best institution building formula. "The basic assumption underlying the decision to test these projects for institutionality is that if an organization is achieving, or has achieved, institutionality, it is probably meeting some specific needs of the HC [Host Country]" (p. 3). In the study an attempt was made to isolate those factors that seemed to have contributed to the institutionalization process or, in the case where institutionalization had not occurred or did not appear to be occurring, those factors that seemed to have impeded the process.

Initially, Derge et al. examined the history and the development of the land grant college in the United States to gain insights into what its role and consequences have been. The organization of the remaining portions of the analysis is built on a 20-cell linkage matrix comprising, on one axis, the institution variables of leadership, doctrine, program, resources, and internal structure and, on the other axis, the linkage variables—enabling, functional, normative, and diffuse. Subsequently, hypotheses are posited for cells in this matrix.

The initial set of hypotheses deals with the interrelationships between leadership and the four types of linkages. After examining the evidence with regard to each of the leadership hypotheses, Derge et al. revised those for which supporting evidence was found. These hypotheses were stated as follows:

Enabling:

A1: Co-membership of leadership of HI [Host Institution] in other government agencies strengthens enabling linkages of HI.

A2: High frequency of interaction between HI leadership and government leadership can serve to strengthen enabling linkages of HI.

A3: HI leadership will be most effectively maximized when change-committed HI leadership is independent from frequent government interference.

A4: When HI leadership is committed to change, acceptance of HI leadership into social, political, and economic elites of HC [Host Country] strengthens enabling linkages and facilitates the broad goals of HI.

Functional:

B1: Interaction between HI leadership and clientele leadership which aggregates the interests of both parties, tends to maximize HI bargaining position and tends to minimize its vulnerability, strengthens functional linkages, and facilitates institution-building.

B2: HI leadership which is personally and professionally acceptable to clientele leadership will be more effective bargaining agents of the HI and thus have the potential to strengthen HI functional linkages.

B3: HI leadership which is able to identify relevant publics within the environment and establish some accommodation with them is vital to the HI's prospects for achieving institutionality.

Normative:

C1: Acceptability or accommodation of HI leadership to social groups which constitute relevant publics themselves, or can have some impact upon relevant publics, functional linkages, or enabling linkages within the HC is essential for attainment of institutionality.

C2: Prospects for HI leadership being effective agents of the HI are greater if it does not transgress the values or deviate from the dominant social consensus of the HC.

Diffuse:

D1: HI leadership which is able to convert favorable public opinion into intrinsic valuation of HI will increase prospects for survival capability.

D2: HI leadership which is able to avert unfavorable public opinion of HI and minimize the effects of negative popular evaluation of HI upon enabling and functional linkages will increase potential for HI survival capability. (pp. 77-78)

In a fashion similar to that followed in testing the leadership hypotheses, the doctrine hypotheses for which support was found were restated.

Enabling:

E1: Where there are other client groups besides HG [Host Government] in the environment, a concept of service, without being tied to any institutional form, can be important for promoting enabling relationships.

E2: The HI doctrine should be at such a level of specificity that, while allowing for personal differences in leadership philosophy and ability, the main thrust of the institution in a national development context will be clearly defined.

E3: The growth and development, i.e., institutionalization, of an HI which is committed to the American land grant concept of service is related to the degree of social mobilization within the society and the resulting number and power of relevant publics in the environment.

E4: In areas having low levels of social mobilization and few relevant publics in the environment outside the HG, the growth and development, i.e., institutionalization, of the HI is related to the ability of the HI staff to achieve a strong working relationship involving mutual respect for the given division of labor with agencies involved in agriculture and rural development.

E5: The ability of the HI to obtain resources and approval from the HG leadership is related to the degree of total and active commitment on the part of the HG leadership to the doctrine of the HI and the HG.

Functional:

F1: The higher the level of specificity of HI doctrine, the less freedom HI leadership has in major policy changes but the more clearly is the HI defined to competing and complementing organizations in the environment.

F2: HI doctrine is meaningless until there is a body of knowledge and information accumulated that will have importance and relevance for the potential clientele groups in the environment.

Normative:

G1: As the relevant publics in the environment increase, the doctrine of the HI will have to be more sensitive to those religious, ethical, and cultural norms prevailing within those publics.

Diffuse:

H1: The interpretation and conveyance of HI doctrine to the environment by the mass media will facilitate achievement of HI goals when that environment is composed of potential clientele groups for HI outputs. (pp. 90-91)

The following are the revised hypotheses concerning program for which supporting evidence was found:

Enabling:

I1: As long as the HG is the major clientele group in the environment, the program of the HI must be responsive to HG leadership.

a. If HG leadership is committed to change and development, the HI program will reflect this commitment.

b. If HG leadership is not committed to change and development, the HI program will reflect this lack of commitment.

I2: As the number of potential clientele groups in the environment increase, the HI program will become more a manifestation of the transaction linkages the HI has been able to establish on the basis of perceived instrumental value of the HI outputs.

Functional:

J1: To the extent the HI program is developed with clientele group needs in mind so as to have "high visibility" of the outputs, the outputs will come to have perceived instrumental value by the clientele group.

J2: National development must be dependent upon a "trickling down" effect in terms of innovations simply on the basis of cost.

a. To the degree that program is designed to maximize this effect, broad national growth can take place but at a very slow pace.

J3: Program should be designed so that it does not come into immediate and obvious conflict with existing and competing programs until the HI has established secure linkages in the environment, i.e., gained some degree of institutionality.

Normative:

K1: The HI program need only be concerned with the normative behavior patterns of relevant publics with which it has or expects to have linkage transactions.

K2: As HI outputs achieve a high perceived instrumental value in the environment and as the index of social mobilization goes up giving rise to more clientele groups in the environment, the HI will be in a position to influence normative behavior on a broad social scale through its program.

Diffuse:

L1: To the degree the HI can support a portion of its program on a charity base, i.e., not cost accounted on an input/output relationship, by providing some service through mass communication media, it can be a force for increasing the social mobilization in the environment. (pp. 98-99)

The revised hypotheses concerning resources for which supporting evidence was found are:

Enabling:

M1: For institutional survival, HG and/or other client groups must provide adequate financial resources after the withdrawal of AID support.

(1) While "adequate" support must increase with increased expectations by clients for the HI outputs, resources must be realistic in terms of national capacities.

(2) While clients, particularly HG, may provide resources to the HI adequate for its survival for reasons unrelated to the desirability of the outputs, e.g., for national prestige, etc., the trade-off for the HI will usually be in terms of its potential for service and change.

M2: The more adequately the personnel resource inputs to the HI are prepared by the HC primary and secondary schools for a college-level experience, the more efficiently can the HI use its limited resources in providing a college-level experience with a consequent higher level of output.

Functional:

N1: Given the low level of social mobilization in most developing countries and the resultant lack of potential client groups for relationships with the HI, most indigenous organizations are dependent on the HG for providing inputs, for consuming outputs, and ultimately for institutionality.

N2: A deliberate attempt by HC secondary schools to provide an input of adequately trained graduates to the HI is an indicator of the normative influence and institutionality of the HI.

Normatives:

O1: The prevailing norms and values of the HG elite may set certain limits on the physical, human, and technological resources which can be allocated to the HI.

Diffuse:

P1: To the extent that relevant publics exist in the environment, efforts expended through the mass media giving the HI a high visibility will serve to create a favorable climate for increased support in terms of human, physical, and technological resources. (p. 112)

The final group of hypotheses tested concerned internal structure. The revised hypotheses for which support was found are:

Enabling:

Q1: The success of the HI is related to an internal structure which maximizes the institution's ability to negotiate with the HG and enabling institutions through one spokesman with political influence in the HG.

Functional:

R1: The higher the degree of social mobilization in a country the better it is to place the project in an entirely new HI free from other institutional control and domination.

R2: The success of the HI is related to how well the internal structure is organized for serving the needs of the HG and other possible clientele groups, and the continuity and stability of the structure.

Normative:

S1: The internal structure of the HI will tend to reflect traditional/ dominancy relationships based on sex, age, ethnic background, tribal groups, and so forth. These usually hinder HI goals. (p. 119)

After testing the hypotheses, Derge et al. returned to the institution building conceptualization. In reflecting on their experience, they conclude that two changes are needed in the approach. The first of these concerns linkages and the other concerns institutionality.

Derge et al. experienced difficulty in operationalizing the categorization of linkages given in the IRPIB working papers. Frequently it was impossible to make clear distinctions between categories of linkages. Further, the same linkage relationship can serve different purposes at different times, and many were multifunctional at any given time. Transactual relationships rather than linkages appeared to be more useful at this stage of the research experience.

A new definition of institutionality is essential, according to the authors. Even as a vehicle for organizing data, the IRPIB definition of institutionality had caused problems. Thus, Derge et al. conclude:

It is only when relevant publics, instrumental accounting, and transactional accommodation cease to be pivotal concerns of organization-institution leadership and the pressure for survival ceases to be the preponderant factor in decision-making that the essence of Esman's approach to institution building becomes relevant as an operational model. For it is then that one meaningfully speaks of intrinsic valuation of the institution. If the society is characterized by a low level of social mobilization, intrinsic valuation is very much secondary to transactional accommodations, instrumental accounting, and utility maximization of relevant publics and clients in general as an index of institutionality. (p. 132)

The report concludes with an appendix entitled "Agriculture, Education, and Rural Transformation in Sub-Saharan Africa."

[32] RIGNEY, J.A.; McDermott, J.K.; and Roskelley, R.W. *Strategies in Technical Assistance.* Technical Bulletin No. 189. Raleigh, N.C.: North Carolina Agricultural Experiment Station, North Carolina State University, 1968. 57 pages. (Part of Committee on Institutional Cooperation and Agency for International Development Rural Development Research Project.)

Another outstanding contribution from the CIC-AID Rural Development Research Project dealt with strategies in technical assistance. This North Carolina Agricultural Experiment Station Research Bulletin contains three closely related research reports that emanated from that project. The first part, entitled "Role of Technical Personnel in the Technical Assistance—Institution Building Process," was written by J.A. Rigney and James K. McDermott. The second part by Rigney is entitled, "Optimum Role for U.S. Overseas Advisors." The final section, "Measuring Institutional Maturity in the Development of Indigenous Agricultural Universities," resulted from the collaboration of R. W. Roskelley and Rigney.

Part I: Role of Personnel in the Technical Assistance-
       Institution Building Process
       by J.A. Rigney and James K. McDermott

The effectiveness of technical assistance programs is largely a function of the quality and magnitude of their components: participant training, capital inputs, and technical assistance as well as the skill with which they are managed and coordinated. While the role of the other components has been reasonably well under-

stood, much confusion and difference of opinion have characterized the role and goals of technical personnel.

On the basis of well over a decade of technical assistance
experience in institution building, J.A. Rigney and James McDermott formulated a construct that describes the role of technical
personnel as a small but critical element of the total process of
technical assistance. In providing an overview of the model, the
authors state:

> The construct views the activity of U.S. personnel at four levels of host
> institution organization for the sake of convenience. Phase A focuses on
> the individual staff member level where the advisor is seeking individual
> acceptance and is relating largely with individuals of the host institu-
> tion. Phase B is the department level, where the contacts are still
> individual-to-individual, but the groups they represent become more
> important. Phase C deals with top administration of the institution and
> the identification of the institution's role in society. Phase D involves
> the linkages between this institution and the other entities in society
> which are important to its development. (p. 3)

Phase A. Noting the crucial importance of the relationship at
this level as both the foundation for the process of institution
building and ultimate justification for that activity, the authors
describe the goals at the level of individual technical relationships
as being (1) to increase the host individual's technical competence
and (2) to form productive attitudes on his part with regard to his
professional and public responsibilities. Since output of the institution occurs at this level, all other phases exist only to facilitate
activity and performance here.

The presence of a foreign technical assistance adviser represents a threat both to an individual, his institution, and even his
country. It engenders the normal defense mechanism of rejection.
In some cases such reaction to foreign assistance precludes initiation of a development process, while in others it gives way to
acquiescence, the prerequisite for succeeding stages.

Stage one, rejection-acquiescence, is followed by the personal
acceptance stage. Within the technical assistance group, personal
acceptance will begin with individual binational pairs. It will be
characterized by the ease and eagerness with which the adviser and
his counterpart from the host institution (HI) associate with each
other. Gaining this acceptance is important not only for the bulk

of the technical assistance group but also at all stages of the life cycle of the project.

Stage three, technical visibility, is characterized by the adviser's demonstration of his technical capacity in the host institution's environment. It results in tangible, visible evidence that the adviser can make contributions toward solving local problems and, thereby, compensate for some of the negative effects of the threat that his presence represents. The visibility of the adviser's technical capacity gives him credit and prestige—the keys to technical acceptance. However, this visibility should also enhance the image of the counterpart, thus ensuring the acceptance of the adviser; visibility for the sake of personal aggrandizement will only impair the adviser's acceptance.

Technical acceptance, stage four, follows technical visibility. A certain level of such acceptance must be achieved as a prerequisite for progress in subsequent stages. Although high and dramatic visibility carries both technical and personal acceptance to a higher intensity in a shorter period of time, the time and sequence relations between personal and technical assistance are not absolute. Progress in one, however, accelerates progress in the other.

Initiation of joint, short-run activities takes place in stage five. After the conditioning activities in the previous stages, which were designed to develop the willingness of the host institution's counterpart to take advantage of the presence of the foreigner, some activities should be initiated in which the two persons are involved as a pair, with their individual success or failure depending upon their joint success or failure. Success of the joint venture is designed to change a lethargic, pessimistic attitude on the part of the host member to one of self-confidence, initiative, and optimism. Probably initiated by the adviser, this initial experience will be followed by a proliferation of joint activities selected to emphasize usefulness and purpose as well as to develop a sense of responsibility to society.

Stage six, consolidation of gains, is needed to ensure that the new experiences and insights are assimilated and integrated into the host's concept of his professional role. Hence, the initiative needs to pass to him from the adviser at this stage. The latter's role is now to encourage and nurture the flow of ideas from his counterpart. The result should be self-confidence rather than dependency. Although overt activities of persuasion and demonstration will decline, they will not stop entirely.

In stage seven, activities become persistent and recognizable to others both within the institutions and outside, thereby formalizing long-run activities.

> The main criteria for projects to be formalized and continued in the long-run are *usefulness* and *relevance* to society. The HI member will have recognized the importance of these criteria as part of his institution's responsibility to the public. It is also in this stage that the pair begins to exhaust its potential for accomplishment without support from a higher echelon in the organization. (p. 6)

Realistic and objective self-analysis tends to develop concomitantly with self-confidence and realization of control over one's destiny. In stage eight the host is able to objectively evaluate his own inadequacies as problems to be systematically solved.

In stage nine, development of an institutional perspective, the adviser recognizes that the host is likely to be strongly tempted to "go it alone" rather than fight institutional battles. He has to be led to recognize that without changes in his institution he soon would be stymied. Hence, he develops an identity with his institution, both in terms of his responsibility to it and his dependence upon it. When this identity is related to the public interest, he develops a genuine sense of personal and professional commitment.

The terminal stage involves the development of a career plan. From this point, the binational pair continues on a peer basis, with emphasis on the professional growth of the host. Thus, the adviser may continue to bring his counterpart into wider contacts with his professional world long after they have been separated physically.

Throughout these steps, effective pairing is implied. Although the host may have the formal designation of counterpart, this is not necessarily the case. Given the existence of effective pairs, the first four stages should be completed in less than six months. In the next six months stages five and six should be accomplished. The entire process should set the stage for a lifetime relationship between peers.

Phase B. Just as individual technical relationships are the focus of attention in Phase A of the model, department-level relationships receive attention in Phase B. Hence, this phase involves group relations at an intermediate level in the organization, as well as intergroup relationships. Nevertheless, interpersonal relationships retain their importance and are joined by other factors. In their roles as representatives of groups, individuals make decisions which have wider implications than for just themselves. Perhaps most critical in this phase are the contacts between the adviser and the department head. However, the adviser's supporting contacts with other members of the department can help to reinforce and enhance development of departmental attitudes and traditions, both important aspects of the process of institutionalization.

The first two of the nine stages in this phase are parallel to the initial phases in Phase A. In this case the focus is on the relationship between the adviser and the department head. But, because personal acceptance involves more than one member of the host institution, a higher risk is associated with this phase. Nonetheless, the adviser must win the confidence of host institution personnel so that he can receive and deal with sensitive information safely and discreetly.

Stage three, program leadership visibility, involves the adviser's actions, activities, ideas, conversations, and a general demonstration of his understanding of local conditions that will tend to inspire the host institution's confidence in his judgment and personal qualifications. This confidence is essential if the adviser is to be able to transfer program management systems to the host institution which involve (1) people and their peculiar personalities and (2) objectives that are often at variance with those implied in the transferred system.

Stage four is that stage of relationships where a provisional technical acceptance develops that is adequate for the department head to begin to assume a small risk in innovation. Technical acceptance will occur when an innovation has proven viable, if not entirely successful. In order to gain such acceptance, advisers at the middle-management level may have to demonstrate competence in a technical area as a prerequisite for their acceptance as program leaders. Regardless of the number of successive advisers, these initial four steps will be common to all in a greater or less degree.

In stage five small, discrete, departmental problems are solved efficiently, and a basis is established for a wider consideration of a total departmental plan. Frequently, this will involve changes not only in the organization but also in attitude—that is, management will move away from authoritarian and dictatorial approaches toward a sympathetic and stimulating style of leadership. Clearly, an appreciable degree of rapport and mutual confidence are essential.

Stage six, initiation of program planning, is similar to the previous stage but is much more directed and comprehensive.

> The modification of attitude and basic philosophy will be the most important input at this level, and those ideas which will be most productive for the department will perhaps require the greatest degree of statesmanship on the part of the HI individual. Therefore, progress in this area will be particularly slow in older individuals who are steeped in the traditions of the existing bureaucracy and who are constrained by a larger number of personal ties. Organizational changes can come faster, but they will contribute much less to the building of an institution in the absence of basic changes in outlook. (p. 10)

When relationships have evolved to the point where the department head accepts the adviser as competent in dealing with the department's program, stage seven has been reached. Although not all of the adviser's ideas will be accepted, the consequences and alternatives of each will be weighed carefully. At this point relationships have become stable and the adviser has achieved status for having maximum influence—if he seizes his opportunities—on the department's organization and program.

In stage eight, awareness of the host country's needs and program requirements, planning begins in earnest. The department head sees the potential role of his department in the development of his institution and his country. Both his growing sense of responsibility to his institution and country and the increases in prestige and satisfaction he has experienced from new activities undertaken with his adviser will contribute to this expanded insight. At this stage the departmental role is both articulated and translated into specific activities, especially by the more innovative and progressive members of the department.

The final and culminating stage will be finished when the department head has enthusiastically participated in the development of a realistic overall plan for his department and has "sold" its accompanying new attitudes, approaches, and perspectives to the staff. The plan will contain priorities and a time schedule for accomplishments. A strong service and problem-solving orientation, typified by land grant institutions, will characterize the new attitudes. Plans for enhancing the productivity of individual staff members will be included as well as plans for their careers within the department.

Phase C. Phase C of the Rigney-McDermott model concerns relationships between top management and the organization. The sequence of personal relationship stages that occurs at the individual and department levels (phases A and B above) also occurs for the team leader at the top management level of the host institution. Stage 1 is an example. In fact, to be effective, the team leader has to achieve a higher level of personal and technical acceptance than other advisers. Although the prestige accorded the position will give him an initial impetus, the team leader must work at gaining acceptance. At times the team can provide support, but more often its effectiveness is determined by his acceptance.

Stage two, contact and rapport with leaders of the host institution, will be marked by close contact between the team leader and the top administrator of the host institution and others in the power structure. Their confidence must be gained and rapport retained by means of continuous contacts, both formal and informal. These also aid in keeping the team leader informed.

> This stage is also marked by the team and team leader identifying with the host institution to the point that the latter is convinced that its problems are of genuine concern to the team leader and the team. The host institution will inevitably begin to regard US team as somewhat distinct from other technical assistance entities and will increasingly consider the team as a component of the HI. (p. 12)

As dialogue about the development of the institution becomes more structured, stage three is reached. The dialogue will concern such things as long-range plans, problems and opportunities, needs of the host country, role of the host institution in meeting the country's needs, needs for and uses of resources, etc.

Some of the political and personal affiliations and ambitions both inside and outside the institution will be exposed and dealt with.

Stage four, perception of the country's needs and definition of the host institution's role, takes place when this dialogue is translated into concrete ideas about the host institution's role in national economic development. Economic development will reflect the host institution as a producer of something the country needs and for which it will be willing to provide support. In the process of focusing and articulating this role, the top management will provide leadership and stimulation within the institution. With the help of the advisory team, a realistic appraisal of the potential of the host institution is developed. Joint adviser-counterpart approaches to external relations contribute to generally high morale. Clearly, the advisory team is expected to make increasingly more sophisticated contributions.

Stage five, development of strategy by the host institution for accomplishing its role in national economic development, requires concentration on ways to serve society rather than to compete with other agencies. Serving society requires (1) an understanding of both the competitors of and collaborators with the host institution and cooperative action where appropriate and (2) recognition that the host institution must develop competence before it bids for additional responsibilities. Hence, plans are made and actions initiated to overcome weaknesses of the host institution, to establish priorities, and to determine where technical assistance is needed. As improvements are made, contracts are obtained from the host government, and efforts are initiated to understand how government leaders analyze the country's needs and the host institution's role.

Logically, the next stage involves execution of the strategy developed in stage five. In the process, advisers and personnel of the host institution tend to function as representatives of a single entity. The emphasis of that entity shifts increasingly to fulfilling the country's needs and efforts are made to bring a higher proportion of the host institution's activities to bear on functions deemed important by the host government and the society at large. "Inherent in this stage is the HI attitude that HI can and must be the prime mover in creating favorable relations with government, business and the general public" (p. 13). This stage marks the end of this phase of the model.

Phase D. The final phase, Phase D, concerns the technical assistance group's relationships with the host government and the public of the host country. During this phase, the technical assistance group is identified with the host institution rather than with the U.S. government. In assisting the host institution in attaining its fullest development, team members come in frequent contact with business and community leaders, as well as with members of the host government. This role is a normal and essential one if the team is to achieve its full potential.

Stage one of this sequence is entitled evaluation of the host institution's previous relationships with the host government and the public. Because the usefulness of approaches based on U.S. conditions has been limited and the relationships between the host institution and the host government as well as other institutions have been tradition-bound, a rational evaluation and understanding of the present and historic situation are needed to develop a palatable and effective set of relationships. In the process, both problems and opportunities are revealed.

The second stage, in which contacts are established with government and public entities, involves a process in which the host institution becomes visible and demonstrates both competence and usefulness in areas that the government and the public consider relevant. Respect for and confidence in the host institution are developed at this stage as a basis for subsequent activities. Likewise, increasing contacts are made by personnel of the host institution with the government and public entities.

Stage three, public realization of the host institution's usefulness, is described as follows:

> Effective and productive relationships at working levels between HI and the government and the public are specifically designed to develop confidence in HI. Specific contacts are made to demonstrate an attitude of cooperation and service instead of a competitive threat to the other agencies. Activities designed to upgrade the competence and enhance the image of government and business technicians develop an atmosphere in which they regard HI as useful to the entire agricultural development process. Widespread contacts with farmers generate public support potential for both HI and government agencies. (p. 15)

Stage four, consensus of both the host institution and the government regarding the host institution's role and responsibility, is well described by its title. The consensus grows out of demonstrations of the host institution's usefulness and contacts which call this usefulness to public attention. Both the host institution and government personnel have an appreciation for the other's viewpoint. However, since relationships are not limited to government, the risk of jurisdictional disputes among agencies is high. Consequently, multilateral relationships must be established carefully.

The maintenance of contact and rapport constitutes stage five. If the rate of turnover of personnel is high, a constant and continuing effort to maintain contacts will be required. The rapport established should enable the personnel of the host institution to know and influence what is happening, what is likely to happen, what the government wants to happen and, reciprocally, what the institution can expect from government. Care must be exercised to identify the institution with the government rather than with the party in power. The public image of the institution as useful to society needs to be developed by assisting society's representatives. All of this requires that the technical assistance team be identified as a significant part of the host institution.

The existence of stage six, publicity for the host institution and the government, explicitly recognizes that deliberate efforts must be made by the host institution's administration to secure adequate funds for its continuance. Just as government has to account to the public because it is a public entity, the host institution must account for itself as an instrument of the public. Public accounting and resource acquisition are intimately related. "An adequate appreciation of the political nature of a publicly supported institution and the development of public information and public relations programs compatible with this nature is a definite stage in institutional development" (p. 16). Specifically, if the host institution has government support, advantages will accrue to it if it makes this support and its own performance known to the public.

The final stage involves the formulation and execution of strategy. At this point consensus is reached between the host institution and the government with regard to what the institution can do in the publicly supported, agrarian program and also what authority, responsibility, and resources government can impart to the institution. In the process of arriving at this consensus, the institution has a responsibility to educate itself and government about such things as cost, consequences, alternatives, and timing with regard to public policy issues. The strategy used may have special implications for the technical assistance group if it involves such things as (1) enabling decision makers to visit viable, productive institutions in other countries, (2) bringing in especially competent executives to advise, or (3) implementing some other similar strategy. When this stage of the process, which should be a never-ending one, can continue through changes in government, one of the necessary criteria of institutionalization will have been fulfilled.

In summarizing their entire model, Rigney and McDermott state, "Since the relationships are presented in the form of a generalized model, they do not represent any single project in its entirety. Furthermore, the relationships cannot be operationalized directly from the construct although there are many implications for the development of an optimum strategy in particular projects" (p. 16).

Part II: Optimum Role for U.S. Advisors
        by J. A. Rigney

This portion of the North Carolina State University bulletin by J. A. Rigney et al. contains a review of the sources of frustrations frequently experienced by U.S. technical assistance personnel and an examination of potential alternative administrative procedures which might "optimize" the role of such personnel.

Frequently, technical assistance personnel arrive at the host institution to find themselves confronted with inadequately described tasks to be performed, a set of conflicting impressions and expectations, and with no experience or guidelines for deciding the most effective routes to be followed. Given this confusion and the fact that the normal two-year tour is a relatively short period of time to carry out a program, there is a tendency to grasp a few relatively familiar activities that can be accomplished with (1) a reasonable degree of assurance of success and (2) minimal reliance on cooperation from others. Usually these activities are selected with little regard to their contribution to institution building.

Upon their completion, an even shorter period of time remains for serious institution building activities.

All too frequently the adviser returns from his overseas tour frustrated and lacking evidence of professional accomplishments. To make matters worse, during his two years abroad he has had no opportunity to pursue his own particular professional interests and has lost contact with both the literature and the developments in his profession.

> Thus the advisor is recruited for a vague and uncertain role, is maintained in this role almost "incommunicado" from a professional point of view, and finally is returned home without the privilege or the necessity of reporting to his peers and colleagues in a professionally disciplined vein. It is for these reasons that participation in technical assistance is so frequently referred to as a two-year interlude in one's professional development. (p. 18)

The purpose of this portion of the bulletin by Rigney is to examine alternatives to such frustrating experiences as these.

In considering alternative roles and attempting to identify the "best" one, several criteria need to be identified explicitly. These include the adviser's (1) early visibility and acceptance, (2) effectiveness in institution building, (3) enhanced professional capability and stature, (4) reentry into the U.S. professional stream, and (5) availability for further technical assistance. Each of these is discussed in turn.

Data gathered from technical assistance projects support the hypothesis that professional acceptance must be achieved as a prerequisite for effective progress by technical assistance personnel in institution building activities. Hence, one of the criteria for an optimal role for a technical assistance adviser involves establishment of his professional visibility and accreditation as early as possible after his arrival at the host institution.

> The accreditation should not only establish the fact that the U.S. advisor is competent in his particular discipline, but that he can bring that competence to bear on the solution of the important problems in the local environment. It should inspire cooperation and incentive to undertake new activities on the part of host nationals. It should open doors for joint activities that would otherwise remain inaccessible to the institutional development process. Therefore, in order to make the advisor's tour of duty most productive, the criteria for an optimum role

must include initial activities which get his program off to an early start. (p. 19)

A second major criterion in optimizing the role of the technical assistance adviser is to ensure that his total effort has maximum effect on institutional development. This means that he needs to help build the capacity of the host institution for producing outputs of value to the society rather than producing end products himself. Many extracurricular activities compete for his time, but the major objective of his activities must be to improve the host institution's leadership, its technical personnel, its organizational structure, its program, its fiscal and physical resources, and its attitude.

A third criterion involves enhancing professional capability and stature. Competent, imaginative, and energetic faculty members are often disinterested in participating in technical assistance programs because they feel they will not be enriched professionally by the experience. Several studies document the fact that faculty members do, in fact, lose ground within their profession if they are away from their university duties for more than a year.

> The criteria for the optimum role of the advisor, therefore, must include activities which will make the assignment more attractive professionally. The optimizing process must seek elements in the role which add to the productiveness of the advisor in institution building at the same time that it provides for enhancing his own professional competence and stature as judged by his professional peers. This will require not only an improvement in his professional capability but also a means for bringing his accomplishments to the attention of his professional peers. (pp. 20-21)

A fourth criterion concerns facilitating the reentry of a staff member into his domestic profession upon return from an overseas tour. In all too many cases, the faculty member, having served in the role of an adviser who gave out professional information, returns home with little evidence that he has expanded his technical competence. This deficiency needs to be overcome so that U.S. university administrators can perceive genuine benefits to their institution, particularly in the form of improved faculty competence, as a consequence of a technical assistance assignment. Such additional competence must be compatible with ongoing programs of the university and not antagonistic to or competitive with them.

> In optimizing the role of the advisor, therefore, it is important to insure that his activities make him more valuable and useful to his home institution upon his return. It is particularly important that he be more useful in his own particular professional field—not just a more widely traveled faculty member with vague impressions of exotic cultures. (p. 21)

The final criterion proposed by Rigney is availability of the staff member for further technical assistance activity. Much of the experience obtained in an initial technical assistance role can be generally applied in the institution building field. Yet relatively few faculty members return for a second tour. In spite of the fact that they could be much more efficient during a second experience, many staff members are unwilling to accept additional tours, partially because of their university's unwillingness to spare them from commitments at home. Second tours have almost certainly been a signal for separation from the U.S. university—an event which would tend to inhibit a staff member's maintenance of his own sharpness, productivity, and attractiveness while overseas.

> A final criterion to be optimized in defining the advisor's role, therefore, is a provision for keeping him in the midstream of his profession to such an extent that he can continue to contribute to it technically while away on assignment, and thereby be able to move quickly back into a productive role at home upon his return. Only under such circumstances can the U.S. University allow him to undertake repeated assignments. (p. 22)

After optimizing the role of the adviser with respect to each of the criteria discussed above, Rigney integrates the criteria in a single role to optimize them jointly.

Part III: Measuring Institutional Maturity in the Development of Indigenous Agricultural Universities by R.W. Roskelley and J.A. Rigney

In the final portion of the North Carolina State University bulletin, R.W. Roskelley and J.A. Rigney address themselves to the problem of measuring progress toward institutional maturity. This problem becomes increasingly important as a technical assistance project matures and decisions are made concerning phasing out or retaining, in some form, a portion of the technical assistance. The authors use the concept of institutionalization defined by Esman and Blaise [20].

> ... "the process by which through the instrument of organization new ideas and functions are integrated and fitted into developing societies, are accepted and acquire the capacity to sustain themselves and in turn influence the larger environment in which they function." (p. 37)

Further, the attempts to measure institutional maturity reported here take cognizance of the dimensions of the process of institution building: (1) institutional variables (leadership, doctrine, resources, program, and internal structure), (2) linkages with the environment, and (3) transactions.

Roskelley and Rigney begin by reflecting on experiences in the Far East, where a number of technical assistance projects were terminated prior to the CIC-AID study. They reach the following conclusions on the basis of the analysis of these terminated projects:

> First, even though progress has been made in some aspects of institutional development, none of the institutions had achieved the kind of overall maturity that was essential for them to sustain a dynamic, self-generative level of performance. . . .

> Second, the criteria used to determine institutional maturity were clearly inadequate. . . .

> Third, each of the institutions experienced a traumatic interlude after the assistance contract was terminated that was characterized by periods of retrogression and loss of competence rather than continued growth.

> Fourth, there was much evidence that neither the U.S. nor the host country would realize the potentially significant dividends from the investments of money, manpower and professional skills which was spent in the institution building program unless additional inputs could be made in key areas where little growth had occurred.

> Fifth, there were many valid reasons which suggested that it was not in the best interest of the U.S. to terminate the contracts at a time when many aspects of the institution were still in the early stages of maturity. (p. 38)

Among other criteria of institutional maturity currently used, the following are suggested as appropriate for a land grant type of institution:

1. The institution conceives its role in society as one of serving the rural community. . . .

2. The service orientation, the devotion to the solution of important agricultural problems and the keen desire to train students in the philosophy and capability, automatically generate a bond of common purpose between professor and student that concentrates on this service orientation and dedication to the solution of problems. . . .

3. The motivation and incentive for individual staff members derive in large measure from a sense of satisfaction of having served the rural people well. . . .

4. To the extent that the service orientation of a Land-Grant Institution makes it a program for the rural people, they in turn generate public support for the institution commensurate with its public service. . . .

5. Since the institution's existence is justified on the basis of its production of useful people and useful information, the internal administrative attitudes and relationships reflect this purpose. (pp. 41-42)

In addition to a list of descriptive variables that could be measured in quantitative terms, the following important variables were added for measuring progress in the land grant model:

A. Teaching
    1. Teacher's attitude toward his major function
    2. Teacher's relationships with students
    3. Teacher's execution of function
    4. Teaching methods employed to achieve objectives
    5. Relationship of subject matter content to country needs
B. Research
    1. Volume and productivity of research
    2. Proportion of projects directed to high priority problems
    3. Capability of staff for documenting the relevance to country needs
C. Extension Education
    1. Definition of Extension Function by the University
    2. Identification of Priority Activities with country needs
    3. Coordination with other agencies
    4. Improvement of System (Organizational Self-Improvement Activities)
    5. Use of such principles and processes as: Group Dynamics, Local Leadership, and Community Organizations
    6. Focus on Best Technology
D. Administrative Incentives
    1. Stimulation of professional improvement

   2. Recognition and reward for excellence
   3. Delegation of authority
   4. Sharing in making professional decisions
   5. Effective use of controls
   6. Development of public support (p. 43)

Subsequently, the rationale for using each of these variables is developed. Finally, a set of survey instruments is presented.

The role and type of technical assistance personnel change as the project moves from initiation to maturity. The authors state:

> The experience from interviews in projects in the NESA region [Near East, South Asia; a region defined by AID] strongly documented the fact that different skills and different length of assignment were indicated at different stages of maturity. Host nationals at the recipient institutions tended to regard U.S. advisors highly and affectionately where the institution was "immature." In the more mature host institutions where the same type of advisor was used the attitude ranged from polite tolerance to restive impatience. These studies strongly point to long term, experienced generalists as the optimum input early in a project, and short term, highly articulate specialists as the most productive in the later stages. Unfortunately, the format of the U.S. input in this respect did not change with institutional maturity in any systematic pattern. (p. 51)

In the initial stages of a project the participant program is, properly, quite rigid in form, concentrating heavily on advanced degree programs. Later, however, the program must become highly flexible and responsive to opportunities that arise. Further, it should concentrate on bringing the institutional leadership into wide and meaningful contact with the scientific and technical world. The institution's leaders will have the difficult task of finding funds for continued travel and communication after outside assistance has been terminated. Progress toward overcoming this obstacle can be made by establishing the initial contacts outside the institution and initiating a flexible program for them.

Although quite important in the early stages of a project, the timing of acquiring support is even more crucial subsequently. After the institution's programs have been more sharply focused, its plans well articulated and documented, and its priorities evaluated and established, crucial inputs of equipment and program operation funds can be quite productive.

An exchange of personnel is highly important to the continuing development of a host institution in its efforts to close the scientific and technological gap. Likewise, U.S. professionals who have had overseas experience find it increasingly attractive to bring professionals from other environments to their campuses to capitalize on their experience and background. Thus, the maturing process of both the host institution and its U.S. counterpart is mutual. Furthermore, complementarity of interest exists in many research areas where testing ideas in a wider environmental context is highly desirable. Under these circumstances, exchanges of professional personnel become mutually attractive.

An opportunity that has been underused in the past has been the technical interchange between the U.S. department and the host institution as the latter shifts into the maturity phase. This potential is described as follows:

> One of the most difficult problems for professionals in the underdeveloped nations is to achieve professional visibility and recognition outside their own limited national circle. The international publication media have been virtually inaccessible to any but the most renowned authors in the developing nations. There are many devices which the assisting U.S. department can use to introduce foreign professionals to the scientific world, including joint authorship, use of widely circulated mimeograph reports, and the widespread listing of good papers published in more obscure media. These are services normally accorded our own graduate students, and they can be equally beneficial to scientists in the developing nations. (p. 54)

Results of the study indicated that far too little attention has been given to phasing out technical assistance in the NESA region. Hence, the following principles are suggested for guidance as the advisory team shifts responsibility to the host institution in the maturity phase: (1) The young professional must be given overt responsibility as rapidly as he is capable of discharging it, preferably while the adviser is still present to guide him. (2) The fact that young professionals learn as much or more from their mistakes as they do from their successes must be recognized. (3) Maintaining rapport and sympathetic contact during this stage is highly important because it facilitates objective examination of experiences as a basis for improvement. (4) The transition should be smooth and gradual rather than precipitous. Throughout, the desire for personal credit on the part of host institution staff members needs to be timed with their ability to assume responsibility for the outcome of the activity.

[33] HILL, Thomas M.; Haynes, Warren; and Baumgartel, Howard. "Management Education in India: A Study of International Collaboration in Institution Building." Harvard University, Cambridge, Mass., 1971. Pages numbered by chapters. (Mimeographed. Preliminary work.)

Although neither a part of the Inter-University Research Program in Institution Building nor the CIC-AID Rural Development Research Project, an institution building analysis of several Indian institutions by Thomas Hill, Warren Haynes, and Howard Baumgartel bears some similarity to the studies summarized above. For example, these authors use an in-depth case study approach with a conceptual framework taken largely from the one developed by Esman et al. They are also concerned about the role of technical assistance personnel. Finally, they are especially concerned about planning in institution building.

The specific objectives of this analysis were: (1) to establish criteria by which the relative success of particular institution building projects of the given class can be gauged and (2) to discover the factors, or input variables, which are important determinants of success in such projects.

The class of projects selected was management education institutions receiving some form of international aid. More specifically, the two case studies focus on the Indian Institute of Management, Ahmedabad (IIMA), and the Indian Institute of Management, Calcutta (IIMC). In addition, some data and analyses are reported for the Administrative Staff College of India at Hyderabad (ASCI).

As a consequence of several evolutionary changes in institutions offering business education in India's postindependence period, the Calcutta Institute and the Ahmedabad Institute were established in the early 1960s. One of the noteworthy "normative spread" effects of these institutions was the introduction of competition into an apparently lethargic system. As a consequence, a number of curricula have been revised, several additional institutions apparently have qualified for additional governmental support, and in virtually all cases the dominant objective seems to have been a curriculum following an American pattern but adapted to local needs.

Drawing on the literature from business policy in their discussion of planning for institution building, Hill, Haynes, and Baumgartel define strategy as the pattern of objectives, purposes, or goals and major policies and plans for achieving these goals stated in such a way as to define what business the institution is in or is to be in and the kind of institution it is to be. Subsequently, the key elements of institutions' strategic planning are defined as (1) identifying and evaluating need; (2) forecasting the institution's capacity to fulfill the need; (3) determining the institution's mission; (4) determining the time dimensions of the development plan; (5) selecting the top leadership; (6) determining leadership style; (7) designing the internal organization; (8) determining the institution's doctrine, especially selecting a model; (9) planning enabling linkages; (10) planning functional linkages; (11) planning relations with similar institutions; (12) planning for coping with environmental constraints; and (13) selecting a site and constructing a plant. In their subsequent discussions of strategic planning of international management education projects, the authors direct their attention to the influence of the agency that is granting financial aid, the technical assistance plan, collaborative relationships, choice of an educational model, a plan for faculty development, participation of faculty and students in major decisions, and planning the product mix. Finally, the strategic planning of both institutes was evaluated not only in terms of these two lists but also as organic entities.

The analysis of costs and benefits of management education is divided into two parts. Initially, a conceptual framework is developed for the measurement and analysis of the private and social costs and benefits of management education in the Indian context. Subsequently, this framework is applied to data for the Indian Institute of Management, Ahmedabad, in making an empirical cost-benefit analysis of the institute. The purpose of making a cost-benefit analysis was to demonstrate the application of the analytical model rather than to evaluate institutional performance.

Hence, the empirical results must be treated as approximations only.

Recognizing that an economic evaluation of any project by no means constitutes a total evaluation of any complex social undertaking, the authors conclude:

> Our analysis does not suffice to answer the question of whether or not the IIMA investment should have been undertaken. It suggests an answer of "yes" if but only if an economic rate of return equal to or greater than the social cost of capital were the sole criterion—which is surely not the case. We therefore believe that the answer continues to depend on evaluation, necessarily largely intuitive, of the non-monetary social returns which we have qualitatively identified but have been unable to quantify. (pp. 5-23)

In focusing on interpersonal and intergroup dynamics, the authors contend that the two institutions suffered from inadequate planning of the distribution of influence. As a consequence, the patterns of authority and power relationships that evolved were often the result of a series of ad hoc decisions and natural events. Not surprisingly, a substantial amount of tension resulted, especially with regard to participation in decision making. One of the major insights derived from the analysis of these two institutions was that the magnitude of tension over the problem of participation varied inversely with the volume of communication between the administrations and the faculties.

Both generic factors, inherent in probably all institution building efforts requiring foreign collaboration, and specific project factors had an effect on the struggle for influence. Generic factors include (1) deficiencies in organizational planning, (2) complications attributable to the participation of foreigners, (3) an inevitable disagreement over institutional doctrine and purpose, and (4) the exacerbating effects of newness on the one hand and rapid growth on the other. Specific project factors include (1) special cultural conditions of India, (2) heterogeneity of the faculty and administration, (3) the high involvement of the faculty, especially the behavioral scientists, in an introspective analysis of the institute's organizational structures, and (4) the particular leadership styles of the directors and their use of seconds-in-command.

On the basis of this portion of the analysis, the authors conclude:

> It should be clear by now that the history of these Institutes, and presumably of a large proportion of new institutions, is significantly influenced by disagreements over the allocation of influence. In some cases conflict over influence may be fatal; it was almost fatal in the Calcutta case. Our experience has been that many persons interested in institution building have a distaste for discussions of influence distribution, which to them seems overly personal and subjective. We believe firmly, however, that no issue is of greater importance in determining the success or failure of new institutions. We ignore such questions of organization and leadership style at our peril. The chief lesson, therefore, is that planners of new institutions must give more attention to the design of approaches which will reduce the dysfunctional effects of unplanned influence distributions. (pp. 6:44-45)

The analysis of relationships between American and Indian project participants and their institutions led to the conclusion that inadequate communication allowed misunderstandings and resentments to accumulate to problem proportions. This is not to say, however, that interpersonal relations between domestic and foreign participants were poor; to the contrary, they were considered to be generally excellent. Nevertheless, the fact that inadequate communication resulted in difficulties was judged by the authors to be sufficiently important to justify recommending a special monitoring device, such as an independent review board.

> The primary function of such a body would be to engage in annual progress reviews with project participants, to assess objectively actual accomplishment relative to that planned, and to report its findings not to sponsoring agencies but to those organizations directly involved in the institution-building process. (pp. 7-49)

To determine the influence of the Institutes at Ahmedabad and Calcutta as well as the Administrative Staff College of India at Hyderabad, a random sample survey of participants in their programs between 1964 and 1967 was undertaken. The survey was designed to provide information about the institutions' functional and normative linkages. The responses of past participants are classified and presented by the programs in which they participated.

In the statistical analysis of the data, certain background and demographic characteristics, especially factors associated with "hierarchial level," were found to predispose certain program populations to more strongly positive or negative evaluations of some program characteristics. The analysis revealed further that executives tended to evaluate their training primarily along two broad dimensions: (1) satisfaction or dissatisfaction with the content of the program engendered by factors, such as course administration and quality of participants, which were important at that time; and (2) perceived benefits (or the lack thereof) in such forms as personal worth and the acquisition of knowledge, probably accurately assessable only after some lapse of time.

On the basis of these analyses the conclusion was reached that programs may be well spoken of—thus serving the important purpose of enhancing the reputation of the sponsoring institution—if judged good by either of these criteria. In addition, with the use of a criterion variable and respondents' reports of their innovative efforts, a relationship was found between the variable and managers who felt they had benefited in particular ways from their training. The organizational climate within which the participant subsequently found himself was also related to his innovative efforts. Both his status within the organization and the quality of the program he attended appeared to have had some bearing on the innovations he attempted. Managers with high status from favorable organizational climates appear most likely to innovate and, for this group, the quality of the training program may especially make some difference. Analysis of the survey data indicated the noteworthy fact that a generally favorable organizational climate existed in the foreign affiliated firms represented by participants, while those public sector enterprises that were represented appeared to be somewhat deficient in this respect.

In concluding the report, Hill, Haynes, and Baumgartel summarize their findings, several of which are especially worthy of consideration. Strategic planning in institution building, however comprehensive, should not be regarded as a one-time activity and should provide for periodic reviews and planned critiques. Ahmedabad Institute's clearly articulated doctrine gave it a strong sense of direction and provided a solid base for faculty collaboration. Although only a part of strategic planning and subsequent evaluation, the cost-benefit analysis methodology developed can help to ensure that decisions are not unduly influenced by the enthusiasm and articulateness of well-meaning proponents or by the special interest of minorities with access to seats of power. Likewise, when used in auditing the consequences of decisions to initiate institution building projects, cost-benefit analysis can help to prevent the expansion or replication of activities that are attractive but not demonstrably cost-effective.

Partially because of inadequate strategic planning, both institutes experienced difficulty with their system of institutional governance and periods of leadership insufficiency. Also as a result of a lack of planning for the orderly diminution of foreign assistance, the belated transition was abrupt and somewhat painful. Further compounding this problem was the inability of both Americans and Indians to fully surmount cultural barriers to effective communication.

Analysis of the sample survey data yielded the following important findings: (1) Those training experiences which provided a sense of accomplishment through acquisition of new knowledge—especially, of knowledge applicable to familiar problems of immediate concern to the trainee—were the ones most highly valued. (2) The effect of management training on management practice is contingent on the receptivity of the user organizations to new ideas. (3) The training efforts of the subject institutions may be too highly spread over too many organizations to have as much effect as if they were focused on a specific set of organizations rather than individuals. Use of the IRPIB tests of institutionality—technical capacity, normative commitment, innovative thrust, environmental image, and spread effect—yielded the conclusion that the Institute at Ahmedabad had the strongest claim to institutionality at the time this study was completed. Finally, the report concluded with suggestions for further research.

[34] THOMAS, D. Woods, and Fender, Judith G., eds. *Proceedings: Conference on Institution Building and Technical Assistance.* Washington, D.C.: Agency for International Development and the Committee on Institutional Cooperation, December 4 and 5, 1969. 164 pages.

The final publication summarized in this section of outstanding contributions with an organizational-institutional focus
could also be classified with the macro-oriented literature to be
summarized subsequently. Because the *Proceedings* of the December 1969 Washington Conference on Institution Building and
Technical Assistance contains some papers that deal with micro
phenomena and others dealing with macro, the summary of this
publication is an ideal transition between the two sections of this
chapter.

The purpose of the conference, the proceedings of which are
summarized here, was:

> ... to develop better understanding of the institution-building process
> among key AID/Washington staff, cooperating U.S. government entities
> and the U.S. university community involved in institution-building
> forms of technical assistance abroad. (Preface)

In the opening paper entitled, "Institution Building: Its Role
in Political, Social and Economic Development," Joel Bernstein
contends that the major variables determining what people do in
developing countries are (1) institutions and (2) government policies. Improving the capability of institutions should, consequently,
be the main purpose of technical assistance. This requires careful
and deliberate planning involving all interested parties. Hence, AID
has supported a number of research efforts, specifically the Inter-
University Research Project in Institution Building and the CIC
Rural Development Research Project, to improve the base of
knowledge for performing this process.

The second chapter, "Institution Building as a Guide to
Action," was written by Milton Esman. In addition to the concepts reviewed in [17], [18], and [19] above, Esman herein emphasizes the need for strategic planning and operational monitoring of
the organization to determine if its actual performance is in accord
with the original intentions and expectations of the plans. He
maintains further that technical assistance can be critical in the
following aspects of institution building: (1) source of change
models, (2) participants in the leadership function, (3) providers
and allocators of valuable resources, (4) transferring and adapting
technology, and (5) operational monitoring. Esman also elaborates
on his previous criteria of institutionalization and includes the

following: (1) technical capacity, (2) normative commitment, (3) innovative thrust, (4) environmental image, and (5) spread effect. Subsequently, the paper was discussed by John Hilliard and Sol Chafkin, followed by discussion from the floor. Finally, Esman recognizes the limitations on the scope of the micro framework formulated by him and others and identifies the boundary conditions under which it is applicable.

George H. Axinn, in his paper "Field Testing the Model," emphasizes William Siffin's contention that institution building is a perspective that can make a contribution to an art. Likewise, he refers to John Hanson's characterization of the approach as a series of lenses [28]. Axinn also refers to Eugene Jacobson's observations [29] as well as to the observations of Jiri Nehnevajsa [22], Guthrie Birkhead [89], William Siffin [88], and Hans Blaise [63]. In the process of summarizing observations about each of the functional characteristics, Axinn alludes to work by Donald Taylor [54] and David Derge [31]. He concludes that the field tests of the model have been promising, although they have demonstrated the need for more research.

Ira Baldwin discussed the topic "Institution Building and Project Planning." He contends that the planning process should be divided into (1) the overall planning prerequisite to establishing an institution building project and (2) planning undertaken for the initiation and conduct of the project. Under the former he discusses the questions of the country's needs, the type of institution required, and the demands on resources. Before turning to the second phase he discusses the role of the donor agency in the first phase. Components of the operational planning phase are (1) joint planning, (2) development of doctrine, (3) evaluation, (4) scale of operations, (5) leadership, (6) program, (7) structure, (8) linkages, (9) improving technical assistance, (10) participants, and (11) strategic planning. Subsequently, the Baldwin paper was discussed by Herbert Rees and Mark Cannon followed by general discussion.

In the paper entitled, "Institution-Building Models and Project Operations," Woods Thomas emphasizes (1) the milieu, (2) recognition and acceptance of project objectives, (3) risk, uncertainty, and project management, (4) doctrine and project operations, (5) the program concept, and (6) the question of tactics. In concluding, he suggests that institution building theory should be extended through appropriate adaptation of decision-making theory and practice. Prior to the general discussion, the paper was discussed by Robert Culbertson and Harold Moss.

J.A. Rigney's paper is entitled, "The Institution-Building Model in Project Review and Maturity Testing." In it he states:

> The *purpose of the project review* is to provide information for administrative decision and action. . . . The *process of project review* involves repeated reassessment of project goals and inquiry into the relevance of the indigenous institution to the real needs of society. . . . The most important *data required for project review* are those indicators of the stage of development of each of the important elements in institution building. . . . Finally, the *assessment of project progress and institutional maturity* involves a judgment as to whether the individual elements of the institution-building process have reached a stage where different forms of technical assistance inputs will be more efficient or, alternatively, a stage where those elements of the institution can progress satisfactorily without further technical assistance inputs. (pp. 89-90)

In discussing project evaluation experience he refers to work by R.W. Roskelley and Rigney [32]. The work by Esman (cited above in [17]) is used as a basis for formulating a number of relevant questions that should be asked in evaluating projects. Later, some of the difficulties encountered in operationalizing the institution building concepts are underscored. Rigney concludes by discussing the following major developments needed to make the institution building concepts operational in evaluation: (1) There is a need to broaden the purpose for which the evaluation is made. (2) More adequate instruments and procedures are needed for measuring the subtleties implied in the concepts. (3) A better understanding is needed of alternative strategies in institution building. (4) Routinely reported data should be distinguished from that needed for project management purposes. Thorsen's discussion paper, which followed this paper, is highlighted in [20]; in addition, this paper is discussed by Roy L. Lovvorn.

Under the heading of "Institution Building and the Institutional Development Agreement," Glen Taggart discusses the background of the Institutional Development Agreement [250] and the reasons for its preparation. The most important contents of the document are summarized and discussed. In concluding, Taggart quotes Dr. John Hannah, AID administrator, as follows:

"New arrangements are being integrated in the Institutional Development Agreement to replace the standard university contract. It is felt that the new agreement is more suitable than the old for joint long-term institution building. . . . At the same time that (the new Institution Development Agreement) gives the universities more authority and more elbow room, it increases their obligations to invest their best talent and management skill to assure the successful attainment of the agreed upon objectives." (p. 127)

After brief discussions of the topic "Next Steps in the Application of the Institution-Building Model" by Joel Bernstein and Willard Cochrane, Siffin's summary report is given. In it, Siffin highlights the presentations made earlier in the conference.

MACRO-ORIENTED LITERATURE

As indicated above, in addition to manuscripts with institutional-organizational orientations, a number of significant contributions have been made concerning macro phenomena. These manuscripts, dealing with aspects of institution building beyond the individual institution, are worthy of the attention of institution builders. The summaries that follow are designed to be sufficiently comprehensive so that the substance of these contributions is apparent.

[35] POWELSON, John P. *Institutions of Economic Growth: A Theory of Conflict Management in Developing Countries.* Princeton, N.J.: Princeton University Press, 1972. 281 pages. Selections reprinted by permission of Princeton University Press.

The book by John P. Powelson, *Institutions of Economic Growth,* warrants initial consideration here. In it, Powelson makes an effort to develop a multidisciplinary theory of institutions and in so doing, he adopts a relatively unique definition of institutions. The term is defined as "any set of relationships between individuals that is designed to resolve their conflicts" (p. 13). The reason for this atypical definition is given in the book's preface.

Why, in some countries, is economic growth stopped by internal quarrels and mistrust? Why, in others, do competitors not only control their conflicts but *use* them to promote growth? In addressing this question, the present volume develops a broad-based theory of institutions. Growth depends, among other things, on a national capacity to build institutions to manage conflicts. This capacity, furthermore, requires national consensus on an economic and a political ideology. These ideologies are defined as the ways in which individuals envisage the economic and political systems—how they operate, and how just they are. Ideological consensus in turn is fostered by a popular nationalism, which therefore plays a positive role in growth rather than the negative one usually attributed to it by economists. (p. ix)

Hence, Powelson adds the effectiveness of institutions in managing conflict to (1) capital and (2) entrepreneurial capacity as potential facilitators of economic growth. The appropriate kind of institution is a location-specific phenomenon; an ideal institution for all circumstances does not exist. In part, the effectiveness of institutions depends upon the particular ideology on which consensus is formed. Such consensus must ultimately emerge or growth will falter.

Initially, Powelson develops a theory of institutions. Subsequently, he deals with implications of the theory. Each is worthy of note.

A potential for conflict occurs whenever two individuals interact and each seeks to satisfy his own needs. The individuals often perceive this conflict even before they sense their mutual goals, especially in the encounters that are part of economic development. Once two or more persons perceive that they have a mutual goal or that separate goals can be achieved only if they work jointly, a formal organization or a normal pattern of behavior emerges. Such institutions are crucial in conflict resolution because the potential for conflict exists whenever a decision must be reached. " . . . Every decision is a conflict resolved" (p. 13). The value or effectiveness of institutions, then, can be measured in terms of their conflict-resolving capacity. This capacity is of utmost importance because conflicts, properly contained and managed, actually propel growth, e.g., labor seeks higher wages which management can pay only if productivity goes up.

Defined as any set of relationships between individuals that is designed to resolve their conflicts, institutions reveal each individual to the other as a reasoning person capable of compromise to achieve mutual goals and with predictable responses. As institutions facilitate conflict resolution, confidence is placed in them, and, subsequently, in the individual parties to the conflict. Given this mutual confidence, the original institution which facilitated its formation may be changed if a more efficient one emerges in the growth process.

Growth requires a division of labor and specialization which, in turn, require different institutions to facilitate exchange. The particular type of institution selected will be determined by benefits and costs of alternative institutions as subjectively judged by members of the power groups capable of forming it. If these groups are growth-sensitive, many of the benefits will be judged by the institution's capacity to achieve growth; its costs will be measured in terms of the pain felt by the power group forming it—that is, in terms of sacrifices of resources, prestige, values, the effort required to overcome resistance of others, or even life itself in the case of a revolution.

In selecting among alternative institutions, the following dimensions are relevant: (1) centralized versus decentralized, (2) authoritarian versus nonauthoritarian, (3) formal versus informal, (4) employees' incentives versus employees' penalties, and (5) neutral versus biased toward specific solutions. The set of dimensional points occupied by any institution depends upon (1) the functions of the institution and (2) the institutional ideology accepted in the country.

Institutional ideology is one of several values that institutions must reflect. In fact, these values change as the society moves from the pretakeoff, through the takeoff, and into the posttakeoff stages. In the process, the transitional nature of the values creates strains for the institutions based upon them. The first institutions of takeoff must conform to existing values or they will not be formed at all. For these institutions to be most effective in light of the existing framework of values, they must embody costly measures to protect contestants against other contestants who are not trusted at the time of takeoff. This means that the institutions are bound to strain values in order to encompass the conflicts which are new at this stage. The amount of strain a society can accept is limited, of course. But after these institutions have existed for some time and have been accepted in the society, values will have changed and new institutions similar to them can be created.

Subsequently, the new institutions can strain values further, to the point where even the pace of the strain may be accelerated. When the society accepts the strain even at the point where the society itself becomes change oriented, the strain involved in change may itself become a value. This evolution of values suggests the profound effect that institutions established early in takeoff have for successive ones: "Values and institutions interact: an institution changes values, then a new institution is formed dependent on the changed values; it changes them further, and so on" (p. 24).

Perhaps more important, however, is the need for ideological consensus within the society as it passes through stages. Optimal consensus probably involves some internal dissension, however, because it serves as a source for institutional vigor and flexibility. Nevertheless, a degree of consensus is a prerequisite for the evolution of any institution. Hence, growth-sensitive power groups seek consensus on ideology. Consensus can be gained directly through numerous media or indirectly by first creating the type of institution desired and then using it as a model for fashioning other institutions. After a society has passed through the takeoff period, all values essential to growth are likely to be called into question. The cultural structure erected to sustain growth is likely to be questioned long before production reaches its physical limits, because once the limitation of supply on growth becomes foreseeable and the pollution predictable, a change in values is likely to occur. Those for whom economic growth is no longer a dominant goal will become desensitized to growth.

> Takeoff is the period in which growth-sensitive groups form and move into positions of power. Landing is the period in which power is sought by groups becoming desensitized to growth. The two periods are symmetrical. In each there is great confusion, as institutions of the previous period are unable to cope with new conflicts arising out of growth (in takeoff) or out of un-growth (in landing). Like takeoff countries, landing countries will find themselves in a severe ideological split. Institutions will weaken through lack of consensus on goals, and effective institutions will not be formed until a new consensus on ideology and goals emerges. (p. 29)

Powelson's theory has implications for both practitioners and scholars of development. Powelson contends that institutional effectiveness rather than the benefit-cost ratio should be the practitioners' principal criterion in selecting a project; that is, those projects most likely to increase a nation's capacity for effective decision making should be given top priority. In challenging scholars to extend the theory, Powelson contends that aggregate institutional effectiveness is a measurable concept that will take on different values in different nations and will be useful in explaining their different rates of growth. Finally, in contrast to (1) builders of models of economic growth who tend to predict infinitely increasing gross national products and (2) classical economists who contend that growth will ultimately stop because the earth's capacity to supply the necessary prerequisites will be exhausted, Powelson contends that economic growth will end for no other reason than that man no longer wants it.

[36] MORSE, Chandler, et al. *Modernization by Design: Social Science in the Twentieth Century.* Ithaca, N.Y.: Cornell University Press, 1969. 426 pages.

A set of perspectives, somewhat similar to John Powelson's in [35], is presented in this book, to which six members of the Modernization Workshop at Cornell University contributed. Representing anthropology, economics, political science, public administration, social psychology, and sociology, these authors indicate that several concepts common to all of them became apparent as their papers were being developed. Chandler Morse, an economist, highlights these concepts.

> In the end it turned out that a common methodological conviction, two leading questions, and an emergent agreement came to influence our work, largely determining the form and content of the essays produced. The conviction was that, in order to be successful, the study of modernization had eventually to proceed at both microanalytic and macroanalytic levels, and in a language that permitted one to move freely between the two poles, as in economic theory. . . .

> The first of the two questions related to the differences between premodern and modern societies, regarded as definably different modal types. To determine and state the crucial distinguishing characteristics of each type thus came to be one of our ambitions. The second and related question, which concerned the manner in which premodern societies were transformed into modern, defined another focus for our intellectual curiosity. . . .

With our interests thus convergent, it soon became apparent that the phenomenon we wanted to examine was different in important respects from that which had given rise to modern, industrialized, high-income countries in the first instance. We found ourselves coming to early agreement that the main difference between the two phenomena (which ought to affect the analysis of modernization far more than it has) was in their origins and modes of evolution. The processes of social change that steadily increased the wealth-creating powers of the North Atlantic nations from the early Middle Ages to the nineteenth century took place in a series of small steps, the cumulative effects of which were not apparant to their initiators. Increasingly complex and formal organizational structures emerged as the cumulative consequence of activities at the grass roots.... The countries that have undergone modernization since the last quarter of the nineteenth century, on the other hand, beginning with Japan (and even Germany), have seen quite clearly the need to initiate indigenous processes of growth and development under forced political draft in order to close in on the early modernizers. Their efforts have been highly organized....these late modernizers have had to start by creating complex, formal institutional structures *de novo,* employing or adapting blueprints derived from Western experience. Modernization in the twentieth century, therefore, is "by design," typically following . . . an "inverse model"....

A second common thread concerned various dimensions of the difference between modern and premodern institutions. We came to believe that an operational understanding of the many dissimilarities and their implications is more important than is generally recognized....the creation of formal organizations and structures leaves many nonformal features of the institutional framework untouched and out of touch with the new formal structures. As a result, the new organizational structures in the emergent modern sector find it necessary, though far from easy, to come to terms with the residual elements of the surrounding context. Related to this . . . is the dual social-psychological problem of building into the processes of developmental intervention a constructive dynamic that will lead to increasingly cooperative interaction, and of preventing such intervention from developing a degenerative dynamic, moving toward conflict. A dilemma of similar content . . . is that politically induced modernization generates various contradictions. The question . . . concerns the extent to which the resulting difficulties can be overcome or must be regarded as setting limits on the feasible scope and speed of modernization by design.

A third thread running through the essays relates to the practical implications of the analyses for the making of policy....

When one looks closely at the low-income countries (or sectors) in the world of today, the limitations of traditional economic explanations and prescriptions and the need for a broader, more flexible approach are even more apparent than before. Economists in increasing numbers, therefore, are looking for an alternative. . . . They are coming to realize that in order to deal with institutionalized poverty wherever it may exist, but especially in the Third World, a somewhat distinctive theory and method, synthesizing the orthodox and less orthodox insights of diverse social analysis, will be needed. The final essay . . . does endeavor to indicate some of the points at which economic and other forms of social analysis intersect and interact. (pp. x-xv)

In the first essay entitled "The Social Limits of Politically Induced Change" John W. Lewis, a political scientist, explores selected problems of political leadership from the perspectives of political science and sociological theory and the experiences of several modernizing nations. He argues that three consequences of any rapid social transformation significantly constrain the speed, types, and numbers of changes that may be politically induced. First, the creation of new roles, institutions, values, and social relationships during the meaningful social transformation produces instability and may lead to anomie. Second, the changes in a society both influence and are influenced by political leadership because social development affects any current distribution of social power. Third, social transformation concerns cultural variation and increasing differentiation and specialization.

Leadership is the pivotal concept in the argument presented in Lewis's chapter. It is tentatively defined as embodied in those authoritative acts of guidance and control, both formal and informal, within any social group, which are required, " 'for the realization of major social goals and for the continuity of social order. . . . Political leadership refers to the formal, upper level leadership exercised by individuals filling roles in what Gabriel Almond calls the 'political system. . . .' " The sociological view of contemporary change, one which has primarily stressed the problems of spontaneous differentiation and role proliferation, is used as a point of departure.

As premodern institutions are transformed into more complex and modern ones, a gradual proliferation of roles occurs. Roles become more specific and specialized. Simultaneously, social cohesion is maintained by means of premodern social relationships and institutions.

A second type of role change occurs when revolutionary or modernizing elites are instrumental in directly transferring specialized organizational forms to their society, thus bypassing the gradual processes of change. This type of change may be viewed as an inversion of the process of spontaneous mutation of agglomerated, unspecialized roles into more highly differentiated ones.

Inverse modernization is brought about partially because nations seek the level of international standing and influence that supposedly follows in the wake of modernization. Political leaders frequently compare their progress with that of already advanced nations and seek to bring about in months or years the kinds of improvements that the older modernized societies took decades and generations to achieve. That is, there are demands for a greater mass knowledge, more flexible uses of resources, better health, etc. The rapid multiplication of industrial organizations is attempted according to preconceived plans. These become instruments for intensive social development.

While these organizations satisfy the elite's desires for symbols of modernity and produce improvements in living standards which placate local segments of the society, they are frequently accompanied by violent political upheaval, strikes, military aggression, depressions, and extremist movements. Hence, disruption and modernization proceed concomitantly. Premodern social relationships provide some social cohesion, but these relationships are often repudiated by revolutionary elites. The elites are further constrained by political competition with the premodern elites and the younger generation of successor subelites.

The new technology, which the elites use as their main instrument for change, generates a demand for well-trained manpower. Consequently, education and training take on new values and tend to displace the sources of status afforded members of the premodern elites. This emphasis on social mobility based on merit and technical expertise becomes a threat even to the less expert revolutionary elites. Especially important at this point is ideology which provides a set of ideas purporting to explain the present state of human action in society. Hence, ideology is used as a partial basis for social cohesion in the new states. However, it comes at a high cost in terms of investment in time and resources.

Nationalism, defined as the acceptance of the state as the impersonal and ultimate arbiter of human affairs, not only is used as an ideology but also has operational connotations. The combination of ideology and nationalism is used by revolutionary elites to justify any action as legitimate. In spite of its limitations, ideology may help a society overcome some of its most difficult crises in the early period. In the long run, ideologies which maintain close contact with evolving aspirations may be more effective than ideology issued as unmitigated dogma.

In countries where nationalist ideology has been substituted for social cohesion, a power struggle frequently results between the revolutionary elites and the successor subelites. In these cases, the revolutionary elite may be inclined toward a nationalistic ideology in which unanimity and retention of control take priority over developmental goals. Frequently the elites in power convert the technology for development into technology for control. Regimentation and discipline become prime organizational techniques as demands for stability and national order replace those for rapid social change. Economic leaders are often replaced by military ones.

After discussing the social limits on politically induced change, Lewis focuses on China as an illustration. He examines the period subsequent to the Communist takeover in light of the propositions concerning difficulties in maintaining order and stability during periods of rapid politically motivated social transformation, the disruptive character of the power struggle that occurs among the competing elite groups, and the distortions that arise from cultural diversity and the breakdown of authority.

In the second essay of Morse's book, William H. Friedland, a professor of industrial and labor relations, emphasizes changes in the social structure that occur during modernization. In particular, he concentrates on social modernization defined in terms of the ability of a society to confront, overcome, and indeed prepare itself for challenges by rearranging its social structure.

Continual specialization of roles and institutions characterizes the self-sustaining process of proliferation. This process takes place by way of innovation and diffusion. The former occurs through differentiation, recombination of existing roles and/or institutions, and introduction of new roles or institutions. Diffusion, on the other hand, can be either piecemeal or can occur through the integrated transference of roles and institutions.

As traditional practices give way to increased structural complexity, formalization increases; that is, there is a continual encompassing of larger areas of behavior within the framework of formal organizations. Not only does increasing complexity increase this formalism, but it also leads to proliferation of decision making and decision makers. In turn, feedback mechanisms are needed to keep upper echelons informed.

In countries late to modernize, the process is significantly different from that in countries early to modernize. While evolutionary change characterizes the latter, late modernizers tend to borrow integrated and formal networks of roles intact. Consequently, problems of institutionalization and maintenance of stability are encountered. These grow out of the dislocations which accompany rapid modernization and unrealistic expectations concerning its benefits.

Chapter 3 of Morse et al. by David B. Macklin, a social psychologist, is entitled "A Social-Psychological Perspective on Modernization." Macklin contends that much of what is important for the understanding and guidance of the modernization process is discovered only at the intersection of the social and psychological systems. Consequently, he presents and illustrates the application of an interaction model in which psychological and social processes play an explicit part. Before turning to the social-psychological interaction, however, Macklin reviews the results of some efforts to develop a grand psychological theory of modernization. Specifically, he deals with work by David C. McClelland, Everett Hagen, Alex Inkeles, and John H. Kunkel.

What follows is Macklin's summary of the essence of McClelland's approach.

A psychological characteristic, technically called "need for achievement" (abbreviated nAch), is the predisposing factor which culminates in economic development whether modern or historical. Need for achievement is regarded by McClelland and by those in the tradition he has established by experimentation and dissemination as "competition with a standard of excellence" . . . , where the individual is personally involved with or emotively oriented to excelling. (p. 90)

In questioning this approach, Macklin concludes that need for achievement is a vastly oversimplified indicator of the conditions that must be satisfied for modernization, and may often be misleading. In fact, he contends, high need for achievement may reflect the extent to which a pattern of modernization has already occurred rather than be a cause of it.

Hagen emphasizes a social event—"withdrawal of status respect"—as the initial impetus for the eventual development of innovative persons who could channel their energies into either economic or noneconomic arenas. Relying on a generally psychodynamic orientation mainly derived from Sigmund Freud involving the production, repression, transformation, and reduction of unconscious rage, Hagen explains changes in personality and social structure. These changes are caused by perception of loss of status; weakening of the father's position and authority; effects of a warm, loving mother on the child; and the influence of a role model. In turn, these changes facilitate the emergence of innovational, striving, achievement-oriented personalities.

On the basis of a survey of literature on development, Inkeles has identified 120 attitude items which, when taken all together, provide an empirical definition of what he calls "sociopsychological individual modernity." A value scale of attitudes designed to operationalize this concept has been used in six developing countries, and Inkeles gives some of the results. These, however, are criticized by Macklin because of the strong Western ideological bias in the approach.

The last contribution that Macklin discusses, by Kunkel, is closely related to that of B. F. Skinner. Kunkel argues that, to promote economic development, behavior needs to be influenced. His intent is to demonstrate that behavior, in relation to the discriminative stimuli, is the phenomenal level from which stem all the terms of social science analyses—especially *personality, values, attitudes,* and *needs.*

The remainder of Macklin's essay is devoted to the interaction of social and psychological levels as manifested in observable interpersonal behavior processes. This interaction is due to the reciprocating interaction in modernization between changes in institutions—the social level—and the psychological strategy.

Macklin presents a model of goal-oriented social action. To

illustrate the model he uses four cases of conflict and cooperation: (1) cooperation within an organization; (2) cooperation between organizations; (3) conflict within an organization; and (4) conflict between organizations.

Because they represent intervention from outside the local social system, many development efforts are a challenge to a set or subset of the local community's norms. There must be sufficient reasons for a change if such challenges are to be accepted permanently. The construction of a social group is needed to legitimize proposed changes if they are to be made. In the Macklin model this social group is labeled the common reference group.

A common reference group is created neither automatically nor by a regular sequence of steps. The interaction of the outsiders associated with a development project and the recipients must establish the foundations of mutual trust and faith. Trust and faith are prerequisites for effective development. Subsequently, Macklin applies his model to the Cornell-Peru project initiated by Allan Holmberg et al. in cooperation with the Indigenous Institute of Peru. Starting by renting the hacienda of Vicos, Peru—thereby becoming the *patron*—Holmberg et al. systematically structured the project to bring about fundamental change in a highly disfavoring environment.

In commenting upon the application of his model, Macklin states:

> First, with the removal of the hacienda system of peonage, a common reference group is formed that welds the Vicosinos together, relatively rather than absolutely and in every detail, into a pattern of cooperative action: Case I. Second, however, vis-à-vis the various extra-community levels of power, they find themselves generally in the "conflict between organizations" situation of Case IV, as they seek to make good on the implications of their increasing independence from their historic circumstances. Lastly, and perhaps it is a significant index of the Vicosinos' evolution from peonage, they were asked to provide advice and credit to other hacienda-Indian groups seeking to follow their lead and were able to do so. . . . This is an example of Case II, cooperation between organizations, with some dimensions of *one* common reference group—Indian status and culture—thus extending toward Case I. Thus, we find progression along the cooperation-conflict continuum in the context of the original-then-changed organization at Vicos, and we find emergent new contexts of intergroup contact, analyzable according to the factors and dynamics proposed, that hold, or held, promise of moving toward the more cooperative role. (p. 146)

In chapter 4 of the Morse book, "Attitudinal Change and Modernization," Douglas E. Ashford, a professor of public and international affairs, relates the explosively expanding environment of the citizen of the developing country to some notions about attitudinal change. He gives special attention to the creation, modification, and effectiveness for development of attitudes toward the concept of "the nation."

Ashford presents some generalizations about attitudes, their components, and how they are changed. He defines an attitude as a predisposition to experience a class of objects in certain ways, with characteristic affect; to be modified by this class of objects in characteristic ways; and to act with respect to these objects in a characteristic fashion. Hence, attitudes have been used by psychologists in explaining characteristics in perception, motivation, and social behavior. Two major views concerning attitudinal change have been identified. One is the dissonance or disequilibrium theory of attitudinal change and the other is an organizational or functionalist theory of the origin of attitudes. The functionalist theory, which focuses on the role of attitudes and values in reconciling the individual to his environment, is used in Ashford's essay because the nature of attitudinal change in developing countries is perhaps more appropriately viewed in this way.

Ashford uses the experiences in educational reforms of Morocco and Tunisia as illustrations of two contrasting approaches that can be framed in the language of attitudinal studies. He states:

> Thus, for the Moroccan and Tunisian policy makers the attitudinal object in the illustration was education; the affective component of attitudes toward education was the profound feeling of Islamic faith reinforced with new patriotic urges; and the cognitive component was the realization that traditional education did not meet the needs of the modern world and would have to be modified, perhaps eradicated. In reviewing the experience of each country since 1956 when both achieved independence, the evidence of social behavior would lead the observer to state that Tunisia had made great progress toward the successful institutionalization of a new education system while Morocco's efforts had fallen far short of being successful. . . .the different experiences of the two countries reflect their different approaches to the situation of attitudinal conflict. . . . (p. 165)

In chapter 5, Fredrick T. Bent, a professor of business and

public administration, makes a comparative analysis of public administration in modern, traditional, and modernizing societies. A high level of competence in public administration is important because accomplishments of such objectives as health, welfare, and education require state financing and public employees. In fact, the alternative modernizing institutions of private business enterprise, secondary associations, and legislative assemblies are frequently looked upon with disfavor or suspicion.

In the process of modernization, public administration must play many roles, including economic, political, and social roles. Above all, bureaucratic innovativeness is essential. Since all government structures do not satisfy this criterion of modernity, a continuum of bureaucratic innovativeness can be formulated. A comparative analysis of three regions of the continuum—the modern and the traditional at the extremes, the transitional in between—is subsequently made in terms of (1) the making of policy, (2) institution building, and (3) policy implementation.

With regard to the type of individual needed for institution building, Bent states:

> . . . it would appear that different ministries have need for different types of institution builders. For those institutions involved in innovation and change, the functionally trained expert is needed at the top. The generalist may be most usefully employed in those ministries concerned with stability and order, particularly the Ministry of Interior. While the management specialist can be profitably used in a subordinate position in all ministries, his talents and skills are particularly necessary in the fiscal, financial, and auditing branches of government. Functional experts clearly are essential to ministries concerned with agriculture, electric power, health, and so on. (p. 214)

Finally, Bent uses a harmonizing-stabilizing continuum as a framework for discussing the functions of integration, mediation, and standard setting. In conclusion, he states:

> What the analysis does attempt to show is that administrative systems in transitional nations are composites of both modern and traditional characteristics: in form and structure, deceptively similar to those found in advanced countries; in spirit and operation, neither modern nor traditional. (p. 236)

Chandler Morse himself contributed the final essay in the book—"Becoming Versus Being Modern: An Essay on Institutional

Change and Economic Development." Morse, an economist, states:

> ... there is need for an approach that, taking off from the indispensable foundations provided by economic theory and fact, will permit modernization to be analyzed more inclusively. A major aim of such an analysis would be to show both the relevance and the limitations of a purely economic approach; to circumvent the limitations by means of appropriate noneconomic analysis; and to indicate how the economic and noneconomic modes of analysis relate to each other. (p. 239)

Institutions can be viewed as comprising three groups of components and a set of hierarchical relationships. The components are (1) conceptual (or cultural), which are largely passive in nature; (2) organizational (or operational), which are inherently active; and (3) personal (or psychological), which strongly influence the quality and intensity of performance of individuals in social roles. The power structure represents the overarching hierarchy composed of relationships such as status, prestige, respect, and so on. Subsequently, Morse constructs a simplified map of the social order on the basis of these elements.

In considering types of institutional change, Morse differentiates between institutionalized institutional change and noninstitutionalized innovation. In noninstitutionalized innovation there are no constraints similar to those in institutionalized change, except those constraints embodied in the personal characteristics of the participants. (Noninstitutional change is categorized as cultural drift, induced change, externally imposed or imperialistic change, internally imposed or radical change, and collective change.) Because of the lack of constraints noninstitutionalized change is often disorderly and unpredictable. "Whether a new order will emerge from such a process, and, if so, whether it will in some identifiable sense be better than the old, is always problematic" (p. 285).

In summarizing this portion of the essay, Morse infers that institutionalization of a wide variety of innovative processes is the central distinguishing characteristic of modern societies. Further, he concludes that modernization is inherently revolutionary in that it involves a change from one system of social order to another. Portions of the rest of the essay examine the implications of these conclusions.

Apropos of the need for the institutionalization of a wide variety of innovative processes, Morse states:

> To put it simply, the very societies that are in need of massive institutional change are those that lack an effective complement of mechanisms for carrying out such change in an orderly, systematic manner. While they have the advantage of being able to imitate the mechanisms found in modern societies, the process of imitation is far from simple. Wherever one looks there are difficulties. (p. 315)

Potential problems are so numerous their very multiplicity inhibits their recognition. Legislation for reform is so cumbersome that it precludes the possibility of change. Agencies responsible for dealing with the problems of change are starved for power, resources, and freedom to maneuver. "In short, the institutional framework, and particularly the power structure, seriously inhibit problem-solving activities in premodern societies" (p. 317).

The final portion of Morse's essay is entitled "Becoming Modern: Process." A prime assumption of the revolutionary modernization model is that radical modernizing elites control the power structure. This group is assumed to be dedicated to changing the basic institutions of the society to create what they perceive to be a more just and progressive social order. In the process of doing so, long-standing barriers to the recognition and solution of perennial problems will be eliminated and mechanisms for dealing with these problems will be institutionalized. The effectiveness of these mechanisms will depend upon the administrative and political capacity of the elite.

The kinds of qualitative changes that must be made in basic institutions are reflected in two value judgments and empirical understanding of the workings of social systems. According to the first value judgment, indigenous ability to maintain a continually rising income in per capita terms is both good and a defining characteristic of economic development. The second value judgment states that increasing equality of wealth and income must occur over time. These judgments suggest the fundamental change of an increase in equality of opportunity and an implied degree of individual and group mobility. Freedom to organize and expand is essential for both entrepreneurs and the other dynamic roles needed in modernizing, such as revolutionaries, reformers, labor and peasant leaders, as well as innovative imperialists in education, science, and technology.

Losses in efficiency are the price that must be paid for the reorganization of activity patterns and redistribution of wealth and income. One such loss occurs as a consequence of devoting more resources to investment than would be justified by the willingness of people, given the freedom of choice, to forego present consumption of goods and services. An objective gain, however, would partially compensate for this in the form of a superoptimal rate of growth of the social product. The second type of efficiency loss results from distortions in prices and misallocations of resources necessary for the structural redistribution of wealth and incomes from more developed to less developed people, sectors, and regions. A consequence of accepting these losses is a higher rate of development.

A radical development strategy will consist of three phases. The developmental growth phase stresses basic institutional change plus a massive increase in the brute capacity to produce. The second phase involves moving the restructured economy onto a new and efficient path. Finally, institutionalization of the progressive growth process is essential.

The reinstitutionalization of a society along modern lines requires a broad and persistent effort if it is to succeed. Piecemeal reorganizations accomplished in typical bureaucratic fashion by many cooperatives, development banks, extension programs, and modern educational systems have resulted in little or no contribution to development. However, once mobilized on a broad front and given time for initial progress, the forces of evolution will eventually begin to take over the modernizing revolution. At some point, the society will have brought into being a new set of basic institutions and the evolutionary process.

Once underway, the process is inevitably altered by continuing forces of evolution and revolution. The new cohort of professionalized occupants of responsible intermediate roles in a modernizing society spells future difficulty for the old modernizing elites, partially because of the difference in values and goals perceived by the two groups and partially because of differences in ideas about the kind of a power structure deemed appropriate.

Regardless of source, an ideological strain is likely to emerge. This is compounded by deepening tension resulting from differences between the flexible norms of individual, organized, consummatory behavior and the proliferation and tightening of productive norms. Finally, as the standard of living improves, the perennial conflict between humanistic and materialistic values will become more conspicuous.

[37] SCHULTZ, T. W. "Institutions and the Rising Economic Value of Man." *American Journal of Agricultural Economics,* 50 (December 1968), 1113-22.

Compared with the two books summarized above, which tend to be theoretical in orientation, T. W. Schultz's outstanding article summarized below is well grounded in an empirical situation. On the basis of observations of changes in institutions resulting from the Green Revolution, Schultz suggests that the effect of a disturbance on the equilibrium of an institutional network is multiplicative.

Schultz addresses himself to the institutional implications of the secular rise in the economic value of man associated with investments in human capital. More specifically, he states:

> My purpose is to show that the rise in the economic value of human agents makes new demands on institutions, that some political and legal institutions are especially subject to these demands, that there are lags in adjusting to the new demands and these lags are the key to important public problems, and that economic theory is a necessary analytical tool in clarifying and solving these problems. (p. 1113)

Schultz suggests the problem.

> We have long known that Ricardian rent is not the fulcrum of economic values; nor is physical capital the critical historical factor, as Marx believed. The institutions governing private rights in land and in other forms of physical capital when Ricardo and Marx made their contributions would be far from adequate in contemporary society with its large investment in human capital. . . . It is currently a mark of sophistication in presenting economic models not to mention institutions. . . . Yet it is obvious that particular institutions really matter, that they are subject to change and are, in fact, changing, and that people are trying to clarify social choices with regard to alternative institutional change to improve the economic efficiency and the welfare performance of the economy. (pp. 1113-14)

Schultz limits himself to institutions that perform economic functions and defines them as behavioral rules pertaining to economic activity. Such institutions include particular political, including legal, institutions that influence in some way, or are influenced in turn by, the dynamics of economic growth, i.e., political economy is the relevant domain. Illustrations of these institutions include (1) those that reduce transaction costs, (2) those that influence the allocation of risk among the owners of the factors of production, (3) those that provide the linkage between functional and personal income streams, and (4) those that establish the framework for the production and distribution of public goods or services. Specific institutions that play important economic roles include private rights in property, contracts, legal rights of labor, organized economic planning by government, and public transfers of income. For many of these, which are susceptible to economic analysis, the guiding principles and appropriate arrangements still are far from settled. The remaining analytical task is to specify the functions of institutions, measure their influence, and determine when they are efficient.

According to Schultz, there are three approaches to the dynamics of economic growth with respect to institutions:

> First, there is the approach that omits or impounds institutions by abstracting from them. . . . Second, there is the approach that treats institutions as subject to change exogenously. . . . Third, I propose an approach that treats these institutions as variables within the economic domain, variables that respond to the dynamics of economic growth. (pp. 1115-16)

In following this approach, Schultz employs the key concepts of (1) the economic value of the function performed by an institution and (2) the concept of an economic equilibrium. Insights into the former, economic value and factors determining it, are gained by assuming that institutions are suppliers of particular services for which demands exist. The latter, the concept of economic equilibrium, is implemented by the assumption that an economy arrives at an equilibrium with respect to each of these economic services of institutions when the rates of return represented by these and other services reach equality.

> By way of summary, then, our theory is designed to explain those changes in institutions that occur in response to the dynamics of

economic growth. The institution is treated as a supplier of a service which has an economic value. It is assumed that the process of growth alters the demand for the service and that this alteration in the demand brings about a disequilibrium between the demand and the supply measured in terms of long-run costs and returns. Although it is possible for the supply of the service of an institution to be altered independently of economic growth considerations, our theory cannot explain such a change in an institution; it can be used, however, to determine the resulting effects of such a change. (pp. 1117-18)

Schultz proceeds to formulate a number of testable propositions with regard to changes in the demand for institutions' services in Asia as a consequence of favorable prices, new varieties, and cheaper fertilizer. Growth momentum is hypothesized to generate changes in farmers' demands for services from credit institutions, as well as tenure and other factor input institutions. "There is, so it seems to me, a growing body of evidence in support of each of these propositions," says Schultz (p. 1118).

With regard to economic incentives for institutional responses engendered by economic growth, Schultz offers several general propositions.

(1) In a market economy which is achieving growth, the demand for the convenience of money shifts to the right. . . . (2) In an economy in which the income per family is rising, the demand for contracts and property arrangements serving the economic activities of the nonfarm sectors increases relative to that associated with the farm sector. . . . (3) As economic growth becomes increasingly dependent upon the advance in useful knowledge, the demand for institutions that produce and distribute such knowledge shifts to the right. . . . (4) When economic development reaches the stage at which the economy requires increasingly more high skills, the demand for high skills that require schooling, including higher education, increases relative to the demand for low skills and for reproducible forms of non human capital. . . . (5) . . . In an economy where growth increases the economic value of human agents, the demands for services of a number of different institutions are altered by this type of growth. (pp. 1118-19)

Schultz concentrates on the last proposition in the remainder of the paper. He illustrates it with examples of increased demands, as the value of human lives increases, for accident safeguards for workers, for health services, for life insurance, for job equality, for less discrimination in access to educational opportunities, as well as for greater equality in access to consumer goods such as housing and family planning information.

Schultz's thesis is that the remarkable secular rise in the economic value of human agents that has been and is occurring in the United States is the source of major disequilibria in the economic functions performed by institutions. He argues that many of the recent legislative and legal developments, in such areas as civil rights and alleviation of poverty, are lagged accommodations to the profound institutional stresses and strains brought about by the marked secular rise in the economic value of human factors. Schultz maintains that additional economic analyses are needed of institutional responses to increases in (1) the market price of work, (2) the rate of return to investment in human capital, and (3) consumers' disposable income.

[38] CENTER for Political Analysis, University of Minnesota. *Bibliography on Planned Social Change: With Special Reference to Rural Development and Educational Development.* 3 vols. 1967. Copies may be purchased from the National Technical Information Service, Springfield, Virginia, 22151. (Part of Committee on Institutional Cooperation and Agency for International Development Rural Development Research Project.)

The final significant contribution to the literature is a bibliography compiled as part of the CIC-AID Rural Development Research Project. It consists of three volumes. The first includes periodical materials; the second is devoted to books and book-length monographs; and the third contains citations to government and United Nations' publications. Most of the citations are annotated.

Selected topics of planned social change are covered. Included are periodicals in English published between 1955 and 1965. About 900 of the most relevant articles are reviewed in order to extract their most important propositions.

3
Selected Contributions to the Central Literature Prior to 1973

CASE STUDIES CLASSIFIED ACCORDING TO TYPE OF INSTITUTION

Agriculture

[39] HUNTER, Guy. "Agricultural Administration and Institutions." Paper presented at the Conference on Strategies for Agricultural Development in the 1970s, Stanford University, Stanford, Calif., December 1971. 25 pages. (Mimeographed.)

The purpose of this paper is to analyze the difficulty emanating from the weaknesses of administrative and institutional tools for implementing a policy conducive to the development of small farmers. Guy Hunter underscores the importance of administration and institutions thus:

The fact is that where the farmer is weak in physical equipment, weak in financial resources, illiterate or semi-literate, bound by constraints of labour supply, by lack of physical investment (roads, water, storage, etc.), often by insecure or oppressive tenure, held in a social system which almost always incorporates at least some values which discourage individualist decisions—in such a case the farmer needs a great deal of external help before he can even stretch out his hand to the opportunities which modern knowledge and organisation could offer him. Further, so many of the services which private enterprise actually competes to supply to the farmer in developed countries are not available to the mass of small farmers before they have the purchasing power and credit-worthiness which would attract suppliers. In consequence, the initial task falls upon public administrative action, public investment, the creation of new farmer institutions stimulated, in one way or another, by public services and persuasion. (p. 3)

Agricultural conditions in developing countries are diverse. This diversity requires (1) substantial delegation in the planning and execution of development programs, (2) better information about farmers' conditions, needs, and capacities, and (3) an understanding that permits the phasing of programs.

A number of faults have characterized central policy in the past. These include lack of appropriate investment in smallholder agriculture, poverty with regard to administration of programs, lavish investment in limited schemes designed to short-cut the whole process, narrowly focused research programs, and imperfect knowledge of the rationale of actual farming systems which leads to overgeneralized campaigns and targets. More important, more complex, more puzzling, more resistant to solution, and far less studied than these problems are a number of other thorny issues. Hunter discusses five of these individually and later combines them under a single framework.

The first of these issues is the lack of coordination within the bureaucratic system. There has to be a deliberately created coordinating mechanism because of the complex nature of agriculture. Efforts to create such a mechanism in the past have sometimes failed because attempts were made on all fronts simultaneously. At other times, district-level coordination has failed because of (1) the lack of coordination at the top and (2) staff loyalty to a department rather than development at the local level. Finally, hierarchies are often too expensive and too complex to meet farmers' needs in a timely and adequate fashion.

A closely related problem grows out of the fact that the citizen's voice is frequently not heard in matters that affect him.

> It is, however, of urgent importance to have some basis of judgment as to which, if any, vital parts of a package of development should be entrusted to "democratic" institutions, and to distinguish between the quality and results of various democratic forms. (p. 12)

Third, market systems replace survival systems as farm incomes rise. The resulting commercial aspects, which rest in ministries—especially marketing, credit, and cooperatives—frequently encounter difficulty. The results are monopolies, single-product organizations difficult for farm managers to deal with, inconvenient credit schemes, and cooperatives characterized more by mythology than a record of successful performance.

Fourth, there is much confusion about the appropriate technology to be used by small farmers in developing countries. Much of this is due to distortions in the price system which cheapen capital-intensive imports. Emotion and Western prejudices also contribute to this confusion.

Finally, poverty at every turn clogs and frustrates the drive for development. Only those choices can be effective which accept the facts of poverty that permeate the infrastructure, human capital, institutions, etc.

In turning his attention to a single framework, Hunter notes the lack of a general theory of organic growth which would (1) constitute a concept of the interacting, sequential processes of growth and (2) provide guidance to the type of assistance which is timely at any one stage of the process in particular environments. However, it is helpful to conceptualize an agricultural development timescale extending from a small traditional community in a survival system to a rural society characterized by commercial agriculture. On this timescale communities in developing countries could be arrayed.

> There is, I suggest, a range of human situations, moving along a line from traditional society to a modernised agricultural economy. There is a range of technical solutions which have to be fitted to this changing local scene, both as to costs and benefits and as to the availability of skills. There is also a range of administrative methods to choose from; and, again, these must be fitted to the attitudes and capacities of the farming community, to the quality of the surrounding economy, and also to the capacity of the administering authority. Recommendations on bureaucracy and politics, on commercial or Cooperative systems, on technology, are inter-dependent, with a common relationship to the general style and achievement of a society at a given time. Nations have flourished long before our era. . . .
>
> We are concerned with mobilising the still under-used resources of land and of human energy. To do so, structures and institutions, the openings and channels, must be at first in a form through which the myriad energies of poor people in a poor country can flow. (pp. 23-24)

[40] MOSEMAN, Albert H., ed. *Agricultural Sciences for the Developing Nations.* Publication No. 76. Washington, D.C.: Ameri-

can Association for the Advancement of Science, 1964. 221 pages. Selection reprinted by permission of the AAAS.

Three of the papers in this proceedings issue for the Section on Agriculture of the 1963 Annual Meeting of the American Association for the Advancement of Science are noteworthy for institution builders. They are: "Institutional Factors Limiting Progress in the Less Developed Countries" by Erven J. Long; "Developing Agricultural Institutions in Underdeveloped Countries" by F. F. Hill; and "Economic Growth from Traditional Agriculture" by Theodore W. Schultz.

Long puts forth the following propositions: (1) economic underdevelopment is itself largely a consequence of institutional underdevelopment; (2) countries wishing to make economic progress must be willing to make fundamental alterations in their institutional structures; and (3) the institutional transformations and development needed in a typical underdeveloped country will be deep, profound, and far reaching.

Long discusses those institutional impediments to rural development which inhibit the play of incentives, those which inhibit the development of capabilities of rural people, and those which inhibit the development and use of science and technology.

If production is to be substantially increased in developing countries, Hill maintains that the following institutions are essential: systematic research and experimentation, an effective system for production and distribution of farm supplies and equipment, easily accessible credit at reasonable costs, as well as an effective extension service and national policies that encourage farmers to accept the risks associated with adopting new practices.

Schultz responds to the question concerning the lack of success in agricultural development programs.

> To find an answer to this question and to indicate what needs to be done, I shall proceed as follows:
>
> First, state the economic basis of traditional agriculture;
>
> Second, show where private profit activities require complementary public activities;
>
> Third, establish the reasons for the lack of success of most programs to modernize agriculture in poor countries;

Fourth, present the essential components of an efficient approach. (p. 186)

On the basis of his analysis, Schultz concludes that an efficient approach to agricultural development must be based on (1) new agricultural inputs which have a relatively high payoff predominantly in terms of improvements in the quality of agricultural inputs; (2) making a supply of these inputs available to farmers; and (3) willingness on the part of farmers to learn how to use the inputs efficiently after accepting them. All have institutional implications.

[41] PROPP, Kathleen McGuire. "The Establishment of Agricultural Universities in India: A Case Study of the Role of USAID— U.S. University Technical Assistance." Unpublished master's thesis, University of Illinois, Urbana, Ill., January 1968. 120 pages. (Part of Committee on Institutional Cooperation and Agency for International Development Rural Development Research Project.)

This is an historical analysis of U.S. university technical assistance rendered under contracts with USAID to Indian agricultural education. It focuses on the ways in which U.S. university staff members and other key Americans encouraged and facilitated the legal establishment of agricultural universities within the Indian environment. In spite of its concentration on the American role, the analysis was not intended to depreciate the accomplishments of the Indians themselves but rather to analyze both the elements of and means employed in the technical assistance effort.

On the basis of the analysis, Kathleen Propp concludes:

The major reason for the development of India's agricultural universities was the determination and commitment on the part of key Government of India officials, state government officials, and college officials. American assistance was secondary to the success of the movement. (p. 96)

However, Propp goes on to draw the conclusion that American assistance was an important factor in making the rural universities a reality in seven states. The reasons for this effectiveness were:

First, on the whole, the key Americans involved were regarded by their peers as very capable individuals. . . .

Second, one cannot help but be impressed with the closeness of formal and informal working relationships between the Rockefeller and Ford Foundation agricultural programs and the USAID agricultural program in India. . . .

Third, each of the key American groups involved in agricultural university development—the U.S. university Team Leaders, USAID officials, and Foundation personnel—served somewhat different functions and operated in a somewhat different role. (pp. 98-99)

[42] HUNTER, Guy. *The Administration of Agricultural Development: Lessons from India.* London: Oxford University Press, 1970. 160 pages. Selections reprinted by permission of Oxford University Press.

This is the last in a trio of books by Guy Hunter, which include *The Best of Both Worlds?* [243] and *Modernizing Peasant Societies* [244]. In the foreword to this book, Anthony Tasker, director of the Overseas Development Institute, of which Hunter is a staff member, states:

In the earlier books Mr. Hunter emphasized the extreme selectivity which is needed in seeking to use, in developing countries, the technologies, the institutions, and indeed the type of economic and social thinking, which reflect the history and stage of development in highly industrialized countries. He went on to suggest, in very tentative terms, a description of the sequences of growth through which a developing country may pass, and the implications for practical policy which these stages may imply.

In this book the argument is brought down to a single, though very large, example—the current system for agricultural development in India—and is carried a step further. For policy has to consider not only the object of change—the rural society in its full dimensions—but the tools which can be expected to work effectively in changing it. (p. 5)

Hunter deals with four main subjects in this book: (1) governmental coordination of administrative action in the provision of a complex set of services to peasant agriculture, (2) changing relationships between services provided by the public and private sectors, (3) the relationship between administrative action and governmental efforts to draw the rural community into the development process, and (4) the twin questions of determining the best type of effort to use in a farming community at each stage of development and, simultaneously, the type of effective organization that a society itself in process of change can apply. Throughout, the focus is on the Indian Extension Service as it deals with small farmers.

Hunter concludes:

> ... despite the constant difficulties and muddles, the policy of Community Development Blocks, the National Extension Service, and Panchayati Raj, embarked upon in 1952, has somehow got through to the Indian cultivator; even the small men know of it, though most of them cannot benefit from it fully. ... Most of them will admit that it was the Extension Service, and particularly the long-suffering and much criticized V.L.W., who brought them a new hope. (p. 91)

After discussing the Intensive Agricultural District Program, Hunter considers the subject of local participation and local politics and concludes:

> Thus countries with an indigenous authoritarian background and large areas of traditional, semi-subsistence local communities may have to proceed slowly and carefully in democratization. The cautious arrangements in India, by which the D.C. retains executive powers, or a veto, or a guiding hand on the elected councils, show exactly this compromise. It is one which is at once nursing rather nervous communities into greater self-confidence, holding the ring for them, so that the new democratic forms are not captured by the old authoritarian leadership, and providing a channel for investment and technical services. Countries with a tribal background may well have been wise in retaining a colonial-type local administration complemented by self-help committees but not yet by Local Government. Countries which have chosen the People's Democracy pattern may find that the authoritarianism of the party, which very easily produces both faction and uncertainty in the village, turns out to be both politically the hardest to manage and economically the least conducive to development, since it is the least tolerant of the discipline which investment and technical aid demand. (p. 121)

Finally, in his concluding statement, the author comments:

> Perhaps the most constantly recurring theme of this book has been the need for adaptation of policy and structures to the movement and change in society, as it passes at quite local levels from poverty, and a traditional adaptation to poverty, towards greater individual prosperity and a stronger cash-economy. It is seen as a transition from necessary and multiple intervention by government to break the circle of dependence and powerlessness to a condition where the farmer, in his greater

security, can choose among the richer variety of services which a richer economy can offer, and thus "coordinate" his own farm-management by himself. The most difficult part of this transition, as an administrative problem, is the earliest stage, where government, possibly weak in personnel and in a poor society, has to assume the maximum task. For in these early stages even the agencies which later on will share that task—Cooperatives, Local Government—are composed largely either of the weak and poor for whom the help is needed, or of the rich and powerful whose position often stands in the way of a wider progress.

The Indian Government has tried to shoulder this task of intervention. But—and this is the second main theme—in seeing it as a task of prescription rather than of enablement, and in setting detailed targets beyond what it has the real power to achieve, it has created an administrative system so complex that it is constantly tripped up in its own tangle, and so rigid that the highly local needs of farmers and the discretions of the Extension staff are excluded. Moreover, it is a system which cannot easily reach more than a small proportion of beneficiaries; indeed, only this small proportion have the means and power to exploit it. Finally, in an intention to move at once to what may be a second stage of the transition, it has endeavoured to use cooperative and democratic agencies prematurely, before either their staff or the political environment in which they work is good enough to give a fair chance of success. (pp. 149-50)

[43] GAUTAM, O. P.; Patel, J. S.; Sutton, T. S.; and Thompson, W. N. *The Punjab Agricultural University: An Assessment of Progress to 1970.* Part II, Joint Indo-American Study Team Report. New Delhi, India: Indian Council of Agricultural Research, April 1970. 153 pages.

Using the methodology presented in Part I [121], the authors analyze the Punjab Agricultural University in India. Fifteen specific recommendations are presented as means of continuing the excellent progress which the study team felt the university had made.

In reaching these conclusions, the team considered the following: the history of the institution; the economy of the state of Punjab; the university's objectives, structure, finances, and personnel; its students and curricula; its methods of teaching and evaluating students; its research program; its extension education program; integration of the teaching, research, and extension functions; individual departments within colleges; the library; students' welfare; faculty development and welfare; communications and printing; the physical plant; linkages with other institutions; and the university's relationship to the rural welfare of the state. Throughout, extensive use is made of survey data gathered on the scene by the binational team who relied heavily on the institution building approach of Esman et al. as a basic framework.

[44] BLASE, Melvin G., ed. *Institutions in Agricultural Development.* Ames, Iowa: Iowa State University Press, 1971. 247 pages. Selection reprinted by permission of Iowa State University Press.

Of special interest to institution builders is the first chapter in which Melvin Blase develops the concept of layered institutional constraints within a sector of an economy.

> In a given country, institution building efforts tend to be centered on one or, at best, a few agricultural institutions. Unfortunately this focus frequently is placed on individual institutions without considering all those which have an influence on agricultural development. Consequently, there is frequently a lack of perspective concerning all institutions constraining the sector's development. Technical assistance and indigenous personnel alike are often frustrated when the development of one institution—designed to remedy a constraint within an economy—does little more than provide an opportunity for another poorly developed institution to substitute as the effective constraint. Consequently, the layering of institutional constraints often misleads individuals who feel the elimination of one institutional barrier represents a panacea for transforming traditional agriculture. (p. 11)

In the remaining ten chapters, competent specialists discuss crucial agricultural institutions with regard to (1) frequently encountered obstacles preventing efficient performance, (2) functions that need to be performed by these institutions, and (3) reform measures for improving the efficiency of agricultural institutions in developing countries.

[45] HANNAH, H. W. *Resource Book for Rural Universities in the Developing Countries.* Urbana, Ill.: University of Illinois Press, 1966. 375 pages.

The purposes of this practical book are:

1. To express as meaningfully as possible and in as many instances as

are appropriate those underlying assumptions and principles which give the land-grant institutions their vitality.

2. To explain and discuss the general structure which seems to have best promoted these underlying assumptions and principles.

3. To provide a reservoir of detailed and factual information about the internal organization and functioning of such a university, from which may spring ideas and answers about what to do and what not to do. (p. ix)

H. W. Hannah recognizes that—in addition to the mechanics, the questions that need to be asked, and the checklists that he provides—important intangible elements remain to be explored.

Finally, there is no substitute for institutional commitment and personal dedication. When these are high and sustained, form becomes relatively unimportant. Despite all the disclaimers that can be made, many people around the world are going to say that America is exporting the land-grant pattern in toto, and if failures occur, they can be regarded as evidence of American short-sightedness. This criterion will not be wholly wrong, but there are two other factors that are more likely to account for failure: the inability of those in charge to live up to the responsibility imposed upon them by a relatively free institution and the heartbreaking task of maintaining a high degree of commitment to the cause of agriculture in a relatively uncommitted environment. Any institutional change that is meaningful and durable must be supported by deep, profound, and far-reaching changes in the society which surrounds it. These changes come slowly, so failure to achieve distinction in a few years is not necessarily a sign of failure. If there had not been faith, this book would not have been written. (p. x)

[46] BELLO, Eduardo S. "Reorganization y Desarrollo de una Institucion de Investigacion Agricola" ["Reorganization and Development of an Agricultural Research Institution"]. Southern Zone of Inter-American Institute for Agricultural Sciences of the Organization of American States, Montevideo, Uruguay, 1971. 59 pages. (Mimeographed in Spanish.)

The Center for Agricultural Research in Uruguay is analyzed for the period 1961 to 1967 with the use of the institution building framework developed by Esman et al. In addition to presenting other findings of interest, Eduardo Bello identifies the systems variables (institutional characteristics) according to their relative importance by years. Initially, leadership, doctrine, and linkages appeared to be decisive, whereas the other variables took on relatively more importance in subsequent years.

[47] WELLS, Oris V. "Some Problems of Agricultural Development." *American Journal of Agricultural Economics,* 51 (December 1969), 1037-45.

O. V. Wells, Deputy Director-General of the Food and Agriculture Organization of the United Nations, enunciates the following provisional set of general principles for planning and appraising requests for assistance in the agricultural field:

[1] Small-scale, piecemeal technical assistance is simply not a sufficiently strong tool. . . .

[2] It is increasingly evident that farming systems as a whole need to be substantially altered or redesigned in many areas, that what is needed is an integrated "package" rather than a "piecemeal" approach. . . .

[3] In addition to developing the necessary "package" of new practices or revised farming systems, ways and means must be found of supplying the necessary production requisites or capital inputs, many of which must come from the outside.

[4] At the same time, ways and means must be found of motivating farmers to adopt the new practices or systems. . . .

[5] Ways and means must be found of assisting or motivating the governments of the developing countries in giving the necessary priority to planning and actually carrying forward a sustained effort to increase agricultural productivity. (pp. 1040-42)

[48] NAIK, K. C. *A History of Agricultural Universities: Educational, Research and Extension Concepts for Indian Agriculture.* Washington, D.C.: Committee on Institutional Cooperation (CIC) and U.S. Agency for International Development (AID), 1968. 230 pages. (Part of CIC-AID Rural Development Research Project.)

The object of this work is to make available a history of education in agricultural sciences in India with special reference to the origin, development and functions of agricultural universities. The book is intended to chart the currents and cross-currents which have marked the development of higher education in agricultural sciences since the days the British ruled India. The traditional university idea did not just suddenly give way to the Land-Grant system in India but was the final outcome of considerable criticism, agitation, and hard work by a large number of persons and agencies. The story of this transformation may also have many lessons of considerable interest and value to educationists in the same field in all parts of the globe. (p. xiii)

[49] KATZ, Saul M. "Administrative Capability and Agricultural Development: An Institution-Building Approach to Evaluation." *American Journal of Agricultural Economics*, 52 (December 1970), 794-802.

In this article, Saul Katz addresses three major questions raised by the increasing recognition of the importance of administrative capability. First, why is administrative ability important? Second, what is its content? And, third, how might it be evaluated as a basis for improvement?

A systems view of an institution building approach is taken to better cope with the difficulties of evaluating administrative capability. Katz identifies the following four subsystems as essential for institutional performance: transformation subsystem, maintenance subsystem, adaptation subsystem, and guidance subsystem. Subsequently, he discusses environmental linkages and then methods of evaluating administrative capability for agricultural development. Throughout, substantial reliance is placed on the institution building framework formulated by Esman et al.

[50] MOSEMAN, Albert H. *Building Agricultural Research Systems in the Developing Nations.* New York: Agricultural Development Council, Inc., 1970. 137 pages.

This paper reviews some pertinent features or components of effective agricultural research programs, with special reference to U.S. experience, and their interrelationships in a functioning national system. In considering national systems of research we should keep in mind the broad scope of disciplines or problem areas, including those in the natural and social sciences and in economics. But for illustrative purposes in this paper, special attention is given to research experience in crop improvement. . . .

If effective national systems of research are to be developed, their requirements must be understood both by officials in each country and by officials of technical assistance agencies. This paper is written with the latter group primarily in mind but may be useful to the former group as well. (pp. 20-21)

[51] ESMAY, Merle L. *Institutionalization of the Facultad de Agron-
      omia [Faculty of Agronomy] at Balcarce, Argentina.*
      Research Report Number 8. East Lansing, Mich.: Institute of
      International Agriculture, Michigan State University, 1971.
      188 pages. (Part of Inter-University Research Program in
      Institution Building.)

      This analysis is based on the conceptual framework for insti-
      tution building developed by Esman et al. and consists of an
      in-depth empirical study of four primary publics of the institu-
      tion: its students, its teaching faculty, outside agricultural leaders
      in the region, and field extension agents. Both summaries of
      empirical data and discussions of cause-and-effect relationships are
      found in the first six chapters. The final chapter transforms some
      of the supportive empirical findings into concepts and inferences
      that may be applicable to other institution building projects.

[52] BLASE, Melvin G. "Discussion: Why Overseas Technical Assistance
     Is Ineffective." *American Journal of Agricultural Economics,* 50 (De-
     cember 1968), 341–44.

      After commenting on the Loomis paper which preceded his,
      Melvin Blase provides an overview of the institution building
      process in a systems context. This approach is developed further in
      [120].

[53] SOUTHWORTH, Herman M., and Johnston, Bruce F., eds. *Agri-
      cultural Development and Economic Growth.* Ithaca, N.Y.:
      Cornell University Press, 1967. 608 pages.

      In this book of readings, Herman Southworth and Bruce
      Johnston (1) review relevant literature, (2) summarize major prob-
      lems in agricultural economic development, (3) evaluate present
      knowledge which is apropos, and (4) suggest priorities for further
      research. Institution builders may be interested in "Toward a
      Theory of Agricultural Development" by William Jones and T.W.
      Schultz; "Traditional Social Structures as Barriers to Change" by
      John Brewster; "The Infrastructure for Agricultural Growth" by
      Clifton Wharton, Jr.; "Education and Training for Agricultural
      Development" by George Montgomery; "Land Reform and Agri-

cultural Development" by Philip Raup; and "The Development of Marketing Institutions" by J. C. Abbott.

Business Administration

[54] TAYLOR, Donald A. *Institution Building in Business Administration: The Brazilian Experience.* MSU International Business and Economic Studies. East Lansing, Mich.: Bureau of Business and Economic Research, Graduate School of Business Administration, Michigan State University, 1968. 205 pages. (Part of Inter-University Research Program in Institution Building.)

This is an accounting of the twelve years of activity engaged in by members of the faculty of the Graduate School of Business Administration, Michigan State University, in Brazil from 1954 to 1965. The principal concern of this technical assistance effort was the institutionalization of the acceptance of business administration education in the Brazilian university system. The three host institutions in which the institutionalizing process was centered were the School of Business Administration at Sao Paulo; the School of Administration, University of Bahia; and the Institute of Administration, University of Rio Grande do Sul. The success in institutionalizing the process by means of these schools will be consummated when the norms and values they espouse are accepted by other educational entities, the business community, the general public, and the potential student body. Considerable progress has been made in this direction as evidenced by the fact that both U.S. and Brazilian authorities consider the institutionalization experience in Brazil one of the most successful anywhere in the world.

The institution building framework developed by Esman et al. is employed in the analysis. More specifically, Donald Taylor describes the methodology thus:

> The research methodology . . . is inferential. Changes in the environment through time are related to those in the change agents through time, and cause and effect relationships are drawn inferentially. This interpretive device makes a time dimension imperative. . . .

As change is observed through time, the changes will be related to a description of the change agent variables at the beginning and end of each time period. In relating changes in the linkage transactions with those in the change agent variables, an attempt is made to understand the nature of the transactions taking place. . . . Through this approach the first purpose of the study is served. Analysis of the environment surrounding each change agent in 1964 serves the second purpose of the study. (pp. 16-17)

In examining the extent of institutionalization, Taylor presents two criteria:

First, is the extent to which the change agents have been institutionalized as establishments through achieving their own capacity to survive. Second, is the extent to which they have been successful in transferring their norms and values to other institutions within the environment. . . . (p. 163)

The evidence indicated that a relatively substantial amount of institutionalization had occurred. The change agents had successfully upheld their values against attack from other institutions in the environment. These attacks greatly diminished over time and the institutions began to achieve acceptance, indicated by greater autonomy of operation. The institutions experienced no difficulty in attracting capable personnel and made considerable progress toward obtaining adequate funding.

Progress was also made toward institutionalizing the discipline of business administration, indicated by the extent to which the change agents had influenced other universities in Brazil. Progress was further exemplified by the passage of the law recognizing the profession of administrator and the resolutions of the First Brazilian Congress of Business Administration. Finally, Taylor states, "As incongruous as it may seem *the values of the change agents are sufficiently well entrenched in the environment to continue regardless of the change agents' presence*" (p. 182).

Subsequently, Taylor deals with the general and specific hypotheses originally proposed for the change management and institutionalizing process. Taylor points to the extensive hostility toward business administration present in Brazil in 1954 and its continuation as late as 1959 as examples of the general hypothesis that environmental hostility at the beginning of an institutionalizing venture will determine the ease or difficulty of achieving success. From the analysis he draws two generalizations:

> First, the participants in any such venture should identify those entities with which the change agent must make positive linkages and assess the hostility in each. . . .
>
> The second generalization concerns the time necessary to achieve success. Failure to recognize that hostility exists and must be overcome results in program statements of objectives and operational methods as described above with no allowance for the time required to alleviate hostility. (pp. 185-86)

Further, Taylor notes that in all three cases, institutionalization with regard to the acceptance on the part of the business community preceded that involving the inner-circle institutions, the higher education system, and the general public. He also calls attention to the need to mold the change agent into an integrated unit at the same time it is engaged in activities to influence the external environment. Clearly, it must be a dynamic unit. All the while, this has to be done under the Brazilian legal structure, which acts as an impediment to the diffusion of new ideas in higher education.

With regard to the specific hypotheses—those which deal with identification of means used by the change agents to reduce conflict among various entities in the environment—Taylor notes the modifications made in the change agent variables to more closely approximate the norms and values of the hostile environment. The suggestion is made that the most effective way for the change agent to influence the environment is by engaging in an iterative process which oscillates from actions representing the change agent's values and norms to actions conforming with the environment, back to the change agent's original position. With regard to this vital point, Taylor states:

> To move immediately to a position that is moderately acceptable to the hostile environment denies the opportunity to familiarize the environment with the ideals of the change agent. It is out of this immediate conflict that the objectives of the change agent are communicated to the environment. The modifications made by the change agent are simply means of gaining a foothold from which it can demonstrate the need for its values and gradually break down the resistance. The ideals

of the change agent which are initially demonstrated and made known eventually become a model to which the environment will gravitate. (pp. 196-97)

[55] CHOWDHRY, Kamla. "Institution Building and Social Change: The Ahmedabad Textile Industry's Research Association." *Indian Journal of Public Administration*, 14 (October-December 1968), 943-61.

In this paper Kamla Chowdhry, a professor of management practices at the Indian Institute of Management at Ahmedabad, presents her insights into the process of institution building and social change in developing countries. Her focus is the Ahmedabad Textile Industry's Research Association and its attempt to introduce scientific methods via technological innovations to a traditional industry.

Much of the successful early growth of the Research Association is attributed to its director and the unique combinations of individuals in different clusters with whom he interacted. Chowdhry considers each of these clusters in turn.

Some tentative conclusions are offered. Because the institution was initiated soon after India's independence, it benefited from the emphasis placed on science and technology as preconditions of national growth. During this period of emergence, there was a readiness on the part of young adults in India to contribute and commit themselves to new, meaningful ventures. Moreover, young people were given an opportunity, which they successfully grasped, to participate in innovative tasks and contribute to the building of the institution. In a cultural setting where age and experience are related to positions of responsibility, this act of faith in using the younger generation of scientists, technicians, and managers involved considerable risk which paid off as one of the prime elements of success in this institution building experience.

[56] OBERG, Winston. "Technical Assistance at the Grass Roots: A Report on the Successful Start of a Point IV Project in Management. Education in Southern Brazil." Department of Management, Michigan State University, East Lansing, Mich., 1962. 39 pages. (Mimeographed.)

Drawing upon personal experience, Winston Oberg attributes the successful initiation of a technical assistance program in business management in a university to the success of an initial short course for top level managers. The utility of the technical assistance program was accepted because of the high visibility given to the short course. The success of that effort was attributed to outside help in preparing curriculum materials, a focus on participants' needs, an emphasis on participation, and an avoidance of an attitude of superiority or of condescension.

Community Development

[57] MILLER, Norman N. "The Political Survival of Traditional Leadership." *Journal of Modern African Studies*, 6, 2 (1968), 183-201.

Norman Miller summarizes his contentions as follows:

In summary, the fundamental argument is this: rural traditional authorities survive in modern times as local political leaders. They do so by serving as intermediaries between modernising bureaucratic authorities and the custom-bound populace. When they fail to serve as intermediaries, a condition of mutual hostility between themselves and modernising authorities develops, and there is a failure to reach bureaucratic goals. When some accord is reached, the situation is in essence syncretistic, that is, the traditional leader serves to balance the demands of the populace and the bureaucratic groups. Syncretism can take the form of alliance or coercion. Under either situation traditional leaders must capitalise on certain culture-bound factors that support traditionalism, and also specifically manipulate such things as local myth, ritual, symbol, and customary law. If this balance is maintained, a tendency toward neo-traditionalism can be expected. When neo-traditionalism persists, the modernising bureaucratic authorities will attempt to check such tendencies as threats to bureaucratic goals. Conflict may be expected because the syncretistic leader tends to rely on the more traditional basis of influence, and in essence to tip the balance in favour of the customary values. This, in turn, causes modernising agents to exert pressure on the syncretistic leader to re-align with bureaucratic goals. The result is either a re-balance under alliance or coercion conditions, or a rupture in relations causing mutual hostility. This over-all thesis may best be illustrated and expanded upon by focusing on a particular nation and a specific ethnic group. (p. 187)

Subsequently, the traditional political system of the Nyam-
wezi, an ethnic group in Tanzania, becomes the focus of analysis.
In this system each chiefdom has a pyramidal hierarchy. Headmen
with territorial jurisdiction serve below the chief (the main decision maker affecting the individual peasant), and, in turn, subhead-
men serve under them with village or neighborhood jurisdiction. In
spite of independence in 1961 and legislation abolishing chief-
taincy in 1963, moderate neotraditionalism continues in Tanzania
because the government is not yet in a position to withdraw
totally the powers of headmen and a few chiefs. These syncretistic
leaders still play the role of intermediary.

Miller reaches the following conclusions:

> Syncretism in political leadership is promoted by the persistence of
> traditional values and attitudes, and the counter-demands of the mod-
> ernising bureaucratic state. The necessary environment for syncretism is
> perpetuated by the specific culture-bound revival of customary values,
> and the manipulation by leaders of symbols, ritual, customary laws, and
> the like. The syncretistic phenomena will continue as long as traditional
> value systems are in conflict with intruding modernising systems. Pre-
> dictably, the traditional system will be changed by the implanting of
> new rural institutions, such as cells, co-operatives, parties, and adminis-
> trative structures, which demand mass participation, which require new
> behaviour patterns, and which establish new goals for rural peoples. The
> success of the rural institutions will depend on the extent to which
> rural people manipulate these structures merely to create new forms of
> old organisations. In some places this will happen; gradualism will hold
> sway, traditional leaders will refuse to be influenced by administrators,
> and the organisational goals will not be reached. In other areas, innova-
> tive local leaders will accommodate the new rural institutions and the
> government's goals will be attained. (p. 198)

[58] GOODENOUGH, Ward Hunt. *Cooperation in Change: An
Anthropological Approach to Community Development.*
New York: Russell Sage Foundation, 1963. 543 pages.

This book deals with the following professional requirements
of a development agent:

1. An agent should be acquainted with scientific theory regarding
   human behavior. He needs to be sophisticated about human motives,
   the subjective factors so important in all human relationships.

2. He should have a clear idea of the nature and properties of what is
   being changed, in this case customs and institutions, ideas and

beliefs. He must understand how these things function in human affairs, the processes by which they undergo change, and the effects of their change on people.

3. He must know how to gain accurate knowledge of the local situation, how to learn what the community's particular resources, customs, institutions, beliefs, and needs are. To do this, he must know what to look for and how to look for it. If he imposes on the local scene a stereotype of underdeveloped communities, he is not likely to discover what the realities are.

4. He must be free to conduct himself in ways that befit his knowledge of the local situation, his general understanding of function and process pertaining to human institutions and customs, and his professional objective as a development agent. This requires that he be aware of the forces and influences that inhibit his freedom of action: his own needs and motives, customs and values; the problems of living and working in a strange social and cultural environment; the organization of his agency; and the interests of other segments of the larger society or nation of which the client community forms a part. (pp. 44-45)

[59] HARRIGAN, Norwell. "Community Development and Institution Building in the British Virgin Islands." College of the Virgin Islands, St. Thomas, 1968. 42 pages. (Mimeographed. Part of Inter-University Research Program in Institution Building.)

This analysis uses the institution building framework developed by Esman et al. in an analysis of the Community Development Service in the British Virgin Islands. The service survived only for two years and the analysis indicates several reasons for its failure to become institutionalized.

[60] EATON, Joseph W. "Community Development Ideologies." *International Review of Community Development*, No. 11 (1963), 37–50.

See [113].

Cooperatives

[61] CHOLDIN, Harvey M. "An Organizational Analysis of Rural Development Projects at Comilla, East Pakistan." *Economic Development and Cultural Change*, 20 (July 1972), 671-90.

Some aspects of the political and ideological context in which the relatively successful rural development projects at Comilla, East Pakistan (now Bangladesh), existed from 1959 to 1965 are discussed. In addition, one of the central programs within the organization, a network of village agricultural cooperatives, is described and analyzed.

The East Pakistan Academy for Rural Development at Comilla was given considerable autonomy and power by its designers. The fact that most of the ten faculty positions were staffed with applied social scientists concerned with rural problems is indicative of the fact that social-science-based solutions were sought to rural problems. These staff members spent a year at an American university studying community development prior to the opening of the academy in 1959. Upon their return to Pakistan, they attempted to educate themselves about rural conditions and problems. In addition, they were officially attached to local officials as development advisers, and the area surrounding the academy was designated an experimental laboratory area. This was largely made possible by an academy director, Mr. Khan, who had high status and operated independently. It enabled the national, Western-educated, elite staff members to work with rural men with high school educations in introducing new ideas.

Despite these complicated relationships, the academy initiated a program keyed to the rural situation which provided for new systems to deal with problems in it. The following series of pilot projects was established: (1) a network of village cooperative societies with a central federation, (2) a reorganization of governmental agencies at the lowest level to coordinate the services they were supposed to be performing, (3) a rural public works program administered through local councils, and (4) an educational program for housewives. These projects, plus others, represented a multifaceted attack on rural social and economic problems.

Administrative structures varied. The smallest project was initially conducted under the administration of the academy. Other projects were undertaken with grants and staff from particular departments. Eventually there was a staff for each particular project. Later a separate campus for the projects was added. Throughout, the director provided the communications link between the pilot projects and the bureaucrats who might expend them as part of their regular programs if they were evaluated to be successful.

The most important of the several ideological commitments at Comilla were (1) that rural life is worthwhile and that living conditions of rural people must be improved and (2) that solution of problems was possible at the local level. Hence, the academy wanted schools to portray village life as worthwhile, or at least to stop denying its worth. Furthermore, they felt that students needed to be taught the elements of applied science that are useful to farmers.

The ideological commitments were reflected in the program. For Comilla projects,

> . . . the main emphases at the local level were in improving the material well-being of the villagers and building viable local governing bodies. The main emphasis within the national government was in making the governmental bureaucracy, the agencies, capable of serving the villagers in an effective manner. (p. 676)

Further examination of individual projects reveals the effect of the value commitment. The rural public works projects, a goat husbandry project, and a contraceptive marketing and advertising scheme were labor-intensive and emphasized the use of local materials. Not only were these projects keyed to locally available resources and patterned according to local traditions, but they were also accompanied by other projects that used imported resources to overcome bottlenecks, e.g., the use of tractors to enable multiple cropping.

Another phase of the program involved cooperatives. Although some failed, a flexible approach was taken and others developed which were notably successful. In contrast to an old cooperative credit system, which in general might be considered a failure, the new cooperative credit system enjoyed considerable success. One of the forces arguing for the success of a number of projects such as this one was an interpretation of Islam as a modernizing force.

Harvey Choldin devotes special attention to the network of agricultural cooperatives. From the start, the faculty members at Comilla established the introduction of new agricultural technology as one of their goals. In order to accomplish it they circumvented some of the traditional problems of working through village level workers by using elected model farmers from villages to serve as local change agents in diffusing new information through weekly educational programs. In addition, the program demonstrated its responsiveness by incorporating the credit program discussed above. Village organizations were used as recipients for group loans and new technology reported by the model farmers. In the case of loans, pressure was applied to ensure that repayments would be made; some supervision was also provided to ensure that funds were used for production rather than consumption.

In responding to the question of whether the projects were an artificial success, Choldin acknowledges the significant contribution of the first director of the academy, who served in that capacity for ten years.

> Throughout history, individual leaders have led others in social changes. In many of these cases, they devised systems which survived and prospered after their own deaths. In other cases, the systems proved to be replicable in other places. The question is whether the system can survive after its inventor is off the scene. The dispensibility of [Akhter Hameed] Khan is tested in each case in which a part of the system is replicated over a territory larger than can be supervised by Khan alone. This has taken place in the rural works program, part of the family planning program, and the thana irrigation program. The question of whether the projects can prosper under different leadership or within a different political context can only be answered in the future. (p. 689)

In a concluding statement, Choldin says:

> In sum, the efforts of an especially talented leader and some favorable circumstances have contributed to the accomplishments. Nonetheless, the accomplishments were achieved where none might have been predicted and where prior programs had failed. (p. 690)

[62] KLAYMAN, Maxwell I. *The Moshav in Israel: A Case Study of Institution-Building for Agricultural Development.* New York: Praeger Publishers, Inc., 1970. 371 pages. (Part of Inter-University Research Program in Institution Building.)

The objectives of this analysis are to (1) construct a model of the moshav—a small landowners' cooperative settlement—in terms of its goals, structure, functions, and interdependencies; (2) analyze the success of the moshav in terms of its economic viability for physical production and financial returns to members; (3) analyze the process by which the moshav has been built as an institution at both the macro and micro levels; and (4) examine the applicability of the institution for the development of the agricultural sectors of underdeveloped countries.

The moshav is one of two basic types of agricultural cooperative settlements in Israel. In contrast to the kibbutz, production and consumption decisions in the moshav are the responsibility of the individual farmer, whereas purchasing, selling, and other services are generally handled cooperatively. Within these general characteristics there are two types of moshav, depending upon whether they were formed in the preindependence (1948) or postindependence period.

In light of the remarkable economic, social, and political success of the moshav, Maxwell Klayman identifies not only the factors critical to its success but also the difficulties it has encountered. The former are divided into exogenous and endogenous factors.

The principal exogenous factors of success are (1) the high quality of leadership; (2) the nature of the institution supporting the cooperative agricultural sector; (3) the unifying bond of Zionist ideology; (4) the quality of government; (5) the prestige and relative position of the cooperative agricultural sector in the economy; (6) the development of a specialized role for the moshav within the cooperative agricultural sector; (7) the financial support provided by worldwide Jewry; (8) a national agricultural policy that has favored cooperative agricultural settlement and has effectively integrated macro agricultural planning with micro planning at the settlement level; (9) favorable economic conditions; (10) the land tenure system; (11) national economic, social, and political goals that favored the development of agricultural structures; (12) the relatively small size of the country; and (13) inheritance of a road and railroad transportation network.

Endogenous factors of success include (1) the flexibility of the moshav; (2) institutionalization of the family farm in a structure operationally consistent with economic, social, and political goals; (3) the inherent nature of the moshav for integrating individualism in a cooperative pattern; and (4) the character and motivation of the settlers.

Klayman describes the difficulties as follows:

> Over and above the financial, organizational, economic, and sociological obstacles of developing merchants and craftsmen from traditional societies into modern farmers, there have been a number of other difficulties. The principal ones have been (1) saturation of the domestic market as a limiting factor to the development of farmers' incomes, and the need to develop products for export to new markets, (2) the Arab blockade that affects the development of export markets and obtaining inputs at lowest prices, (3) the limitation of water supplies, (4) the constant peril of Arab marauders in border settlements, and (5) the economic prosperity that has increased the competition for a limited labor supply from the industrial and services sector. (p. 248)

In considering the applicability of moshav principles to developing countries, Klayman initially concludes that this institutional approach would be limited in the most primitive underdeveloped countries and those where the principal barrier to development is the bad proportioning of the factors of production—models one and three respectively, according to John Kenneth Galbraith's classification. However, in model-two countries, where the principal barrier to advance is the social structure, this institutional form has much to offer.

After analyzing, by means of case studies, the application of moshav principles in Venezuela and Iran, Klayman reaches the following conclusions:

> The first of the moshav principles, comprehensive, coordinated, and integrated planning, rests on the package approach to development. Complementary as opposed to activity concentration has been questioned in planning agricultural-development strategy. It seems that those who are directly concerned with the implementation of development favor the complementary approach while some, primarily concerned with economic research, are more critical. The package, complementary approach, however, has gained wider acceptance in recent years.

> The evidence indicates that the moshav approach, under certain circumstances, can provide an effective developmental package integrating planning and implementation, particularly in category 2 countries and in the framework of national land-reform and agricultural-development programs. It can be most effective where there is an urgent desire for agricultural development in a relatively short period of time. The

application of moshav principles can be a factor in increasing food supplies, modernizing peasant agriculture, raising rural incomes, and improving the amenities of rural life. (p. 349)

Educational Institutions

[63] BLAISE, Hans C., and Rodriguez, Luis A. "Introducing Innovation at Ecuadorean Universities." Graduate School of Public and International Affairs, University of Pittsburgh, Pittsburgh, Pa., undated. 135 pages. (Mimeographed. Part of Inter-University Research Program in Institution Building.)

The initial seven chapters present a chronological perspective of university education in Ecuador from 1962 until 1967. Although other universities are alluded to, prime focus is on the Central University of Ecuador in Quito. During the period under study, this institution, aided by a University of Pittsburgh technical assistance team, experienced a number of changes. The most important of these was the formation of a Faculty of Basic Studies. This and other aspects of the institution are analyzed in the final chapter.

In terms of the institution building framework of Esman et al., institution building at the Ecuadorean universities essentially began after the arrival of the foreign technical assistance groups. That process was quite closely related to and considerably affected by the political developments in the country. Hence, the following three time periods were identified: (1) the period prior to the military coup in July 1963, (2) the period of the reign of the military junta, and (3) the period subsequent to March 1966, when the military junta was replaced by an interim civilian government. These periods were used in discussing the institutional variables of the analytical framework.

Leadership

In the case of the Central University, two of the most notable aspects of leadership were its lack of centralization and its unity of purpose. The leadership structure included university authorities, student leaders, some professors, and technical assistance team members. Students, because of the extent of their membership on various governing bodies, held a strong, formal position of leadership. Hence, their support was needed for change to be initiated.

Because authorities and student leaders were elected, only those generally acceptable to the electorate stood a chance of being placed in positions of power. In order to retain that position they could not deviate substantially from established norms or aspirations of the electorate. Consequently, change was possible only when it was viewed as being desirable by a large group of individuals in the institution. An exception to this occurred, however, during the reign of the military junta (July 1963-March 1966), when student power was reduced.

Only in the postjunta period did a non-Communist ascend to the presidency of the most important student organization. Shortly thereafter the traditional student solidarity broke down and evidence began accumulating that student groups were moving toward more independent action.

Hans Blaise and Luis Rodriguez summarize the attributes of leadership at the institutions as:

> (a) elected authorities indebted to and influenced by their electorate; (b) lack of discretionary powers and resource control on the part of the authorities; (c) student leaders with considerable influence on and control over student action. (p. 99)

(These apply to the state universities rather than to the Pontifical Catholic University in Quito, where students did not participate directly in the leadership of the institution and authorities were not elected.)

Blaise and Rodriguez summarize the attributes of the technical assistance team members co-opted as part of the institutions' leadership.

> (a) lack of direct influence on the institutions' governing bodies, offset by a lack of accountability; (b) respect enjoyed among those leadership elements they assisted; (c) control over resources. (p. 100)

Doctrine

As a source of motivation and justification, doctrine can be perceived only by (1) looking at the values and objectives underlying an institution's social structure and action and (2) subsequently comparing these with formal statements of doctrine. To consider the latter only would be quite misleading, e.g., to consider the law of higher education in Ecuador as a statement of doctrine of universities.

Neither students nor faculty members expressed dissatisfaction with the aims and programs of the universities. Furthermore, no significant changes could be observed in the institutions' doctrine with regard to the broad purposes and goals of the universities during the three periods of study, except changes in autonomy—meaning noninterference by government or other external agencies in university affairs. Although the military junta initially violated this autonomy during its rule, its interference only strengthened the university community's opposition to the military regime, which subsequently contributed substantially to the junta's downfall.

Another noteworthy element of doctrine was manifest in the cogovernment and election system, as a result of which considerable consensus was needed in the university for any action to be taken. Internal politics tended to influence the selection of university authorities, who had relatively little power and frequently little inclination to deviate from established patterns. With regard to its implications for introducing change, the authors summarize this system of selecting university authorities as follows:

> (1) the need to achieve consensus, either ideologically or by demonstrating benefit to all groups concerned; (2) strengthening effective control by authorities without violating the basic concept of co-government; (3) establish internal political alliances to combat opposition groups. (p. 106)

A final element of doctrine was political action. Students, who represented the most formidable power group, were divided along political-ideological lines. Political orientation, autonomy, and cogovernment were of greater importance in guiding social action at the universities than the doctrinal elements concerned with the functions and academic programs of the institutions.

Program

In the program area the actions of the external change agents were focused on (1) academic and professional programs of the universities, (2) extension programs and functional relationships in other organizations, and (3) administration. The most noteworthy academic program was the creation of a basic studies faculty at the Central University. Because change agents had not developed a formula for promoting basic institutional change through program reform, this faculty was eventually eliminated and retrenchment became necessary, which limited both the scope of the program and the political power of the unit. Meanwhile, innovations were introduced in the engineering faculty, which conformed considerably more to existing aspirations and patterns. Through the introduction of these acceptable innovations into the program a foundation was built within the faculty for more fundamental institutional changes later.

The second area of program action, extension programs and functional relationships with other organizations, was initiated deliberately to foster change during the reign of the military junta. Alienation between university participants and the government thwarted this effort. However, in the postjunta period this action was intensified, and indications of institutionalized change became apparent.

The final program area which served as a target for change was that of university administration. The ineffectual administration that had existed previously was the subject of reform during the reign of the junta. One of the manifestations of that reform was the 1965 law of higher education. A number of the administrative changes initiated in this reform were continued in the postjunta period.

Resources

One of the contraints placed on changes in the program was the lack of adequate resources. Evidence suggests that this was the overriding factor in the universities' initial request for technical assistance. Blaise and Rodriguez describe the situation as follows:

> Although there were a few leaders at the universities who were oriented toward programmatic, structural and procedural reforms, the majority of the leadership elements were looking for additional financial, equipment and manpower resources to carry out the existing university programs. Contrary to this orientation, the technical assistance team members were fundamentally change oriented, viewing their participa-

tion in university teaching as well as the resources at their disposal for equipment purchases, for scholarships abroad, etc., as aids and instruments to bring about change. (p. 113)

In this situation the single most important factor in effecting change was the technical assistance team's accessibility to and control of these resources. Nevertheless, Blaise and Rodriguez caution:

If, however, institutional change is intended, then physical inputs appear to be only effective as an instrument of change if there is a strong motivation for change internal to the institution, if internal and/or external pressures for change exist, and if there is sufficient internal and/or external control over implementation. (p. 114)

The authors continue:

Resource availability and control appear to have been a powerful weapon in the hands of the change agents. Although this would be difficult to document, there are strong indications that the prospect of receiving resources for program implementation has in a number of instances caused the decision makers at the universities to accept recommendations for change from the technical assistance groups. In other words, the preference of the donor for a certain institutional rearrangement carried more weight when accompanied by the actual or implied promise of resources than without this. Conversely, a strong desire to acquire physical resources enhanced the change receptivity on the part of the universities' decision makers . . . . this process has encouraged and rewarded entrepreneurship; it has increased the scarce resources of the universities; it has allowed progressive forces to bring about change without being constrained by traditionalism and political conflicts. (pp. 114-16)

Especially in an established institution with little receptivity to change, the availability of additional resources may constitute an important component of a technical assistance team's strategy. However, if they are deliberately used to circumvent limitations in doctrine, leadership, and internal structure, the resources must be sufficiently stable and legitimate to prevent conflict in terms of the character of the other variables.

Perhaps the most important of all resources are those called human resources. In the Ecuadorean case, university authorities and administrative personnel had little influence on the operation of the universities or on the introduction of change. The same cannot be said for the professors, however. In light of the facts that (1) motivation for and receptivity to change among them appeared to be closely correlated with professional competence and the amount of time they spent working at the university, and (2) most of them were part-time staff members and were judged by both students and foreign professors to be of limited competence in a majority of cases, this group had considerable capacity for negating institution building efforts. Likewise, both in terms of quality and orientation, the students could not be viewed as a positive element for institution building. In light of these barriers, external assistance at the universities was viewed as indispensable for institution building. The technical competence of external teams and their access to material resources made them one of the most influential forces in promoting institutional change.

Internal Structure

The introduction of change in an institution is affected by two aspects of internal structure: (1) the number of persons involved in the decision-making process as well as their location in the institution and their relative power, and (2) the extent to which decision makers can cause the change to be accepted and implemented. Especially at the relatively decentralized Central University, the Ecuadorean institutions were organized so that many people were involved in the decision-making process. Furthermore, the decision makers had relatively little influence on acceptance and, once an innovation was adopted, its implementation. Under such circumstances, internal structure can significantly inhibit institution building. Blaise and Rodriguez summarize these constraints as follows:

> Our study has indicated that a number of characteristics of the internal structure of the Ecuadorean universities constituted impediments to the introduction of change:
>
> 1. Decentralization;
> 2. decision making on virtually all institutional matters by representational bodies;
> 3. elected officials without discretionary powers;
> 4. lack of administrative services;
> 5. excessive influence of student organizations;
> 6. lack of communication. (p. 125)

Institutional Linkages

This analysis focused on enabling, functional, normative, and diffused linkages in accord with the institution building conceptualization. Each of these will be discussed briefly.

The universities' most important enabling linkage was with the national government. One important aspect of this linkage was the autonomy of the universities, which has been strengthened over recent years except during the reign of the military junta. Another important aspect of this linkage was financial resources, since the state universities were primarily dependent upon the central government for their budgets. Unfortunately, this allocation was the result of a political process which could hardly be said to have any relation with objectively determined, technically analyzed university and national needs. The third aspect of enabling linkages revolves around the group of international organizations which provided technical assistance and economic resources. Where physical inputs were provided by these agencies and control over the allocation of them was vested in the technical assistance personnel also provided, the influence of the donor agency on the recipient institution was considerable.

Blaise and Rodriguez summarize their findings with regard to enabling linkages as follows:

> On the basis of the circumstances described, we can only conclude that the relationships of the universities with the enabling linkage institutions within Ecuador, i.e., the executive and legislative branches of the Ecuadorean government, had little if any positive effect on institutional change. This is true both from the universities' and from the enabling institutions' viewpoint. On the other hand, from both the universities' and from the foreign assistance institutions' viewpoint the enabling linkage existing between them could and did contribute positively to the institution building process. (p. 129)

Although some efforts were made late in the study to improve the functional linkages of universities, they remained weak during most of the study period. Incoming students were inadequately prepared. A substantial proportion of the professors lacked the required competence. The universities had negligible influence on organizations that might employ their students and professional associations and vice versa. Finally, competition among the universities was all too real and frequently detrimental, leading to wasteful duplication of programs and facilities.

With regard to normative linkages, institutions and individuals in the society widely accepted such norms and values as cogovernment and autonomy as time honored traditions, as a cultural pattern. These were so firmly rooted that most leaders would rather accept their negative aspects than their abolishment. Leaders knew that tampering with the established traditions would invite the wrath of the university community, with dire consequences for the attacker. Further complicating the problem were the normative linkages between university participants and political parties, which were clearly detrimental to the institution building process.

Both because the universities had their own channels to exert pressure and in recognition of the limited influence of public opinion, universities did not attempt to gain broad public support. Only toward the end of the study did they begin to render more direct services to the community and seek additional sources of financial support.

Blaise and Rodriguez summarize their study as follows:

> As an evolutionary process, change and modernization will undoubtedly take place at the Ecuadorean universities. During the few years that groups of change agents have been actively engaged in introducing deliberate change at those universities, they have demonstrated, albeit on a modest scale, that this evolutionary process can be accelerated. (p. 135)

[64] DE KIEWIET, C. W. "The Emergent African University: An Interpretation." American Council on Education, Overseas Liaison Committee, Washington, D.C., December 1971. 58 pages.

This manuscript, intended to serve as useful background for those planning and directing institutional development in Africa during the 1970s, was written by the long-standing chairman of the Overseas Liaison Committee, which operates under the aegis of the American Council on Education (ACE). In reflecting on the African universities, C. W. de Kiewiet states:

> At the end of the sixties higher education is engaged in a process of disengagement from its past, or more positively, in a search for an

institutional identity, with a pattern and objectives in accord with the realities of Africa, ethnic, historical, geographical and economic. (p. 2)

De Kiewiet concludes:

Many of the problems of costs and the national effectiveness of education, many of the issues of neglect and imbalance, are closely connected with dislocation and lack of coordination in the total realm of education. The university was an institution with insufficient linkings with government, with the rest of education, with the major imperatives of national development. Separations which could be endured in the metropolis became a damaging compartmentalization of jurisdictions, drawn into collision or driven apart by competition or possessiveness. Out of such dislocations and divided jurisdictions arose some of the most serious criticisms. The accusation that the universities were too little concerned with development and productivity finds some of its explanation in the fact that some of the best instruments were not in their hands.

In the territory that has been traversed in a long essay there is no pattern that is clear or correct or inevitable. African universities stand on a line that goes from a conviction that the university can achieve an acceptable level of adjustment, innovation and relevance in its own environment by means internal to itself, securing support from without but without enduring a mandate from without. Or the same result may be achieved by the exercise of the authority of the state in setting up the form of education which it considers best suited to the national interest. Between the two extreme points lies a range of alternatives and approximations. There lies encouragement and reassurance, and the room for debate and varied decision. (pp. 57-58)

[65] NORMINGTON, Louis W. *Teacher Education and the Agency for International Development.* Washington, D.C.: American Association of Colleges for Teacher Education, 1970. 186 pages.

The research for this volume was sponsored by the American Association of Colleges for Teacher Education (AACTE) out of its concern for the improvement of teacher education in America and its increasing involvement in technical assistance programs abroad.

The two major functions of the study are: (1) to describe the extent of AID's involvement in teacher education, including an examination of the types of assistance given, the institutions involved, the operational methods used, the difficulties encountered, and the elements contributing to success or failure; (2) to see if generalizations can be extracted, with particular reference to the factors underlying success or failure, that may be useful as guidelines to AID or to other institutions participating in similar projects in the future.

After stressing the fact that this should be regarded as a "modest beginning" or a "first phase of a much broader survey," Louis Normington presents a concise picture of the AID programs in education in 1967. Of special interest to institution builders is chapter 3, which is summarized briefly below.

Chapter 3 is entitled "The Technical Assistance Program: Past, Present, Future." After listing numerous trends in the technical assistance projects throughout the last decade, Normington attempts to analyze the factors underlying success and failure. He stresses the fact that, because of many unknown variables, the absence of a rigorous research design when programs were initiated, and the difficulty in defining criteria for success of an institution, "it is virtually impossible to pinpoint the effect of the American input" (p. 39). He then explores the strengths and weaknesses of technical assistance projects concluded from progress and termination reports of team members and judgments of people interviewed who were involved in some fashion with the program.

The following four clusters of crucial factors are discussed:

I. Factors relating to the project—its selection, planning, and timing:

    A. Clear understanding and agreement among the various parties as to the purposes of the project;

    B. Commitment to the goal of establishing an indigenous educational system and not imposing an American model;

    C. The project is developed as an integral part of an overall program for economic and social development;

    D. Major projects are conceived, from the beginning, as long-term and plans made accordingly;

    E. Major focus is toward investment in people rather than investment in commodities—buildings, equipment, and so forth;

    F. Effective timing.

II. Factors relating to the support of the project by the host country, AID, and the home institution:

    A. Firm commitment to the project and capacity to carry it out by the institution accepting the contract;

       B. The National Government is stable, and the Ministry of Education is not only committed to the project, but can gain support for its proposals;

       C. Support to the project is both adequate and carefully timed.

III.   Factors relating to the contract team:

       A. The contract team has operating authority for day-to-day decisions;

       B. Chief of party is able to exert leadership;

       C. Sensitivity to the cultural factors influencing change;

       D. Team members have a clear idea of their responsibilities;

       E. An effective program of orientation is carried on for new team members.

IV.   Factors relating to the carrying out of the project:

       A. Plans are clear—they involve in their preparation all those concerned and the planning process is continuous throughout the project;

       B. Adequate provision is made for the selection, training and re-employment of counterparts and participant trainees;

       C. Relevant research is made an integral part of technical assistance in teacher education. (pp. 40-52)

Normington then makes 21 recommendations, most of which are adjuncts of the above factors.

[66] PORTER, Willis P. "College of Education, Bangkok, Thailand: A Case Study in Institution Building." Graduate School of Public and International Affairs, University of Pittsburgh, 1967. 218 pages plus appendixes of 179 pages. (Mimeographed. Part of Inter-University Research Program in Institution Building.)

Willis Porter, who, from 1954 to 1957, served as chief of party of the Indiana University Contract Team which provided technical assistance to the Thai College of Education, describes this report as follows:

In the first chapter an attempt is made to describe the educational environment in 1954 and the conditions which the doctrine of the College was designed to change. This is followed by a summary of conditions indicating readiness for a college and a description of the College of Education at two periods, 1954 and 1964, with certain additions to bring the data up to 1967. There follows in Chapter III a discussion of the extent to which the institution-building process conformed to the Inter-University Committee's concepts of leadership, doctrine, program, resources, and internal structure. This is further elaborated in Chapter IV which is a detailing of the main strategies employed in technical assistance in moving the College from a teacher training institution of little stature to a degree-granting institution approaching university status. In the summary and conclusions, Chapter V, an effort is made to recapitulate the institution-building process at the College with special reference to criteria suggested by Esman growing out of his review of Hanson's study. (p. iv)

Using the Hanson-Esman criteria of (1) use of services, (2) survival, (3) support, (4) respect and approval, (5) normative spread, (6) autonomy, and (7) innovative thrusts, the author concludes that the process of institution building at the college, albeit incomplete, has been successful.

[67] SIMON, Herbert A. "The Business School: A Problem in Organizational Design." *Journal of Management Studies*, 4 (February 1967), 1-16.

The central thesis of this paper is sufficiently simple so that no lengthy conclusion is needed. Organizing a professional school or an R & D department is very much like mixing oil with water: it is easy to describe the intended product, less easy to produce it. And the task is not finished when the goal has been achieved. Left to themselves, the oil and water will separate again. So also will the disciplines and the professions. Organizing, in these situations, is not a once-and-for-all activity. It is a continuing administrative responsibility, vital for the sustained success of the enterprise. (p. 16)

[68] McNEIL, Kenneth, and Thompson, James D. "The Regeneration of Social Organizations." *American Sociological Review*, 36 (August 1971), 624-37.

Kenneth McNeil and James Thompson maintain that regeneration is a significant element in the dynamics of virtually all types of social organization. They present an index of regeneration which reflects the fact that social organizations often contain many overlapping cohorts. In addition, they deal with (1) how and why regeneration processes vary, (2) the potential consequences of such variations, and (3) how social organizations deal with regeneration phenomena. Illustrative data are presented for the University of Tennessee and Vanderbilt University. Subsequently, the discussion is expanded to include other complex organizations, families, nation-states, and cities.

[69] ASHBY, Eric, et al.*Investment in Education: The Report of the Commission on Post-School Certificate and Higher Education in Nigeria.* Nigeria: Federal Ministry of Education, 1960. 140 pages.

Known as the Ashby Report, this publication contains 64 conclusions and recommendations presented to the Nigerian government on the eve of its independence. In addition, it contains a series of special reports in which the substantive details of the general report are discussed.

[70] MORTIMORE, Fredric J. "Diffusion of Educational Innovations in the Government Secondary Schools of Thailand." Unpublished Ph.D. dissertation, Michigan State University, East Lansing, Mich., 1968. 250 pages.

With the use of survey data, Fredric Mortimore tests components of the broad hypothesized relationship that, for Thai government secondary school teachers, awareness time, adoption time, and beneficiality perceived as deriving from adoption of selected innovations (dependent variables), were related to demographic, sociometric, communication, technical, and personality considerations (independent variables). Each of the independent variables were disaggregated to 50 and in each case, 17, 20, and 30 were found to correlate significantly with awareness, adoption, and perceived beneficiality of innovation, respectively.

Government Operations

[71] MONTGOMERY, John D.; Hughes, Rufus B.; and Davis, Raymond H. *Rural Improvement and Political Development: The JCRR Model.* Comparative Public Administration Special Series Number 7. Washington, D.C.: American Society for Public Administration, 1966. 39 pages.

John Montgomery, Rufus Hughes, and Raymond Davis constituted a survey team sponsored by AID which studied the Sino-American Joint Commission on Rural Reconstruction

(JCRR). The function of this institution has been to administer aid of all kinds—loans, grants, and technical assistance—to agricultural, rural health, and related projects. Not only have funds been obtained from appropriated sources but also from the Chinese counterpart account, the source of 94 percent of all JCRR expenditures.

The authors conclude that many of the institutions created as a consequence of JCRR activities will survive the presently living participants because of the increases in initiative, resourcefulness, and managerial capabilities that resulted as a consequence of the program. These long-range effects can be expected from the research institutions, training programs, revised statutes, land reform, farmer associations, family planning projects, and overseas Chinese technical assistance projects.

Numerous factors influenced the effectiveness of JCRR. One was its joint character which enabled it to review a wide variety of project requests from numerous sources without the impediment of political pressure. Further, the "sponsoring agency" approach— e.g., JCRR allocating project funds to numerous organizations throughout the country—enabled those entities responsible for projects selected to have entire control of their management and operations. This stimulated many potential sponsors to initiate development proposals and take responsibility for activities designed to improve the living standards of their constituents.

[72] PINTO, Aluizio L. "The Brazilian Institute of Municipal Administration (IBAM): A Case Study of Institution Building in Brazil." Unpublished Ph.D. dissertation, University of Southern California, Los Angeles, Calif., 1968. 444 pages.

This study has the following specific aims: (1) to utilize, with the appropriate modifications, the institution building model developed by the Inter-University program in order to determine the degree of organizational institutionalization of IBAM; (2) to identify the basic strategies of institutionalization, in the light both of cultural factors and of intrinsic characteristics of the Institute, and their implications for the permanence of the organization, as used by IBAM in the past, present, and for the future; (3) to contribute to the task of model development and, ultimately, to increase knowledge in the field of institution building as a whole. (p. 13)

As a result of the analysis, Aluizio Pinto reaches the conclusion that IBAM can be considered well advanced in the process of organizational institutionalization. It ranks high both with regard to individual indicators of institutionalization and in the general tests of institutionalization suggested by Esman et al. Thus it has a high degree of institutionalization with regard to survival, environmental acceptance, and normativeness.

Pinto concludes:

> A point of theoretical importance, but with many practical implications, pertains to the proposition that all organizations carry within themselves the seeds of institutionalization. Successful institutionalization consists in the constant "infusion" of these values in an ever-growing number of individuals. The faster this process occurs, the stronger the possibility of the organization to resist entropic forces and consolidate its linkages in the early stages of its formative development. The creation of sub-system leadership from the very beginning could alleviate the problems of expansion or leadership crisis. (pp. 430-31)

[73] QURESHI, A. U. "California State Training Division: A Study in Institution Building." Unpublished Ph.D. dissertation, University of Southern California, Los Angeles, Calif., 1967. 647 pages. (Part of Inter-University Research Program in Institution Building.)

This dissertation is divided into two parts. Part I includes a detailed examination of organization theory, its relationship to the institution building model, and a history of the training division in California. Part II contains a discussion and analysis of empirical data from the training division. Part II is of particular interest to institution builders.

The broad objective of the study is to determine the process through which a typical public training organization in an advanced society can become an institution. The two main hypotheses are: (1) The training division has become an institution. It has developed a normative character and is prized and valued by the environment, which ensures its continuity in terms of survival for an indefinite period of time. (2) Institutionality has existed in the training division in varying degrees during the different phases of its history.

A. U. Qureshi uses the conceptual framework developed by

Esman et al. Data were gathered by means of a comprehensive survey of historical records of the division, a number of interviews with persons who have been in close contact with the division, and three questionnaires administered to three different sets of people. Qureshi uses continua scales to measure such institutionalization qualities as survival, valuation by the environment, and the normativeness of patterns.

Several conclusions are worth noting.

The California Training Division was concluded to be a semi-institution—that is, one oscillating between institutionalization and noninstitutionalization over time. During one period in its history, it showed capabilities of becoming institutionalized, but after the particular leader at that time left, its prestige decreased. During a survey in 1962-63 support for the program tended to be greater than knowledge of it (a sign of institutionality), whereas in 1965-66 it had difficulty surviving an attack by a legislative analyst. This leads to the conclusion that the relationship between the leader and the doctrine and program is important to the survival of an institution. The personality and skills of the leader are also important.

Another sign of institutionality is autonomy. Qureshi points out that it is difficult for a state institution to become institutionalized because of its dependence on the state for funds for personnel and program. It does not have the flexibility of a private institution.

From its beginning, the training division emphasized decentralization. Training was seen as a line function which was to be performed at place of operation.

> The story of the Training Division, in brief, is that it has accomplished the purpose for which it was created; it has established and popularized training in the State of California. There was a need for replacing its purpose and making certain changes and modifications with regard to that purpose. This need was not fulfilled. (p. 527)

One of Qureshi's key conclusions is that the Esman framework can be used in both developing and advanced societies. "The variables and linkages stipulated in the model exist in all organizations in every society" (p. 538). Two of the limitations he sees are (1) the problem of precision in measurement, and (2) inadequate emphasis on the variable of time.

[74] IZMIRLIAN, Harry, Jr. "Institutionalization of Political Values and Structure: An Indian Example." Syracuse University, Syracuse, N.Y., 1967. 46 pages plus appendixes. (Mimeographed. Part of Inter-University Research Program in Institution Building.)

This report is based on data gathered from three villages during two years (1961-62, 1965-66) of field research in Punjab, India. The institutional frame is the Panchayati Raj (PR), a three-tiered system of local government involving districts and blocks. In 1957, a government report (Mehata Report) noted that the rural population was not supporting the Community Development Program (CDP). The villagers felt that their participation was kept to a minimum and that the program was bureaucratically imposed from above. In an attempt to overcome this criticism, a new program was initiated in the PRs. However, this program also has not been uniformly successful.

Harry Izmirlian, an anthropologist, is concerned with the importance of political communication in this setting as a force of influence in nonpolitical aspects of villages. His point of departure is Esman and Fred Bruhn's observation that a few responsible and influential villagers convinced of the value of innovation can muster support for it.

The research methods were anthropological, involving observations, personal interviews, census cards, and structured questionnaires. The political communication of the three villages studied was classified thus: (1) in village A leaders had informal contacts with leaders at the district and state level; (2) in village B leaders were locally oriented and isolated from wider networks; and (3) in village C, the only key village, leaders had formal connections with block and district bodies.

From the data presented, cultural and social change is related to the nature of the political structure of the village. Where leaders in the village have political access, the involvement of the total agricultural population is maximized. Thus 80 percent of the nonactives in A were utilizing improved methods of agriculture; in B, only 30 percent. For C, we must remember that we have a disproportionate number of actives, which may in part be due to the high politicization in this village. In this context then, PR as an institution appears to have a catalytic effect, fostering greater political access in villages where such is to some extent already the case. What I am suggesting then, is that PR accen-

tuates political processes already present, sharpening political align-
ments, mobilizing villagers toward greater action in competing for
rewards and finally intensifying communication outside and within the
village. Such processes ultimately restructure ideas as well as action. (p.
46)

[75] CHOWDHRY, Kamla, and Sarabhai, Vikram. "Organization for
Developmental Tasks: Atomic Energy Commission of India."
Indian Journal of Public Administration, 14 (January-March
1968), 1-22.

In providing an overview of this article, which focuses on one
institution, the authors state:

At one level it is the story of atomic energy in India, at another level
the story of [Dr.] Bhabha, the great innovator and organizer, and yet at
another level, of the growth of institutions and the introduction of
change based on advanced technologies. (p. 1)

In summarizing the factors that contributed to the success of
this institution, Kamla Chowdhry and Vikram Sarabhai emphasize
the strategy which provided for the building of organizations
around men who, in this instance, possessed a sense of trust and a
sense of the significance of their role in building society. Second,
they note the unusual combination of policy-making, executive,
and scientific roles that accorded the institution's top administrator important power, freedom, and authority. Third, in the crucial
early years of the institution, considerable benefit was derived
from the transfer of a large group of scientists with a homogeneous culture from the predecessor institution. Fourth, as in
many other professional groups, motivation and control were
contained in professional commitments and exercised through
both discussions and the judgment of peers. Fifth, the body to
which the top administrator referred for policy and strategic
decisions was compact in size and consisted of members chosen
for their expertise and roles. Sixth, by wearing several hats at
different times, key individuals in the institution participated in
the interplay among basic science, technology, and industrial practice so that economic progress could result. Finally, personnel
were motivated as professionals through the autonomy, mobility,
and interaction with their peers which they were afforded.

[76] BUKHALA, James A. "The Process and Strategy of Promoting and Developing an Audiovisual Programme in Kenya." Unpublished Ph.D. dissertation, Syracuse University, Syracuse, N.Y., 1969. 241 pages. (Part of Inter-University Research Program in Institution Building.)

This is an analysis of Kenya's abortive attempts to develop an integrated audiovisual program with which James Bukhala previously had been affiliated. Drawing both on his own experience and the theoretical literature, he focuses on change phenomena, institution building, methods of introducing innovations, and characteristics of successful innovations and innovating institutions.

On the basis of a conceptual model of change developed for the Kenyan context, various propositions emerged. These propositions provided a basis for the development of the following independent variables which mediated success in the development and promotion of integrated audiovisual programs: an institution's desirability, viability, innovative capacity, acceptance, innovative diffusive thrust, and reciprocal relationships with its environment. Bukhala contends that the order of these variables is important because each of the succeeding subordinate variables mediates the success of the next variable. In addition, each variable incorporates action strategies which are transferable and should be integrated with those belonging to the next variable. Finally, these variables are considered crucial in the formulation of a model for cumulative strategy which Bukhala develops.

[77] MOREHOUSE, Ward. *Science in India: Institution Building and the Organizational System for Research and Development.* Administrative Staff College of India Occasional Papers, Hyberabad. Bombay, India: Popular Prakashan, 1971. 144 pages.

This essay, written while its author was a visiting professor at the Administrative Staff College of India, is designed as a conceptual outline rather than a detailed application of this framework to Indian scientific organizations. It provides a way of looking at the organizational system of Indian science to pose some hypotheses about the growth of the system and to indicate some of the investigations needed to test these hypotheses. In addition to this major purpose, the book is also designed to bring together some of the basic data on the organization of Indian science and its growth since India's independence.

As a way of looking at institutions, Ward Morehouse uses the institution building conceptualization of Esman et al. Using the tests of institutionality of that approach, he concludes that Indian science has developed so rapidly in the past two decades that it has not become sufficiently institutionalized to function as a major factor in the achievement of national goals. Following from this conclusion are a series of hypotheses concerning different aspects of the institution building process in Indian science. Subsequently, a synoptic view of the organizational landscape of Indian science is presented as general background material for the further empirical research which Morehouse recommends.

[78] MOREHOUSE, Ward. "Analytical Elegance or Relevant Analysis: Institution-Building and Public Policy for Science in India." Paper prepared for Symposium on Education and Development in India, Duke University, Durham, N.C., November 1971. 96 pages. (Mimeographed. Preliminary work.)

In this paper the institutional experience of the Indian Institute of Science is examined. After detailing the historical development of the institute, Ward Morehouse applies the institution building conceptualization developed by Esman et al. and then the criteria of institutional maturity. In concluding the analysis Morehouse states:

> In sum, then, the institution-building model provides a helpful way of looking at complex phenomena but thus far has demonstrated limited relevance to policy makers because of its limited predictive power (save in special circumstances such as decisions regarding external aid). It is limited in predictive power not so much because the model is faulty but because we have not yet developed sufficiently sharp analytical tools to find answers to what policy makers need to know and to provide comparability in data between different organizational entities. In short, the institution-building model, at its present stage of refinement, is more analytically elegant than relevant to the real world of public policy in India. (p. 90)

[79] HERMANO, Ramon A. D. "The National Science Development Board and Its Environment—A Case Study of Institution

Building." Unpublished Ph.D. dissertation, University of Pittsburgh, Pittsburgh, Pa., 1968. 329 pages.

Ramon Hermano analyzes the Phillippine National Science Development Board with the use of the institution building concepts developed by Esman et al. In addition, he uses five indicators of support for the institution provided by its environment, on the premise that institutionality is manifest by the level of such support. These indicators were the extent to which the environment (1) provides authority and resources, (2) makes demands for the organization to process, (3) uses the organizational outputs, (4) approves and respects the organization, and (5) incorporates the values and norms of the organization.

In summarizing the results of the analysis Hermano states:

> It was revealed that a positive relationship seemed to exist between the organizational capability to elicit environmental support on one hand, and the following factors on the other: the political viability and personality of its leadership; availability of resources; and flexibility of structure. A negative relationship seemed to exist between the reliability of the Board's program and its capacity to elicit support.

> The study also indicated that a positive relationship seemed to exist between high support and a strategy with a perspective which viewed all elements in the environment as capable of being changed, and which emphasized (1) the establishment of inter-personal linkages with influentials as a change tactic, (2) the use of emotional appeals, (3) the creation of needs and new allies in the environment, (4) dependence on a diffuse doctrine, and (5) the utilization of conflicts to propagate a change doctrine.

> From the study, two organizational elements seem to stand out as critical factors: (1) the leadership style and political viability; and (2) the manipulation of structure as a tactical element to build up strong linkages with the environment. (Preface)

[80] JREISAT, Jamil E. "Provincial Administration in Jordan: A Study of Institution-Building." Graduate School of Public and International Affairs, University of Pittsburgh, Pittsburgh, Pa., September 1968. 217 pages. (Mimeographed. Part of Inter-University Research Program in Institution Building.)

This analysis of the Balqa Provincial Administration (BPA) in Jordan uses the institution building framework developed by

Esman et al. Data for the analysis were gathered on site by the author.

Among other things, Jamil Jreisat comments on the usefulness of the institution building framework as a research tool. Its limitations include (1) the difficulty of implementing the concept of institutionalization, (2) the difficulty of analyzing transactions separately from linkages, and (3) the difficulties in investigating concepts dealing with values and norms, including their operationalization. He sees the strengths of the framework as (1) its utility in providing an understanding of the internal processes of administration of the institution, (2) its emphasis on environmental interactions and their effects on the institution, (3) its utility for studying institutions in developing countries, (4) its usefulness in identifying obstacles to effective performance of the institution, and (5) its utility for providing a basis for intertemporal and interspacial comparisons of institutions.

[81] HEAPHEY, James J. "Technical Assistance in the Administration of Legislatures: Problems of Theory and Concepts." Prepared for presentation at the annual meeting of the American Society for Public Administration, March 1972. 32 pages. (Mimeographed. Preliminary work.)

Initially, three theoretical aspects of legislative development are discussed. Subsequently, the merit of viewing legislative improvement as institution building is stressed. Finally, the program in legislative development of the Comparative Development Studies Center of the State University of New York at Albany in cooperation with U.S. state legislatures and those in developing countries (the latter supported by a grant from the United States Agency for International Development) is described.

[82] PINTO, Rogerio F. S. "The Political Ecology of the Brazilian National Bank for Development (BNDE): A Study of Politics, Development and Public Administration." Unpublished Ph.D. dissertation, Department of Political Science, University of North Carolina, Chapel Hill, N.C., 1967. 214 pages.

The institution building framework of Esman et al. is partially used in this study of a development bank. The decades of the 1950s and 1960s represent the time frame of the analysis, and the various Brazilian administrations which held office during this period are analyzed with regard to the bank.

In drawing conclusions, Rogerio Pinto compares the characteristics of leadership, doctrine, program, resources, and structure of the bank during each administration with those characteristics of these variables which would be necessary if the bank were regarded as an autonomous government institution. This analytical approach facilitates comparison of these variables among administrations.

[83] ESMAN, Milton J. *Administration and Development in Malaysia: Institution Building and Reform in a Plural Society.* Ithaca, N.Y.: Cornell University Press, 1972. 341 pages.

This book is largely based upon Milton Esman's experiences while serving as senior adviser to the prime minister's department in Malaysia from September 1966 to August 1968. During this period he was instrumental in the formation of the Development Administration Unit in the prime minister's department. As primary adviser to this new, innovative institution, Esman used his institution building approach as a framework of operation. In doing so, he employed several approaches to strategies of institution building which might be useful in other situations.

In summarizing his findings, Esman states:

> The institution-building perspective proved to be a useful strategy for guiding administrative reform in Malaysia. Intellectually, it was able to account for the problems that arose and for the successes and failures that were experienced in the early years of the Development Administration Unit. Operationally, it provided a model of the processes to be pursued, a check list of factors to be taken into account, a method of mapping the terrain, and a set of criteria for guiding decisions. The institution-building orientation is particularly useful for induced and guided change in relatively stable bureaucratic systems. (pp. 292-93)

[84] ANDERSON, D. Craig. "The Grasshopper Flat Controversy." Office of International Programs, Utah State University, Logan, Utah. November 1971. 19 pages. (Typewritten.)

Three basic observations are made as a consequence of this case study of conflict between a public institution, the U.S. Forest

Service, and one of its clientele groups, the Ashley Reservoir Company. First, the environment of a bureaucracy has a pronounced effect on its organizational structure and determines, to a large degree, bureaucratic effectiveness. Second—and this is consistent with James D. Thompson [358]—a bureaucracy that is responsible to the public, when in a situation of differing value orientations, cannot deal in absolutes but must, rather, consider degrees. Third, where the public will conflicts with bureaucratic goals because of value differences, compromise is essential if reconciliation is to be effected.

Planning Organizations

[85] SIEGEL, Gilbert B. "Development of the Institution Building Model." Graduate School of Public and International Affairs, University of Pittsburgh, Pittsburgh, Pa., 1966. 69 pages. (Mimeographed. Part of Inter-University Research Program in Institution Building.)

The objective of this paper is to determine the nature and interaction of clusters of institutional variables and environmental linkages on the basis of an analysis of organizational ecology drawn from the experience of the Brazilian Administrative Department of the Public Service (DASP). Gilbert Siegel first studies the institution as the basis for an organizational history and then applies the institution building framework of Esman et al. to the data.

Siegel operationalizes three tests of institutionalization—survival, valuation by the environment, and normativeness. Continua are developed as follows: (1) survival: (a) sacrifice of innovative elements and (b) dependence upon founding structure; (2) valuation by the environment: (a) autonomy to deviate from parent system, (b) autonomy to acquire resources based upon intrinsic value, (c) autonomy to rely on intrinsic value for defense against attacks and encroachment, and (d) ability to influence decisions in functional areas and to enlarge sphere of action; and (3) normativeness: relations and action patterns that are normative for other social units.

Siegel's analysis revealed a strong suggestion of linear development of the institutionalization process through the stages of noninstitution, semiinstitution, and institution. Tests of survival and normativeness tend to characterize the semiinstitution stage, while influence and autonomy appear to be related to the institutionalized end of the continuum. If the principle of linearity of these tests is valid, then appropriate clusters of organizational linkage variables should be relatable to each of them and the continuum as a whole. Subsequently, Siegel combines the four types of linkages with the five types of institution variables in different combinations for each test performed on the institutionalization continuum.

[86] WOODWARD, Weldon E. "The Building of CORDIPLAN." Unpublished Ph.D. dissertation, University of Pittsburgh, Pittsburgh, Pa., 1969. 387 pages. (Part of Inter-University Research Program in Institution Building.)

The purposes of this study were (1) to contribute, by means of a case study of the growth of the Venezuelan Central Office for Coordination and Planning (CORDIPLAN), to the understanding of the process whereby effective planning institutions are built, and (2) to contribute to the development of more useful concepts and hypotheses in the fields of institution building and administration of national planning. To accomplish these objectives, the principal hypothesis tested was that CORDIPLAN had become a development institution. For testing the hypothesis data were gathered on site during a 15-month period approximately ten years after CORDIPLAN was initiated.

Weldon Woodward concludes that CORDIPLAN has become firmly established within the Venezuelan social system as a norm-setting organization which performs services that are valued in the society and which makes a significant contribution to national development. Factors contributing to the institution's development of its capacity have been (1) the quality and continuity of its leadership; (2) the stability, technical competence, and political neutrality of its technical staff; (3) the technical excellence of the law creating it; (4) its close relationships with the President of the Republic; (5) its cooperative relationship with the minister of finance; (6) its strategic position as a focal point of public expenditures; (7) its manipulation of organizational resources and its efforts to shape its own environment, especially by means of institutional investments; and (8) its multifaceted doctrine. Not to be overlooked is the fact that the institution enjoyed a relatively stable environment that provided time to acquire and train a competent technical staff and time for the staff to establish all-important personal relations with counterparts in other agencies. Further, the institution has had time to experience considerable learning as an organization. Finally, Woodward presents several hypotheses for further research, suggested by the analysis of CORDIPLAN, which may contribute to institution building theory.

[87] NAYAR, P.K.B. "Bureaucracy and Socio-Economic Development: A Case Study of Planning Departments in Two Indian States." Unpublished Ph.D. dissertation, University of Pittsburgh, Pittsburgh, Pa., 1967. 210 pages. (Part of Inter-University Research Program in Institution Building.)

This report presents the results of an analysis of the planning departments of Andhra Pradesh and Kerala, two Indian states, using the institution building framework developed by Esman et al. Data were obtained from relevant documents as well as by means of interviews with personnel in those departments. These data were used to test five hypotheses. Noteworthy among the findings was the fact that leadership was the most important of several factors upon which the effectiveness of planning departments depends.

Public Administration

[88] SIFFIN, William J. "The Thai Institute of Public Administration: A Case Study in Institution Building." Graduate School of Public and International Affairs, University of Pittsburgh, Pittsburgh, Pa., 1967. 275 pages. (Mimeographed. Part of Inter-University Research Program in Institution Building.)

This analysis was conducted between 1965 and 1966 and was focused on the Institute of Public Administration (IPA) at Thammasat University in Thailand. IPA had been in existence for approximately ten years at the time of the analysis. During almost the entire period the institute received technical assistance from a University of Indiana team. Eighteen months after termination of that assistance the institute was absorbed into a new and more comprehensive organization, the National Institute of Development Administration. In many respects, the latter was a product of the former. Hence, the institute was a victim not of failure but of growth.

After providing a thumbnail sketch of the historical development of the institute, William Siffin turns to an examination of its staff. Their attitudes, perceptions, and activities are viewed as essential features of the organization as an institution.

While only about 37 percent of the Thai trainees financed by the Indiana contract returned to become staff members of the institute, they did represent a core group and, through their acquaintance with the other participant trainees who had returned, formed a subtle linkage with the institute's social environment. However, the institute was marked by a high rate of turnover, which was in part due to the more attractive positions available within the established bureaucracy. The result was that an adequate academic staff was never built.

Although most staff members perceived that the institute's support came from political sources, there was no clear-cut, widely shared perception of (1) adequate support relationships on the one hand and (2) insufficiently met needs for support on the other. Thus, the staff seemed rather satisfied with its supportive linkages. These seemed to be regarded as more or less fixed and determined rather than subject to challenge and change.

In 1965 the staff also perceived the institute's role as a passive one. The institute was not viewed as a thrusting instrument of bureaucratic change. Although the staff felt that their students developed a critical attitude toward the bureaucracy, they saw the bulk of the institute's effects as relatively diffuse. Clearly, the institute was not perceived as a continuing innovator.

The staff seemed to be divided into two groups with regard to leadership, one traditional and the other more innovative. The innovators had shared extensive and relatively stressful sets of experiences as participant trainees in the United States. The traditional faction, on the other hand, headed by the dean, had been able, through him, to establish legitimacy for the institute as well as build and maintain linkages with the bureaucracy. The two groups were divided on such matters as whether or not the dean should be a full-time leader of the institute. The American advisers, who were part of the innovative faction, maintained that full-time leadership was essential. The dean contended that in the Thai context a full-time dean would be likely to be a relatively weak person, not possessed of status sufficient to establish and maintain the necessary linkages. He felt that, in the best Thai fashion, the dean should have a wide network of involvements and relations within the government and a suitably high status. This problem was partially resolved by the eventual appointment of a full-time associate dean.

Students and alumni of the institute regarded program as valued but only in a relative way. Completion of the program was not considered the absolute key to success, and it was not totally preferable to certain perceived alternatives. But the program had some impact upon the perceptions of the students. As a result of it they saw themselves as being somewhat more able to function and thrive in the bureaucratic milieu—somewhat more skilled, more perceptive, and perhaps more critical. They were aware of prospects of change and probably inclined to favor change, but did not perceive themselves as major vehicles of these changes.

Evidence suggests that the content and doctrine of the institute's executive development and inservice training programs were accommodated to the normative-cognitive set of the participants. Siffin states:

> The accommodation consisted of the establishment of a viable process, or a merchandisable product—one which is not conceived in the IPA as inconsistent with doctrine and broad goals; and one which is perceived by the customers as meaningful and useful, although not necessarily in terms of the substantive norms or doctrine presumably held by the IPA Inservice Training Division management and the top-level of the IPA. (p. 243)

This accommodation evolved over time, especially in the latter part of the decade of the institute's existence.

Although the key to initiation of the executive development

program, which did not begin to flourish until 1961, was the impetus provided by foreign advisers, the ground had already been prepared by a pre-existing training division. Its series of activities had more or less established a precedent and a diffuse acceptance, and, thereby, legitimacy of the activity.

At the culmination of his analysis Siffin concluded that between 1955 and 1965 the institute had become established in the sense that it was a going concern with a program, a staff, a set of clients, an acceptable identity, and a stable supply of resources sufficient to enable it to continue. Although not clearly articulated, the doctrine used in this process was a series of postures toward the Thai bureaucracy—attack, adjust, accept, and explain. Its doctrine was such that, even after ten years, the institute had not produced forceful evidence that it had reached into the environment and set performance standards and process patterns which were guidelines for other organizations in the society. In general, the institute was accepted rather than highly valued by its environment.

With regard to leadership, Siffin contends that the Thai institute represents a vivid illustration of a central problem of building institutions.

> Effective leadership must relate the organization to its environment in a way that will enable survival and appropriate growth. It must procure and maintain mandates, get resources, and allocate them within the enterprise in ways that will largely determine its nature. It must produce an effective adjustment between the needs of the organization and the environmental norms and values that are reflected in such things as operating rules and regulations. Ultimately the leadership must claim and establish the legitimacy of the organization. The initial leadership of the IPA did these things, the organization became a going concern. At a price, of course. That price was essentially a doctrinal orientation less than wholly compatible with the intended aims of certain other parties to the institution-building effort. (pp. 253-54)

The greatest resource problem of the institute was the inadequacy of professional staff resources. The instructional staff was never sufficient. Moreover, the institution's ability to acquire resources was never commensurate with its needs. Another facet of this problem was the need to reinforce and sustain professional personnel who were operating in a highly corrosive environment—

one which quickly used up professional capital and drew personnel off into a variety of nonprofessional activities in quest of income, status, and identity. Siffin's analogy between small businesses, which founder because of failure to anticipate capital needs, and institution building efforts, which likewise fail because of insufficient resources, is meaningful at this point.

With regard to linkages, he states:

> In the set of transactional relations between the Institute and its environment there seems to be one suggestive lesson: Environmental support depends upon the ability to appeal to premises which induce support—and not necessarily upon doctrine. (p. 259)

In summarizing the analysis, Siffin states:

> By 1965 a relatively stable transactional pattern had been established, quite sufficient to assure the continuance of the organization. In a sense, the IPA had become "institutionalized." It had acquired sufficient acceptance and meaningfulness in its setting to be relatively free from threats. But its meaningfulness did not lie in its perceived value as a significant innovative institution, nor was it a function of its ability to confer important changes in status upon its clients. Internally, the IPA was faced with a sharp split in the structure of its leadership.

> In short, and in conclusion, the outcome of the effort to build the IPA was mixed. The aim had been to create an organization embodying new values, functions, and technologies, which would stimulate tendencies toward normative change in its bureaucratic environment. It was a bold vision, marked by hope and the innocence that often attends such ventures. That it was never fully achieved is no indictment: there are vast gaps between visions and ventures. If a study of its failures as well as its successes contributes to the effectiveness of other efforts at institution-building, then even the IPA's failures will to some extent be justified. (p. 269)

[89] BIRKHEAD, Guthrie S. "Institutionalization at a Modest Level; Public Administration Institute for Turkey and the Middle East." University of Syracuse, Syracuse, N.Y., 1967. 126 pages plus appendixes. (Mimeographed. Part of Inter-University Research Program in Institution Building.)

Approximately two years prior to the initiation of its first course in March of 1953, the Public Administration Institute for Turkey and the Middle East (PAITME), Turkey, and the United Nations agreed to set up a training program for the public service in Turkey and neighboring nations. During part of this interim period a working group composed of four United Nations consultants and a number of Turkish representatives met to make plans for the institution. In summarizing the work of this group, Guthrie Birkhead states:

> The Working Group had been presented with a general commission, and its members rendered to the United Nations and Turkey a most general report. They raised or identified at least as many questions as they answered. "Public administration"—content, clientele, or training methods—was left unidentified. PAITME was to be an autonomous body, and its location in the hierarchy of administration was not mentioned. Categories of potential students were only broadly identified. All possible courses the new institute might teach were listed. One concrete recommendation was made in the report that the internal organization of PAITME be modeled after a "faculty." This was a wish of the Turkish members. (p. 30)

Describing the leadership of PAITME the author states:

> No dean to this day has devoted his full time and attention to the Institute. Problem-solving, program-planning, internal decision-making have failed to hold their attention. No dean even spent much time physically in the Institute until it was moved in 1959. Only on a very few occasions was a dean motivated to accept and work for "public administration" ideas urged on him by U.N. personnel. And even these related mainly to the need for passing the law and improving the outside relationships of the Institute. (p. 53)

Although most U.N. experts were quite knowledgeable in the field of public administration, they were handicapped by relatively short tours of duty. Many of the institute's shortcomings were attributed to these short tours, which resulted in the failure of the "counterpart" system.

The program of the institute, which suffered little through the years from shortages of resources, consisted of both short- and long-term courses in addition to a research component. Although initially staffed by U.N. experts, the latter phase of the program was gradually taken over by Turkish researchers. The most impressive and probably the most useful product of this phase was an organizational manual of the whole government which resulted from a comprehensive organizational survey.

In spite of the fact that the original plans called for it to do so, the documentation and publication section of the institute still, by 1966, had not obtained status comparable with that of teaching and research. This was due partly to the difficulties of the Turkish language, but was also attributable to the lack of interest and attention to this function by the U.N. and Turkish staff.

In 1958 the law formally establishing the institute passed under pressure of potential U.N. withdrawal of assistance and as a result of the efforts of a Turkish leader in the institute. While there were no dramatic changes in the institute after it gained its law, there were a number of gradual improvements. These included an increase in the number of full-time staff members, broadening of the course offering, continued increases in budget, acquisition of its own building, and expansion of the number of applications of students for its general course. However, whether its reputation was enhanced by having a law was impossible to test.

In spite of the fact that the institute was to serve not only Turkish needs but also those of the other Middle Eastern countries, the latter were very infrequently represented in the student body. In discussing the problem, Birkhead states:

> In reality the Turks never gave regionalism a try. Like so many ideas for the Institute, it faded for lack of enthusiasm and active support, particularly from among Turks directly associated in the endeavor. Verbal support from the Foreign Ministry was not enough; somebody had to do some work. Today regionalism remains only in the name of PAITME. (p. 92)

Another complicating factor in the history of the institute was the assistance that the U.S. government, via contract and direct-hire personnel, provided to it and the faculty of which it was initially a part. Competition developed between U.N. and U.S. technical assistance advisers with both positive and negative consequences. But apparently the arguments among the foreigners influenced events very little.

Birkhead summarizes his impressionistic account of the PAITME experience in terms of the institution building framework of Esman et al., specifically in terms of leadership, doctrine, program, resources, and linkages. During the institute's initial years, its leadership allowed it to drift ever so casually into the hands of the faculty of political science. Even after passage of the law separating the institute from the faculty, the only serious candidates for the general directorship continued to be political science professors. Hence, the author states:

> Before the law the general director was the Faculty's steward for Institute affairs, and since the law there has never been an overt threat of PAITME competition with the Faculty. Therefore one concludes, to this extent, that this is a case of an existing institution which succeeded in embracing a new institution to effectively suppress or at least control its development. (p. 102)

Making something of the institute, developing and enlarging it, never seemed to infect the imagination of the Turkish general directors before or after passage of the law. They did not try to build an empire from the institute. They were content with the minor kingdom it represented. Although this was not necessarily the case with regard to the codirectors (U.N. personnel) there were practically no long-range results of their efforts, although their reception by higher officialdom was uniformly polite.

During the early years of the institute, at least, the content of its doctrine was so inchoate as to be highly ineffective. The technical assistance personnel tended to believe that some kind of public administration doctrine could be evolved over the years, primarily through research. Indeed, research was among the first commissions given the institute. However, it chose to emphasize teaching and did not make research the first item on its agenda. Only much later did analyses begin to produce the substance on which academic efforts might have been founded. Yet, at the time of this study there had not been any noticeable refinement of the vague public administration doctrines initially provided the institute.

By asking strategic questions, Birkhead is able to operationalize the institution building conceptualization with regard to categories of linkages. The relatively small number of contacts made by the institute with outside groups so categorized may be interpreted by some to mean it has a good reputation and enjoys the confidence of higher officials, while others would argue that higher officialdom is ignoring it.

[90] SHERWOOD, Frank P. "Social Exchange in the Institution-Building Process: Rewards and Penalties in the Brazilian School of Public Administration." Graduate School of Public

and International Affairs, University of Pittsburgh, Pittsburgh, Pa., 1967. 67 pages. (Mimeographed. Part of Inter-University Research Program in Institution Building.)

This technical paper on the social exchange process in institution building is based on empirical work of Jose Silva de Carvalho and Alberto Guerreiro Ramos, faculty members at the Brazilian School of Public Administration (EBAP). In contrast to the theory which explains membership cohesion by consensus on norms and values, this work is premised on the assumption that individuals participate in activities because they calculate the rewards of group membership to be greater than the penalties. This approach draws heavily on economics and behavioral psychology in viewing social behavior as exchanges between two or more people which, regardless of whether the objects are tangible or intangible, the participants find to be more or less rewarding and/or costly. In this formulation, social approval can play the role of money while the other item of exchange is interaction. In a small group, rewards and penalties are a function of direct relationships among participants, whereas in large organizations the reward or penalty generated by an action is more contrived and the reward-penalty relationship more indirect. Frank Sherwood argues that an institution, if it is to survive, must provide sufficient rewards to individual members for them to maintain it. In many respects, this approach is similar to that of Mancur Olson [140].

With the use of the survey data mentioned above, Sherwood analyzes the inducements EBAP can provide its faculty in order to secure participation. He found:

> There is considerable general satisfaction with membership in the organization. . . .

> Though the base salary for professors is low and commonly accounts for only about 45 percent of total income, EBAP has been able to fashion a pattern of material inducements that . . . permit essentially full-time dedication to the work of the organization. . . .

> Inducements that are indirect and organizational in nature also seem to be an important part of the non-material reward system. (pp. 40-41)

In exchange for these rewards and inducements the institution secures, among other things, a noteworthy return in terms of the number of hours worked by its faculty.

On the basis of the above findings and other findings based upon similar analyses of data obtained from the administrative staff, the students, and the alumni, Sherwood concludes:

> In general the investigation appeared to be fruitful. While there is no absolute point at which one might claim that an organization's non-material rewards are sufficient to earn it the designation of institution, it certainly is evident that a high proportion of EBAP's rewards to the faculty and administrative people is non-material. In the case of the students, there is a need to recognize that virtually all rewards are non-material and that they relate to a future time. The student is asked to engage in an exchange where his gratifications from the arrangement are almost entirely deferred. The exchange with alumni could be potentially important; but the present exchange is more hypothetical than real.
>
> In the overall, it appears that the concept of social exchange can suggest important strategies to the leader seeking to build an institution. If he accepts the major premise that rewards must in the long run be greater than the cost of membership, the system of analysis should then enable him to think more innovatively and more rigorously about the ways in which he can create a climate of profitable exchange for the organization's members. (pp. 66-67)

[91] BRUHNS, Fred Charles. "The Roles of Values in the Management of Institutional Doctrine: The Institution Building Experience of an African Regional Organization." Graduate School of Public and International Affairs, University of Pittsburgh, Pittsburgh, Pa., 1969. 315 pages. (Mimeographed. Part of Inter-University Research Program in Institution Building.)

The overall purpose of this study is to contribute to a model of doctrinal change in institutions and, thus, to test and develop further the conceptual framework developed by Esman et al. However, rather than consider doctrine as a stable reference point as Esman did, Fred Bruhns views it "as a combination of a number of different and frequently heterogeneous elements which, in regard to stability, differ from each other in change proneness or propensity; some might be more, others less, stable" (p. 5). In this sense doctrine is hypothesized to be an important tool that institutional leadership can manipulate to (1) make institutional adjustments and adaptations to the environment in order to overcome resistance and gain acceptance therein, and (2) build, maintain, and strengthen the internal cohesion and organization of the institution for making a greater impact upon the environment.

To accomplish the objectives of the analysis and test its hypotheses, Bruhns studied the African Training and Research Center in Administration for Development (CAFRAD) at Tangier, Morocco. Prior to reporting the results of the empirical analysis, however, Bruhns identifies the conceptual framework with approaches used by Elton Mayo, Chester I. Barnard, Dwight Waldo, Richard Cyert, James March, Fred W. Riggs, and especially Philip Selznick.

In summarizing the culmination of differences concerning doctrine in the institution, Bruhns states:

> When it finally became manifest on the level of bureaucratic action involving leadership personnel, an effort attempting to rationalize value dissonance had been set in motion in each group and the dissonance on level III became so irreconcilable that a most serious and disruptive crisis ensued for CAFRAD. (p. 242)

Evidence was found which supported the principal hypothesis in the following restated form:

> It is the main function of institutional doctrine to serve as an important tool of, and for, the organization's leadership. The tool will be manipulated for two main purposes: (1) to increase the institution's acceptability in the external environment by gaining support therein and by overcoming resistance and indifference; . . . and (2) to build, maintain or strengthen the internal cohesion and organization of the institution in order to enhance organizational production and goal performance. (p. 264)

In referring to the other two hypotheses tested, the author states:

> In fact, the CAFRAD data indicated that, on the whole, the actors did not *view* and *perceive* organizational doctrine as the researcher did; they had not even much thought about it as an integrated whole. On the other hand, the data also show clearly that the actors indeed *handled* doctrine not as a monolithic whole or "the stable reference point of the institution and of its interaction with the environment" as the "Guiding Concepts" of the I.B. Program suggested (Esman and Blaise, 1966, p. 10), but as a flexible combination of different elements. (p. 265)

[92] WEIDNER, Edward W. *Technical Assistance in Public Adminis-tration Overseas: The Case for Development Administration.* Chicago, Ill.: Public Administration Service, 1964. 247 pages.

The objectives of the research, the results of which are presented in this book, were to (1) describe major programs of technical assistance in public administration, (2) broadly examine their effect, and (3) reach some conclusions about their signifi-cance. In reporting his findings, Edward Weidner addresses the following topics: goals, agencies, personnel, academic effects, effects on host governments, environment of public administra-tion, educational perspectives, development administration, and strategy for technical assistance programs.

Although Weidner concentrates on describing the public ad-ministration institutes and their interaction with technical assis-tance teams, he does reach some conclusions such as, "The aca-demic programs of the institutes of public administration have had only small influence on the host governments" (p. 118). Subse-quently, he deals with explanations for the limited impact of technical assistance in public administration. He concludes, "if technical assistance in public administration is to make a maxi-mum contribution to the national development of the less favor-ably situated countries of the world, it should be restructured along development administration lines. Development administra-tion requires the right kind of political and administrative bases" (pp. 218-19). The author maintains further that the development of a philosophy and a strategy for encouraging change is an essential prerequisite for any technical assistance agency to have a meaningful program that will result in maximum impact.

[93] BJUR, W. E. "Technical Assistance and Institution Building: A University Experience in Brazil." Unpublished Ph.D. disserta-tion, Claremont Graduate School, Claremont, Calif., 1967. 293 pages.

In this analysis—closely related to research in Brazil by Frank Sherwood [90], in California by A. U. Qureshi [73], and in Brazil by Jose Silva de Carvalho [94]—W. E. Bjur identifies some of the shortcomings of the institution building conceptualization of Esman et al. They are (1) the need to focus on indigenization rather than institutionalization, (2) the lack of explicit consideration of time, and (3) the need to focus on indigenization of innovations rather than organizations. Subsequently, an indigenization model is developed that provides for the following four stages in the process of indigenizing innovations: (1) charismatic stage, (2) professionalization stage, (3) legitimation stage, and (4) institutionalization.

The first necessary step in the charismatic stage is an assessment of the relative receptivity of the environment to the innovation or to the institutional doctrine that bears it, and to the leadership that proposes it. For a new organization to provide more than it is demanding from its environment it is nearly always forced to resort to charisma as an indispensable element. Likewise, nonmaterial rewards frequently constitute the most important inducement for employees of a new organization. Especially in instances where the environment is relatively unreceptive, pure charisma of a personal nature, found in some indigenous, non-affiliated leader is preferred. This stage is illustrated for the host institution studied by Bjur.

Sooner or later the first stage of charisma must be gradually replaced by professional competence, vis-à-vis the functions which the organization is designed to carry out. This functional competence is indispensable in acquiring resources, among other things, but functional competence is also required within the organization so that performance can be rewarded by increased professional prestige. Again, this stage is illustrated by the Brazilian host institution.

> The goals of indigenization are reached when the innovation has become "normal practice" for the client system, when the organization or group carrying on the function is seen by the larger society as carrying on the task which belongs to it, which it has the right to do. (p. 271)

As with the other two stages, Bjur subsequently illustrates this one.

The final stage of institutionalization is discussed with the assistance of criteria for obtaining resources from the environment developed by Esman et al.

[94] CARVALHO, J. Silva, de. "EBAP: An Experiment in Institution Building." Unpublished Ph.D. dissertation, University of Southern California, Los Angeles, Calif., January 1968. 642 pages. (Part of Inter-University Research Program in Institution Building.)

In this analysis of the Brazilian School of Public Administration (EBAP) the major hypothesis is that organizations can be differentiated from institutions on the basis of the following capabilities: (1) to enhance survival, (2) to exert influence, (3) to innovate, (4) to engage in self-determination, (5) to infuse its internal population with values, and (6) to respond to norms and values prized by the environment. The four sets of working hypotheses used in the analysis were based on the first, third, fifth, and sixth of these capabilities.

In summarizing the results of the inquiry, J. Silva de Carvalho concludes that institutionalization is a process which is to be understood in terms of degree. The process can further be considered from the perspective of a syndrome of symptoms of institutionalization. More specifically, he states:

1. The symptoms of institutionalization which have been identified in this study—often called institutionalizing forces, or ultimate tests of institutionalization—seemed to have been demonstrated in the case of EBAP as a useful theoretical device. . . .

2. EBAP's experience has shown that institution-building theory cannot be, by its nature, value-free. . . .

3. EBAP's experience emphasizes two key elements in the process of institution building: goals and leadership. In fact, leadership at EBAP was the single most important factor which brought about the transformations which ultimately affected the character of the School. . . .

4. Goals are an expression of the group and they serve to demarcate areas in which there is a declared intention to exercise influence. (pp. 567-70)

Trade Union

[95] SUFRIN, Sidney C. "Transactions of Trade Unions and Government in Developing Societies." Graduate School of Public and International Affairs, University of Pittsburgh, Pitts-

burgh, Pa., undated. 306 pages. (Mimeographed. Part of Inter-University Research Program in Institution Building.)

This economic analysis develops the contention that unions provide a point of synthesis between the frustrations of development and the aspirations of new elites in developing societies. Almost inevitably this arrangement demands political adjustments to social and economic issues. These political adjustments are further necessitated by the unions' financial dependence upon government and political parties, the impracticability of lengthy strikes, and the need for labor leaders to be involved in the political arena in order to secure financial security for their unions.

In light of the above, three multivariable regression equations are hypothesized for the following dependent variables: (1) number of industrial disputes as a percentage of nonagricultural employment; (2) number of man-days lost as a percentage of nonagricultural employment; and (3) number of workers involved as a percentage of nonagricultural employment. The models are tested with the use of data collected from the United Nations' sources and the International Labor Organization.

Although the results indicate that there are no regularities in the relationships between the variables under consideration and among countries, several conclusions are reached. First, trade unions and government in the Third World arrive at adjustments in the political arena over such economic issues as wages and social overhead expenditures. Second, this process of political accommodation may result in a wide range of treatments for unions, ranging from outlawing them to giving them freedom of action. Third, there is no clear indication that these political accommodations have had an adverse effect upon activities related to growth and development. Finally, the forms of labor protest used in developing societies appear to have stronger effects on wages and budget expenditures than in the four developed countries analyzed.

Youth

[96] EATON, Joseph W., in collaboration with Michael Chen. *Influencing the Youth Culture*. Beverly Hills, Calif.: Sage Publications, 1970. 256 pages.

This book is a case study of a comprehensive effort to get young people in Israel to identify with the core ideals of their parents' generation through youth organizations. Part I discusses general issues of planning within youth culture and the role of youth organizations in the process of generational transition. Part II presents the research setting and the findings of an extensive field study of Israel's youth programs.

Of special interest is Chapter 8 entitled "Institution Building: The Gadna." The Gadna, or youth corps, organized in 1939, is reviewed as a case study in institution building:

> The planful establishment of a new organizational arrangement to serve purposes which are thought to require more and different resources than those which can be allocated by already existing administrative units. (p. 140)

Because of the military situation in 1939, Jews in Palestine were involved on three fronts: against Germany, against the British, and against Arab guerillas. Jewish adolescent manpower was thought to be a valuable resource to prepare in case of need. A decision was made to establish a physical education program (Hagam) to serve as a legal cover for what was a proscribed activity, a youth corps in high schools. The youth corps evolved into a permanent administrative organization combining educational with military requirements, linked to two major institutions: school and army.

After establishment of Israel (1948), the need for a clandestine youth corps disappeared. When an institution attains its goals, how does it continue? To avoid an "achievement crisis," it is necessary to adapt, to continually reevaluate programs. In the case of the Gadna, paramilitary objectives were supplemented by social welfare, educational, and developmental goals. Consequently, it has survived as a nonpolitical youth program. It is partly compulsory during school, but offers a wide range of extracurricular activities. Since it is sponsored by both the Ministries of Defense and Education, it has a highly flexible program, but has retained a stable organizational structure since its beginning. (This information on Gadna also appears in citation [213].)

[97] COE, Richard L. "The Kenya National Youth Service: A Study in Institution Building." Syracuse University, Syracuse, N.Y.,

undated. (Mimeographed. Part of Inter-University Research Program in Institution Building.)

The emphasis in this report is on prerequisites to an organization becoming institutionalized. Toward this end, the author analyzes the development of Kenya's National Youth Service (NYS) from mid-1964 to late 1966.

Richard Coe discusses at length the different groups which were motivated to have a youth service. The four major groups were: (1) the Kenya African National Union (KANU) Youth Wing; (2) the pressured groups, including the trade unionists and party members who are under direct pressure from the youth and unemployed; (3) the expatriate commercial farming and business community—expatriate whites who were subject to destructive activities of KANU youths and unemployed, landless Kenyans; and (4) the governing elite—those elected officials who formulated policy in government.

The second major condition considered was the unemployment crisis. Although there was an unemployment problem before independence, the people expected great changes after independence. From 1961 to 1963, the number of wage earners actually decreased. From January to March, 1964, there were a series of demonstrations in Nairobi. Again, the time was ripe. The government announced the establishment of NYS. The general objectives, set forth by the governing elite were (1) to put unemployed young people in an environment promoting good citizenship and contributing to social and economic development of the country; (2) to promote national unity by recruiting youths from all of Kenya; (3) to provide employment, education, and training for future productive employment; (4) to contribute to the economy of the country by developing Kenya's natural resources.

On August 16, 1964, the Nairobi Training Unit began. Coe studies the NYS from mid-1964 to late 1966 when he concluded his work in Kenya. He reviews the difficulties encountered by the NYS during this period.

For evaluation purposes, Coe uses several mapping procedures including (1) the blueprint map, which indicates the form that the institution is intended to take; (2) the operations map, which gives data pertaining to what actually occurred; and (3) the image map, showing how individuals perceive the institution as working. Since the researcher was unable to obtain access to certain groups vital to the image mapping, he concentrated on the blueprint and operations mappings.

Coe observes several sources of degradation: (1) Expecting too much of the institution too soon. The haste in starting the program resulted in deficiencies in both staff and planning. (2) Lack of available resources in the form of advisers and equipment, especially in the vocational training program. In theory (on blueprint) monies and equipment were available from various external sources, but problems were encountered in obtaining them. (3) A possible degradation which Coe foresees is that the size and scope of NYS might be too expensive for the government of Kenya.

CROSS-SECTIONAL ANALYSIS OF INSTITUTIONS

[98] BALDWIN, I. L., Project Director; Rigney, J. A.; Roskelley, R. W.; and Thompson, W. N. *Building Institutions to Serve Agriculture.* Lafayette, Ind.: Committee on Institutional Cooperation, Purdue University, 1968. 236 pages. (Part of Committee on Institutional Cooperation and Agency for International Development Rural Development Research Project.)

In the foreword, I. L. Baldwin et al. state:

Under the sponsorship of the Committee on Institutional Cooperation and supported in large part by A.I.D. funds, some thirty-five senior staff members of nine state universities have been engaged for the past three years in various aspects of a broad study of the factors affecting the success of the A.I.D.-supported university projects with the developing nations in the field of institutional and rural development. The studies reported here were confined to the technical assistance efforts of United States universities in the field of building institutions to serve agriculture; however, many of the findings may be found useful to technical assistance efforts in other fields. (p. xiii)

In the overall summary the authors contend that the technical assistance programs in agriculture have been good enough to justify their continuation and expansion but poor enough to require prompt action from the Agency for International Development and the universities for their improvement. The authors urge that continuation and expansion move in the direction of flexible, long-term programs that are goal oriented.

The specific recommendations resulting from the investigation are:

> 1. There should be a stronger commitment on the part of all participating agencies to an expanded and long-term program of building institutions to serve agriculture. (p. 4)

> 2. More flexible project agreements and improved liaison between A.I.D. and the university community would effect needed improvements in A.I.D.-university relations. (p. 7)

> 3. Research on the institution building process should be significantly increased and existing knowledge should be utilized more effectively. (p. 9)

> 4. The basic ideas that underlie the land grant type institution are highly relevant in technical assistance projects if properly understood and employed. (p. 10)

> 5. Agreement on goals and commitment to an overall strategy by host and U.S. personnel should be strengthened by wider participation in project planning and review. (p. 12)

> 6. Those aspects of technical assistance programs which have contributed to the highly negative attitudes of many university staff members and department heads should be changed. (p. 14)

> 7. There should be fundamental changes in orientation programs in order to prepare team members adequately for their overseas assignments. (p. 17)

> 8. Programs of participant training should be more carefully planned and more adequately supported so that they conform to the developmental needs of host institutions. (p. 19)

> 9. The university community should exert its leadership in developing a fuller public understanding of international technical assistance. (p. 21)

> 10. A.I.D. and the universities should cooperate in strengthening the international capabilities of U.S. universities. (p. 22)

In addition, the authors give more specific details for most of the recommendations.

The recommendations above are given in the first chapter; the chapters that follow are "The Problem," "The Background,"

"Effects on Host Institutions," "Effects on U.S. Universities," "Development of the Project," "Operation of Contract Programs," "Basic Factors Conditioning Success," and "Overall Costs and Accomplishments."

The book includes a wealth of information, among which are the following factors that are associated with successful projects:

1. The preproject planning was better than average. . . .

2. The sponsoring institution in the U.S. was a strong university with a staff large enough to field the size of team that was necessary to make change possible and meaningful.

3. The U.S. university field teams were, in general, technically well-trained. . . .

4. There was evidence that team members on successful projects knew something of the varied and subtle aspects of institutional development. . . .

5. Home campus backstopping was good. . . .

6. There was continuity of leadership of project operation by the major parties.

7. The technicians stayed on the job long enough to discover a job that needed to be done and worked in a meaningful fashion to complete a task before returning home. . . .

8. All long-term projects did not succeed in building mature institutions, but all of the more mature institutions had participated in project operations for eight years or more. . . .

9. Good participant training programs, involving significant numbers of the staff with many obtaining higher degrees, were often a great source of change within the institution. . . .

10. Desires of host nationals were an important factor in determining success of projects. . . .

11. Successful projects showed a significant increase in outputs—more students, more graduates, additional graduate programs, research projects related to vital local and national problems, and significant off-campus educational activities.

12. Some of the more important changes associated with institutional growth involved changes of attitude and commitment. (pp. 62-64)

In the summary to the final chapter, Baldwin et al. state:

Although there are wide variations in the effectiveness of various projects, it is clear that the university contract program in agriculture has made important contributions abroad at comparatively small cost to the United States in money, manpower, and interruption of domestic programs. The overall past record demonstrates that the use of U.S. university teams to assist a less developed nation build an institution to serve agriculture can be very productive abroad and well managed at home. Unfortunately not all have been equally productive abroad and well managed at home. The challenge now is to make better use of the experience which we have gained to improve the performance both abroad and at home. Most of the needed improvements will require cooperative action by A.I.D. and the universities. The program should be improved, continued, and expanded. (p. 230)

Finally, the publication contains references to the individual research reports of the project cited herein as [31], [32], [38], [41], [48], [99], [100], [101], [102], [103], [105], [106], [107], [108], [109], [120], [136].

[99] THOMPSON, William N.; Guither, Harold D.; Regnier, Earl H.; and Propp, Kathleen M. "AID-University Rural Development Contracts and U.S. Universities." University of Illinois, Urbana, Ill., 1968. 192 pages. (Mimeographed. Part of Committee on Institutional Cooperation and Agency for International Development Rural Development Research Project.)

This portion of the CIC-AID Rural Development Research Project was undertaken by a multidisciplinary team at the University of Illinois. The objectives of their portion of the project were:

1. To evaluate the effects of participation in international technical assistance activities upon U.S. universities' domestic and foreign program capabilities.

2. To determine how and to what extent AID and U.S. universities' policies and practices influence technical assistance project effectiveness.

3. To establish criteria for determining the types of projects appropriate for U.S. university implementation. (pp. 2-3)

In turn, these objectives were divided into the following ten subprojects:

... contract team characteristics and personnel practices; campus back-stopping organizations and practices; the role of executive visits to overseas projects; impacts of AID contract programs on university departments; impacts of programs on the international work of universities; participant training effectiveness; commodity assistance in overseas projects; project evaluation policies and practices; university contractor/AID relations; and the role of universities in international rural development. (p. 3)

Data were obtained from (1) university-AID contract project files, (2) university personnel, (3) AID personnel in Washington, D.C., and (4) the four overseas research analysts who spent approximately 18 months in each of 4 major regions of the world. Data were obtained from university personnel through interviews at 32 universities. Likewise, selected AID/Washington personnel were asked to complete several questionnaires. In addition, the overseas research analysts obtained data through interviews with university contract team members and team leaders, AID mission personnel, and representatives of host institutions and host governments.

The authors present the findings of this inquiry in the following order: (1) a description of university involvement with AID contracts in the 68 projects, (2) university support of the overseas projects, (3) effects of the contract programs in U.S. universities, (4) analyses of university technical assistance programs and recommendations for their improvement, and (5) technical assistance programs as a means of improving university competence for international work in the future.

In the summary chapter the authors focus on (1) the general effectiveness of universities; (2) the varying degrees of university commitment to international activities; (3) integration of organized overseas projects into campus programs; and (4) the future role of universities in international activities. The authors point out that the overseas research analysts rated eight of the overseas university projects outstanding and seven excellent in terms of their effectiveness. Although all factors responsible for these levels of performance were not identified, there was a relationship between effectiveness and the depth of university commitment to international work.

The following evidences of involvement in international activities by universities with commitment were found:

(1) The university is interested in developing its stature in the international area and recognizes international work as a legitimate concern of the university deserving added resources. (2) Faculty members are involved in an organized way in major policy decisions on international work. . . . (3) On-campus personnel are actively engaged in determining policies and strategies for the university's contribution to overseas projects. . . . (4) International work is an integral part of the work of the departments. . . . (5) There is an administrative organization to give leadership in the international area with effective means of communication among faculty members and among administrators at different levels—university, college, and department—and across college and departmental lines. . . . (6) Faculty members who have returned from overseas assignments are using their experience to build university programs and competence in the international area. . . . (7) University personnel policies encourage faculty members to accept foreign assignments with assurance that their positions with respect to rank promotion, salary, position upon return, and fringe benefits are not jeopardized. (p. 166)

With regard to integrating international contract programs with overall campus activities, the authors found that there were many unexploited opportunities to use faculty members' experiences abroad to improve university international programs. Much of the reason for this is due to the nature and objectives of contract projects. Hence, overseas service-oriented contracting arrangements must be complemented and supplemented to strengthen university competence in international development.

The following criteria were formulated for determining the appropriateness of university involvement in future AID contracts:

1. The university must have strength and competency in the area or discipline in which the work is to be done.

2. The project should involve institution building—the building of organizational competence, traditions, and attitudes which make for a sense of purpose. The host institution may be a university, research station, an extension service, credit agency, or a government department.

3. The program should enable the university to derive some benefit and establish some continuing relations.

4. The project should enable individual staff members to perform in the areas of work that they know best—teaching, research, extension, and as consultants in their specific technical fields.

5. The project should enable Americans to train host country citizens so that they can carry on specific activities without American assistance. (pp. 171-72)

[100] WARNKEN, Philip F. "Strategies for Technical Assistance." University of Missouri, Columbia, Mo., 1968. 75 pages. (Mimeographed. Part of Committee on Institutional Cooperation and Agency for International Development Rural Development Research Project.)

Philip Warnken describes the approach taken by USAID technical assistance contractors as follows:

> The traditional and standard approach to institution building . . . has been to employ a bevy of technicians, line them up with host counterparts and then hope that, somehow, some way, something magic will take place and an institution will be built. (p. 67)

In summarizing the results of an analysis of this approach he states:

> In conclusion, the traditional institution building approach is a generally unsatisfactory means of accomplishing the perceived desired objectives. Not only is it unsatisfactory, it is also far more expensive than it need be. Cost could be considered a rather insignificant matter if there was not rather overwhelming evidence that superfluous and redundant resources often tend to be destructive to the very purpose of institution building. And on this question there can now be little debate. (p. 71)

In analyzing potential strategies of technical assistance, Warnken focuses on the alternative technical assistance inputs of U.S. cash and commodities, stateside training for personnel, and direct assistance of U.S. technical personnel. In formulating a mix of these alternatives to be employed under a strategy the following criteria were considered: dependency, acceptability, feasibility, urgency, and economy. In addition, attention is called to the fact that the following elements must be affected in the institution building process: leadership, organizational structure, program content, technical competence, fiscal and physical resource base, and the institution's aggregate attitude. Warnken summarizes the results of his analysis of strategy as follows:

> The real functional role of individual technical inputs must be the focus of concern. It was determined that few constraints are imposed on cash and commodity inputs. The functional role of these inputs, however, is indeed limited: only one institution building element—the fiscal and physical resource base—is notably affected. Hence, other than affecting this one element, cash and commodity inputs have no significant role to play in institution building efforts.
>
> Participant training programs are the most flexible of all input forms. Training can be utilized to affect each critical institution building element selectively through deliberate program design. Leadership qualities, including organizational and program content considerations can be modified effectively through the use of short-term, non-technical tours. Technical competence can be upgraded through specialized short-term training. Long-term participant training, while generally used to enhance technical competence, often has even greater long run impacts on other institution building elements. Coupling participant training with short tours for U.S. technical personnel is generally a more effective means of assisting the development of institutions than using numerous long-term resident technical personnel. Participant training aided by an integrated relationship with the assisting U.S. university should be looked upon as a crucial institution building input.
>
> U.S. technical personnel have been attractive inputs in technical assistance activities largely because their *potential* influence on various institution building elements is great. There is, however, evidence that this *potential* is seldom realized. Too many constraints surround their use for technical personnel inputs to be effective. And shifting the function of such personnel from an advisory role to a participating role in the host institution only exaggerates present difficulties. This implies that the use of highly specialized resident technical personnel should be avoided. Instead a very limited number of very high-level U.S. advisory personnel should be employed to assist host institution leadership in organizational and program content matters. In addition, subject matter specialists can be turned to on a short-term basis for the upgrading of specific technical areas. For maximum impact, long-term leadership advisors and short-term specialists should be intimately coupled with participant training programs. (pp. 72-73)

[101] POTTER, Harry R. "Criteria of Progress and Impacts of Technical Assistance Projects in Agriculture." Purdue University, Lafayette, Ind., 1968. 56 pages. (Mimeographed. Part of Committee on Institutional Cooperation and Agency for

International Development Rural Development Research Project.)

In the first portion of this analysis several criteria were developed and used to highlight changes that have occurred in agricultural institutions that have hosted a U.S. technical assistance team. These criteria were grouped into the following categories: (1) facilitating mechanisms, (2) inputs and outputs, and (3) relationships between the institution and society. In summarizing the findings of 25 projects, Harry Potter states:

> Most of the indicators show changes that are consistent with the institution building approach at most of the institutions. The majority show increases in inputs of students and staff, and in outputs of number of graduates, extension and research work. There are exceptions to this, as noted. There also have been changes in facilitating mechanisms. Teaching, research and extension programs have increased either through the addition of programs or through increased relationships with other agencies, although there are cases where university staff members have little participation in research or extension work. Explanations for these changes can be found in the attitude and commitment of the faculty and administration to the conduct of research and extension, and in the location of these activities in the university or in the Ministry of Agriculture. There is evidence of improved relationships with other organizations in the society at many of the projects, which has facilitated an increase in outputs and program. The increase in physical facilities has also been beneficial in increasing outputs. However, in some areas at some institutions there have been relatively few changes; some are a long way from resembling a Land Grant institution. (p. 33)

In the second portion of the analysis the evaluations of the host institutions made by the senior overseas researchers (SOR) of the CIC-AID research project are summarized. The following are highlights of that summary:

> Generally, the SOR's indicated improvement on most criteria, although the quality of entering students and sense of problems by host institution personnel seemed especially resistant to improvement. There was also a high percentage of projects where extension and research were rated as currently being not very useful. High ratings on improvement of quality and adequacy of physical facilities suggest that material changes were most easily achieved. Ratings on projects that have been in existence eight years or longer were compared with ratings on shorter-term projects. This also represented a comparison of projects

with larger and smaller expenditures of AID funds and USU [United States University] manpower. To some extent, the ratings on longer-term projects reflect greater progress than the shorter-term projects on most criteria, but there are exceptions. As might be expected, ratings on the quality and adequacy of physical facilities reflect only slight differences between the longer-term and shorter-term projects which seems to indicate that this is one of the first and easiest changes to make. Ratings on extension and research show some improvement in practicality for longer-term projects over shorter-term projects, but many longer-term projects retain low ratings. Ratings on sense of problem indicate paradoxically that this is better developed in shorter-term projects than longer-term projects. Quality of entering students seems to have improved more for the longer-term projects. Quality of education seems to present the most consistent evidence of greater improvement at longer-term projects. . . .

The data indicate the importance of time in the institution building process. On four criteria, quality of students, quality of education, practicality of extension and practicality of research, the longer-term projects were rated higher than the shorter-term projects. It takes time for the relationships between the institution and other segments of society to be initiated, stabilized and crystalized. This suggests that short term projects should be limited to solving specific technical problems or providing physical facilities, but that institution building requires long-term commitments. (p. 49)

In the overall summary of the report Potter calls attention to the most significant changes in the host institutions. Three factors seemed to be important in effecting these changes. The first of these was the role played by participant trainees who had returned to the host institution. As a consequence of not only their training but also of the understanding they gained about the organization and program of land grant universities, these individuals add greatly to the indigenous staff. The second factor was the development of a research program. Institutions appeared to progress more rapidly if they had a research component, which enabled them to produce visible outputs of utility to society as well as increase the competence of their instructional staff. The third important factor was the nature and extent of relationships the host institution had with outside organizations. Those institutions showing greater progress tended to have established more cooperative relationships with other agricultural institutions and these, in turn, reciprocated by providing opportunities for the university, as well as increasing its responsibility for information and services. Finally, two common problems were (1) the lack of continuity of leadership in the host institution, the technical assistance team, and the Ministry of Agriculture, and (2) the inadequate duration of many technical assistance projects. Potter repeatedly stressed the fact that institution building takes time.

[102] ROSKELLEY, R. W. *Pre-Contract Planning*. Logan, Utah: Utah State University, 1968. 15 pages. (Part of Committee on Institutional Cooperation and Agency for International Development Rural Development Research Project.)

From the standpoint of a sociologist with administrative experience, R. W. Roskelley examined precontract survey reports and their consequences as part of the CIC-AID research project. In only 3 cases out of the 42 studied was any attention given to the consideration of the more subtle aspects of institution building, such as essential value systems, norms, and patterns of human relations. Further, the evidence suggested that the precontract reports were largely unilateral and afforded the host country nationals no opportunity to either concur in or disagree with the material they contained.

On-site interviews revealed that no one below the organizational level of dean had been involved in precontract planning in selected Asian universities. This failure to involve more people resulted, in some cases, in mediocre project performance and, in others, lack of accomplishment altogether. Both members of the host institutions and groups responsible for funding university activities failed to understand what end products were sought as a consequence of technical assistance efforts.

An examination of end-of-tour reports prepared by technicians and contract termination reports provided very little insight about precontract planning. In most instances there was no mention of the role played by preliminary planning in subsequent activities related to institutional development.

In place of the conventional approach to precontract planning Roskelley suggests that planning operations be divided into two segments. The first would be a three- to four-month feasibility study and the second a bilateral, in-depth, precontract planning study to last one year. They should be designed to develop a spirit of mutual trust, confidence, and understanding among the representatives of the two countries. Further, they should result in blueprints that would spell out the ultimate goals, the steps necessary to achieve these goals, and the roles and responsibilities of the different parties to the developmental process.

[103] ATKINSON, J. H. "U.S. University Field Team and AID-Field Relationships." Purdue University, Lafayette, Ind., 1968. 20 pages. (Mimeographed. Part of Committee on Institutional Cooperation and Agency for International Development Rural Development Research Project.)

In this companion report to "Extent of Administrative Unity Within the Technical Assistance Complex" by David Ellsworth [108], the most important propositions with regard to identification of problems by members of the Technical Assistance Complex are presented and discussed. The following seven statements summarize the responses to these propositions obtained from the AID field team (AID-F), AID personnel based in Washington (AID-W), U.S. university contract field team members (USU-F), and U.S. university personnel based in the United States (USU-C):

1. There was substantial agreement by all administrative entities except AID-F that problems of agreement on or understanding AID-F and USU-F working relationships impaired project performance. AID-F did not feel this problem as acutely as the other units.

2. AID entities view USU's as impairing field unit working relations by exercising undue independence while USU's accuse AID-F of impairing working relations by regarding USU-F as operationally subordinate.

3. All of the administrative units are alert to the possibility that emphasis on operational matters may cause neglect of larger problems but field units are much less concerned than the U.S. based entities.

4. USU's feel that project performance is impaired by relationships between USU-F and AID-F which even seem to place USU-F in a subordinate role. The USU entities expressed only slight agreement to disagreement with this notion.

5. All groups expressed nearly complete or substantial agreement with the idea that the contract alone can create proper working relation-

ships. USU team members and AID-F respondents seemed to have more confidence in the contract than other groups.

6. All groups tended to favor more peer, collaborative and cooperative relationships between USU-F and AID-F, but they recognized some of the difficulties involved in establishing such relationships.

7. Only USU-C expressed some agreement with the idea of transferring problems of conflict between field units to their U.S. based counterparts. (p. 16)

The following remedial measures are suggested:

First, an effort should be made, at the USU-C, AID-W level to identify those problems which can be solved "by decree.". . .

Second, it should be recognized that no joint effort can long endure which does not result in greater achievement of the objectives of both parties than if they had acted alone. . . .

Third, much more effort needs to be devoted to means of accumulating and using the experience gained by USU team members. . . .

Fourth, means to promote collaborative relations between USU-F and AID-F need to be established. . . .

Finally, the matter of how to communicate demands more attention. (pp. 17-18)

[104] DUNCAN, Richard L. "Technical Assistance and Institution Building." *International Development.* Edited by H. W. Singer, Nicolas De Kun, and Abbas Ordoobadi. Dobbs Ferry, N.Y.: Oceana Publications, Inc., 1967. Pp. 113-20.

In reflecting on the nearly completed study of the administration of technical assistance at the Maxwell School, Syracuse University, Richard Duncan uses two broad categories to illustrate the way technical assistance has influenced institution building: demonstration and exhortation. Within the latter he identifies the following specific activities by which advisers have influenced institution building: (1) Long-term technical assistance, ten to twenty years in length, has tended to characterize successful projects. (2) When only a few advisers are used, impetus is placed on mobilizing local resources. (3) Close identification of advisers with their host institutions appears to be important during an early period of development. (4) Success has been facilitated by the use of a saleable doctrine. (5) Advisers have had an effect on institutional survival when they have been able to promote constructive relationships between the host institutions and other organizations in the environment.

[105] MILLER, William L. "Team Leader." Purdue University, Lafayette, Ind., 1968. 17 pages. (Mimeographed. Part of Committee on Institutional Cooperation and Agency for International Development Rural Development Research Project.)

> This paper is divided into three major sections. The first section examines the theory of leadership, management, and organization related to the task of a team leader in an institutional building environment in a developing nation. The second section describes the function and special problems of team leaders working in a developing country. The third section synthesizes the theoretical framework of the first section and the empirical information from the second section to develop suggested modifications in the environment, selection, and training of team leaders to improve team leader performance. (p. 1)

Although difficult to describe, several characteristics of team leaders seem to be essential from a theoretical point of view. One of these is that leaders should have the ability to develop the respect and trust of the team members. Another is that leaders should have drive and a capacity for hard work. In addition, successful leadership is facilitated by effective communications. Finally, the leader's span of control should not be so large as to prevent effective communications.

The following functions of team leaders are discussed: (1) relating the foreign team to the indigenous society, (2) developing a plan of work related to project goals, (3) ensuring high team morale, and (4) handling the routine administrative matters.

Two broad conclusions are reached. One is that there is a substantial need for improvement in the communication of ideas and information by team leaders. Several alternative methods for improving the communications process are given. The other broad conclusion is that the goal of linking the technical assistance team to the indigenous society should have top priority with regard to a team leader's activities. Again suggestions are given concerning methods of accomplishing this goal.

[106] WAYT, William A. "AID, Agriculture, and Africa: A Perspective on University Contract Projects." Ohio State University, Columbus, Ohio, 1968. 103 pages. (Mimeographed. Part of Committee on Institutional Cooperation and Agency for International Development Rural Development Research Project.)

William Wayt addresses this report to the administrators of the Agency for International Development and of U.S. universities who have undertaken commitments to provide technical assistance in agriculture in Africa under AID contracts. He states:

> This report is an attempt to try to draw generalizations from the experiences of practitioners, discuss problems indicated by such practitioners as being important in influencing the course of project developments together with recommendations for improvements in programs. (p. 1)

The report is based on an eighteen-month analysis of sixteen college contract programs for agriculture in Africa. Diversity characterized both the projects and the region itself.

After discussing operational problems of technical assistance in detail, Wayt concludes:

> In this region with changing personnel in host government, changing goals and objectives as expressed by that government, and the long term nature of some of the kinds of projects desired; it would appear that close working relationships are required between the USAID Mission in the field and contractor entities attempting to carry out specific objectives. These conditions would also seem to place limitations on the extent to which specific very long term objectives can be enunciated and pursued. This would seem to place the emphasis on development of projects or programs with a degree of flexibility in their implementation.
>
> There is need both for more realistic timetables in pursuit of stated goals and of better devices for measurement of rates of progress or accomplishment toward those objectives. (p. 103)

[107] McDERMOTT, J. K. "Administrative Procedures and Strategies of the Technical Assistance Complex in Institution Building Contracts." Purdue University, Lafayette, Ind., 1968. 31 pages. (Mimeographed. Part of Committee on Institutional Cooperation and Agency for International Development Rural Development Research Project.)

This report contains some tentative generalizations on three important aspects of contracting for institution building. These statements were developed from the experiences, observations, and opinions available to the researchers who studied approximately fifteen years of technical assistance contracting experience compiled by the late 1960s.

> These are: (1) the organizational relationships that exist between the Agency for International Development and the Contracting University throughout the contracting endeavor, (2) the processes involved and the Host Institution changes sought in the institution-building activity itself, and (3) the conduct of the Contracting University's field team in the actual accomplishment of the institution building. (p. 2)

Subsequently, the institution building concepts developed by Esman et al. are summarized. Finally, the initial conceptualization of the technical assistance institution building process prepared by McDermott et al. (see [32]) is presented.

[108] ELLSWORTH, David F. "Extent of Administrative Unity Within the Technical Assistance Complex." Purdue University, Lafayette, Ind., 1968. 33 pages. (Mimeographed. Part of Committee on Institutional Cooperation and Agency for International Development Rural Development Research Project.)

This report—a companion report to "U.S. University Field Team and AID-Field Relationships" by J. H. Atkinson [103]—contains the results of an analysis of administrative unity found in technical assistance complexes in the late 1960s. For purposes of this analysis a technical assistance complex includes USAID Missions, AID/Washington, contracting university's field team, and the campus complex of the contracting university. Administrative unity is interpreted to mean the degree to which these entities agreed upon a given proposition.

A list of propositions was mailed to selected individuals of the four components of the technical assistance complex. Subsequently, the data were analyzed. Those propositions upon which there was the greatest and the least administrative unity were chosen for discussion.

Two propositions are of special interest: the one upon which there was the least degree of administrative unity and the one upon which there was the most unity. The former proposition reads:

> The most common threat to productive, cooperative relations between the field units of AID and USU [United States University] from USAID/M [USAID/country mission] is its tendency to regard USU field team as operationally subordinate. (There is no question of USAID's authority on general policy matters.) (p. 5)

The latter proposition was:

> TAC [Technical Assistance Complex] bargaining personnel need to know almost as well as HC [Host Country] people the bargain the Host Country can accept and fulfill. If it doesn't, it runs the risk of forcing bargains the HCC (Host Country Complex) [host government and institution] cannot live with which could cause loss of respect and trust. (p. 30)

Subsequently, each of these and the other propositions presented are discussed and conclusions about their implications are drawn.

OTHER RELEVANT LITERATURE

Analytic Reviews

[109] RICHARDSON, John M., Jr. *Partners in Development—An Analysis of AID-University Relations, 1950-1966.* East Lansing, Mich.: Michigan State University Press, 1969. 272 pages. (Part of Committee on Institutional Cooperation and Agency for International Development Rural Development Research Project.)

Part I of the book, "From Genesis to Harmony—A History of Stability and Change in Agency-University Relations," is divided into the following chapters: "The Agency-University Relationship: An Overview"; "The Period of Genesis (1949-1953)"; "The Period of Proliferation (November 1953-June 1955)"; "The Period of Retrenchment (July 1955-September 1957)"; "The Period of Inertia (September 1957-September 1961)"; "The Interregnum (September 1961-December 1962)"; and "The Period of Harmony (1963-1966)." Part II, "Persistent Issues, Environmental Constants and Behavioral Patterns: An Analysis of Stability and Change in Agency-University Relations" contains three more chapters: "Persisting and Unresolved Issues"; "Historical Patterns and Individual Behavior: A Framework for Analysis"; and "The Statics and Dynamics of Agency-University Relations."

After tracing the history of AID-university relations, John Richardson examines in detail five persisting and unresolved issues: equal partnership, university autonomy versus agency control, contractual form, project length, and personnel clearance. The last of these is described as a partially resolved but persistent issue.

The following statements capture much of the essence of the findings of the analysis:

> In conclusion, it seems appropriate to examine briefly the major policy implications of this study. Perhaps the most significant finding to emerge is the degree to which the persistence of divisive issues in Agency-university relations must be attributed to the factors which have been labeled "environmental variables" and to the structural characteristics which have been caused by these factors. Unless there is a considerable increase in the knowledge about technical assistance and development or a major shift in Congressional attitudes, it is difficult to see how there can be a significant, long-term change in Agency-university relations. Moreover, policy changes which attempt to alter the "intervening variables" without altering the factors which influence them are likely to be no more effective in the future than they have been in the past. An exceptional [AID] administrator, such as David Bell, may be able to affect some moderate improvements for a short time but these are likely to be no more than transient phenomena.

> This conclusion leads to a second important finding regarding the changes which have occurred. From the standpoint of the university-contract program, these might almost be called chance occurrences for the goals of the program have not been influential premises for the key decisions which were made. Whether or not a particular decision had unintended effects, good or bad, on the university-contract program was simply not a major consideration in the decision-making process by which administrators were selected and major Agency policies were determined. For example, there is no evidence to suggest that David Bell's favorable attitude toward university contracting and unique ability to communicate with university officials was a factor which led to his selection as administrator. Nor for that matter was [ICA director] John Hollister's disinterest in university projects and inability to communicate with university officials a significant factor affecting his selection. Moreover, considerations related to the university-contract program were rarely taken into account in the major organizational

changes which have occurred. Thus, to understand what has happened and not happened to Agency-university relations during the past seventeen years, it is essential to recognize that the university-contract program has been a very small frog in a rather large and often turbulent puddle. (pp. 204–5)

[110] BLAISE, Hans C. "The Literature on Institution Building (A Bibliographic Note)." University of Pittsburgh, Pittsburgh, Pa., June 1964. 13 pages. (Mimeographed.)

This represents one of the initial efforts to deal with definitions of terms such as *organization* and *institution*. Also, the pertinent literature that existed at the outset of most of the institution building research is identified.

Hans Blaise states:

. . . the various authors who have specifically concerned themselves with the concept institution building identify the following points of origin of institution building efforts:

(a) the emergence of new social goals and values

(b) the identification of pressing problems which require solutions

(c) the increasing understanding of the underlying causes of social problems—which may lead to institution building in an area indirectly related to the problem situation

(d) the differentiation of social functions, inherent in the development process

(e) the introduction of new social, economic, political, and administrative activities

(f) the introduction of new physical and social technologies—which may be introduced either for the more efficient and effective performance of existing services and functions, or as a part of other changes taking place. (pp. 5-6)

Blaise also discusses the origin of institution builders and their universe. He notes that the existing literature stresses the significance of the origin, position, orientation, and other characteristics of indigenous innovators engaged in institution building. He emphasizes the following points about their universe:

(a) The design and structuring of organizations which embody and adapt new values, functions, and technologies is not a mere technical problem of effective and efficient organization. . . .

(b) An institution cannot, however, be viewed in isolation. . . .

(c) . . . Institutions are viewed as mechanisms and channels through which new technologies, patterns and norms are spread to other segments of the society. (pp. 8-10)

In summarizing the need for systematic research, Blaise states:

> The literature on institution building consists at the present time almost entirely of insightful though isolated observations by scholars and practitioners who have substantial experience in guiding and analyzing the national development process. They identify institution building as highly significant to the achievement of development, and to the rendering of technical assistance in particular. However, as Goldschmidt states, "little systematic work has been done on the problem of how to create institutions and stimulate their growth. . . ."

> One of the major tasks of a research program in institution building is to adapt and reinterpret much of the existing knowledge of social change, drawn primarily from the experience of Western industrial societies, to the situations created by the pressures for rapid and purposeful change in the less developed countries. (p. 11)

[111] EATON, Joseph W. "The Inter-University Research Program in Institution Building: A Review of Phase I, 1964-1968." Graduate School of Public and International Affairs, University of Pittsburgh, Pittsburgh, Pa., December 1, 1968. 36 pages. (Mimeographed. Part of the Inter-University Research Program in Institution Building.)

This report describes the accomplishments of the Inter-University Research Program in Institution Building (IRPIB) under the following headings: "Comparison of Case Studies"; "Inference Formulation"; "Hypothesis Testing"; "Communication of Findings"; and "Application of Findings." Each of these areas was attended to in the first four years of the program. The studies have begun to have an effect on researchers and practitioners. Joseph Eaton suggests the need for a second phase which would address itself especially to the application of findings. The report refers to [17], [26], [21], [234], [66], [60], [113], [91], [89], [54], [88], [22], [33], and [101]. In addition, the appendixes contain a summary of the conceptual framework formulated by Esman et al., a set of definitions, and citations to reports either completed or in process that were sponsored by or grew out of the IRPIB.

[112] SIMMONS, Roger J. "Rural Local Governance and Agricultural Development: An Inventory of Propositions and Some Research Notes Preliminary to the Construction of Institution Building Research Designs." Unpublished master's thesis, University of Pittsburgh, Pittsburgh, Pa., 1969. 162 pages. (Part of Inter-University Research Program in Institution Building.)

The first part of this study consists of an inventory of propositions gathered from the literature. These are classified according to the major components of the institution building conceptualization developed by Esman et al. Consequently, the study represents a broad survey of rural local governance phenomena posited as significant for agricultural development. While the inventory was being compiled, a collection of research notes was accumulated, which constitute the second portion of the thesis. Within it, two major themes can be observed: (1) the need for a multidisciplinary approach and (2) the need for action-oriented institution building studies.

Conference Proceedings

[113] THOMAS, D. Woods, et al. *Institution Building: A Model for Applied Social Change.* Proceedings of Summer Workshop on Agricultural College and University Development, Purdue University, Lafayette, Ind., July-August 1969. Cambridge, Mass.: Schenkman Publishing Co., 1972. 296 pages. (Draft papers reviewed and quoted prior to release of book in mid-1972.)

In a paper entitled "Meeting the Need for Professional Agriculturalists," Ira Baldwin emphasizes the need for a dramatic increase in the number and quality of professional agriculturalists in developing countries in light of the world food problem. In discussing methods of meeting this need he emphasizes the importance of a system of institutions to serve agriculture; the need for graduate programs in agriculture in most developing countries; the need for improvements in participant training programs as they are reduced; and the requirement for viable institutions with high-quality leadership, clear objectives, and strong linkages. Finally, he makes several suggestions for improving institution building efforts.

"Agricultural Policy and National Development" is the title of Willard Cochrane's paper. He uses a hypothetical economy to trace changes that occur as it proceeds along the path of development. Emphasis is on the content and interrelations of agricultural policies.

Arthur Coutu addresses the subject of the needs and available resources of a country. He focuses on the following broad issues: (1) a brief criticism of past and emerging guidelines for institutional development in agricultural education and research establishments, (2) some specific guidelines for educational and research institutional development, (3) possible phases of the institutional development process, particularly as it is related to U.S.-host university relationships, and (4) three basic instrumental changes for U.S. university programs abroad. One of the central arguments of the paper is that a country's basic need is depth in departmental structures that will lead to productive research and technical developments in critical institutions. Finally, several new and expanded technical assistance instruments are suggested.

"Utilization of Technical Assistance by Host Governments and Host Institutions" is the title of O. P. Gautam's paper. On the basis of his experience with the planning and operation of technical assistance in India, he offers a number of suggestions for increasing the efficiency of that assistance. For example, he suggests that the periodic reviews of the progress made and of new needs of the institution should be carried out jointly.

Joseph Eaton's paper entitled "Institution Building: The Case of the Gadna Youth Corps of Israel" is similar to his book annotated in [96].

In the paper entitled "Planning and Development: An Ideological Typology," Eaton distinguishes between ideal type concepts, which go beyond that part of reality that can be observed through sense organs and instruments, and empirical concepts. Ideal type concepts are helpful in foreign aid because they enable the most relevant ideas of an institution to be abstracted from a culture. In this regard three ideological models have been distinguished in explanations of how planning and development proceed: the social Darwinist approach, the expert approach, and the mutualist approach. Each is discussed.

For the essence of Milton J. Esman's paper entitled "Some Issues in Institution Building Theory," see [34].

The paper entitled "Strategic Planning of Management Education Institutions" was written by Warren Haynes. In it he presents a condensed version of the report annotated in [33].

In his paper, Eugene Jacobson contends that if institution building is successful as a change process, one of the measures of its success will be the emergence of unanticipated combinations of events, circumstances, and products. Since institution building involves human values, beliefs, aspirations, and competence, and the tools of institution building include interpersonal influence, human communication, and management of the learning process, the criteria of success will inevitably be complex, difficult to quantify, and measurable only within broad margins of error. Goals and objectives are not only likely to change in detail but also even in terms of major components.

Jacobson enumerates the generalizations and implications resulting from the field research cited in [29]. Likewise, he repeats his three recommendations about the relationship between institution building and research on that process.

In "Philosophical Differences in Approaching Agricultural Technical Assistance," Erven Long raises questions about the method, substance (content), and structure of different approaches to technical assistance. With regard to the first of these, he raises questions about the desirability of the adviser-role concept. With regard to content or substance of technical assistance, he contends that the first phase of institution building has been completed and the present task is to put genuine substance into the activities of assisted institutions. Finally, with regard to the structure of technical assistance, Long contends that the challenge is to find ways that developing countries can participate more fully in scientific, technological, and economic growth.

In his paper entitled "Strategies and Levels of Operation in University Institution Building Projects," J. K. McDermott emphasizes sources of items of strategy in cases where projects have imaginative leadership. In those projects objectives are clear. The role of the U.S. team is perceived as one that will help transmit and interpret U.S. experience in meeting the demands of economic development. It is important for the U.S. and host institution personnel to highly respect each other and for the U.S. team to identify with host personnel. Communications between the two teams are essential. Building external relationships is perhaps as important as building internal ones. In the process of discussing these matters, McDermott discusses the four strategies annotated in [32].

"Identifying and Meeting Institutional Needs of Colleges of Agriculture in the Developing Countries" is the title of William Miller's paper. His discussion focuses on students, the curriculum, the staff, the facilities, research, extension, and public service. Throughout, he assumes that (1) an educational institution's program must be continuously related to the country's qualitative and quantitative needs for trained manpower and development plans through a systematic process of effective communication among planning groups, government ministries, industry leaders, and education officials, and (2) the land grant model, with its emphasis on teaching, extension, and research activities that are truly germane to a country's agricultural needs, is appropriate, given necessary adjustments, as a guide for thinking and planning.

Harry Potter summarizes his paper entitled "Criteria of Institutional Change as Guidelines for Assessing Project Maturation" as follows:

> How do technical assistance personnel on institution building projects know that they are accomplishing their goals? This paper has attempted to specify some problems and some criteria to be considered in answering this question. An initial consideration is the distinction between project goals and the related but not identical institutional goals. Confusion on this point can lead to confusing project maturity with institutional maturity.
>
> One of the things that is needed is adequate base line indicators describing the host institution at the beginning of the technical assistance project. These indicators should not only describe inputs and outputs, but should also describe organizational characteristics and relations with the environment. The central theme of institution building theory is the development of viable organizations with a relatively high degree of interaction with clientele and an orientation toward helping solve the problems of that clientele. A technical assistance-

institution building project, then, should be concerned with the development of these characteristics in the host institution. The goal of the project is to help provide a significant increase in these characteristics within the institution. When this occurs the project matures in the sense of reaching an end-state; the institution is maturing in the sense of acquiring the ability to perform its tasks more adequately within its environment. (pp. 17-18)

J. A. Rigney addresses questions concerning strategies and perspectives that will achieve the greatest institution building results from technical assistance efforts. His paper is entitled "Team Strategies and Functions." He touches on techniques for establishing rapport and professional credibility. Subsequently, the role of the team is discussed in terms of its objectives of developing leadership of the host institution, forming technical competence in its personnel, improving its organizational structure, strengthening the content of its program, obtaining more resources for the institution, and helping to establish an institutional tradition and attitude. Later, Rigney considers the team leader's functions from a number of perspectives. The importance of offering opportunities for professional development of team members is also touched on. Finally, both observed and optimal patterns of continuing collaborative activity are described.

William Siffin concludes his paper, "The Institution-Building Perspective: Properties, Problems and Promise," as follows:

There is no magic in institution-building. Under certain conditions—and they are not easy to know—the IB perspective makes sense as the source of a strategy of social change action—more sense than the narrower perspectives it seeks to supplant.

The IB perspective, however, remains limited and incomplete. The key to its enhancement is to refine and enlarge the heurism. But data collection and analysis are also important, and both tasks should be undertaken. IRPIB studies, the CIC/AID project, and other studies offer valuable data. Interpreted and related within an analytical framework, the findings could be presented in training manuals, planning guides, and speculative analyses. The process could be set up to cumulate knowledge over time.

The results will never add up to a broad, determinate theory of institution-building. The IB perspective, however enhanced, can never meet the hard tests of empirical theory. Nor can any other comprehensive scheme for helping deal with novel, indeterminate, elusive but

ineluctable problems of social change. Not even in retrospect will the
University of Pittsburgh be able to know determinately whether it is
possible to have restructured the Central University of Equador. . . .

Sensitivity to important qualities of the Central University might have
led to a better subjective judgment about a contemplated project or a
better action-strategy. Yet the IB perspective, in either present or
future form, could never produce a firm prediction that "the institution
as an entity could not be directed." It could never crank out a precise
and accurate answer to a "go-no go?" question in Equador, or anywhere else. It could have helped decision-makers better identify and
assess the evidence on which to base a decision. And the evaluation of
the Equadorian experience, through the lens of an institution-building
perspective might contribute to wiser judgmental action in other times
and other places. And this is all we can hope for—and strive for. (pp.
40-41)

Glen Taggart discussed the role of the university in international affairs. In outlining a minimal role for a university he
enumerated (1) the need to impress students with the knowledge
of other world cultures and (2) the need to develop both a spirit
of educational cooperation among the scholars of the world and
the interrelation of educational programs of American colleges
with institutions in other countries. He concludes by stating that
the role of universities in international affairs is limited only by
the resources available to it and its own lack of vision.

In discussing relationships between home and host campuses,
William Thompson summarizes the main threads of his arguments
as follows:

1. Building the international dimensions of U.S. universities is a task
   coordinate with the task of building agricultural institutions in other
   countries. We have been more successful at the latter than the
   former.

2. U.S. university capacity to serve effectively to assist in a foreign
   agricultural institution building project on a continuing basis is
   dependent upon developing program, professional, and administrative relationships that provide for "gaining" as well as "giving"
   throughout, and beyond, the life of the project. Simply stated, the
   U.S. university that gains the most will serve best.

3. Institution development project planning and evaluation should consider both the foreign and U.S. university institutional development
   goals and objectives and means for attaining them. Home campus

and host campus leaders, as well as cooperating organization personnel, should be actively engaged in the "two-way" institution development process.

4. Institution building concepts that are appropriate in building foreign
institutions should be equally applicable in building the international dimension of the U.S. University. It is a curious fact that the
concepts have been tested more overseas than in the U.S. (pp. 5-6)

George Axinn summarizes the highlights of the conference,
emphasizing similarities and differences among authors' perspectives with regard to institution building and technical assistance.

[114] RIGNEY, J. A., and Cummings, R. W. *A Report on the Asian
Agricultural College and University Seminar.* Raleigh, N.C.:
North Carolina State University, 1970. 112 pages.

From September 20 to October 5, 1970, a traveling seminar
was held in Thailand and India. This report contains the proceedings of that seminar. The seminar was designed to expose a
carefully selected group of Asian agricultural leaders to newly
formulated institution building concepts and give them an opportunity to use these concepts as an analytical frame for viewing
institutional development strategies and progress. Twenty-four
prominent agricultural leaders from ten Asian countries participated.

The underlying assumptions of the seminar were stated as
follows:

Experience strongly suggested that Asian Agricultural institutions have
progressed in their development to a point where agricultural leaders in
that region could learn as much or more from studying each other's
experiences as they could by visiting in the more developed countries.
There were also strong suggestions that new perspectives in institution
building could greatly facilitate such a study. (p. 7)

Abstracts of the three basic papers by George Axinn, J. A.
Rigney, and Ira Baldwin are presented in addition to summaries of
the seminar discussions.

The appendix contains a list of participants, the program
outline, the basic papers by Ralph W. Cummings, K. A. P. Steven-
son, Axinn, Rigney, and Baldwin, and reports of the eight commit-
tees.

The institution building concepts in the papers by Axinn and Rigney have been noted elsewhere—see [18], [34], and [32]—but Baldwin's contribution has not. His central thesis is that a system of services from a number of agencies is necessary to support agricultural development. Each of these services must make its proper contribution at the proper time if the rate of development is to be optimized. While there is no correct formula for bringing this about, the following hypotheses were discussed in the seminar:

I.   The rate of agricultural development is dependent on the degree of effectiveness of the various services supporting agricultural development and on the degree to which they function as an integrated system.

II. The education of professional agriculturists and the development of an indigenous agricultural research service in the early stages of agricultural development deserve high priority in the allocation of scarce resources.

III. The effectiveness of agricultural extension and public service programs can rise no higher than the level of the availability of locally adapted, improved agricultural practices and the supply of professionally trained workers.

IV. Improved practices can be only marginally effective without the development of an effective and efficient infrastructure to supply the necessary inputs—credit, seed, fertilizer, pesticides, machinery, etc.—and the necessary marketing structure—preservation, storage, transportation and capital.

V.   Agricultural development depends on the development and adoption of improved practices; adoption of improved practices is largely dependent on the probable profit to be gained by the adoption of the improved practice; profitability is often dependent on governmental policies, on prices, credit, taxation, import-export controls, etc.

VI. The development of an effective educational program for professional agriculturists in a developing country requires a faculty with both an interest in and an opportunity of assisting in finding solutions to the important problems facing agricultural development.

VII. To serve adequately the agricultural development of a nation, its agricultural colleges should continually survey the emerging needs of the nation for agriculturists with various types and levels of training and make the necessary programmatic changes to meet such needs.

VIII. In developing countries with large rural populations the elementary and secondary schools should be responsive to the needs of agricultural development and the agricultural colleges have a responsibility to assist in the development of appropriate agricultural educational programs in such schools.

IX. The agricultural college has a responsibility to assist in upgrading all agricultural workers whether in education, research, extension, public service or infrastructure activities through noncredit lecture, seminar, workshop, etc. programs, as well as by formal credit programs.

X. Where the resources—trained men and materials—available for agricultural research are in short supply heavy emphasis should be placed on applied adaptive and projective research both in agricultural colleges and in agricultural research stations.

XI. The agricultural research service has a responsibility to make information readily available to professional workers, in education, extension, etc. about progress being made in providing answers to critical agricultural problems.

XII. Since many important decisions affecting agricultural development—such as taxation, pricing, transportation, quarantine, water and soil conservation policies—are made at the highest levels of government, frequently with inadequate factual information, those directing agricultural research programs should give high priority to securing the data needed to enable the establishment of sound policies.

XIII. Many aspects of agricultural education, agricultural research and agricultural extension can be most efficiently and effectively managed at the Federal level and many others at the State level; and agricultural development will be best served by the development of integrated Federal-State programs.

XIV. The absence of adequate linkages among related but separate services often renders ineffective the independent services of each; and coordinated integrated programs are necessary to support rapid agricultural development.

XV. Strong viable linkages between associated agricultural services must be based on mutual respect for the assigned tasks of the services and on the development of the programs which bring significant benefits to each party. (pp. 23-24)

[115] PETER, Hollis W., ed. *Comparative Theories of Social Change.* Ann Arbor, Mich.: Foundation for Research on Human Behavior, 1966. 374 pages.

This book of readings is primarily composed of papers presented at a symposium on comparative social change planned by the Foundation for Research on Human Behavior and financed by AID. The chapters and their authors are: "Summary" by Hollis W. Peter; "Toward a General Theory of Directed Value Accumulation and Institutional Development" by Harold D. Lasswell and Allan R. Holmberg; "Toward a Theory of Power and Political Structure" by Karl W. Deutsch; "Wealth and the Economy" by Everett E. Hagen; "Health and Well-Being Values in the Perspective of Sociocultural Change" by Charles C. Hughes; "Social Change Skills and Creativity; Enlightenment and Communication" by Daniel Lerner; "General Equilibrium Model of the Social System" by Walter Isard and C. Peter Rydell; "Applying Behavioral Science for Organizational Change" by Warren G. Bennis and Hollis W. Peter; and "Institution Building in National Development: An Approach to Induced Social Change in Transitional Societies" by Milton J. Esman and Fred C. Bruhns [129].

In summarizing the symposium, Peter states that no satisfactory general theory of social change has been agreed upon by social scientists. Advances in recent years toward the formation of such a theory have been made, however. A number of partial theories were presented, but the symposium did not satisfactorily integrate them, partially because of the different meanings attached to terms such as *values* and *institutions* by the social scientists represented. Other reasons included differences with regard to distinguishing progress from change and different roles of social scientists.

A number of themes and common issues run through the papers. One recurrent theme is the interactive linkages between micro and macro systems. Also, the importance of technology as a major factor in shaping the direction, nature, and speed of social change is acknowledged in the papers. The importance of time in the modernizing process is also recognized. Finally, one member of the group interpreted the symposium discussion about suggested guidelines for needed research on social change as including the need for (1) cross-national research teams, (2) interdisciplinary approaches, (3) practitioner guidelines, (4) practitioner-researcher dialogue, and (5) research on change-agent roles.

[116] SMART, Lyman F., ed. *Proceedings of the Regional Conference on Institution Building.* Logan, Utah: Utah International Education Consortium, Utah State University, and the United States Agency for International Development, 1970. 173 pages plus appendixes.

This publication contains the twelve papers or portions thereof, seven committee reports, and the summary presented by members of the conference. Following the introductory paper by S. Lyman Tyler, an abstract of Milton Esman's paper is given which contains concepts described in [17]. The résumé of the paper by Woods Thomas alludes to these concepts and to the findings of the CIC-AID Rural Development Research Project (see [98]), as well as to the Institutional Development Agreement (see [250]). J. K. McDermott stresses the utility of institution building models in his paper. César Garcés describes the experience in institution building of the Inter-American Center for Integrated Land and Water Resource Development in Mérida, Venezuela. Likewise, José Marull describes the experience of the Inter-American Institute of Agricultural Sciences Program at Turrialba. Melvin Blase's contribution is cited in [120]. Similarly, the essence of William Thompson's contributions are found in [43] and [121]. J. A. Rigney reviews some of the lessons learned in technical assistance, drawing on the CIC-AID findings and experiences of North Carolina State University in Peru. Glen Taggart summarizes the Institution Development Agreement in [250]. Walter Sedwitz summarizes the activities of the Organization of American States in institutional development and some other projected activities. Under the headings of "Selection," "Orientation," and "Preparation," Bruce Anderson discusses the overseas worker prior to his departure. Focusing especially on the committee reports, George Axinn summarizes the conference as having deepened understanding, tested concepts, and provided a shared experience from the perspectives of both institution building and technical assistance.

[117] MINISTRY of Agriculture and Livestock of El Salvador and United States Agency for International Development in El Salvador. *Proceedings of the Institutional Development Seminar (Seminario Sobre Desarrollo Institucional).* San Salvador, El Salvador: The Ministry, 1971. 156 pages. (Available in both Spanish and English.)

After the introductory paper in which Bruce Anderson explains the purpose of the seminar, George Axinn draws heavily on work by Milton Esman ([17], [18], [19], and [129]) in discussing institution building concepts. In focusing on strategies and techniques suggested by institution building concepts, J. K. McDermott frames questions that need to be asked in designing a strategy for institution building. In addition to the concepts annotated in [120], Melvin Blase suggests the use of the Program Evaluation and Review Technique (PERT) in developing a time-phased strategy of institution building. Irving Tragen contends that (1) project identification and resource mobilization are part of the same process and (2) development can only be achieved by a cohesive, long-term effort which is joined by and meaningful to as broad a spectrum of the body public as possible. William Thompson summarizes the material annotated in [43] and [121]. In discussing the role of technical assistance in institution building, McDermott states that two distinct functions can be expected from foreign technical assistance: technical services and assistance in institution building. In his paper entitled "A System of Services to Support Agricultural Development," Axinn describes the six major functional components of a rural social system as production, supply, marketing, governance, research, education/extension, as well as the linkages among them. Charles Loomis [142] uses the results of a sociometric analysis in Costa Rica as well as data from other nations in discussing cultural variables and institution building. Finally, in his discussion of key problem areas in world agriculture, Marshal Fox describes a number of U.S. Department of Agriculture research projects being undertaken for the Agency for International Development.

[118] CENTRE for Economic Development and Administration. *Proceedings: Seminar on Institution Building and Development, June 26 to June 30, 1971.* CEDA Study Series Seminar Paper

No. 1. Kirtipur, Kathmandu, Nepal: The Centre, 1971. 200 pages.

The papers and summaries of participant's discussions in this proceedings issue contain the ideas of Nepalese and American scholars and officials who attended the conference in June 1971.

Robert Holt presents a hypothetical example of problems faced by newly created development agencies. Prachanda P. Pradhan attempts to analyze the degree of institutionalization and development in the Centre for Economic Development and Administration (CEDA) in light of institution building theory. Shri Bihari K. Shrestha also applies the Esman conceptualization in order to understand the development of the Panchayat Training Organization and to examine the utility of the Esman approach in such a situation. Mohammad Mohsin discusses the climate in Nepal and the direction education hopes to take.

Among the papers and the summaries, the papers of Norman Uphoff, George Axinn, and James Green are noteworthy.

Uphoff states that an organization becomes an institution when it demonstrates the value of its functions over time and others accept them as important and significant. In the process, the organization becomes more stable and secure, more capable of performing its functions, and ensures that its rising productivity is incorporated into the society's "regular" activities and beliefs. Uphoff proceeds to use the institution building concepts of Esman et al. in discussing institution building. He expands upon their concept of leadership to indicate that both entrepreneurship and management are required.

> The entrepreneur who cannot manage will probably not be able even to demonstrate satisfactorily the worth of his innovations, while the manager who cannot conceive of innovations will not be able to advance the organization he manages toward institutional status. (p. 29)

Likewise, he amplifies the concept of doctrine by drawing an analogy to military doctrine.

> Institutional doctrine serves similar purposes, in communicating to all persons within an organization what the strategic objectives of the organization are, what defenses must be maintained or strengthened against interference from outside, what are the preferred modes of initiative and response. (p. 29)

He also expands the concept of resources to include the factors of institutional production (see [24]).

After touching first upon environment and linkages and then upon institution building strategy, Uphoff turns his attention to what institution building can do. While it can provide a starting point for development activity, it cannot establish national priorities because of its micro rather than macro nature.

Subsequently, Uphoff discusses situational variables that have an effect on the outcome of institution building efforts and institution building as an intellectual orientation.

The following is Axinn's definition of planning:

> To plan, as I think of the word, means to study the past and the present in order to be able to make some kind of forecast of the future; and in light of that forecast of the future, to determine alternative courses of action; and then, to forecast the likely consequences of each of the alternative courses of action, in order to make the best decision among the alternatives as to which course of action should be followed. To me, this is the heart of strategic planning, and these are the types of questions I would put in the context of institution building. (p. 140)

After making several basic assumptions, Axinn lists the following aspects of the process by which an organization becomes institutionalized: (1) innovation, (2) rejection, (3) legitimation, (4) acceptance, (5) normality, (6) entrenchment, and (7) rigidity. Subsequently, the institution building variables of leadership, doctrine, internal structure, program, and resources are considered in regard to selected strategic questions. Finally, Axinn stresses the importance of linkages as follows:

> Thus the strategic decisions here hang on the ability of the new or changed institution to maintain and further develop linkages. The alternative is inability to develop linkages. Keep in mind the probability of competition, if not rejection, by those organizations and individuals on the other side of each linkage. (p. 154)

In his paper Green sets for himself the following objectives: (1) to examine societal pressures for continuity of institutional activities; (2) to discuss two forces for change which increase institutional effectiveness in development; and (3) to suggest some strategy whereby some institutions may become innovative forces for development.

Examination of established institutions reveals that rather

than continuing to innovate they are designed to reliably repeat prescribed operations and, in the process, they turn out more or less standardized products. Since these end products are valued by society, instilling institutions with innovativeness for development as the key feature is a very difficult task, not only because old institutions are powerful and control many resources but also because the ability to launch and institutionalize organizations is slow relative to the growth of developmental needs of developing countries. Hence, the only feasible alternative, if innovations are to be made, appears to be rejuvenating existing institutions. A second force working for the preservation of the status quo is the structural fact that organizational maintenance goals are usually more operational than are those of an institutional, substantive nature.

In contrast to forces strengthening preservation of the status quo are two societal forces for institutional change: consequentiality and institutional innovativeness. The former can be determined by end-product analysis (EPA), which identifies the products of an established institution, follows them into the society, and determines their consequences for the components of the society of which they have become a part. The latter is pertinent in that an institution must incorporate innovations relevant to the changing needs of its society which, in turn, must accept them if the institution is to continue to exist.

In the remaining portions of the paper, which focus on strategies for rejuvenation, Green discusses end-product analysis as a methodology for studying the roles played by the end-products of an institution in light of the needs of its society. For purposes of illustration an educational institution is assumed. First an in-depth role analysis is suggested for each of the institution's graduates included in the sample. The second step involves attempting to understand the structural context of need-dispositions of the role as understood by the community.

> When the data on the sample of graduates and of their respective societal entities have been summarized the analyst will be able to determine with considerable certitude the *consequentiality* of the institution for the larger society. Although the objective of the EPA will have been achieved, the institution with which one began will be little affected, assuming that the field analyses will have been carried out by

an outside analyst. In the event that an outside analyst is used to make the study he then proceeds to an *analysis of the institution itself* using the procedure briefly described above to analyze in depth each position-role in the institution. The reason for putting the institution last is that the analyst is better able to focus on the most relevant elements and issues in the institution using his intimate knowledge of the graduates, their roles and the needs of their respective societal units as cues. As with the field analyses, he is attempting to understand each role-position in the institution as it is understood by its occupant, and in sum to understand the institution from its own viewpoint. (pp. 110-11)

One of the major purposes of end-product analysis is to provide an internal impetus for change in an institution. In the process, an institution's doctrine is reformulated in operational terms. Likewise, restructuring the internal order of the institution is essential if new programs are to be offered.

Thus, if this happy sequence of events should occur, the institution would again, or perhaps for the first time in its existence, have a *substantive goal* as a *legitimizer*, a real *guide to program* and action and a *standard for evaluating* its future operations. (p. 112)

End-product analysis will also increase the opportunities for establishing linkages between the institution and other organizations and individuals in the society. In addition, members of the institution are likely to become more linkage-conscious and change their action patterns accordingly. To supplement the end-product analysis, another study of existing and recommended linkages should be made by the institution or its representative.

In other words, the methodology of building and maintaining linkage relationships is not self-evident but must be created by each institution, taught to its personnel, made an integral part of the planning process, and managed by the leadership with the same zeal as given to other aspects of institution-building. (pp. 113-14)

Finally, the following selected conclusions are given by Green:

1. The building of an innovative developmental institution is never finished, i.e., it must always be in a process of rebuilding itself, of *rejuvenating its innovative powers*, if it is to be a meaningful agent of development.

2. The concepts of the IB model are a useful general framework within which to conceptualize the rejuvenation process, but additional concepts are required. The greatest utility of the model for already-established institutions is the same as that for new institutions, namely, providing *guidance in devising IB strategies.*

3. A large part of institutional resistance to change and subsequent *atrophy as an innovative force* for development lies in (a) the commitment by most institutions to reliable repetition of prescribed operations; and, (b) the greater complementarity and operationality (the attainment process is known and criteria for measuring attainment are available and applied) of organizational maintenance goals, as compared to institutional substantive goals.

4. The key to attaining and maintaining a high level of institutional productivity lies in *maximizing the consequentiality of the institution's products to the societal units in which these products serve. . . .*

5. *Effective linkages require management* with the following characteristics: (a) periodic resurveys of all linkage possibilities; (b) acceptance of responsibility for specific linkages by each staff member; and (c) staff planning of transaction strategies based on mutuality of benefits. (p. 116)

[119] EAST-WEST Technology and Development Institute. *Proceedings of Research Seminar on Innovative Leadership and Institution-Building.* Honolulu, Hawaii: East-West Center, April 3-6, 1972.

The proceedings of this seminar will be published as working papers of the East-West Technology Development Institute. The papers were presented by: Hans C. Blaise, Suk-choon Cho, Richard P. Suttmeier, Ward Morehouse, and Daniel Kie-Hong Lee.

Methods of Analysis

[120] BLASE, Melvin G. "Institution Building as a Component of the Development Process." Agricultural Economics Departmental Paper No. 1972-24. University of Missouri, Columbia, Mo., 1971. 35 pages. (Mimeographed. Preliminary work.)

The objectives of this paper are: (1) to conceptualize an institution building theory as a systems process and, hence, provide insight into public sector development; (2) to apply conventional principles of micro-economic analyses to the question of optimum use of resources by institutions, especially with respect to their development as vehicles for growth in the larger society; and (3) to formulate a conceptual basis for deriving a strategy for institution building.

Much of the paper is based on the systems model of institutional performance and development which is presented. The model depicts three classes of institutional output: current services, influence, and institutional reinvestments. In order to produce some mix of these products the model specifies that the institution must recombine a series of intermediate products produced within it. These internally generated services, largely based upon the conceptualization of Esman et al., are leadership, internal structure, doctrine, program, linkages, technology, and resource acquisition. Further, the model specifies that in order for these seven intermediate products (services) to be produced within the system, the institution must consume a series of flow inputs and, in the process, combine them with the services of a set of stock resources. Flow inputs are classified as unrestricted budget, restricted budget, and commodities. The stock resources of an institution are listed as its propensity for change, its opportunities, and its institutional capital. Consequently, the model depicts an institution as a two-stage production process.

The dynamics of institutional development are incorporated by portraying the systems model as recycling through time. As this recycling occurs, the institutional reinvestment class of outputs adds to or, if a negative quantity, detracts from the institution's capacity to produce represented by its stock resources. Meanwhile, the other classes of outputs, current services and influence, are injected into the using society which, in turn, provides (1) the flow inputs into the system in successive periods and (2) constant feedback.

Given this systems model, micro-economic theory can be applied to obtain insights into the optimal use of resources by an institution. Initially, optimal output is envisioned as being specified by the point of tangency between (1) indifference curves of key decision makers in the society and (2) the institution's production possibility curve. In turn, this specification of optimal quantities of each class of outputs identifies the optimal point on the production function for each. These functions depict the transformation of the seven intermediate products into the system's final outputs. Having identified the quantity needed of each of the intermediate services produced within the system, the quantity of each category of flow inputs and stock resources required can be identified in terms of their derived demands. Hence, the systems model provides a framework for using micro-economic theory to deal with the questions of the optimal output mix for the institution, optimal factor-product relationships, and optimal combinations of classes of inputs.

The discussion of strategy formation for institution building is introduced with the following definition: "Strategy is defined here as a series of predetermined actions, including an alternative action to defer a decision to a subsequent time period, designed to enable accomplishment of a specific objective" (p. 28). In order to deal with the implied problem of time sequencing, Melvin Blase suggests the possible use of a PERT framework.

> Regardless, the strategy needs to consider at every point the full systems ramifications of each individual decision. Further, such a strategy should be based on the assumption that effective institutions do not grow "like Topsy" but rather their development needs to be deliberately structured. Finally, the need for pragmatism must be recognized in the formulation of strategy in light of the uncertainty that must be faced at a number of points. (p. 29)

This paper is similar to others by Blase cited in [52] and [116]. Likewise, the model bears some similarities to that discussed in [136].

[121] GAUTAM, O. P.; Patel, J. S.; Sutton, T. S.; and Thompson, W. N. *A Method of Assessing Progress of Agricultural Universities in India.* Joint Indo-American Study Team Report, Part I. New Delhi, India: Indian Council of Agricultural Research, April 1970. 128 pages.

> The purposes of this report are threefold: first, to present a broad outline of the essential elements of an institution and to illustrate the applicability of this framework to a university that is to serve the rural society; second, to present the essential features of an agricultural university; and third, to set forth methods and procedures for obtaining and analysing information that will lead to meaningful judgements

regarding the effectiveness of an agricultural university in fulfillment of its goals. (p. 1)

The authors use the institution building approach of Esman et al. as a framework for their analysis. After discussing the special and essential features of an Indian agricultural university, the authors develop an outline of methods and procedures to be followed in assessing the progress of such an institution. Finally, questionnaires are presented in the appendixes for obtaining data to perform such an analysis. In a companion publication, *The Punjab Agricultural University* [43], the same authors present the empirical results of such an investigation.

[122] EPLEY, David W. "The Institute of Administration, Zaria, Northern Nigeria, 1946-1967; A Study in Development Administration." Unpublished Ph.D. dissertation, University of Pittsburgh, Pittsburgh, Pa., 1967. 328 pages.

For both methodological and organizational reasons, David Epley found the institution building framework of Esman et al., which had been selected originally as the approach to the analysis, unsatisfactory.

> But the further into events that one went, the more it appeared that instead of under-standing and revealing reality, the variables were standing-in-the-way. To put it otherwise, the research had become too concerned with affirming the variables and not enough concerned with listening to the data, which seemed to be saying things which the institution-building model did not help to hear. (pp. iii-iv)

Consequently, Epley followed a more inductive approach wherein, as trends, themes, or threads of dominant interest emerged and were traced, concepts were selected eclectically to articulate and interrelate them. Although some of these concepts were the same as the variables in the approach of Esman et al., others were not.

Data gathered on the scene by Epley emphasize the 1957-67 period in the life of the Institute of Administration in Zaria. Using a chronological framework largely, but not entirely, Epley makes these and other historical data the basis for much of the dissertation. Finally, the institute's experience is viewed from the perspective of a structural model consisting of cultural, social, personal, and natural interrelated systems.

[123] ANDERSON, Robert C. *A Sociometric Approach to the Analysis of Inter-Organizational Relationships.* Technical Bulletin B-60. East Lansing, Mich.: Institute for Community Development, Continuing Education Service, Michigan State University, October 1969.

This analysis adapts the conventional sociometric form of analysis to apply it to identifying interorganizational relationships. Initially, the total universe of relevant organizations was identified in the Upper Peninsula of Michigan, the area for which the analysis is made. Second, individuals in positions of authority within each of the organizations were asked to respond to the question, "What organization does your organization deal with in carrying out its business?" Respondents also selected one of three categories to indicate frequency: frequently, occasionally, or never. Third, these scores were used to identify both the interorganizational relationships that existed and also constellations of organizational relationships that characterized the area. Conclusions were also drawn about the relative importance of major economic sectors. For example, in the Upper Peninsula the sociogram indicated that the tourism sector contained organizations with high interaction frequency scores. These were interpreted to mean that the sector had relatively strong bonds—i.e., bonds with higher intensities than others—with other economic sectors in the region.

The methodology described in this publication provides a valuable analytical approach to identifying linkage relationships among institutions. It can be easily applied to the institutions in an area or particular economic sector at a low resource cost relative to the information obtained.

[124] CHURCHMAN, C. West. *The Systems Approach.* New York: Delacorte Press, 1968. 243 pages.

This book provides an overview of the "systems approach" as a methodology. It is useful not only because it provides a systems view, but also because it discusses such functions as planning and program budgeting within organizations.

[125] JOHNSON, Knowlton W. "Police Interaction and Referral Activity with Personnel of Other Social Regulatory Agencies: A

Multivariate Analysis." Unpublished Ph.D. dissertation, Michigan State University, East Lansing, Mich., 1971. 148 pages.

This analysis provides both a methodology for and an example of an analysis of linkages among institutions. Of special interest is the statistical analysis which includes multivariate analysis of variance and "Q" analysis as well as multiple regression techniques.

[126] SEIDMAN, Robert B. "Law and Development: A General Model." *Law and Society Review* (February 1972), 311–42.

After pointing out the need for a general model relating law and social change, Robert Seidman proceeds to discuss (1) the definition of the problem, (2) its parameters, (3) an heuristic model, and (4) a variety of "middle-level" hypotheses. The discussion focuses on Africa.

[127] DAYAL, Ishwar, and Thomas, John M. "Operation KPE: Developing a New Organization." *Journal of Applied Behavioral Science*, 4 (1968), 473-506.

In this article, the authors report the results of their consultantship with a new company, the K. P. Engineering Corporation in India. The key problem areas that commanded the consultants' attention were grouped into individual, group, and organizational issues.

A new method of group development, the role analysis technique, was applied to the problem of interdependence, which was especially important at the group level. In using the technique, the following steps evolved in the scenario:

> The focal role individual initiates discussion and the group begins an analysis of the purpose of the role in the organization, how it fits into the overall objectives of the company, and its rationale.

> The focal role individual lists on the blackboard the activities which he feels constitute his role; other members discuss this and ask for clarification; additions and subtractions are often made to this list. . . .

> The focal role individual then lists his expectations from each of those other roles in the group which he feels most directly affect his own role performance. . . .

Each role sender then presents his list of expectations from the focal role. . . .

Upon concluding an individual role analysis, the focal role incumbent is held responsible for writing up the major points evolved during the group discussion. . . .

Briefly, at the next meeting, before another focal role is taken up, the previous role write-up is discussed and points are clarified. (pp. 487-88)

The paper concludes with a discussion of three general issues which affect the future growth of the new organization:

. . . (a) the importance of developing concurrently at individual, group, and organizational levels; (b) the importance of evolving a norm of self-consciousness about processes of growth; and (c) the dual relevance of differentiation and integration for effective organization development. (p. 473)

Position Papers

[128] GANT, George F. "The Institution Building Project." *International Review of Administrative Science,* 32 (1966). (Also a Ford Foundation Reprint.)

For purposes of this analysis, an institution building project is defined as an undertaking by a developing country to establish or strengthen an educational institution or discrete part of such an agency with the assistance of a foreign aid organization. The authority in the host country, usually its government, and the aid agency must agree not only on the importance and nature of each project but also on priorities among them. Further, George Gant states:

The components of an institution building project are easily named. They are the buildings, equipment and library; the staff and its development; the foreign specialist personnel; and the funds to maintain staff and plant at an adequate level. All such components should be assured if the project is to have any real chance of success. (p. 2)

However, not even these components automatically assure that a viable institution will result. Another essential element is a carefully prepared process of synthesis, which might be outlined in a plan of development. In the joint development of such a plan, opportunity will exist for the host country and the aid agency to reach understandings about objectives and methods as well as about their respective roles.

The most promising institution building projects will then be administered and financed primarily by the host country. Especially important is the selection of the institution's staff, which should be left in the host country's realm of decision making. To supplement the adequately trained personnel in the host country expatriates should be recruited and other personnel sent abroad for training. Twice as many personnel as there are positions to be filled should be sent abroad for training to ensure that an adequate supply of competent participants return to staff the institution.

Especially during the interim before a sufficiently large and experienced staff is available, foreign consultants can be of appreciable assistance. They can both function as consultants and do some teaching and research, if time permits, to demonstrate the proper performance of these tasks. Obviously, such consultants need to be qualified not only in their profession but also as institution builders. Individuals who devote three to five years to such an assignment are much more productive than short-time specialists. Before they initiate their assignments, however, these professionally competent individuals with personal sensitivity should have the benefit of an orientation program. If a foreign language is required, adequate time should be allocated for the specialist to obtain a facility in it. In addition, the orientation should cover the nature and process of the institution building project.

Once on the job, a foreign consultant should have a clear and mutual understanding about the relationships among the institution, the aid agency, and consultants such as himself. His identification with and loyalty to the host institution are essential and are facilitated if the foreign staff is given the same type of office facilities, housing, and official transportation as the regular staff of the institution.

Since institution building requires that life be breathed into a complex process, a developed university can provide the necessary resources, leadership, and support to an overseas project and its foreign personnel. Further, it can provide the training for the foreign students. It can provide support in numerous other ways as well. In the process, the university itself can benefit.

> Most institutions, in their growth, reach a defined plateau of compe-
> tence and performance, after time, at which level they can do very well
> without massive assistance. Rather than to continue to rely upon
> external assistance, when the plateau has been reached, it is preferable
> that the institution proceed on its own, even though there might be
> some slippage in the program. At some later time perhaps, when the
> institution is ready to move toward a higher plateau of excellence or of
> program coverage, a new assistance project might be considered. During
> the interim period, or when the project comes to a close, a thread of
> relationship should be maintained between the institution and the
> university. A modest exchange of professors and students and of
> publications gives returns much larger than the costs in terms of
> research and teaching at both ends of the connection. (p. 8)

[129] ESMAN, Milton J., and Bruhns, Fred C. "Institution Building in National Development: An Approach to Induced Social Change in Transitional Societies." Graduate School of Public and International Affairs, University of Pittsburgh, Pittsburgh, Pa., 1965. 34 pages. (Mimeographed. Part of Inter-University Research Program in Institution Building. Published also in *Comparative Theories of Social Change*, edited by Hollis W. Peter, 1966, 318–42. See annotated citation number [115].)

After defining essential terms, as in [337] and [27], the authors use them as the basis for the following assumptions:

(a) Development, or more modestly, social change, and the con-
    comitant new values, functions, technologies and action patterns,
    cannot be effectively introduced and sustained in transitional soci-
    eties unless they are embedded in a supportive network of social
    structures, processes, and norms. In short, these innovative values,
    functions, and technologies must be institutionalized.

(b) This process takes place in and through institutional organizations
    which must either be newly created or adapted and restructured for
    this purpose.

(c) Institutional development need not be a "natural" or evolutionary
    process which occurs independently of human design. In this era,
    new technologies and new institutional forms are almost every-
    where deliberately induced and directed. This sense of deliberate

human purpose and human direction warrants the use of the phrase "institution building" and suggests a key role for modernizing elites.

(d) Institution building is thus an approach to the development process which relies heavily on the concept of "social engineering" and which stresses the leadership functions of modernizing elite groups within that process and the alternative action strategies available to them.

(e) As development occurs, social functions or technologies become increasingly specialized. With specialization, interdependencies develop. The institutions incorporating innovations are thus involved in a network of complementary and competing relationships in their environment on which institution building research must focus.

(f) Institution building is conceived of as a generic social process. There are elements and actions that can be identified as generally relevant to institution building, even though their expression will differ depending on the type of institution and the social environment.

(g) It is possible, through systematic and comparative analysis of institution building experiences, to derive elements of a technology of institution building that will be useful to persons engaged in introducing innovation into developing societies, whether they be indigenous change agents or foreign advisors. (pp. 6-7)

Milton Esman and Fred Bruhns note that the institution building approach is (1) interdisciplinary and (2) can draw few insights from Western organization theory. Rather than assume that the prerequisites associated with organizational efficiency prevail in traditional societies, institution building research begins with the assumption that deliberate efforts must be made to introduce radical innovations into traditional societies whose cultural values and social structures, in addition to economic and political interests, may not initially be supportive of these changes. After these preliminary comments, the tests of institutionality and conceptual scheme are presented, as in [18].

The institution building approach is addressed to situations in developing countries where nation building and socioeconomic progress are overriding goals. Hence, these goals constitute normative guides and regulators of official doctrine and, as such, influence public policy and programmed action.

Our task or action oriented model now begins to emerge, incorporating the following components: a governing, goal-oriented elite which bears the major responsibility for initiating and directing the process of modernizing change; a doctrine, or set of action commitments, which establishes, communicates, and legitimizes norms, priorities and styles for operating programs; and a set of action instruments through which communication with the community is maintained and operating programs are implemented. . . . (p. 22)

In short, institution-building provides the means by which a change oriented leadership can articulate with an organized community and the community can participate in the struggle to achieve the twin goals. (p. 23)

This then, is the larger goal and action-oriented model for nation building and socioeconomic development.

Subsequently, Esman and Bruhns comment on the research methodology used in the institution building approach described in [22]. They conclude with remarks about the limitation of the approach, the expectations with regard to the findings of field research, and the need for further inquiry.

[130] ZALD, Mayer N., and Ash, Roberta. "Social Movement Organizations: Growth, Decay and Change." *Studies in Social Movements: A Social Psychological Perspective.* Edited by Barry McLaughlin. New York: The Free Press, 1969, pp. 461-85. (Reprinted in full from "Social Movement Organizations," by Mayer N. Zald and Roberta Ash, *Social Forces,* 44 (1966), 327-41.) Selections reprinted by permission of both the Macmillan Co. and the University of North Carolina Press.

In this essay on theoretical synthesis, Mayer Zald and Roberta Ash contend that the Weber-Michels model (stemming from ideas of Max Weber and Roberto Michels) is incomplete as a statement of the transformation of (social) movement organizations (MO). In simplified terms, that model predicts changes in organizations stemming from changes in leadership positions and leadership behavior. In addition, it predicts what organizational changes lead to changes in organizational behavior. This approach, Zald and Ash maintain, can be subsumed under a more general approach to MOs, which specifies the conditions under which alternative transformation processes take place.

Using an institutional analysis approach similar to that of Philip Selznick's in [337], Zald and Ash contend that large-scale organizations can be viewed as collections of groups harnessed together by incentives of various kinds to pursue relatively explicit goals. These organizations may experience internal conflicts but, more importantly, they exist in a changing environment to which they must adapt. This may require changes in goals and in the internal arrangement of the institution. Hence, goals change in response to both internal and external pressures. This methodological approach is useful because it focuses on conflict, environmental forces, and the ebb and flow of organizational viability.

On the basis of this general approach, the authors formulate the following hypotheses for testing:

> Proposition 1: The size of the organizational potential support base, the amount of societal interest in the social movement and its MO's, and the direction of that interest (favorable, neutral, or hostile) directly affect the ability of the organization to survive and/or grow.

> Proposition 2: The more insulated an organization is by exclusive membership requirements and goals aimed at changing individuals, the less susceptible it is to pressures for organizational maintenance or general goal transformation.

> Proposition 3: Goal and tactic transformation of a MO is directly tied to the ebb and flow of sentiments within a social movement. The inter-organizational competition for support leads to a transformation of goals and tactics.

> Proposition 4: MO's created by other organizations are more likely to go out of existence following success than MO's with their own linkages to individual supporters.

> Proposition 5: MO's with relatively specific goals are more likely to vanish following success than organizations with broad general goals.

> Proposition 6: MO's which aim to change individuals and employ solidary incentives are less likely to vanish than are MO's with goals aimed at changing society and employing mainly purposive incentives.

> Proposition 7: Inclusive organizations are likely to fade away faster than exclusive organizations; the latter are more likely to take on new goals.

Proposition 8: A becalmed movement is most likely to follow the Weber-Michels model because its dependence on and control of material incentives allows oligarchization and conservatism to take place.

Proposition 9: Inclusive MO's are more likely than exclusive MO's to participate in coalitions and mergers.

Proposition 10: Coalitions are most likely to occur if the coalition is more likely to achieve goals or lead to a larger resource base—when success is close or when one indivisible goal or position is at stake.

Proposition 11: The less the short-run chances of attaining goals, the more solidary incentives act to separate the organization into homogeneous subgroups—ethnic, class, and generational. As a corollary, to the extent that a becalmed or failing MO is heterogeneous and must rely heavily on solidary incentives, the more likely it is to be beset by factionalism.

Proposition 12: The more the ideology of the MO leads to a questioning of the basis of authority the greater the likelihood of factions and splitting.

Proposition 13: Exclusive organizations are more likely than inclusive organizations to be beset by schisms.

Proposition 14: Routinization of charisma is likely to conservatize the dominant core of the movement organization while simultaneously producing increasingly radical splinter groups.

Proposition 15: If a leadership cadre are committed to radical goals to a greater extent than the membership-at-large, member apathy and oligarchical tendencies lead to greater rather than less radicalism.

Proposition 16: An exclusive organization is almost certain to have a leadership which focuses on mobilizing membership for tasks, while the inclusive organization is readier to accept an articulating leadership style.

Proposition 17: the MO oriented to individual change is likely to have a leadership focused on mobilizing sentiments, not articulating with the larger society. Organizations oriented to changing the larger society arè more likely to require both styles of leadership, depending on the stage of their struggle. (pp. 469-83)

[131] HUNTINGTON, Samuel P. "Political Development and Political Decay." *World Politics*, 17 (April 1965), 386–430.

According to Samuel Huntington, it is useful to distinguish political development from modernization and to identify political development with the institutionalization of political organizations and procedures. Rapid increases in mobilization and participation, the principal political aspects of modernization, undermine political institutions. In brief, rapid modernization produces not political development but political decay. In order to liberate the concept of development from the concept of modernization, political development is defined as the institutionalization of political organizations and purposes. This institutionalization can be measured by an organization's adaptability, complexity, autonomy, and coherence.

In light of the necessity for effective political institutions for stable and eventually democratic governments and as a condition for sustained economic growth, Huntington suggests strategies of institutional development.

Two general considerations affecting the probabilities of success in institution building are recognized: (1) that the psychological and cultural characteristics of people differ markedly and, with them, peoples' abilities to develop institutions, and (2) that institutions are the products of conscious, purposeful effort.

There are two methods of furthering institutional development. One is to slow social mobilization, which presumably creates conditions more favorable to the preservation and strengthening of institutions. Three methods of doing this are (1) to increase the complexity of the social structure, (2) to limit or reduce communications in the society, and (3) to minimize competition among segments of the political elite. The other method is to develop strategies and directly apply them to the problem of institution building. This creates a dilemma in that the would-be institution builder needs personal power to create institutions, but he cannot create institutions without relinquishing some of this personal power.

In the absence of traditional political institutions, the political party is the only modern organization that can become a source of power and that can be effectively institutionalized. Regardless of the type of institution involved, the danger of overextension of its resources in the institution building process is considered analogous to the danger involved in overextending troops in a military campaign.

[132] NEHNEVAJSA, Jiri; Siffin, William J.; Hanson, John; Montgomery, John D.; and Butts, R. Freeman. *Institution-Building and Education: Papers and Comments.* Bloomington, Ind.: Comparative Administration Group, Department of Government, Indiana University, undated. 35 pages. (Part of Inter-University Research Program in Institution Building.)

In his paper entitled "Institution-Building: Elements of a Research Orientation," Jiri Nehnevajsa discusses the institution building approach of Esman et al. [18]. Subsequently, he touches on the types of mapping discussed in [20].

William Siffin's paper entitled "Institution Building Research in Thailand" is based primarily upon the research on the Institute of Public Administration described in [88]. This institution building experience resulted in the following lessons:

A. The central object of any educational institutional development is to embody a doctrine in an organization. This doctrine includes norms as well as skill and/or knowledge content. . . .

B. The ability to interpret doctrine and to make innovative applications of it in operating and developing a program of activities is probably the key indicator that the doctrine has been institutionalized. . . .

C. The development of an innovative institution depends upon the creation of a structure of institutional leadership. . . .

D. Protecting and maintaining an institutional leadership structure, plus a supporting cadre, in a hostile environment may be more difficult than establishing it in the first place. . . .

E. It is entirely possible to mobilize environmental support for an innovative institution even if there are sharp inconsistencies between the institution's doctrine and the value orientation characteristic of that environment. . . .

F. . . . A full determination of the institutionalization of an educational entity such as the IPA must consider the impact upon the organization's clientele and, ultimately, of the clientele upon the environment. (pp. 12-16)

In his paper "Institutionalization of the College of Education of the University of Nigeria," John Hanson highlights the findings in [28]. In addition, he elaborates on some of the difficulties encountered in the field while undertaking the project. These problems are discussed under the headings of environment, people, reference points, timing, and innovation or innovating.

Although entertaining some doubts about the universality of the institution building approach of Esman et al., John Montgomery recognizes that the preoccupation with doctrine does call attention to an important range of activities that are sometimes neglected in institution building. He defines doctrine as the self-propelling, self-renewing value system that gives an organization a life line independent of the corporate sum reached by adding up the qualities of its individual members. In comparing the two institutions described by Siffin and Hanson he notes that the problem in Thailand was getting the society to change while in Nigeria it was getting the professionals to accept the appropriateness of the demands of society. Both cases suggest the need for an institution to develop a cadre of committed professional individuals. Finally, he acknowledges that the institution building approach expands the knowledge available to the administrator and, hence, reduces the role he has to leave to chance.

R. Freeman Butts notes that the institution building enterprise is a peculiarly appropriate means of bringing sociology and political science to bear upon the problems of education. However, he argues that the "environment" of an educational institution is not only the political, economic, and social setting of its particular locality, region, or nation, but also embraces the larger supranational environment represented by the world of knowledge, the international canons of scholarship, and the practice and performance of professional behavior that transcends national boundaries. In addition, he maintains that the implicit assumption that the direction of change in institution building should progress from the relatively less to the relatively more modern should be made explicit and dealt with accordingly.

[133] SUFRIN, Sidney C. "Economists and 'Institution Building' (The Little Men Who Weren't There)." Syracuse University, Syracuse, N.Y., 1964. (Mimeographed. Part of Inter-University Research Program in Institution Building.)

Economists, says Sidney Sufrin, have not considered it their task, by and large, to recommend how new institutions should be formed; economics on the whole has been analytical rather than synthetic. Several economists (such as Alfred Marshall, Frank H. Knight, and Joseph Schumpeter) are quoted with regard to the analytical nature of economics.

General

[134] RIGNEY, J. A.; Bumgardner, Harvey L.; Ellis, Walter; Lynton, Rolf P.; Jung, Christian W. "A Guide to Institution Building for Team Leaders of Technical Assistance Projects." North Carolina State University, Raleigh, N.C., 1971. Pages numbered by chapters. (Mimeographed.)

This publication contains the following chapters: "About the Guide"; "The Team Leader's World of Work"; "Basic Concepts of Institution Building"; "Implementation of Basic Concepts"; "The Team Leaders and the Host Institution and Host Government"; "The Role of Technical Assistance in Institution Building"; "The Team Leader and the Team"; "The Team Leader and the Home Institution"; "The Team Leader and the External Assistance Agency"; "Participant Training"; "Project Assessment and Planning"; "The Team Leader's Role and His Preparation."

The "Guide" is largely focused on the institution building type of technical assistance and makes use of past research findings (e.g., [17] and [120], much of which was financed by AID, on both (1) institution building and (2) methods of maximizing the effectiveness of technical assistance programs. Team leaders or project managers are the prime audience for which the publication was written.

[135] PHILLIPS, Hiram S. *Guide for Development: Institution-Building and Reform.* Praeger Special Studies in International Economics and Development. New York: Praeger Publishers, Inc., 1969. 282 pages.

This analysis is limited to those institutions that have organizational entities which can contribute to development. It discusses institutions and change, case studies of institutional development, and policy and operations.

After discussing the overview, the role of institutions, framework for action, climate for reform, and the institutional environment, Hiram Phillips uses many of the concepts developed by Esman et al. in his treatment of the building of institutions. He also writes on the evaluation of results.

In the second part of the book the following case studies are discussed: land reform in Taiwan; research to improve production of corn in Asia; tax modernization in Chile; and fiscal management in Thailand.

This highly readable handbook for development concludes with a set of recommendations for foreign assistance agencies. For example, Phillips proposes that foreign assistance agencies set up programs to train present and future leaders who will be able to promote an environment for development through devising programs of reform in their own countries.

[136] JONES, Ronald W. "Information-Search as an Aid to Technical Assistance Strategy Planning." U.S. Agency for International Development, Washington, D.C., August 1971. 191 pages. (Mimeographed. Preliminary work.)

This manuscript is an outgrowth of the Committee on Institutional Cooperation and the Agency for International Development Rural Development Research Project. In it Ronald Jones urges that technical assistance strategy planning be given a more scientific bent, thereby enhancing the quality of such planning through a more systematic approach to the search for decision-making information. A systems model is used to facilitate a discussion of a behavioral theory of technical assistance. Finally, an information-search technique is presented and illustrated. Throughout, the focus is on locating strategic constraints to the performance of the technical assistance system.

Jones' generalized behavior model of an organization system depicts inputs of men, money, and material interacting with action variables categorized as will, opportunity, and means. In turn, these variables interact with functional characteristics of linkages, leadership, doctrine, program, and internal structure. Three categories of proximate outputs are depicted in the model: current services, institution building, and influence. These are injected into the environment as intermediate outputs, and there they are transformed into ultimate outputs. This model is used as the basis for a schematic outline of a donor strategy model. Using the same categories as in the generalized behavior model, the strategy model depicts the interaction of the technical assistance complex with the host institution system. This type of modeling is also used by Melvin Blase in [120].

[137] FOSTER, George M. "An Anthropologist's View of Technical Assistance Methodology." University of California, Berkeley, Calif., 1972. 56 pages. (Mimeographed. This and [138], [139], and [159] were prepared as background reading for participants in the technical assistance methodology seminars sponsored by the Methodology Division, Technical Assistance Bureau, U.S. Agency for International Development, held during 1972.)

Technical assistance is a form of directed cultural change in contradistinction to evolutionary change. It presupposes professional specialists who command useful skills that can be directed toward the solution of problems by bringing about changes in individuals, groups, and/or corporate behavior. Although sponsored in many ways, the processes and methodologies of technical assistance are pretty much the same. However, relatively few of the traditional models developed by sociologists are applicable to the study of these phenomena. Nevertheless, there are some interdisciplinary concepts worthy of note.

In order to achieve the most effective technical assistance, the social, cultural, and psychological dimensions of (1) the innovating organization, (2) the technical specialists who execute projects, and (3) the client or target group must be understood.

After summarizing the major assumptions of technical assistance that appear to have evolved, George Foster notes two anthropological concepts: (1) sociocultural systems are logically integrated wholes, and (2) implicit premises or subconscious assumptions underlie the cultural forms and individual behavior of members of a group.

He also examines some aspects of problems in technical assistance rooted in the client group, in the bureaucracy, and in the personality of the technical specialist. With regard to client groups, in many peasant societies one person's gain with respect to any good must be necessitated by another's loss. In order to guard against being the loser, people in these closed, static, unexpanding systems opt for an egalitarian, shared-poverty, equilibrium, status-quo style of life in which no one can be permitted major progress with respect to any good. This goes a long way toward explaining the fatalism of many rural peoples, their apparent apathy, their reluctance to cooperate with their fellows, and their insistence on using resources for traditional rituals.

Most bureaucracies as client groups are strikingly like a natural community such as a tribe or peasant village with a real society and a real culture. Any analysis of such client groups should concentrate not only on their cultural and institutional forms but also the premises that underlie bureaucratic dynamics. Here, too, the following anthropological caution applies:

> Significant change in any social institution or phase of culture occurs only when accommodation is made in those institutions or phases that impinge upon it, and the degree of possible change is limited by the extent to which these accommodations occur. (pp. 12-13)

The technical specialist shares premises and values with fellow citizens and has been enculturated both into a profession and a bureaucracy. All professionals tend to be ethnocentric. As bearers of the premises and values of their national cultures, as well as their professional subcultures and innovating bureaucracies, technical specialists tend to be influenced thereby with regard to role definitions, tasks incumbent to these roles, and evaluation of role performance. More often than is realized, the technical specialist's strategy, at least subconsciously, is directed toward pleasing himself rather than members of the client group. For example, the goals he sets for himself are frequently those that, if accomplished, would bring approbation in his home country.

In concluding, Foster states:

> It is important to continue our efforts better to understand the structure, the dynamic forces, the values, and the premises of client groups, better to be able to bridge what has been called the "cultural chasm" that usually separates specialist from people. But it is even more important to recognize that the next major step in perfecting a technical assistance methodology is to direct attention to the innovating bureaucracy, and to its personnel, to its premises and to its rationale. (pp. 49-50)

[138] SEIDMAN, Ann. "An Economist's Approach to Technical Assistance." Land Tenure Center, University of Wisconsin, Madison, Wis. Paper prepared in conjunction with the seminars on technical assistance methodology sponsored by U.S. Agency for International Development, 1972. 56 pages. (Mimeographed.)

Ann Seidman explains why static economic analysis is of limited value in planning for economic development. Since it does not include provisions for institutional structural change, it fails to address the essence of the development problem in many countries in general, and in African countries in particular. African countries have inherited an institutional structure developed on the foundation of and which reinforces a distorted pattern of resource allocation.

> The dominant feature of the export enclave is the group of oligopolistic foreign private trading, and in some cases mining and plantation firms, and associated banking, insurance and shipping interests. In the days of outright colonial rule, the entire political-economic institutional structure of government—from the administrative departments to the money and banking system—was shaped primarily to facilitate the operation of these firms and associated interests. Since independence, with few exceptions they have continued to dominate the export enclave. They seek to maximize their profits primarily by producing or purchasing crude materials for their home industries in accord with patterns shaped in the past. (pp. 13-14)

Technical assistance in the field of economics would contribute more to meaningful development policies if a problem-solving approach were taken. Seidman suggests the following problem areas for analysis: (1) industrial development, (2) agricultural development, (3) trade expansion, (4) financing development, and (5) regional integration.

A paradigm formulated by students of law and development to direct rigorous interdisciplinary research to determine how a new working rule affects the behavior of a given role-occupant is illustrated by an attempt of a legislature to channel the sales of a cash crop through a new institution, a marketing cooperative. This approach suggests that technical assistants should urge consideration of proposed institutional changes, not merely in terms of costs and benefits measured in monetary terms, but also in terms of their overall implications for national development goals. It provides a framework within which physical and social scientists working together with lawyers as a multidisciplinary team can evaluate the probable consequences of proposed institutional changes.

> Several concrete proposals emerge from the foregoing discussion of the necessity of reorienting technical assistance to a problem-solving approach:
>
> First, technical assistance within a given country should be provided in the context of multi-disciplinary teams in which local counterpart personnel participate as colleagues in formulating and testing hypotheses for explaining and solving particular problems. . . .
>
> Second, technical assistance might help establish interdisciplinary problem-oriented training programs for local personnel, like district planners, rural development officers and industrial managers, to work with local citizens in dealing with the range of problems which may plague the particular area with which they are likely to be concerned. . . .
>
> Third, U.S. technical assistance might be directed to encouraging U.S. universities to offer interdisciplinary, problem-solving programs for students from less developed countries seeking to pursue their studies further. . . .
>
> Fourth, technical assistance could contribute to the institutionalization of on-going evaluative research, preferably in national educational and research institutions of higher learning. . . .
>
> Fifth, technical assistance could contribute to the establishment of internationally operated data banks for collecting the cumulative results of national on-going evaluative research. (pp. 52-55)

[139] HAVENS, A. Eugene. "The Sociologist's Approach to Technical Assistance Methodology." University of Wisconsin, Madison, Wis. Paper prepared in conjunction with the seminars on technical assistance methodology sponsored by U.S. Agency for International Development, 1972. 43 pages. (Mimeographed. Preliminary work.)

The major approaches to the sociological study of societies can be divided into two broad camps: equilibrium models and conflict models. A. Eugene Havens contends that the former are not appropriate for most developing countries. Rather, technical assistance methodology must begin with determining the structural arrangements of the country in question. These arrangements frequently do not allow the broad masses of people to participate in either new technological changes or their benefits. Hence, changing structural arrangements becomes a prerequisite for development. In these situations technical assistance is probably best given by establishing what the structural arrangements are and what groups they exploit. As a consequence, an understanding can be obtained about the required change and the plans needed to bring it about.

[140] OLSON, Mancur, Jr. *The Logic of Collective Action.* Cambridge, Mass.: Harvard University Press, 1965. 176 pages. (Reprinted in 1971.) Selection reprinted by permission of Harvard University Press.

This analysis challenges the widely held view that groups of individuals with common interests can be expected to act on behalf of their common interests much as single individuals can be expected to act on behalf of their personal interests. Mancur Olson's conclusion is that unless the number of individuals in a group is quite small, or unless there is coercion or some other special device to make individuals act in their common interest, rational, self-interested individuals will not act to achieve their common or group interest. Hence, the widespread view common throughout the social sciences that groups tend to further their interests is accordingly unjustified, at least when it is based on, as it usually is, the assumption that groups act in their self-interest because individuals do.

> The proofs of all of the logical statements that have been made above are contained in Chapter I, which develops a logical or theoretical explanation of certain aspects of group and organizational behavior. Chapter II examines the implications of this analysis for groups of different size, and illustrates the conclusion that in many cases small groups are more efficient and viable than large ones. Chapter III considers the implications of the argument for labor unions, and draws the conclusion that some form of compulsory membership is, in most circumstances, indispensable to union survival. The fourth chapter uses the approach developed in this study to examine Marx's theory of social classes and to analyze the theories of the state developed by some other economists. The fifth analyzes the "group theory" used by many political scientists in the light of the logic elaborated in this study, and

argues that the theory as usually understood is logically inconsistent. The final chapter develops a new theory of pressure groups which is consistent with the logical relationships outlined in the first chapter, and which suggests that the membership and power of large pressure-group organizations do not derive from their lobbying achievements, but are rather a by-product of their other activities. (p. 3)

[141] WOLF, Charles, Jr. "Institutions and Economic Development." *The American Economic Review,* 45 (December 1955), 867-83.

In this article Charles Wolf, an economist, makes some preliminary observations and suggestions concerning a framework for institutional programming designed to serve as a catalyst of development in economically less-developed areas. He uses *institution* to refer to organizations and policies in order to select those elements in the existing or potential social context that can be incorporated into institutional programs, accompanying and supplementing investment, and technological programming. This is consistent with his view of the role of institutions as possible constraints to the development process.

> The inadequacy of technology and capital formation may be due less to a shortage of information about techniques or of potential savings, than to shortages of the "right" kinds of institutions—"right" implying those kinds of institutions which permit or stimulate, rather than impede, the adoption of new techniques and the formation of productive capital. (p. 867)

Institutions may stimulate or impede behavior leading to economic growth by their following effects: (1) the direct calculation of costs and benefits; (2) relationships between production and distribution (output and income); (3) the order, predictability, and probability of economic relationships; (4) knowledge of economic opportunities; and (5) motivations and values. Wolf discusses each of these in turn.

[142] LOOMIS, Charles P. "Cultural Variables and Institution Building: The Strategy and Conceptualization of Directed Change—As Illustrated by a Case from Costa Rica and Survey Data from 5 Nations." Michigan State University, East Lansing, Mich. (Mimeographed. Prepared for the Institutional

Development Seminar, El Salvador, 1971.) 63 pages. See [117] also.

This paper is organized according to the processually articulated structural (PAS) model. It is presented as an analytical tool that provides some of the basic concepts for institution building and processes of change as well as the interrelation between them. The model incorporates both social structure and process of change. It is used to furnish a basis for possible comparisons among activities in institution building and to organize certain findings that are relevant for agricultural development.

[143] DE VRIES, Egbert. *Man in Rapid Social Change.* New York: Published for the World Council of Churches by Doubleday and Co., Inc., 1961. 240 pages. Selection reprinted by permission of the World Council of Churches.

In setting the tone for the book, Egbert De Vries states:

> In this study, we want to refrain from a hypothetical or philosophical approach which would "explain" all behaviour patterns as the result of social organization or methods of production. In many cases the spirit of people prevailed over institutional patterns.
>
> However, we would not deny the profound influence which social institutions have upon the attitudes, the motivations, and behaviour of man. Especially in cases where the new elements are of foreign origin, as is so often the case in areas of rapid social change, we may expect tensions and contradictions, the outcome of which may depend upon mental attitudes as well as institutional forces. (p. 45)

De Vries maintains that the following forces, which he categorizes as prime movers, have brought about changes: economic forces, technological forces, spiritual forces, sociocultural forces, and political forces. His list of main catalytic forces that accelerate change include: reward-awareness; generation tension; prophetic pronouncement; moral indignation; emotional mass movement; and curiosity. The following inhibiting forces that retard change are given: fear of taking risks, generation-to-generation perpetuity, the sacred nature of the existing order, rejection of individual deviation, and xenophobia.

After discussing the change process, De Vries examines specific issues of rapid social change and the common responsibility that it involves. Examples of specific issues studied are family life, education, and rural development.

[144] EISENSTADT, S. N. "Institutionalization and Change." *American Sociological Review*, 29 (April 1964), 235–47.

S. N. Eisenstadt concludes that the process of institutionalization of a system creates the possibility of opposition systems within it. While their nature and strength may vary, in opportune situations opposition systems constitute important foci of change even though they may often remain latent for long periods. In spite of these opposing systems, the main system might perpetuate itself by accommodating different subsystems and through a hierarchy of norms. While the nature and timing of the institutionalization process may be unique to each institution—to its nature, values, norms, organization, as well as the internal and external forces to which it is especially sensitive—the very process itself contains the basis for possible conflict.

[145] BOULDING, Kenneth E. *The Organizational Revolution*. New York: Harper & Brothers, 1953. 286 pages.

Although not at the core of the institution building literature, this book is of interest because of the economic and ethical perspectives with which Kenneth Boulding views organizations and their evolution. He examines both the supply and demand forces operative in the formation of organizations. Further, he deals with some of the ethical implications of the resulting organizational changes. Among others, labor unions and farm organizations are discussed in light of the economic and ethical framework developed in earlier sections of the book. Finally, critical comments are offered by a theologian, other scholars, and representatives of various interest groups as well as Boulding's response to them.

[146] BUCKLEY, Walter, ed. *Modern Systems Research for the Behavioral Scientist*. Chicago: Aldine Publishing Co., 1968. 525 pages.

This book of previously published articles brings together both physical and social scientists' perspectives of systems research. It is organized into the following parts: (1) "General Systems Research: Overview"; (2) "Parts, Wholes, and Levels of Integration;" (3) "Systems, Organization, and the Logic of Relations"; (4) "Information, Communication, and Meaning"; (5) "Cybernetics: Purpose, Self-Regulation, and Self-Direction"; (6) "Self-Regulation and Self-Direction in Psychological Systems"; and (7) "Self-Regulation and Self-Direction in Sociocultural Systems." Of special interest to the novice at applying systems analysis to institution building are the two chapters "General Systems Theory—The Skeleton of Science" by Kenneth E. Boulding, and "Definition of System" by A.D. Hall and R. E. Fagen.

[147] LIPPITT, Ronald; Watson, Jeanne; and Westley, Bruce. *The Dynamics of Planned Change.* New York: Harcourt Brace Jovanovich, Inc., 1958. 312 pages.

This book presents an analysis of change in psychological processes, social relations, interpersonal processes, problem-solving procedures, and social structures. It focuses on the role of change agents in the process of initiating change, fostering it, and institutionalizing change processes in large organizations, as well as in small groups and/or individuals.

[148] TRUMBO, Don A. "Individual and Group Correlates of Attitudes Toward Work-Related Change." *Journal of Applied Psychology,* 45 (1961), 338-44.

Don Trumbo presents some of the findings of a study of the correlates of employees' attitudes toward change as a general job-related phenomena.

[149] BENVENISTE, Guy, and Ilchman, Warren, eds. *Agents of Change: Professionals in Developing Countries.* New York: Praeger Publishers, Inc., 1969. 252 pages.

For discussions of universities and research institutes, attention is called to chapters 14 and 15, "Institution Building in Developing Countries" by Raul Deves Jullian and "The International Institute Approach" by Vernon W. Ruttan.

[150] SIFFIN, William J. "Institution Building and Administrative Problems." *Administrative Issues in Developing Economies.* Edited by Kenneth J. Rothwell. Lexington, Mass.: D.C. Heath and Co., 1972.

This statement of the strengths and weaknesses of the institution building framework of Esman et al. is somewhat similar to [20].

4
Supporting Literature

[151] ADELMAN, Irma, and Morris, Cynthia. "An Econometric Model of Socio-economic and Political Change in Underdeveloped Countries." *American Economic Review*, 58 (December 1968), 1184–218.

[152] ADELMAN, Irma, and Morris, Cynthia. *Society, Politics and Economic Development*. Baltimore, Md.: Johns Hopkins University Press, 1967. 307 pages.

[153] AGENCY for International Development; U.S. Department of Agriculture; and Association of State Universities and Land-Grant Colleges. *Proceedings of the Conference on International Rural Development*. Washington, D.C., July 27–28, 1964. 185 pages.

[154] AHMED, Manzoor. "Mobile Trade Training Schools of Thailand— Case Study No. 6." International Council for Educational Development, Essex, Conn., June 1972. (Preliminary work.)

[155] AHMED, Manzoor, and Coombs, Philip H. "PAACA: Education in an Integrated Agricultural Program—Case Study No. 10." International Council for Educational Development, Essex, Conn., June 1972. (Preliminary work.)

[156] AHMED, Manzoor, and Coombs, Philip H. "Training Extension Leaders at the International Rice Research Institute—Case

Study No. 12." International Council for Educational Development, Essex, Conn., June 1972. (Preliminary work.)

[157] ALEXANDER, Yonah. *International Technical Assistance Exports: A Case Study of the U.N. Experience.* Praeger Special Studies. New York: Praeger Publishers, Inc., 1966. 233 pages.

[158] AMUZEGAR, Jahanger. *Technical Assistance in Theory and Practice: The Case of Iran.* Praeger Special Studies. New York: Praeger Publishers, Inc., 1966. 275 pages.

[159] APTER, David E. "The Development of AID." Yale University, New Haven, Conn. Paper prepared in conjunction with the seminars on technical assistance methodology sponsored by U.S. Agency for International Development, 1972. 50 pages. (Mimeographed.)

[160] ARENSBERG, Conrad M., and Niehoff, Arthur H. *Introducing Social Change.* Chicago: Aldine Publishing Co., 1964. 214 pages.

[161] ARGYRIS, Chris. *Integrating the Individual and the Organization.* New York: John Wiley and Sons, Inc., 1964. 330 pages.

[162] ARGYRIS, Chris. *Interpersonal Competence and Organizational Effectiveness.* Homewood, Ill.: Dorsey Press, Inc., 1962. 292 pages.

[163] ARNON, I. *Organization and Administration of Agricultural Research.* New York: Elsevier Publishing Co., Ltd., 1968. 342 pages.

[164] ARRINGTON, Leonard J. *Great Basin Kingdom: Economic History of the Latter Day Saints, 1830–1900.* Lincoln, Nebr.: University of Nebraska Press, 1958. 534 pages.

[165] ASHBY, Eric. *African Universities and Western Tradition: The Godkin Lectures at Harvard University.* Cambridge, Mass.: Harvard University Press, 1964. 113 pages.

[166] ASHBY, Eric (with the assistance of Mary Anderson). *Universities: British, Indian, African.* Cambridge, Mass.: Harvard University Press, 1966. 558 pages.

[167] BAKKE, E. Wight, and Argyris, Chris. *Organizational Structure and Dynamics: A Framework for a Theory.* New Haven, Conn.: Yale University Labor and Management Center, 1954. 38 pages.

[168] BANFIELD, Edward C. *The Moral Basis of a Backward Society.* Chicago: The Free Press, 1958. 204 pages.

[169] BASS, Lawrence W. *The Management of Technical Programs: With Special Reference to the Needs of Developing Countries.* New York: Praeger Publishers, Inc., 1965. 138 pages.

[170] BEAL, George M., et al. *Social Indicators: Bibliography I.* Sociology Report No. 92. Ames, Iowa: Iowa State University of Science and Technology, 1971.

[171] BECKER, Howard S., et al., eds. *Institutions and the Person: Papers Presented to Everett C. Hughes.* Chicago: Aldine Publishing Co., 1968. 372 pages.

[172] BELL, David E. "On the Future of Technical Assistance." *Industrial Organization and Economic Development.* Edited by Jesse W. Markham and Gustav F. Papanek. Boston: Houghton Mifflin Co., 1970. 422 pages.

[173] BELSHAW, Cyril S. "Evaluation of Technical Assistance as a Contribution to Development." *International Development Review,* 8 (June 1966), 2–6, 23.

[174] BENDIX, Reinhard. *Nation-Building and Citizenship: Studies of Our Changing Social Order.* New York: John Wiley and Sons, Inc., 1964. 314 pages.

[175] BENNIS, W. G.; Benne, Kenneth D.; and Chin, Robert, eds. *The Planning of Change: Readings in the Applied Behavioral Sciences.* New York: Holt, Rinehart and Winston, Inc., 1961. 781 pages.

[176] BHABHA, H. J. "Science and the Problems of Development." Lecture delivered at the International Council of Scientific Unions, Atomic Energy Establishment, Trombay, Bombay, India, January 1966. 12 pages.

[177] BLACK, Cyril Edwin. *The Dynamics of Modernization: A Study in Comparative History.* New York: Harper and Row, Publishers, 1966. 207 pages.

[178] BLASE, Melvin G., and Goodwin, Joseph B., eds. *Readings in International Agricultural Economic Development.* New York: MSS Educational Publishing Co., Inc., 1970. 205 pages.

[179] BLASE, Melvin G., and Paulsen, Arnold. "The Agricultural Experiment Station: An Institutional Development Perspective." *Agricultural Science Review,* 10, 2 (1972), 11–17.

[180] BLAU, Peter M. *Exchange and Power in Social Life.* New York: John Wiley and Sons, Inc., 1964. 352 pages.

[181] BLUME, Hans. *Organizational Aspects of Agro-Industrial Development Agencies: 9 Case Studies in Africa (Tea, Cotton, Oil-Palm).* München, Germany: Weltforum Verlag, 1971. 239 pages.

[182] BRAIBANTI, Ralph, ed. *Political and Administrative Development.* Durham, N.C.: Duke University Press, 1969. 688 pages.

[183] BREITER, A. E. "Institution Building Applied to a Top Management Development Program." Unpublished master's dissertation, Massachusetts Institute of Technology, Cambridge, Mass., 1969. (Microfilm.)

[184] BROOKINGS Institution. *Development of the Emerging Countries—An Agenda for Research*. Washington, D.C.: The Institution, 1962. 239 pages.

[185] BRUMBERG, Stephen F. "*Accion Cultural Popular:* Mass Media in the Service of Colombian Rural Development—Case Study No. 1." International Council for Educational Development, Essex, Conn., April 1972.

[186] BRUTON, Henry J. *Principles of Development Economics*. Englewood Cliffs, N.J.: Prentice-Hall, Inc., 1965. 376 pages.

[187] BUNTING, A. H., ed. *Change in Agriculture*. New York: Praeger Publishers, Inc., 1970. 813 pages.

[188] BURNS, Tom, and Stalker, G. M. *The Management of Innovation*. London: Tavistock Publications, 1961. 269 pages.

[189] BYRNES, Francis C. *Americans in Technical Assistance: A Study of Attitudes and Responses to Their Role Abroad*. New York: Praeger Publishers, Inc., 1965. 156 pages.

[190] CAIDEN, Gerald E. *Administrative Reform*. Chicago: Aldine Publishing Co., 1969. 239 pages.

[191] CHAMBERS, Robert. "The Small Farmer Is a Professional." *Ceres* (March–April 1980), 19–23.

[192] CHAUDHURI, K. N. *The English East India Company: The Study of an Early Joint-Stock Company 1600–1640*. London: Frank Cass & Co., Ltd., 1965. 245 pages.

[193] CHOLDIN, Harvey M. "The Development Project as Natural Experiment: The Comilla, Pakistan, Projects." *Economic Develop-*

ment and Cultural Change, 17 (July 1969), 483–500. (Article No. 4167, Michigan Agricultural Experiment Station, Michigan State University, East Lansing, Mich.)

[194] CHOLDIN, Harvey M. "Urban Cooperatives at Comilla, Pakistan: A Case Study of Local-Level Development." *Economic Development and Cultural Change,* 16 (January 1968), 189–218. (Article No. 4073, Michigan Agricultural Experiment Station, Michigan State University, East Lansing, Mich.)

[195] CHOWDHRY, Kamla Kapur. "Social and Cultural Factors in Management Development in India and the Role of the Expert." *International Labour Review,* 94 (August 1966), 132–47.

[196] CIRIACY-WANTRUP, S. V. "Water Policy and Economic Optimizing." *American Economic Review,* 67 (May 1967), 179–89.

[197] CLEVELAND, Harlan, and Mangone, Gerard J., eds. *The Art of Overseasmanship.* Syracuse, N.Y.: Syracuse University Press, 1957. 150 pages.

[198] CLEVELAND, Harlan; Mangone, Gerard J.; and Adams, John Clarke. *The Overseas Americans.* New York: McGraw-Hill Book Co., Inc., 1960. 316 pages.

[199] COMMONS, John R. *Institutional Economics.* Madison, Wis.: University of Wisconsin Press, 1961. 921 pages.

[200] COPLIN, William D., ed. *Simulation in the Study of Politics.* Chicago: Markham Publishing Co., 1968. 365 pages.

[201] COWAN, L. Gray; O'Connell, James; and Scanlon, David G., eds. *Education and Nation Building in Africa.* New York: Frederick A. Praeger, Inc., Publishers, 1965. 403 pages.

[202] CROZIER, Michel. *The Bureaucratic Phenomenon.* Chicago: University of Chicago Press, 1964. 320 pages.

[203] DeGREGORI, Thomas R. "Technology and Economic Dependency: An Institutional Assessment." *Journal of Economic Issues*, XII, 2 (June 1978), 467–76.

[204] DE VRIES, Egbert, and Casanova, P. Gonzales, eds. *Social Research and Rural Life in Central America, Mexico and the Caribbean Region.* Proceedings of a seminar organized by UNESCO in cooperation with the United Nations Economic Commission for Latin America, Mexico City, October 17–27, 1962. Paris: UNESCO, 1966. 257 pages.

[205] DEWEY, John. *Logic: The Theory of Inquiry.* New York: H. Holt and Co., 1938. 546 pages.

[206] DE WILDE, John C. "Nonformal Education and the Development of Small Enterprise in India." International Council for Educational Development, Essex, Conn., January 1972. (Preliminary work.)

[207] DOBYNS, Henry, et al. *Methods of Analyzing Cultural Change.* ERP Document Number VII-12. Ithaca, N.Y.: Cornell University, 1957.

[208] DOBYNS, Henry, et al. *Strategic Intervention in the Cultural Change Process.* ERP Document Number VII-11. Ithaca, N.Y.: Cornell University, 1967.

[209] DOMERGUE, Maurice. *Technical Assistance: Theory, Practice and Policies.* New York; Praeger Publishers, Inc., 1968, 196 pages.

[210] DORNER, Peter, ed. *Land Reform in Latin America: Issues and Cases. Land Economics.* Monograph Series No. 3. Madison, Wis.: University of Wisconsin Land Tenure Center, 1971. 276 pages.

[211] DOWNS, Anthony. *Inside Bureaucracy.* A Rand Corporation Research Study. Boston: Little, Brown and Co., 1967. 292 pages.

[212] EASTON, David. *A Systems Analysis of Political Life.* New York: John Wiley and Sons, Inc., 1965. 507 pages.

[213] EATON, Joseph W. "Gadna: Israel's Youth Corps." *Middle East Journal* (August 1969), 471–83. See citation [96] for a summary.

[214] EATON, Joseph W. "Reaching the Hard-to-Reach in Israel." *Social Work,* 15 (January 1970), 85–96. (Part of Inter-University Research Program in Institution Building.)

[215] EISENSTADT, Samuel N. "Review Article: Some New Looks at the Problems of Relationships between Traditional Societies and Modernization." *Economic Development and Cultural Change,* 16 (April 1968), 451–69.

[216] ENSMINGER, Douglas. "Overcoming the Obstacles to Farm Economic Development in the Less-Developed Countries." *Journal of Farm Economics,* 44 (December 1962), 1367–87.

[217] ETZIONI, Amitai, ed. *A Sociological Reader on Complex Organizations.* 2nd ed. New York: Holt, Rinehart and Winston, Inc., 1969. 576 pages. (First published in 1961 under the title *Complex Organizations: A Sociological Reader.*)

[218] FAUNCE, William A.; Hardin, Einar; and Jacobson, Eugene H. "Automation and the Employee." *Annals of the American Academy: Special Issue,* 340 (March 1962), 60–68.

[219] FOSTER, George M. *Traditional Cultures, and the Impact of Technological Change.* New York: Harper and Row, Publishers, 1962. 292 pages.

[220] FRIEDMANN, John. "The Institutional Context." *Action Under Planning.* Edited by Bertram M. Gross. New York: McGraw-Hill Book Co., Inc., 1967. Pp. 31–67.

[221] FUSFELD, Daniel R. "The Development of Economic Institutions." *Journal of Economic Issues*, XI, 4 (December 1977), 743–83.

[222] GARDNER, John W. "AID and the Universities." A Report to the Administrator for the Agency for International Development. Washington, D.C.: U.S. Agency for International Development, 1964. 57 pages.

[223] GETZELS, J. W., and Guba, E. G. "Role, Role Conflicts, and Effectiveness: An Empirical Study." *American Sociological Review*, 19 (April 1954), 164–75.

[224] GILPIN, Clifford, and Grabe, Sven. "Programs for Small Industry Entrepreneurs and Journeymen in Northern Nigeria—Case Study No. 7." International Council for Educational Development, Essex, Conn., April 1972. (Preliminary work.)

[225] GITTINGER, J. Price. *The Literature of Agricultural Planning*. Planning Methods, Series No. 4. Washington, D.C.: Center for Development Planning, National Planning Association. 136 pages.

[226] GLICK, Philip M. *The Administration of Technical Assistance—Growth in the Americas*. Chicago: University of Chicago Press, 1957. 390 pages.

[227] GRABE, Sven. "The Cooperative Education System of Tanzania—Case Study No. 9." International Council for Educational Development, Essex, Conn., April 1972. (Preliminary work.)

[228] GRABE, Sven. "The Rural Education System in Upper Volta—Case Study No. 14." International Council for Educational Development, Essex, Conn., April 1972. (Preliminary work.)

[229] GRILICHES, Zvi. "Research Costs and Social Returns: Hybrid Corn and Related Innovations." *Journal of Political Economy*, 66 (October 1958), 419–31.

[230] GROSS, Bertram M. *The Managing of Organizations: The Administrative Struggle.* 2 vols. New York: Free Press of Glencoe, 1964. 971 pages.

[231] GUITHER, Harold D., and Thompson, W. N. "Agricultural Economics in Overseas Development Assistance and the Impact upon U.S. Universities." *American Journal of Agricultural Economics,* 50 (December 1968), 1313–25.

[232] GUITHER, Harold D., and Thompson, W. N. *Mission Overseas: A Handbook for U.S. Families in Developing Countries.* Urbana, Ill.: University of Illinois Press, 1969. 294 pages.

[233] HAGEN, Everett E. *On the Theory of Social Change—How Economic Growth Begins.* Homewood, Ill.: Dorsey Press, Inc., 1962. 557 pages.

[234] HAMBIDGE, Gove, ed. *Dynamics of Development: An International Development Reader.* New York: Frederick A. Praeger, Inc., Publishers, 1964. 401 pages. Chapter 13, "Institution Building in National Development" by Milton Esman (pp. 140–51), is of special interest to institution builders.

[235] HAMILTON, William B., ed. *The Transfer of Institutions.* Durham, N.C.: Duke University Press, 1964. 312 pages.

[236] HANSEN, Gary. *Regional Administration for Rural Development in Indonesia: The Bimas Case.* East-West Center Working Paper Series No. 26. Honolulu: Technology and Development Institute, 1972. 21 pages. (Mimeographed.)

[237] HART, Henry C. *Campus India: An Appraisal of American College Programs in India.* East Lansing, Mich.: Michigan State University Press, 1961. 217 pages.

[238] HAVELOCK, Ronald G. *Planning for Innovation through Dissemination and Utilization of Knowledge.* Ann Arbor, Mich.: Center for Research on Utilization of Scientific Knowledge, Institute for Social Research, 1971. Numbered by chapters. (The larger bibliography upon which part of this publication is based can be obtained as ED #029172 from the same source.)

[239] HAYAMI, Yujiro, and Ruttan, Vernon W. *Agricultural Development: An International Perspective.* Baltimore, Md.: Johns Hopkins Press, 1971. 367 pages.

[240] HILLS, R. Jean. *Toward a Science of Organization.* Eugene, Oreg.: Eugene Center for the Advanced Study of Educational Administration, University of Oregon, 1968, 122 pages.

[241] HIRSCHMAN, Albert O. *Journeys Toward Progress: Studies of Economic Policy-Making in Latin America.* New York: Twentieth Century Fund, 1963. 308 pages.

[242] HIRSCHMAN, Albert O. *The Strategy of Economic Development.* New Haven, Conn.: Yale University Press, 1961.

[243] HUNTER, Guy. *The Best of Both Worlds?: A Challenge on Development Policies in Africa.* London: Published for the Institute of Race Relations by Oxford University Press, 1967. 132 pages.

[244] HUNTER, Guy. *Modernizing Peasant Societies: A Comparative Study in Asia and Africa.* London: Published for the Institute of Race Relations by Oxford University Press, 1969. 324 pages.

[245] HUNTINGTON, Samuel P. *Political Order in Changing Societies.* New Haven, Conn.: Yale Univesity Press, 1968. 488 pages.

[246] ILCHMAN, Warren F., and Uphoff, Norman Thomas. *The Political Economy of Change.* Berkeley, Calif.: University of California Press, 1969. 316 pages.

[247] JALAN, B., ed. *Problems and Policies in Small Economies*. New York: St. Martin's Press, Inc., 1982. 275 pages.

[248] JOHNSON, Richard A.; Kast, Fremont, E.; and Rosenzweig, James E. *The Theory and Management of Systems*. New York: McGraw-Hill Book Co., Inc., 1963. 513 pages.

[249] JOHNSTON, Bruce F., and Clark, William C. *Redesigning Rural Development: A Strategic Perspective*. Baltimore: Johns Hopkins University Press, 1982. 311 pages.

[250] JOINT Committee of the National Association of State Universities and Land Grant Colleges, and the Agency for International Development. *The Institutional Development Agreement: A New Operational Framework for AID and the Universities*. Washington, D.C.: Agency for International Development, 1970. 88 pages.

[251] JONES, Garth N. *Planned Organizational Change: A Study in Change Dynamics*. London: Routledge and Kegan Paul, 1969. 243 pages.

[252] JONES, Stephany Griffith. *The Role of Finance in the Transition to Socialism*. Totowa, N.J.: Allanheld, Osmun & Co. Publishers, 1981. 194 pages.

[253] KALUSEN, A. M. *Kerala Fishermen and the Indo-Norwegian Pilot Project*. Oslo, Norway: Universitetsforlaget, 1968. 201 pages.

[254] KATZ, Daniel, and Kahn, Robert L. *The Social Psychology of Organizations*. New York: John Wiley and Sons, Inc., 1966. 498 pages.

[255] KATZ, Saul M. "A Systems Approach to Development Administration: A Framework for Analyzing Capability of Action for National Development." Papers in Comparative Public Administration, Special Series No. 6. American Society for Public Administration, Washington, D.C., 1965. 59 pages.

[256] KAZEMIAN, Gholam H. *Impact of U.S. Technical Aid on the Rural Development of Iran.* Brooklyn, N.Y.: Theo Gaus' Sons, Inc., 1968. 729 pages.

[257] KREININ, Mordechai E. *Israel and Africa: A Study in Technical Cooperation.* New York: Frederick A. Praeger, Inc., Publishers, 1964. 206 pages.

[258] KROEGER, Louis J., ed. *Reflections on Successful Technical Assistance Abroad.* Washington, D.C.: Agency for International Development, 1957.

[259] KULP, Earl M. *Rural Development Planning: A Systems Analysis and Working Method.* New York: Praeger Publishers, Inc., 1970. 664 pages.

[260] LAUFER, Leopold. *Israel and the Developing Countries: New Approaches to Cooperation.* New York: Twentieth Century Fund, 1967. 298 pages.

[261] LAWRENCE, Paul R., and Lorsch, Jay W. *Developing Organizations: Diagnosis and Action.* Reading, Mass.: Addison-Wesley Publishing Co., 1969. 101 pages.

[262] LEAGANS, J. Paul, and Loomis, Charles P., eds. *Behavioral Change in Agriculture: Concepts and Strategies for Influencing Transition.* Ithaca, N.Y.: Cornell University Press, 1971. 506 pages.

[263] LIKERT, Rensis. *The Human Organization: Its Management and Value.* New York: McGraw-Hill Book Co., Inc., 1967. 258 pages.

[264] LIKERT, Rensis. *New Patterns of Management.* New York: McGraw-Hill Book Co., Inc., 1961. 279 pages.

[265] LIN, Nan. "Innovation Internalization in a Formal Organization."

Unpublished Ph.D. dissertation, Michigan State University, East Lansing, Mich., 1966. 117 pages.

[266] LINDHOLM, Richard W. "A Tested Program for Third World Economic Development." *American Journal of Economics and Sociology,* 36, 2 (April 1977), 165–68.

[267] LIU, Shao-Chi. *How to Be a Good Communist.* New York: New Century Publishers, 1952. 64 pages.

[268] LOOMIS, Charles. *Social Systems: Essays on their Persistence and Change.* Princeton, N.J.: D. Van Nostrand Co., Inc., 1960. 349 pages.

[269] LOOMIS, Charles. "Toward a Theory of Systemic Social Change." *Inter-professional Training Goals for Technical Assistance Personnel Abroad.* Edited by I. T. Sanders. New York: Council on Social Work Education, 1969. 198 pages.

[270] LOOMIS, Charles P., and Rytina, Joan. *Marxist Theory and Indian Communism: A Sociological Interpretation.* East Lansing, Mich.: Michigan State University Press, 1970. 148 pages.

[271] LOOMIS, Ralph A. "Why Overseas Technical Assistance is Ineffective." *American Journal of Agricultural Economics,* 50 (December 1968), 329–41.

[272] McCLELLAND, David C. *The Achieving Society.* Princeton, N.J.: D. Van Nostrand Co., Inc., 1961. 512 pages.

[273] MADDISON, Angus. *Foreign Skills and Technical Assistance in Economic Development.* Paris: Development Centre Studies, Organization for Economic Cooperation and Development, 1965. 104 pages.

[274] MADDISON, Angus; Stavrianopoulos, Alexander; and Higgins,

Benjamin. *Foreign Skills and Technical Assistance in Greek Development*. Paris: Development Centre Studies, Organization for Economic Cooperation and Development, 1966. 169 pages.

[275] MALONE, Carl C., and Johnson, Sherman E. "The Intensive Agricultural Development Program in India." *Agricultural Economics Research*, 23 (April 1971), 25–35.

[276] MANAGEMENT Development Working Group Office of Rural Development and Development Administration, Development Support Bureau, U.S. Agency for International Development. *Management Development Strategy Paper: AID's Response to the Implementation Needs of 1980s*. Washington, D.C.: U.S. Agency for International Development, June 1981. 40 pages. (Mimeographed.)

[277] MARCH, James G., ed. *Handbook of Organizations*. Chicago: Rand McNally and Co., 1965. 1247 pages.

[278] MARCH, James G., and Simon, Herbert A. (with the assistance of Harold Guetzkow). *Organizations*. New York: John Wiley and Sons, Inc., 1958. 262 pages.

[279] MARTIN, Roscoe C. "Technical Assistance: The Problem of Implementation." *Public Administration Review*, 12 (1952), 258–66.

[280] MARTIN, Roscoe C., ed. *TVA The First Twenty Years: A Staff Report*. Knoxville, Tenn.: University of Alabama Press and University of Tennessee Press, 1956. 282 pages.

[281] MARTINDALE, Don Albert. *Institutions, Organizations, and Mass Society*. Boston: Houghton Mifflin Co., 1966. 576 pages.

[282] MEADOWS, Paul. "Institution Building: A Sociological Perspective." Syracuse University, Syracuse, N.Y., 1964. 15 pages. (Mim-

eographed. Preliminary work. Part of Inter-University Research Program in Institution Building.)

[283] MEEHAN, Eugene J. *Science and Policy Making.* Proceedings of the Wisconsin OAPEC and Arab Fund Seminar, Vol. 1. Madison, Wis.: n.p., 1978. 8 pages. (Mimeographed.)

[284] MILLIKAN, Max F., and Hapgood, David. *No Easy Harvest: The Dilemma of Agriculture in Underdeveloped Countries.* Boston: Little, Brown and Co., 1967. 178 pages.

[285] MONTGOMERY, John D., and Siffin, William J., eds. *Approaches to Development: Politics, Administration and Change.* New York: McGraw-Hill Book Co., Inc., 1966. 299 pages.

[286] MOORE, Wilbert E. *Social Change.* Englewood Cliffs, N.J.: Prentice-Hall, Inc., 1963. 120 pages.

[287] MOREHOUSE, Ward. "Plato and the Sarkari Scientist: Government Administration and Scientific Research in India." *Journal of the Administrative Staff College Association,* 14 (March 1970), 22–43. This journal is published by the Administrative Staff College of India, Hyderabad.

[288] MOSHER, Arthur T. *Creating a Progressive Rural Structure: To Serve a Modern Agriculture.* New York: Agricultural Development Council, Inc., 1969. 172 pages.

[289] MOSHER, Arthur T. *Getting Agriculture Moving: Essentials for Development and Modernization.* New York: Published for the Agricultural Development Council by Praeger Publishers, Inc., 1966. 191 pages.

[290] MOSHER, Arthur T. *To Create a Modern Agriculture.* New York: The Agricultural Development Council, Inc., 1971. 162 pages.

[291] MYRDAL, Gunnar. *Asian Drama: An Inquiry into the Poverty of Nations.* 3 vols. New York: Twentieth Century Fund, 1968. 2284 pages.

[292] NAIR, Kusum. *Blossoms in the Dust: The Human Factor in Indian Development.* New York: Praeger Publishers, Inc., 1961. 206 pages.

[293] NAIR, Kusum. *The Lonely Furrow: Farming in the United States, Japan, and India.* Ann Arbor, Mich.: University of Michigan Press, 1969. 314 pages.

[294] NORTE, Zona. *Esqueme de Analisis Institucional.* IICA, May 1976.

[295] NYERERE, Julius K. "On Rural Development." Address to the Food and Agriculture Organization, World Conference of Agrarian Reform and Rural Development. Rome, Italy: 1979. 15 pages. (Mimeographed.)

[296] O'CONNELL, Jeremiah J. *Managing Organizational Innovation.* Homewood, Ill.: Richard D. Irwin, Inc., 1968. 199 pages.

[297] OLSON, Mancur. *The Rise and Decline of Nations.* New Haven and London: Yale University Press, 1982. 273 pages.

[298] ORGANIZATION for Economic Cooperation and Development. *Aid to Agriculture in Developing Countries.* Paris: The Organization, 1968. 184 pages.

[299] ORGANIZATION for Economic Cooperation and Development. *Catalogue of Social and Economic Development Training Institutes and Programmes 1970.* 2 vols. Paris: The Organization, 1970. 533 pages and 412 pages respectively.

[300] ORGANIZATION for Economic Cooperation and Development. *Regional Project of Kosovo–Metohija, Yugoslavia.* OECD Technical Assistance Evaluation Studies. Paris: The Organization, 1968. 94 pages.

[301] ORGANIZATION for Economic Cooperation and Development. *Technical Assistance and the Economic Development of Spain.* Paris: The Organization, 1968. 108 pages.

[302] OWEN, Marguerite. *The Tennessee Valley Authority.* New York: Praeger, 1973. 275 pages.

[303] PAAUW, Douglas S., and Fei, John C. H. "The Institutional Approach to Economic Growth." M-9422. A working paper for the National Planning Association, Washington, D.C., 1968. 88 pages.

[304] PAAUW, Douglas S., and Fei, John C. H. *The Transition in Open Dualistic Economies.* 2 vols. M-9859. Washington, D.C.: Center for Development Planning, National Planning Association, 1970. 715 pages.

[305] PAPANEK, Gustav F. "The Economist as Policy Adviser in the Less Developed World." *International Development Review,* 11 (March 1969), 7–13.

[306] PERLMUTTER, H. V. *A Conceptual Guide for the Organization Building Process.* Mimeo No. HPBE 109. Lausanne, Switzerland: Institute des Études de Méthodes de Direction de l'Entreprise, 1965.

[307] PERLMUTTER, H. V. *Towards a Theory and Practice of Social Architecture.* Tavistock Pamphlet No. 12. London: Tavistock Publications, 1965.

[308] PHILLIPS, Hiram S. "Foundation Stones and Building Blocks of Institutional Development." Agency for International Development, Washington, D.C., 1965. 16 pages. (Mimeographed.)

[309] PONSIOEN, J. A. *National Development: A Sociological Contribution.*

The Hague: Mouton, 1968. 286 pages.

[310] PROPP, Kathleen M.; Guither, Harold D.; Regnier, Earl H.; Thompson, William N. "AID-University Rural Development Contracts 1951–1966." University of Illinois, Urbana, Ill., June 1968. 95 pages. (Part of Committee on Institutional Cooperation and Agency for International Development Rural Development Research Project.)

[311] PYE, Lucian W. *Aspects of Political Development.* Boston: Little, Brown and Co., 1966. 205 pages.

[312] RAHMAN, A. T. R. "Theories of Administrative and Political Development and Rural Institutions in India and Pakistan." SEADAG papers, No. 21. Paper presented at the meeting of the Southeast Asia Development Advisory Group (SEADAG) Development Administration Seminar in Carmel, Calif., November 23–25, 1967. New York: SEADAG. 26 pages.

[313] RAPER, Arthur F., et al. *Rural Development in Action: The Comprehensive Experiment at Comilla, East Pakistan.* Ithaca, N.Y.: Cornell University Press, 1970. 351 pages.

[314] RICE, E. B. *Extension in the Andes: An Evaluation of Official U.S. Assistance to Agricultural Extension Services in Central and South America.* Agency for International Development Evaluation Paper 3A. Washington, D.C.: Agency for International Development, 1971. 552 pages.

[315] RIGGS, Fred W. *Administration in Developing Countries—The Theory of Prismatic Society.* Boston: Houghton Mifflin Co., 1964. 477 pages.

[316] RIGGS, Fred W., ed. *Frontiers of Development Administration.* Durham, N.C.: Duke University Press, 1971. 623 pages.

[317] RIGNEY, J. A.; Bumgardner, Harvey L.; Ellis, Walter; Lynton, Rolf P.; and Jung, Christian W. "A Guide to Institution Building for Team Leaders of Technical Assistance Projects." North Carolina State University, Raleigh, N.C., 1971. Reprint ed., South East Consortium for International Development, Chapel Hill, N.C., 1981. Pages numbered by chapters. (Mimeographed.)

[318] RIVKIN, Arnold, ed. *Nations by Design: Institution Building in Africa.* Colloquium on Institution Building and the African Development Process, 1967. Garden City, N.Y.: Doubleday and Co., Inc., 1968. 386 pages.

[319] ROBERTS, Richard. *Economic Development, Human Skills and Technical Assistance: A Study of I.L.O. Technical Assistance in the Field of Productivity and Management Development.* Geneva, Switzerland: Librairie E. Droz, 1962. 157 pages.

[320] ROGERS, Everett M.; Joyce, Richard E.; et al. "Diffusion of Innovations: Educational Change in Thai Government Secondary Schools." Michigan State University, East Lansing, Mich., 1969. 179 pages. (Mimeographed. Part of Inter-University Research Program in Institution Building. Shorter form available by same authors: "The Diffusion of Educational Innovations in the Government Secondary Schools of Thailand," 1968. 59 pages. English and Thai.)

[321] ROGERS, Everett M., and Shoemaker, F. Floyd. *Communications of Innovations: A Cross-Cultural Approach.* New York: The Free Press, 1971. 476 pages. (First edition of this book was entitled *Diffusion of Innovations,* 1962.)

[322] ROSE, Arnold, ed. *The Institutions of Advanced Societies.* Minneapolis: University of Minnesota Press, 1958. 691 pages.

[323] RUTTAN, Vernon W. *Agricultural Research Policy.* Minneapolis: Uni-

versity of Minnesota Press, 1982. 370 pages.

[324] SANDERS, John H., and Johnson, Dennis V. "Selecting and Evaluating New Technology for Small Farmers in the Colombian Andes." *Mountain Research and Development*, 2, 3 (1982), 307–16.

[325] SANTOS, Gerald Santos. *CEPLAL, Comissão do Plano de Lavoura Cacueira, Um caso de Desenvolvimento Institucional.* Getulio Vargas Foundation, 1979.

[326] SCHAFFER, B. B., ed. *Administrative Training and Development.* New York: Praeger, 1974. 445 pages.

[327] SCHILLER, Herbert I. "Authentic National Development Versus the Free Flow of Information and the New Communications Technology." Paper prepared for Panel V of the International Symposium on Communication: Technology, Impact and Policy. Annenberg School of Communications, University of Pennsylvania, March 23–25, 1972. 22 pages. (Mimeographed. Preliminary work.)

[328] SCHILLER, Herbert I. "Madison Avenue Imperialism." *Transaction,* 8 (March/April 1971), 55–58, 64. (This article is also in *Communications and International Politics.* Edited by Richard Merritt. Urbana, Ill.: University of Illinois Press, 1972.)

[329] SCHILLER, Herbert I., and Smythe, Dallas. "Chile: An End to Cultural Colonialism." *Society,* 9 (March 1972), 35–39, 61.

[330] SCHULTZ, Theodore W. *Economic Crises in World Agriculture.* Ann Arbor, Mich.: University of Michigan Press, 1965. 114 pages.

[331] SCHULTZ, Theodore W. *Transforming Traditional Agriculture.* New Haven, Conn.: Yale University Press, 1964. 212 pages.

[332] SCHUMPETER, Joseph A. *The Theory of Economic Development: An Inquiry into Profits, Capital, Credit, Interest, and the Business Cycle.* Translated from the German by Redvers Opie. Cambridge, Mass.: Harvard University Press, 1961. 255 pages.

[333] SCHURMANN, Franz. *Ideology and Organization in Communist China.* Berkeley, Calif.: University of California Press, 1966. 540 pages.

[334] SCHUTJER, Wayne A., and Coward, E. Walter, Jr. "Planning Agricultural Development—The Matter of Priorities." *Journal of Developing Areas,* 6 (October 1971), 29–38.

[335] SCHUTJER, Wayne A., and Weigel, Dale. "The Contribution of Foreign Assistance to Agricultural Development." *American Journal of Agricultural Economics,* 51 (November 1969), 788–97.

[336] SEERS, Dudley. *The Rehabilitation of the Economy of Uganda: A Report by a Commonwealth Team of Experts.* 2 vols. London: Commonwealth Secretariat Publications, 1979. 383 pages.

[337] SELZNICK, Philip. *Leadership in Administration: A Sociological Interpretation.* New York: Harper and Row, Publishers, 1957. 162 pages.

[338] SELZNICK, Philip. *TVA and Grass Roots.* Berkeley, Calif.: University of California Press, 1953. 274 pages.

[339] SHAFER, Robert Jones. "Institution Building and Innovation in Mexican Business Associations." Graduate School of Public and International Affairs, University of Pittsburgh, Pittsburgh, Pa. (Mimeographed. Part of Inter-University Research Program in Institution Building. Preliminary work.)

[340] SHAFFER, James D. "On Institutional Obsolescence and Innovation—Background for Professional Dialog on Public Policy."

American Journal of Agricultural Economics, 51 (May 1969), 245–67.

[341] SHERWOOD, Frank P. *Institutionalizing the Grass Roots in Brazil: A Study in Comparative Local Government.* San Francisco, Calif.: Chandler Publishing Co., 1967. 173 pages.

[342] SIFFIN, William J. "Institution-Building: Some Notes Concerning Theory." 1962. 12 pages. (Mimeographed.) For later works of same author see [88], [150], and [343].

[343] SIFFIN, William J. *The Thai Bureaucracy—Institutional Change and Development.* Honolulu, Hawaii: East-West Center Press, 1966. 291 pages.

[344] SIMON, Herbert A. *Administrative Behavior: A Study of Decision-Making Processes in Administrative Organization.* New York: Macmillan Co., 1945. 259 pages.

[345] SIMON, Herbert A. *The New Science of Management Decision.* New York: Harper and Row, Publishers, 1960. 50 pages.

[346] SIMON, Herbert A. *The Sciences of the Artificial.* Cambridge, Mass.: Massachusetts Institute of Technology Press, 1969. 123 pages.

[347] SINGER, Hans, and Ansari, Javed. *Rich and Poor Countries.* 3rd ed. London: George Allen and Unwin Ltd., 1982. 239 pages.

[348] SMITH, Eldon D. "University Assistance in Building Agricultural Research Institutions in Southeast Asia—A Case Analysis." *Southern Journal of Agricultural Economics* (December 1970), 61–67.

[349] SOFER, Cyril. *The Organization from Within.* London: Tavistock Publications, 1961. 178 pages.

[350] STAUFFER, Elam K., and Blase, Melvin G. "Institutional Disequilibria in the Development Process." *Economic Development and
Cultural Change*, 22 (January 1974), 265–78.

[351] STIFEL, Laurence D.; Black, Joseph E.; and Coleman, James S., eds.
*Education and Training for Public Sector Management in Developing
Countries*. New York: Publication Office, The Rockefeller Foun-
dation, 1977. 147 pages.

[352] SUFRIN, Sidney C. *Technical Assistance—Theory and Guidelines*. Syracuse, N.Y.: Syracuse University Press, 1966. 111 pages.

[353] TASK Force on International Developmental Assistance and International Education of the National Association of State Universities and Land-Grant Colleges. "International Developmental
Assistance: A Bibliography." 1969. 39 pages.

[354] TAYLOR, Carl C., et al. *India's Roots of Democracy: A Sociological
Analysis of Rural India's Experience in Planned Development Since
Independence*. New York: Frederick A. Praeger, Publishers, Inc.,
1965. 694 pages.

[355] TEAF, Howard, M., Jr., and Franck, Peter G. *Hands Across Frontiers:
Case Studies in Technical Cooperation*. Ithaca, N.Y.: Cornell University Press, 1955. 579 pages.

[356] THOMPSON, Carey C., ed. *Institutional Adjustment: A Challenge to a
Changing Economy*. Austin, Tex.: University of Texas Press,
1967. 184 pages.

[357] THOMPSON, James D. "Organizations and Output Transactions."
American Journal of Sociology, 68 (November 1962), 309–324.

[358] THOMPSON, James D. *Organizations in Action*. New York: McGraw-
Hill Book Co., Inc., 1967. 192 pages.

[359] THOMPSON, James D., and McEwen, William J. "Organizational Goals and Environment: Goal-Setting as an Interaction Process." *American Sociological Review,* 23 (February 1958), 23–31.

[360] TINBERGEN, Jan. *Development Planning.* Translated from the Dutch by N. D. Smith. London: Weidenfeld and Nicolson, 1967. 256 pages.

[361] UNITED Nations, Public Administration Division. *Appraising Administrative Capability for Development: A Methodological Monograph Prepared by the International Group of Studies in National Planning (INTERPLAN).* New York: United Nations, 1969. 116 pages. "Additional Note 4" by Katz will be of special interest to institution builders.

[362] USEEM, John, and USEEM, Ruth. "The Interfaces of a Binational Third Culture: A Study of the American Community in India." *Journal of Social Issues,* 23 (January 1967), 130–43.

[363] VECTOR Corporation, Oak Brook, Illinois. "Afghan Karakul Institute: A Method for Administering US/AID Technical Assistance." Research Study A-002. May 1969. 35 pages.

[364] VILLANUEVA, Benjamin. "Institutional Innovations and Economic Development, Honduras: A Case Study." Unpublished Ph.D. dissertation, University of Wisconsin, Madison, Wis., 1968. 288 pages.

[365] VRANCKEN, Fernand. "Technical Assistance in Public Administration: Lessons of Experience and Possible Improvements." Paper from the XII International Congress of Administrative Sciences, Brussels International Institute of Administrative Sciences, 1963.

[366] WEATHERLEY, Richard, and Lipsky, Michael. "Street-Level Bu-

reaucrats and Institutional Innovation: Implementing Special-Education Reform." *Harvard Educational Review*, 47, 2 (May 1977), 171–97.

[367] WEIDNER, Edward W., ed. *Development Administration in Asia*. Durham, N.C.: Duke University Press, 1970. 431 pages.

[368] WEITZ, Raanan, ed. (with the assistance of Yehuda H. Landau). *Rural Development in a Changing World*. Cambridge, Mass.: Massachusetts Institute of Technology Press, 1971. 587 pages.

[369] WHYTE, William F. *Participatory Approaches to Agricultural Research and Development: A State-of-the-Art Paper*. Ithaca: Rural Development Committee, 1981. 111 pages.

[370] ZEFF, Stephen A., ed. *Business Schools and the Challenge of International Business*. Papers presented at the Conference on Education for International Business, November-December 1967. New Orleans, La.: Tulane University Graduate School of Business Administration, 1968. 292 pages.

PART II
Key Concepts:
Substance and Definition

Guide to Part II

The authors cited in Part I represent many broad disciplines. Many of the variations in the concepts they use stem from differences in the definitions used, not only among disciplines but also within each of them. The resulting confusion over the central body of literature on institution building therefore justifies this effort to identify schools of thought associated with specific definitions of specific concepts. If one dominant definition prevails in the literature, the reader's attention is called to that fact. More frequently, however, several schools of thought are represented by the definitions of concepts presented in the discussion which follows.

5
Selected Concepts

A review of the central literature on institution building reveals that nine essential or key concepts are worthy of elaboration. Each of these will be examined in depth, with emphasis on comparative perspectives and definitions. This will be followed by definitions of other terms that appear frequently in the literature. Only when the differing connotations that characterize these concepts and terms are understood does the institution building literature begin to take on meaningful form rather than appear as an amorphous mass of disjointed ideas.

INSTITUTIONS AND THE DEVELOPMENT PROCESS

A segment of the central literature addresses the question of why institutions should be considered with regard to the development process. The concept is developed that institutions play a strategic role when the focus is on development rather than growth. Joel Bernstein develops this concept as follows:

> The term "institution" is used in many ways. In this particular case, I am referring to the organized capability to perform the important economic, social, or political functions in a society. In performing these functions, institutions are particularly important in providing not only the opportunities for developmental action, but also the necessary incentives to encourage individuals to react to changing conditions in the desired manner. This reflects the interdependency of institutional arrangements and policy determination and implementation. For example, government price policy may provide incentives to produce more of a particular type of commodity, but the individual entrepre-

neur cannot respond in a meaningful way to this incentive without access to adequate credit, marketing, and other institutional services.

Moreover, the quality of institutions is an important aspect that must be considered. It is not enough that an institution simply exists in a static sense. Rather, it is imperative that the institution be a viable, dynamic unit generating the proper conditions for orderly change in the society through time. The influence of institutions on the societies they serve can either catalyze or retard economic and social progress.

Let me summarize the previous discussion in this way. Institutions along with government policies are the major variables determining what people do in developing countries. They are prime determinants of the course of political, social, and economic progress and offer the greatest potential for influencing the direction of development. ([34], pp. 5-6)

Note that Bernstein refers to development rather than growth. John Powelson makes the distinction between economic growth and economic development and emphasizes noneconomic factors.

Economic growth is a state of increase in the national product, without reference to income distribution. Per capita economic growth occurs when the percentage increase in national product is greater than the percentage increase in population. Economic development, on the other hand, is economic growth combined with the nurture of those culture objects (norms, institutions, and values) necessary to make growth continuous. ([35], p. 7)

Likewise, Hans Blaise refers to Joseph Schumpeter in making a similar distinction. "In Schumpeter's terms, development involves 'qualitatively new phenomena,' while growth is a process of adaptation within the existing framework" ([27], p. 18).

Chandler Morse calls attention to different types of institutions in considering their role in development.

"Modernization," then, is the process of acquiring both economically progressive institutions and other types of progressive institutions as well. To acquire progressive institutions, and thus to become modern, is very different from having and operating such institutions, and thus to be modern. ([36], p. 246)

In the process of introducing their concepts of institution building as a component of economic development, Milton Esman and Fred Bruhns provide additional details about the role of institutions.

(a) Development, or more modestly, social change, and the concomitant new values, functions, technologies and action patterns, cannot be effectively introduced and sustained in transitional societies unless they are embedded in a supportive network of social structures, processes, and norms. In short, these innovative values, functions, and technologies must be institutionalized.

(b) This process takes place in and through institutional organizations which must either be newly created or adapted and restructured for this purpose.

(c) Institutional development need not be a "natural" or evolutionary process which occurs independently of human design. In this era, new technologies and new institutional forms are almost everywhere deliberately induced and directed. This sense of deliberate human purpose and human direction warrants the use of the phrase "institution building" and suggests a key role for modernizing elites. ([129], p. 6)

The concept *institution building* will be further defined and discussed later; but, first, the term *institution* requires attention.

DIVERGENT DEFINITIONS OF INSTITUTIONS

Although some authors define institutions in a way that is compatible with the roles envisioned by Esman and Bruhns, others find the multiple connotations of the word confusing. Hiram Phillips' definition is akin to that of Esman and Bruhns.

The term "institutions," as used in this work, refers to organizations staffed with personnel capable of carrying out defined, but evolving, programs contributing to social and economic development and having enough continuing resources to assure a sustained effort for establishment, acceptance, and application of new methods and values. ([135], p. 20)

Amitai Etzioni, on the other hand, finds the term confusing.

Institution is sometimes used to refer to certain types of organizations, . . . Sometimes institution refers to a quite different phenomenon—namely, to a normative principle that culturally defines behavior such as marriage or property. Because of these two conflicting usages, this term has probably caused more confusion than *formal organization* and *bureaucracy* together. All three might well be avoided in favor of the simple term, *organization.**

---

* From *Modern Organizations* (Englewood Cliffs, N.J.: Prentice-Hall, Inc., 1964), p. 3. For other work by Etzioni, see [217].

Others, however, maintain that the terms *organization* and *institution* are not synonymous. Included in this group are the analysts of the Inter-University Research Program in Institution Building (IRPIB), who, in differentiating between the terms, refer to Philip Selznick's definition.

> In what is perhaps its most significant meaning, "to institutionalize" is to *infuse with value* beyond the technical requirements of the task at hand. The prizing of social machinery beyond its technical role is largely a reflection of the unique way in which it fulfills personal or group needs. Whenever individuals become attached to an organization or a way of doing things as persons rather than as technicians, the result is a prizing of the device for its own sake. From the standpoint of the committed person, the organization is changed from an expendable tool into a valued source of personal satisfaction. . . .
>
> To summarize: organizations are technical instruments, designed as means to definite goals. They are judged on engineering premises; they are expendable. Institutions, whether conceived as groups or practices, may be partly engineered, but they have also a "natural" dimension. They are products of interaction and adaptation; they become the receptacles of group idealism; they are less readily expendable. ([337], pp. 17, 21–22)

In keeping with Selznick's distinction, Esman and Bruhns formulate the IRPIB's definition of an institution as

> . . . an organization which incorporates, fosters, and protects normative relationships and action patterns and performs functions and services which are valued in the environment. Thus, while all institutions are organizations of some type, not all organizations are institutions. ([129], p. 5)

Others in the IRPIB school of thought make similar distinctions. For example, Norman Uphoff maintains that

> An institution is more than an organization and more than a cultural pattern. It attracts support and legitimacy from its environment so that it can better perform its functions and services. This is the essential dynamic of Institutional Building. ([118], p. 24)

He also states, "To the extent that an organization succeeds over time in demonstrating the value of its functions and having them accepted by others as important and significant, the organization acquires the status of an 'institution'" ([118], p. 23).

Still other members of the IRPIB group call attention to the uniqueness of their definition. Richard Duncan and William Pooler emphasize that

It should be recognized at the outset that institutions, as used in the context of this research, are defined in a particularistic manner. They are specific formal organizations which over time have developed a capacity to act as agents for the larger society by providing valued functions and services. More than this, they serve as models for defining legitimate normative and value patterns, conserving and protecting them for the larger society. In dealing with the problem of how to introduce innovative techniques in developing societies, we assume that an effective way to do this is by creating and supporting formal organizations which utilize these innovations and corresponding technology in such a manner that, over time, given changes in the existing institutional complex of the society, these organizations take on the mantle of institutions. ([20], pp. 183–84)

Finally, Esman presents a shortened definition of *institution* as "a new or remodeled organization which induces and protects innovations" ([34], p. 22).

Hollis Peter comments on the uniqueness of the IRPIB definition.

Esman emphasized that the group concerned with research on institution building did not refer to institution as a set of pattern norms, the conventional sociological meaning referred to by Lasswell and Holmberg, Stein and Lerner. Rather, institutions are special types of organizations which embody certain values and norms, represent them in society, and promote them. In this special meaning, organizations do not qualify as institutions if they perform technical functions which are purely instrumental and which do not embody values that become normative in society. Institutions are thus a sub-class of large-scale organizations which have explicit, overt, purposeful programs of discriminating and promoting certain sorts of values. ([115], p. 343)

The IRPIB's unique definition of institution is the modal one in the institution building literature because of the heterogeneity of other definitions. Eric Ashby defines an institution as "the embodiment of an ideal" ([166], p. 3). Ward Goodenough, an anthropologist, takes a somewhat similar position.

The recipes, stockpiles, materials and social arrangements, and schedules to which people commit themselves acquire value as ends in themselves. Alternatives are devalued accordingly. These publicly valued procedures and arrangements to which such commitment has been made, and all of the things associated with them, make up a community's *institutions*. ([58], p. 344)

William H. Friedland takes still another perspective.

"Institutions" are, for purposes of the present discussion, defined as well-established and understood organized constellations of roles which fulfill functions for society or groups within a society. The point that must be stressed is that institutions are organized networks of roles with distinct social consequences. No single role represents an institution; it is the patterned organization of roles in an inseparable complex which makes the social institution meaningful. ([36], p. 44)

Not only do definitions of *institution* vary widely among disciplines but also within them. The fields of economics and sociology can be used as illustrations.

In an *American Economic Review* article, Charles Wolf states:

. . . the term "institution" refers to *organizations* and *policies*, both governmental and private. This limited definition is used in order to select those elements in the existing or potential social context which can be incorporated in institutional programs, accompanying and supplementing investment and technological programming. Such programs are conceived as groups of integrated and consciously planned institutional innovations designed to stimulate those kinds of behavior by management, farmers, labor, consumers, savers, investors, and innovators which can be expected to initiate and sustain growth. ([141], pp. 868-69)

In his classic work, John Commons defines *institutions* as "collective action in restraint, liberation, and expansion of individual action" ([199], p. 73). T. W. Schultz defines an institution as a behavioral rule ([37], p. 1113). Morse states:

Institutions are bounded, integrated, and internalized sets of social components: ideas, concepts, symbols, rules, statuses, relationships, and so on. By "bounded" we mean that the relevance of the set of components is restricted in certain commonly understood ways: for example, to people in a certain geographical area or kinship group, to those belonging to certain formal or informal organizations, to those engaged in certain kinds of behavior or present at certain times or places, and so on. By "integrated" we mean that there is a logical, an empirically necessary, or an historically sanctioned interdependence, consistency, and appropriateness among institutions and among the components of a given institution. By "internalized" we mean that the individuals whose behavior is guided by an institution understand its components and their interdependence and that, through emotional attachment or intellectual appreciation, there is a measure of commitment to the institution. Institutions thus establish and coordinate behavior patterns, making social action meaningful. ([36], pp. 268–69)

Finally, J. K. McDermott, referring to a particular type of institution, states:

Perhaps what distinguishes . . . an institution from . . . an organization, is whether or not it can influence other entities in the economy, or whether it is limited to the programs it can execute directly. . . . The fact is that institutions are not built in a vacuum. They are built only through an active, even aggressive participation in an economy. ([44], p. 160)

Even more variation with regard to the term is found in the sociological literature. Hans Blaise deals with this at some length.

Sociologists are often neither clear nor in agreement on the meaning of the term "institution." There are those who, like MacIver, restrict the term to refer to "the established forms or conditions of procedure characteristic of group activity." This implies that every group in a society has its own characteristic values, meaning, and forms of procedure or, as MacIver puts it, "every association has, in respect of its particular interest, its characteristic institutions." MacIver views an institution as symbolic, "we cannot *belong to* an institution." MacIver is not consistent, however, in the use of this term. Later in his work he speaks of political and religious institutions in the sense of social structure or organizations in such a manner that it conflicts with these earlier definitions.

Another conceptualization is provided by Parsons, who defines institution as "generalized patterns of norms which define categories of prescribed, permitted and prohibited behavior in social relationships for people in interaction with each other as members of their society and its various subsystems and groups." Following this definition, Parsons states that "thus we may speak of complexes of institutional patterns as regulating all the major functional contexts and group structures of a social system, economic, political, integrative, educational, cultural, etc." Thus, Parsons does not use the term with respect to specific functional units or organizations, but rather with regard to general societal functions and classes of units. Institutions in this context are, for instance, the family, education, property, government, etc.

In a third use of the term we find that the term institution has been used both to denote specific units or collectivities in the society, and with regard to generalized meanings, values and broadly shared norms of social structure and conduct. The outstanding example here is Stuart Chapin. Chapin distinguishes between "diffused-symbolic institutions" and "nucleated institutions." The first type refers to the meaning and value content of diffused concepts like art, law, ethics, science, etc., whereas the second possesses tangible aspects. The nucleated institutions identified by Chapin include among others local government, local business enterprise, newspapers, the school, the family, etc. He refers to the nucleated institutions as "cultural concretions" and explains their origin under five points: "First, a social institution arises out of and as a result of repeated groupings of interacting human individuals to elemental needs or drives (sex, hunger, fear, etc.). Second, common reciprocating attitudes and conventionalized behavior patterns develop out of the process of interaction (affection, loyalty, cooperation, domination, subordination, etc.). Third, cultural objects (traits) that embody symbolic values in material substances are invented or fabricated and become cue stimuli to behavior conditioned to them (the idol, cross, ring, flag, etc. are charged with emotional and sentimental meanings). Fourth, cultural objects (traits) that embody utilitarian values in material substances are invented or fabricated and become the means of satisfying creature wants for warmth, shelter, etc. (buildings, furniture, etc.). Fifth, preserved in oral and written language, externally stored and handed down from one generation to the next, there is description and specification of the patterns of interrelationship among these elemental drives, attitudes, symbolic culture traits, and utilitarian culture traits (codes, charters, constitutions, franchises, etc.)."

Variations on this classification, which distinguishes between institutions as norms of value and conduct and specific collectivities of people in organized interaction, can be found in the work of other social scientists. Perroux, for instance, distinguishes between institutions as norms (*institutions-règles du jeu*) and institutions as collectivities (*institutions-organismes*).

Arnold Rose, noting the differences in interpretation of the term "institution" has suggested that, where we speak of an integrated group of socialized individuals we can use the term group and institution interchangeably. In that case, namely, the interacting members of the group "have learned to predict each other's behavior fairly well . . . through common meaning and values." This is one of the characteristics of an institution, and with regard to the interacting members the group itself is an institution. It is the cluster of common meanings and values, regulating the action of individuals and having a permanence and universality in terms of action within that environment which can make a collectivity an institution. . . .

Regardless of the definitions and uses of the concept institution, it appears that there is basic agreement on certain elements of the phenomenon. Thus, the concept refers to a set way of perceiving and doing things; institutions prescribe the norms of behavior. Secondly, institutions have a degree of regularity and permanence independent of individual actors. Thirdly, the patterns of norms as referred to in the definitions may apply to a small group of interacting individuals or to an entire society.

Adhering to these basic elements, but deviating in some respects from the traditional sociological definitions, we shall define institutions in this context as organizations which embody, foster, and protect normative relationship and action patterns and perform functions and services which are valued in the environment. Organization as used here refers to a consciously designed and controlled set of actions and relationship patterns among persons in interaction toward the achievement of certain objectives. ([27], pp. 72–76)

Clearly, enough variation in the connotation of the term *institution* exists to require careful reading to determine the meaning each author attaches to it. The IRPIB definition of the term has much to recommend it: it is useful in considering the role of institutions in the development process and it is used modally in the literature. However, to read all the institution building literature with only that unique definition in mind would distort the meaning of a majority of the works. While a single, all-purpose definition of *institution* would be convenient, it does not exist, and the literature is not mature enough for its formulation at this time. At best, several common threads run through some of the literature.

One such thread deals with the "value" dimension of institutions. Attention is now turned to the concept that institutions, according to many writers, connote value.

INSTITUTIONS, VALUES, AND IDEOLOGY

Not surprisingly, the IRPIB school of thought, more than other authors, has developed the concept that values represent important dimensions of institutions. For example, Fred Bruhns initially quotes Saul Katz with regard to a definition of *value* and then explains its importance.

"Values are assertions about facts, and determining facts depends on values . . . values cannot be rationally established or defended but can be rationally discussed, analyzed, and understood."

This definition of values and the process of value formation eliminates "facts" as an opposite of "values"; as a result, the value-fact controversy loses much of its substance. Why then bring it up in the first place? There are three reasons. First, there seems to be much accumulated evidence that values play indeed a most important role in the decisions and transactions of most organizations, especially if we include in our definition of values not only positive forces such as goals, preferences, or the desire to reach certain future states of affairs, but also negative forces such as fears, doubts, or the rejection of certain future states of affairs. If values are important factors in organizational or administrative behavior, then the problem of handling or managing values and value congruence or dissonance also becomes important; this constitutes a challenge for both organizational theory and practice. The second reason is that dichotomous thinking, even if it reflects reality insufficiently as we have seen in the value-fact issue, can have its usefulness as an analytical device in detecting dynamic trends and in providing direction. It seems that viewing *forces* as flowing between opposite poles is an analogy not alien to reality, provided one views forces in flow and not static or momentary manifestations of a force. The third reason, when concerned with organizations, is that the rather untenable value-fact dichotomy leads us to a more fruitful dichotomy which, when used as an analytical device, seems to provide directions for value-management in organizations which we could not find in the value-exogenous perspective of organizations. . . . ([91], pp. 30–31)

Milton Esman and Fred Bruhns further develop this concept, primarily by reflecting on Hans Blaise's writings.

Thus, an organization is primarily a technical instrument, a means to reach certain objectives, but never an end in itself. In contrast, as our colleague Hans Blaise has observed, "the institutional approach emphasizes not only the instrumental characteristics; nor is the focus of analysis and action primarily on the structural, functional and behavioral elements which are internal to the organizational system though these are essential also. In institutional analysis, we are concerned with purposes and values which extend beyond the immediate task at hand," with the spreading of "norms which affect participants and clientele beyond the functional and productive specialization of the institution." Thus, institutional values and "specific relationship and action patterns governing the performance of functions within the institution become normative beyond the confines of the institution itself . . . (and) stable points of reference both within the organization and for the environment." It goes without saying that influences flow simultaneously in the opposite direction, from the environment to the institution, affecting the latter both in its structure as well as its performance. ([129], pp. 5-6)

In a similar vein Charles Wolf suggests that institutions can influence economic development by means of motivations and values. By values he means

... individual and collective judgments (or assumptions) concerning what is desirable. In "rational" human behavior, values provide the motivations which impel men to choose or avoid particular types of voluntary action. ([141], p. 880)

In attempting to identify the psychological effect of ideological differences, Douglas E. Ashford states that a compilation of very general values or attitudinal objects represents ideology ([36], p. 176). Further, John W. Lewis states, "Typically, ideology is the favorite tool in the hands of the revolutionary elite" ([36], p. 13). The reason for this can be seen in John Powelson's definition of ideology.

Ideology is the individual's view of society that best enables him to fit into it. . . . This sociopolitical concept of ideology implies a psychological reason for the individual's selection. He must create his niche in society. Either he must shape himself to fit society, or he must form his concept of society to fit his concept of himself. Most of us do a bit of each. ([35], p. 147)

Finally the importance of ideology in developing countries is underscored by Powelson, who cites Seymour M. Lipsit as follows:

"Ideology and passion may no longer be necessary to sustain the class struggle within stable and affluent democracies, but they are clearly needed in the international effort to develop free and political institutions in the rest of the world. It is only the ideological class struggle in the West which is ending. Ideological conflicts linked to levels and problems of economic development and of appropriate political institutions among different nations will last far beyond our lifetime, and men committed to democracy can abstain from them only at their peril. To aid men's actions in furthering democracy in then absolutist Europe was in some measure Tocqueville's purpose in studying the operation of American society in 1830. To clarify the operation of Western democracy in the mid-twentieth century may contribute to the political battle in Asia and Africa." ([35], p. 145)

The question of how appropriate institutions can be built is the essence of the fourth concept in the literature that deserves attention.

INSTITUTION BUILDING PROCESS

A variety of definitions of *institution building* can be found in the literature, but the most frequently encountered or modal one is that used by the IRPIB scholars. Before focusing on that one, however, several other definitions of this concept are worth noting.

The orientation of several authors is indicated by their definition of *institution building*. Thomas Hill, Warren Haynes, and Howard Baumgartel state, "More specifically, we are concerned . . . with *institution building*, by which term we mean to identify the process involved in deliberately forming a new institution or reforming an existing one" ([33], p. 1:2). Emphasizing that institution building requires more than establishment of a new organization, Edward Weidner states, "It must fit into local ways of doing things, be staffed, supported, and wanted by host country nationals, and perform a useful function for the society" ([92], p. 74). Richard P. Suttmeier emphasizes the role of institutions as change agents.

> The idea of institution building is to fabricate organizations in environments needing and perhaps desiring change. Through accumulating necessary resources, persisting over time, and most importantly impacting its environment, these organizations are to be agents for change. "Institution" is understood in Parsonian terms as referring to " 'normative patterns which define . . . proper, legitimate or expected modes of action or social relationships,' " and also as a " 'change inducing and change-protecting formal organization' ". . . . ([119], pp. 9–10)

Many of the above concepts are incorporated in the IRPIB definition of *institution building*, which is,

> . . . the planning, structuring, and guidance of new or reconstituted organizations which (a) embody changes in values, functions, physical and/or social technologies, (b) establish, foster and protect normative relationship and action patterns, and (c) attain support and complementarity in the environment. ([18], p. 2)

This definition is shortened subsequently by Milton Esman to,

"Planning and guiding organizations which induce and protect innovations, gain support, and thus become viable in their society" ([34], p. 22).

Several members of the Inter-University Research Program in Institution Building (IRPIB) group discuss the crucial aspects of institution building. According to Norman Uphoff,

> Institutional Building involves the introduction and establishment of *organizations* which in turn induce changes in patterns of action and belief within a society. Most commonly, these changes are associated with new *technologies*, both physical and social. The crux of the Institution Building process is moving *from* introduction *to* establishment, . . . ([118], p. 21)

Hans Blaise and Luis Rodriguez clarify the use of the term.

> It is frequently difficult to distinguish between institutional change and institution building. Changes in external and internal conditions, in leadership and resources make all organizations change and adapt over time. An organization which does not have this adaptive capacity is not likely to survive. Assuming that the functions it fulfills are still required by society it will be replaced by another organization or organizations which are more responsive to the changing needs. Such adaptive change of organizations, however, is conceptually different from institution *building*. Institution building refers to the deliberate infusion of fundamentally different values, functions and technologies requiring changes in the institution's doctrine, in its structural and behavioral patterns. ([63], p. 95)

One member of the group suggests a change in terminology.

> In general, it can be said that organizational institutionalization is more meaningful than the expression "institution building" because of its neutral connotation. For one thing it avoids the modernizing bias contained in the rationale of institutional building studies, thus increasing the universalistic value of the model developed so far, and it allows the latter to be applied to a wider array of organizations that may not have any connection with modernization in the cross-cultural, comparative administrative sense. ([72], p. 11)

Regardless of the specific terms used, the institution building process conceptualized by Esman et al. contains the basic elements of institution variables, linkages, and transactions. The first of these will be discussed in the next section and the remaining two in the following section.

INSTITUTION VARIABLES

Initially in this section the major institution variables will be defined in both extensive and shortened form. Subsequently, additional definitions of each of the major institutional variables will be provided. Throughout, the focus will be on parameters internal to an institution.

Viewing them as the elements necessary and sufficient to explain the systemic behavior of an institution, Milton Esman defines and describes the five institution variables as follows:

(a) *Leadership,* defined as "the group of persons who are actively engaged in the formulation of the doctrine and program of the institution and who direct its operations and relationships with the environment." Leadership is considered to be the single most critical element in institution building because deliberately induced change processes require intensive, skillful, and highly committed management both of internal and of environmental relationships. Leadership is considered primarily as a group process in which various roles such as representation, decision-making, and operational control can be distributed in a variety of patterns among the leadership group. The leadership group comprises both the holders of formally designated leadership positions as well as those who exercise important continuing influence over the institution's activities. A number of leadership properties are identified as variables, among them political viability, professional status, technical competence, organizational competence, and continuity. High ranking on each of these properties is expected to correlate with leadership success.

(b) *Doctrine,* defined as "the specification of values, objectives, and operational methods underlying social action." Doctrine is regarded as a series of themes which project, both within the organization itself and in its external environment, a set of images and expectations of institutional goals and styles of action. Among the sub-variables which seem to be significant for the effectiveness of doctrine are specificity, relationship to (or deviation from) existing norms, and relationship to (emerging) societal preferences and priorities.

(c) *Program,* defined as "those actions which are related to the performance of functions and services constituting the output of the institution." The program thus is the translation of doctrine to concrete patterns of action and the allocation of energies and other resources within the institution itself and in relationship to the external environment. The sub-variables which were identified as relevant to the program or output function of the institution are consistency, stability, and contribution to societal needs.

(d) *Resources*, defined as "the financial, physical, human, technological, (and informational) inputs of the institution." Quite obviously the problems involved in mobilizing and in ensuring the steady and reliable availability of these resources affect every aspect of the institution's activities and represent an important preoccupation of all institutional leadership. Two very broad sub-variables are identified in the original conceptualization—availability and sources.

(e) *Internal Structure*, defined as "the structure and processes established for the operation of the institution and for its maintenance." The distribution of roles within the organization, its internal authority patterns and communications systems, the commitment of personnel to the doctrine and program of the organization, affect its capacity to carry out programmatic commitments. Among the sub-variables identified in this cluster are identification (of participants with the institution and its doctrine), consistency, and adaptability. ([17], pp. 3–4)

Elsewhere Esman provides the following shortened definitions of the major institution variables:

a. *Leadership:* The group of persons who direct the institution's internal operations and manage its relations with the external environment.

b. *Doctrine:* The expression of the institution's major purposes, objectives, and methods of operations.

c. *Program:* The activities performed by the institution in producing and delivering outputs of goods or services.

d. *Resources:* The physical, financial, personnel, informational, and other inputs which are required for the functioning of the institution.

e. *Internal Structure:* The technical division of labor, and distribution of authority, and the lines of communication within the institution through which decisions are taken and action is guided and controlled. ([34], p. 22)

Leadership

Since numerous volumes have been written on the subject of leadership, the term cannot be treated extensively here. Rather it will be considered from a few selected points of view. One of these is Philip Selznick's: "The art of the creative leader is the art of institution-building, the reworking of human and technological materials to fashion an organism that embodies new and enduring values" ([337], pp. 152–53).

In his study of an African educational institution John Hanson used the term *leadership*

> . . . to refer to those persons who formulated the doctrine and program of the University and its College of Education, who directed their operations, and who were by virtue of office responsible for establishing relationships with the *environment*. ([28], p. 147)

Hans Blaise identifies the following elements as determinants of the value of leadership:

1. Functional role. . . . In short, the role or position of the leadership in the social structure bears on its channels of communication, its power and influence in the functional area and the environment. . . .

2. Status—While functional role refers to the formal position in the hierarchy, status refers to the ascribed power and influence position. . . .

3. Motivation. . . . Beyond the actual motivation of the leadership, we are also concerned with the motivations ascribed by the environment. . . .

4. Functional competence—This refers to the technical competence in the functional area of the institution as it is represented in the leadership group. . . .

5. Organization competence—By organization competence is meant what Harlan Cleveland has called "a talent for combining personnel and resources into dynamic, self-sustaining enterprises.". . .

6. Role distribution . . . which indicates whether the potentially available complementarity among the members of the leadership unit is in fact fully used. . . .

7. Continuity. . . . Without continuity in the leadership group there are likely to be changes in values and approaches which are detrimental to the consistent and systematic building of an institution. Besides, it hampers the development of the necessary competences and their application to a given situation. ([27], pp. 196–99)

Finally, Norman Uphoff and Warren Ilchman describe some aspects of the institution builder as

... not simply the counterpart of *homo economicus.* He does not merely buy cheap and sell dear. Rather he is an *entrepreneur,* combining factors of organizational production in such a way as to produce valued outputs. These in turn yield him resources which may be used to further the process of organizational growth. He is one who has a canny sense both of his market opportunities and his own objectives. He finds new *sources* of resources and support, new *combinations* which are more productive, or new *uses* for them which yield greater value of output. . . .

The characteristic of leadership, then, which distinguishes it with success is an acute faculty for strategy, that is, the use of resources *over time.* A person occupying a position of authority who lacks a sense of the productivity of time may well squander or dissipate the resources which accrue to his position. Many persons in positions of authority have resources at their disposal. Yet often by neither seizing nor making opportunities for organizational growth they forfeit the possibility of strengthening the organization—by increasing its outputs or increasing its inputs. ([24], pp. 9–11)

Doctrine

Since doctrine has proven to be a difficult concept because of its abstract nature, the following statement by Thomas Hill, Warren Haynes, and Howard Baumgartel is not surprising.

Some of the recent literature on institution building has used the term "doctrine" instead of "mission" or "objectives." At first we were tempted to avoid this term as less familiar and more ambiguous than the alternative terms which have become well established in the literature on administration, particularly on business policy. On second thought, however, it appeared to us that doctrine is a useful concept; it goes beyond the broad objectives, which normally are short statements of the major goals to be sought. The doctrine takes the objectives and converts them into a more concrete set of policies and guidelines which give definite direction for the institution's activities. ([33], pp. 2:11-12)

In explaining his use of the term, J. Silva de Carvalho states:

Doctrine is used as synonymous with ideology, more specifically "applied ideology." Put in this way, doctrine is closely associated with autonomy in the sense that doctrine may also mean rules and values which are built in the organization in such a way as to justify its functions and existence. ([94], pp. 32–33)

John Montgomery presents a similar but shorter definition of *doctrine* as "the self-propelling, self-renewing value system that gives an organization a life line independent of the corporate sum reached by adding up the qualities of its individual members" ([132], p. 28).

Finally, John Hanson discusses the functions performed by doctrine in the African university as follows:

> It was the function of doctrine to establish normative linkages between the old and the new, between establishment and innovators, such as would legitimize innovations which came with the new organization. Doctrine itself could not perform this function; yet it could provide connections which made organizational innovations appear less new, less threatening, and correspondingly more legitimate. It could tip the balance. At the same time that it might perform this function with those publics who would ultimately either institutionalize or reject innovations, it could also provide University leaders with norms or standards which could guide them in projecting programs, establishing priorities, and assessing accomplishments. It could provide a sense of solidarity and progress so important to morale. ([28], p. 99)

Program

Uphoff and Ilchman state:

> Program represents the translation of doctrine into practical activities of organization. Given the scarcity of resources, a program represents a statement of *priorities* or a sequence of resource allocations judged to be most productive for attaining organizational goals. ([24], p. 16)

Reflecting on his experience using the framework developed by Esman et al., William Thompson defines *program* as

> Those planned and organized actions that are related to the performance of functions and services, i.e., the production of the outputs of the institution (teaching, research, extension). Programs are designed to fulfill the goals of the organization as set forth in legal mandates, official doctrine, and needed and demanded by the environment to be served. ([117], pp. 146–47)

Finally, Blaise lists the following determinants of the program variable: consistency, stability, feasibility, and substantive contribution to needs ([63], pp. 203–204).

Resources

O. P. Gautam et al. define *resources* as

... the inputs of the organization that are converted into products or services and into increases in institutional capability. It includes not only financial resources that can be used for construction of physical plant, equipment and facilities and employment of personnel services, but also such intangibles as legal and political authority and information about technologies and the external environment. ([121], p. 3)

Blaise states that there are two dimensions of the resource variable:

1. Resource availability—The physical and human inputs which are available or can be obtained for the functioning of the institution and the performance of its program.

2. Sources—The sources in the environment from which resources have been obtained and alternative sources to which the institution has access. ([27], p. 206)

Jiri Nehnevajsa comments on resources as follows:

In this approach we think of *resources* as the physical, human, and technological inputs of the institution. Their availability to the innovative organization is at the crux of our studies, as is the identification of the actual and alternative sources of these resource flows, and changes in them. ([132], p. 5)

Internal Structure

With regard to internal structure, Blaise states:

Our concern is here with the mechanisms and modes of control, communication, and decision making within the institution. The structure of the institution, i.e., role specification, and the distribution of authority and decision making, affects program performance and maintenance of the system. Similarly, the structure of the institution and the processes of communication and decision making affect the identification with the institution on the part of the participants, as well as the control and influence exercised by the leadership. Where organizational structure and process deviates from the established norms within the environment, the institution's internal structure will affect the relations of the institution with the external world. It can be stated, then, that internal structure is a significant element for institution building analysis in at least four areas: (1) program performance; (2) system maintenance; (3) identification of the participants with the institution; and (4) relationships with the environment. ([27], pp. 207–208)

Reflecting on their analysis, David Derge et al. state, "Adaptability and consistency are considered to be the two most important qualities in an effective internal structure" ([31], p. 123).

William Thompson presents a comprehensive view of internal structure in the following definition:

> That organization of resources into formal and informal patterns of authority, division of responsibility among the different units of the organization, channels of communication, and means of resolving differences and formulating consensus on priorities, policies, and procedures. ([117], p. 145)

LINKAGES AND TRANSACTIONS

Richard P. Suttmeier underscores the importance of linkages and transactions.

> Because the basic purpose of the institution is to induce change in its environment linkages and transactions take on a particular importance, and indeed the conscious attention given to this thrust towards the environment has given the IB perspective a distinctive appeal. ([119], p. 10)

Before he discusses them, Milton Esman defines *linkages* as

> ... "the interdependencies which exist between an institution and other relevant parts of the society." The institutionalized organization does not exist in isolation; it must establish and maintain a network of complementarities in its environment in order to survive and to function. The environment, in turn, is not regarded as a generalized mass, but rather as a set of discrete structures with which the subject institution must interact. The institution must maintain a network of exchange relationships with a limited number of organizations and engage in transactions for the purposes of gaining support, overcoming resistance, exchanging resources, structuring the environment, and transferring norms and values. Particularly significant are the strategies and tactics by which institutional leadership attempts to manipulate or accommodate to these linkage relationships. To facilitate analysis, four types of linkages are identified: (a) *enabling linkages* "with organizations and social groups which control the allocation of authority and resources needed by the institution to function"; (b) *functional linkages,* "with those organizations performing functions and services which

are complementary in a production sense, which supply the inputs and which use the outputs of the institution"; (c) *normative linkages,* "with institutions which incorporate norms and values (positive or negative) which are relevant to the doctrine and program of the institution"; and (d) *diffused linkages,* "with elements in the society which cannot clearly be identified by membership in formal organizations." ([17], p. 5)

Subsequently, Esman succinctly defines the terms involved as follows:

Linkages: Patterned relationships between the institution and other organizations and groups in the environment. These relationships comprise the exchange of resources, services, and support and may involve various degrees of cooperation or competition.

a. *Enabling:* Relationships with organizations that control the allocation of authority to operate or of resources.

b. *Functional:* Relationships with organizations that supply needed inputs or which take outputs.

c. *Normative:* Relationships with organizations that share an interest in social purposes.

d. *Diffuse:* Relationships with individuals and groups not associated in formal organizations. ([34], pp. 22–23)

Several IRPIB scholars have amplified these concepts. Hans Blaise states:

For the creation of a new institution which introduces new values, relationship and action patterns, and social and physical technologies, the institutional linkages are highly significant. The process of institution building depends to a large extent on the number and kinds of linkages which the organization has with its environment and how these linkages are affected. . . .

A significant aspect of institution building is the structuring of an environment which supports and is complementary to the values, functions and services of the new institution. The creation of a new institution or the reconstitution of an existing institution will affect the role boundaries of the interdependent complex of functionally complementary organizations. Innovations which are introduced within and by the new institution will affect the external relations and internal processes of one or more organizations in the functional complex. Thus, concomitant changes may be required in the environment if the new institution is to adhere to its values, carry out its program, and attain its objectives. ([27], pp. 210–11)

Still other IRPIB scholars clarify the concept of linkages. Norman Uphoff and Warren Ilchman state:

> The more discriminating description by Esman of environment, . . . directs attention to the elements of an organization's environment which may resist, i.e., prevent or make more costly, the desired changes. The term "linkages" may itself also be too abstract. What is implied in that description is *exchange relationships*—exchanging resources, gaining support, establishing legitimacy, etc. This conceptualization points up the consideration most critical for institutionalization—the establishment and maintenance of "interdependencies which exist between an institution and other relevant parts of the society." It also makes clearer, on the one hand, the importance of *reciprocity*, and, on the other hand, of *asymmetry* in relationships which characterize institutions. The notion of "enabling linkages" cloaks both these distinctions. An institution provides something in return for its inputs, whether it is tangible and immediate or not. But it is more an institution and less an organization to the extent that others are more dependent on it than it on them. ([24], p. 22)

Elsewhere in the literature Uphoff provides the following clarification:

> At some points in the literature on Institutional Building, it appears that the term *linkage* refers to the *source* of resources from the environment. This ambiguity is to be avoided by identifying resource exchanges or flows as linkages and by speaking separately of groups, organizations or sectors in the environment with which linkages can be established. ([118], p. 26)

Finally, Thomas Hill, Warren Haynes, and Howard Baumgartel, who draw heavily on the Inter-University Research Program in Institution Building (IRPIB) concepts, draw an analogy from a business management perspective.

> The chief distinction between the institutions we are considering and business enterprises is that the market is not usually expected to provide full financial support. The institution is dependent upon government subsidies, foundation grants, and private donations to supplement whatever fees it collects. Winning support from the market requires a wide range of marketing activities which must be planned. Winning support from government agencies requires an analysis of points of access to the governmental structure and the planning of negotiations with the appropriate agencies. Similarly, plans must be made for approaches to foundations or private donors. ([33], p. 2:13)

Although some IRPIB researchers experience difficulties with the particular categorization of linkages formulated, these categorizations have tended to predominate in the literature emanating from that consortium. Several members of the group have amplified the concepts suggested by the four types of linkages. The following statement by Jiri Nehnevajsa illustrates this group:

> Some of the systemic linkages bind the organization to other organizations and social groups in an *enabling* manner. Some organizations, groups, and personalities control the decision-making processes which bear on the allocation of authority and resources which are essential for the innovative organization to function at all. Through these enabling linkages, the change agents seek to further their cause. The innovative organization is dependent entirely in its continued functioning on the maintenance of minimally satisfactory relations with other societal units with which it is linked in an enabling sense.

> There are also *functional linkages*. These bind the organization with others who may be performing functions and services complementary to the innovative organization. They supply the inputs, and the organizational outputs are directed to such functionally-linked units. Both inputs and outputs are generally some mixes of symbols, people, and materials. Patterns of support become manifest in inputting the right kind, of the right quantities, and at the needed times. Patterns of support will also become manifest in the acceptance and utilization of the outputs of the organization.

> There are also *normative linkages*. They specify the organization's relations with institutions which incorporate norms and values relevant to the doctrine and program of the organization. Many norms and values are thus protected by existing religious and political organizations even though they are not tied to the innovation in either an enabling or functional sense. Depending on the characteristics of the linkages, they may enhance or hamper the institution-building process.

> Finally, there are *diffused linkages*. Certain patterns of dependency exist vis-à-vis the various population aggregates. The innovative organization is either directly or indirectly affected by diffused support or resistance. The problem of diffused linkages thus concerns such issues as those of public opinion, and the relations with the larger public as mediated by the various mass media of communication and other channels for the crystallization of individual and aggregate opinion not reflected in formal institutions of a society. ([132], pp. 6–7)

A concept closely related to linkages is that of transactions.

William Siffin, one member of the IRPIB group, explains what this concept means.

It is possible to conceive of the entire process of organization—environment relations in terms of "transactions"—exchanges of goods and services, and of power and influence. From an organization viewpoint, transactions are the relational activities through which resources and mandates are procured and purposes are pursued. Transactions are the substance of an entity's linkages with its environment; they may lead to organizational growth or attenuation; and they shape as well as manifest institutional qualities. ([88], p. 266)

Subsequently, Esman provides the following short definition of transactions: "Exchanges of goods and services or of power and influence" ([34], p. 22).

A. U. Qureshi lists four purposes of transactions: (1) gaining support and overcoming resistance, (2) exchanging resources, (3) structuring the environment, and (4) transferring norms and values ([73], pp. 30–31).

INSTITUTIONALIZATION

The question of when the institution building process has been completed frequently arises. Criteria for identifying that point have been suggested by a large number of scholars in the field. In fact, a substantial portion of the institutional-organizational literature deals with this concept of institutionalization.

David Derge et al. succinctly deal with the concept.

The thrust of the institution building theory concerns the "locking in" of the organization into its environment. . . . As the outputs come to have perceived instrumental value by clientele groups in the environment and/or as the organization acquires intrinsic value *vis à vis* those clientele groups, it is becoming institutionalized in the environment. ([31], p. 4)

Samuel Huntington, a political scientist, defines institutionalization as "the process by which organizations and procedures acquire value and stability" ([131], p. 12). On the other hand, Charles Loomis, a sociologist, states, "Institutionalization is the process through which human behavior is made predictable and patterned" ([269], p. 182).

William H. Friedland states that institutionalization consists of the following three basic processes: (1) the organization of new clusters of roles, (2) the diffusion of the symbolic meaning of roles and clusters of roles, and (3) the infusion with value, a process in which, as the newly organized patterns continue to be successful, they take on value in and of themselves. Friedland adds:

> In recent times it has become common to refer to the assistance provided by technologically advanced countries in organizing administrative structures in developing countries as "institution building." This monstrosity of administrative nomenclature reflects ignorance of the sociological meaning of institutions. Buildings can be built—as can hierarchies of formal roles within formal institutions; institutions are complexes of roles that develop in spontaneous processes. Formal administrative units are usually the product of conscious and rational behavior; institutions are only rarely so. Formal organizations become institutionalized, however, when they take on symbolic and normative meaning. ([36], p. 74)

Finally, in summarizing one of the institution building conferences, George Axinn states:

> Harry Potter gave us yet another approach to the definition of institutionalization by quoting Talcott Parsons, in suggesting that the integration of expectations of the actors is a matter of the degree, not a matter of pressure, and that integration comes through a high degree of interaction. But Harry also said that when an organization became an institution, then the organization had been transformed into something with greater values and relevance to its own society. ([113], p. 7)

While the above definitions provide an indication of the heterogeneity of connotations of institutionality, the homogeneity which exists in the literature with regard to this term is indicated by the IRPIB's use of it, which is modal. Milton Esman states:

> The concept of institutionality denotes that "at least certain relationships and action patterns incorporated in the organization are normative both within the organization and for other social units, and that some support and complementarity in the environment have been attained." Within this rather generalized definition a number of tests of institutionality are identified, among them ability to survive—a necessary but not sufficient condition of institutionality; being viewed in its environment as having intrinsic value which in turn can be tested by the autonomy the institution has gained; the influence which it exercises; and the spread effect of its activities—whether specific relationships and action patterns embodied in the organization have become normative for other social units with which it interacts. ([17], pp. 5–6)

Subsequently, Esman provides the following concise definition of *institutionality:*

> The end-state of institution-building efforts characterized by the following conditions: (a) a viable organization has been established which incorporates innovations; (b) the organization and the innovations it represents have been accepted and taken up by relevant groups in the environment. ([34], p. 22)

Elsewhere Esman and Fred Bruhns quote Philip Selznick: "To institutionalize is to *infuse with value* beyond the technical requirements of the task at hand" ([129], p. 5).

As various IRPIB scholars attempted to operationalize the concept of institutionalization they developed additional dimensions of the concept. Several of these are worthy of note.

Hans Blaise places the definition in perspective.

> The process through which values and goals come to be shared and social relationships and actions become normatively regulated is defined as institutionalization. In other words, when values, goals, social relationships and processes evoke patterned responses among the participants in an interaction process, they have been institutionalized. The definition given here is somewhat more inclusive than the definitions of institutionalization found in much of the sociological literature. Loomis, e.g., defines institutionalization as "the process through which organizations are given structure and social action and interaction are made predictable." In a later work he states that "through institutionalization human behavior is made predictable and patterned, social systems are given the elements of structure and process of function. As each invention or practice is accepted or rejected as part of [the group's] life, institutionalization of relationships concerning it takes place." Two points should be noted with regard to Loomis' definitions. First, he limits the concept institutionalization to the patterning of social structure and processes. It appears that he does not view the value aspect of a new invention or practice as being institutionalized. In our view the acceptance of an invention or practice is in itself an institutionalization process. The acceptance of a new technology is not only a cognitive, rational process. It involves attaching significance, utility, or value by the members of the group, so that their behavior toward it can be determined and relevant social structures and processes can develop. This is how we interpret Selznick when he states that " 'to institutionalize' is to *infuse with value* beyond the technical requirements of the task at hand." The second point is that Loomis refers to institutionalization, i.e., the establishment of norms, as taking place *in organizations.* Although institutionalization is an important process in organizations, it seems too restrictive to specify in a definition that

institutionalization is a process which occurs in organizations. Rather, it takes place in and among collectivities of people involved in interaction. ([27], pp. 84–85)

John Hanson discusses the importance of the concept to the development process.

One of the most unfortunate residues from colonialism in developing nations is the fact that colonial institutions often came to be valued for their own sakes, to be seen as having some intrinsic value which raised them above the challenge of assessment in terms of their usefulness in fulfilling social purposes. Once an institution is so viewed, attempts to alter it become singularly difficult. The near-mystical sense of intrinsic value which has been generated precludes a call upon rational bases for change, and outmoded institutions remain as barriers to development. The important ingredient in the "institutionality" sought for development purposes is that the organization, while retaining its own identity, not lose its capacity to adapt to changing circumstances. One of the most difficult tasks which the University of Nigeria faced as an agency for social change was that of *de-institutionalizing* educational patterns which many strategically placed persons continued to justify as having merit in themselves rather than as having relevance in a particular social context or being answerable to the instrumental test of how well they served social purposes. ([28], p. 305)

Hanson also states:

When . . . we speak of *institutionality* it is of . . . a human phenomenon that we are speaking; of the success of a human organization in meeting the hopes and aspirations of the people it serves, in capturing or being captured by their dreams, in becoming *valued*. Institutionality is, of course, not only a matter of what professional educators who have devoted a lifetime to the shaping of society think and feel; it is a matter of what the new generation of teachers think, what the politicians and kingmakers accept, expect, and reward. It is a matter of what its own immediate offspring (or "products" in the terminology of the modern economic world) feel and think about their parent. ([28], pp. 5–6)

William Siffin provides still another perspective of the concept of institutionality.

The essence of institutionality is "meaningfulness." An entity is an institution to the extent that it is meaningful to its participants—to those directly involved in it, and those who perceive themselves as being affected by it.

"Meaningfulness" is not itself a highly meaningful term. In a broad manner of speaking, a meaningful entity *confers* something upon its participants and it is valued as a source of value. An institution may grant status. More basically, it may interpret existence and grant identities which have status components. It may articulate and enforce acceptable rules by which to regularize conduct and premises by which to perceive and interpret phenomena. An institution may confer competence upon participants who may value it for its personal effects upon themselves—their personalities and their abilities to attain fulfillment. It may be a prime means for the assertion of values cherished by participants particularly those with important roles within the institution. To the extent, however, that an organization is merely perceived as one of a series of alternative instruments by which values may be asserted and conferred, and to the extent that the particular instrument is seen as having few distinguishing attributes that make it more desirable or preferable to equally available means for the enhancement of value—to the extent that this circumstance attains, prospects for distinctive institutionalization are limited. ([88], pp. 4–5)

Weldon Woodward suggests another dimension to the concept.

Thus, it is helpful . . . to define as institutionalized capacity the work that an organization can perform under specific future conditions which is not fundamentally dependent upon the incumbency of any particular individual within the organization. This capacity inherent in the organization stands in sharp contrast to what might be called *personalized capacity* which depends essentially upon the incumbency of particular individuals. ([86], p. 9)

Donald Taylor reaches several conclusions.

In summary, the institutionalizing process adheres to certain postulates. First, society consists of an institutional structure in which the institutions interact with each other. Second, as a result of the relationships between institutions, values and norms emerge which determine the functional behavior and structural composition of the institutions. Third, it is a process in which change may be consciously introduced through creating new institutions for this very purpose. ([54], p. 8)

Tests of Institutionality

Initially, the IRPIB group articulated three tests of institutionality. Jiri Nehnevajsa discusses these.

One test of institutionality consists in an organization's ability to survive. This may, of course, not suffice. Survival at the cost of compromising and forfeiting most of the innovative elements would hardly establish the viability of innovative organizations. Furthermore, the survival of an organization *qua* organization need not be at issue at all. Other institutional arrangements may become the receptacles and protectors of the new values, functions, actions, and technologies. The original organizational format may come to an end of its useful societal function, and its redesign or even the dissolution of the organization may become both necessary and desirable.

The second test of institutionalization, as a process, concerns the extent to which an innovative organization comes to be viewed by its environment as having intrinsic value. Some of the parameters of this test include *autonomy* and *influence.* The former has to do with the capacity of the organization to control its own destiny, and thus to establish rules and procedures which may be independent from the larger system of which it is a part; the latter deals with an organization's capacity to acquire and use resources without being subject to detailed scrutiny of specific operational items; and it has to do with the organization's ability to defend itself against attacks and encroachments on its values and its patterns of behavior by falling back on the acknowledged intrinsic value of the organization.

The problem of influence, in turn, has to do with the degree of impact which an innovative organization can wield within the society in its particular functional area of responsibilities, and with the extent to which it can enlarge or confine its sphere of action both within the organization and outside.

Finally, the third major test of institutionality concerns the extent to which the innovative patterns embodied in the organization become normative for other social units. This is a way of looking at the diffusion- or spread-effect of the innovations thus introduced into the larger social system. ([132], pp. 3–4)

Without doubt, Hanson has made a greater contribution toward operationalizing and expanding the concept of institutionality than others. Viewing the concept of institutionality in terms of the extent to which an institution's relevant publics prize it, he develops the following criteria of institutionality:

... (1) the use made by publics of organizational outputs and services, (2) verbal approval from these publics, (3) survival and growth of the organization, (4) support from other organizations, (5) autonomy, and (6) spread of innovative norms to others within the environment. ([28], pp. 305–306)

Specific indexes are suggested for each of these criteria in his book.

TECHNICAL ASSISTANCE IN INSTITUTION BUILDING

A rather extensive amount of literature exists concerning technical assistance. Only that portion of it that is explicitly focused on institution building is included here. Even within this limited range of the literature, however, considerable variation exists with regard to the meaning of the concept of technical assistance. Several perspectives will be considered.

Richard Duncan and William Pooler provide a discussion and definition of technical assistance that are used by Philip Warnken. They state:

> *Technical assistance is first of all purposive;* it can be easily separated from traditional diffusion and acculturation which has been occurring among cultures for thousands of years.
>
> *Technical assistance is cooperative.* It requires agreement on purpose and means, between a donor agency and a recipient government. Either party participating in technical assistance is free to withdraw or to allow activities to languish until they are terminated.
>
> *Technical assistance involves an international transfer of knowledge and skill through individuals or agencies of a donor, and with a defined relationship to individuals, groups or organizations of a recipient in the accomplishment of mutually agreed objectives.* ([26], p. 10)

Prior to presenting their model of technical assistance for institution building, J. A. Rigney and J. K. McDermott define the term as follows:

> "Technical assistance" carries the distinct implication that: 1) The change is to be facilitated by a group of foreign technicians for the specific purpose of building or altering an indigenous institution. 2) The change process is to be deliberate, induced and rapid. The significance of this can be appreciated by observing that intercultural change is common in history and institutions are continually changing, even autonomously. The characteristic of technical assistance programs that make them unusual is that they specifically set out to telescope these long-time, autonomous processes into a short-run, deliberate procedure, largely under the volition of the changer. ([32], pp. 1–2)

An abbreviated definition of technical assistance is provided by George Axinn: "By technical assistance, we refer to inputs, usually coming from a second country, which are designed to assist an organization as it goes through the development process on its way to institutionalization" ([113], p. 6).

Finally, in discussing the process of modernization, John W. Lewis presents a suggestion for direction of technical assistance.

> Revolutionary elites have frequently sponsored the transference of many kinds of nonindigenous organizational forms, notably factories, armies, bureaucracies, and schools. In these, officials have endeavored to create by mass education the requisite occupational skills with little thought given to the subtle connections between discrete occupational roles or to the social relationships of workers and staff. Technical assistance programs should deal with these social connections, but most often training focuses on inculcating the required technical skills and not on the interactions among individuals possessing those skills. ([36], p. 7)

SYSTEMS, STRATEGIES, AND TACTICS

In a small but significant portion of the literature institution building is viewed from a systems perspective. As a consequence, some of the concepts of systems analysis are worth defining. Likewise, the terms *strategy* and *tactics,* frequently but not always employed in connection with systems analysis, should be discussed.

One of the foremost writers in this area, Herbert Simon, provides the following definition of a system:

> Roughly, by a complex system I mean one made up of a large number of parts that interact in a nonsimple way. In such systems, the whole is more than the sum of the parts, not in an ultimate, metaphysical sense, but in the important pragmatic sense that, given the properties of the parts and the laws of their interaction, it is not a trivial matter to infer the properties of the whole. In the face of complexity, an in-principle reductionist may be at the same time a pragmatic holist. ([346], p. 86)

Daniel Katz and Robert Kahn also define systems, emphasizing open systems.*

> System theory is basically concerned with problems of relationships, of structure, and of interdependence rather than with the constant attributes of objects. In general approach it resembles field theory except

---

* Selections from [254] reprinted by permission of John Wiley and Sons, Inc.

that its dynamics deal with temporal as well as spatial patterns. Older formulations of system constructs dealt with the closed systems of the physical sciences, in which relatively self-contained structures could be treated successfully as if they were independent of external forces. But living systems, whether biological organisms or social organizations, are acutely dependent upon their external environment and so must be conceived of as open systems. ([254], p. 18)

Elsewhere they state:

Our theoretical model for the understanding of organizations is that of an energic input-output system in which the energic return from the output reactivates the system. Social organizations are flagrantly open systems in that the input of energies and the conversion of output into further energic input consist of transactions between the organization and its environment. ([254], pp. 16–17)

Viewing systems from an administrative perspective, Saul Katz states:

The use of "system" here, as an assemblage of elements that have ordered and recurrent patterns of interrelationships built around definable objectives or purposes, is not dissimilar to its usage by economists and sociologists. . . . The systems view may be used at different levels of aggregation and for various purposes. Organizations, and often, groups of organizations, interact as systems. ([20], p. 154)

Finally Hans Blaise presents a definition of system:

In this context we shall define a system as a bounded, goal-directed social unit consisting of a set of interdependent elements and maintaining an exchange relationship with the environment. Interdependence specifies the determinate relationship among the variables as contrasted with random variability. Elements refers to all physical and social phenomena, be they concrete physical objects, structural relationships, or processes necessary for the operation of the system. For analytical purposes we are only concerned with conceptually identifiable variables, either given to measurement or definable in some other meaningful manner.

A feature of the system approach is that it clarifies the relationship of functionally related phenomena, regardless of the categorization of the variables in the system by classes of objects, processes or functions in the aggregate sense in a larger universe. Another aspect of the system approach is that it allows for the analysis of interaction and interdependence of otherwise conceptually disparate elements and the effect of changes of one variable on others. Although the elements or variables of a system are interacting and interdependent, they are not viewed as being in a state of constant equilibrium. If, however, the state of one variable in the system undergoes a change, then—to continue functioning—one or more other elements must also change, either in nature or in their intra-system relationship. This, in fact, helps to define the system.

Two more specifications must be made about systems in terms of their relevance to development theory. In the first place development is action-oriented. Thus, we are more concerned with the dynamic aspect of production or output of the system, acting upon certain inputs. The system in which we are interested, in other words, is an instrumentality with goal-orientation. Secondly, our systems are "open," they are in interaction with their environment; the variables are subject to influences from outside, while the systems as entities interact with other systems. ([27], pp. 66–67)

West Churchman summarizes by identifying four schools of thought about what really constitutes *the* systems approach:

(1) The advocates of *efficiency;* they claim that the best approach to a system is to identify the trouble spots, and especially the places where there is waste, e.g., unnecessarily high costs, and then proceed to remove the inefficiency. (2) The advocates of the use of *science* in approaching a system; they claim that there is an objective way to look at a system and to build a "model" of the system that describes how it works. The science that is used is sometimes mathematics, sometimes economics, sometimes "behavioral" (e.g., psychology and sociology). (3) The advocates of the use of human feelings, i.e., the *humanists;* they claim that systems are people, and the fundamental approach to systems consists of first looking at the human values: freedom, dignity, privacy. Above all, they say, the systems approach should avoid imposing plans, i.e., intervention of any kind. (4) The *anti-planners,* who believe that any attempt to lay out specific and "rational" plans is either foolish or dangerous or downright evil. The correct "approach" to systems is to live in them, to react in terms of one's experience, and not to try to change them by means of some grandiose scheme or mathematical model. There are all kinds of anti-planners, but the most numerous are those who believe that experience and cleverness are the hallmarks of good management. ([124], pp. 13–14)

One element of systems analysis that tends to be common in each of these schools of thought (at least in the first three) and that is applicable for institution building is feedback. James Bukhala, partially drawing upon Robert Chin's work, discusses this from the perspective of an IRPIB researcher.

As the system affects the environment, "Systems gather information about how they are doing. The information is then fed back into the system as inputs to guide and steer its operation." This feedback is essential for the maintenance of goodwill between the system and its environment. Thus institutions aspire to attain both internal and external equilibrium, and goodwill for their own survival. ([76], p. 42)

Likewise, Garth N. Jones discusses feedback.

The basic element of this feedback process involves: (1) the orderly collection of information about the functioning of a system (2) the reporting of this information into the system (3) the use of information for making further adjustments.

The agent of change places himself into a position to receive and evaluate information about the significance of the client system's behavior. He then transmits this information to the client system in order to stimulate an awareness of the need for change. ([251], p. 205)

Although not always used in a systems context, a number of definitions of *strategy* and, to a lesser extent, *tactics* are found in the literature. Several of these are worthy of note.

Focusing on a technical assistance strategy for institution building, Philip Warnken states:

For the effective use and maximum impact of technical assistance resources, something more than gross guesswork is needed in institution-building efforts. Borrowing from military terminology, perhaps what is really required is a strategy—a technical assistance institution-building strategy. As commonly used, a strategy is a planned dynamic sequence of actions directed toward the achievement of determinate objectives. Or, as [R. W.] Jones [136] notes, a plan which "represents an *a -priori* choice among future alternatives." He further adds that strategy is "future-oriented, sequential, goal directed, time bound, and reflects the full sweep of cognitive and valuational considerations." For technical assistance projects, strategy thus denotes a plan for sequencing technical assistance activities to achieve specific institution-building objectives.

The concept of a technical assistance strategy is applicable at several different levels within any given institution-building project. One type of strategy might govern the day-to-day actions of technical personnel. Such a strategy would serve as a "cookbook" for individual technicians. It would consider aspects such as personal adjustment to foreign cultures, establishing social and technical rapport with host institution personnel, developing effective counterpart relationships, guidelines for effective advisory techniques and the like.

Another type of strategy might serve as a guide to administrative personnel in institution-building projects. Its concern would be optimal institutional organization, personnel administration, program structure and similar issues. H. W. Hannah's [45] recent work provides a rather excellent example of strategy guidelines for host institution administrators. Additionally, research being undertaken by Rigney and others [32] will provide insights for technical assistance personnel. ([100], p. 6)

Again drawing upon business administration concepts, Thomas Hill, Warren Haynes, and Howard Baumgartel state:

One definition of strategy is "the pattern of objectives, purposes, or goals and major policies and plans for achieving those goals, stated in such a way as to define what business the company is in or is to be in and the kind of company it is to be." This definition will serve our purpose if we substitute the word "institution" for the word "company." Strategy is concerned with the major decisions, usually long-term in their implications, which set the general direction of the institution. ([33], p. 2:3)

Subsequently, they state:

Another purpose of strategic planning is well expressed by Learned et al.: "From the point of view of implementation, the most important function of strategy is to serve as the focus of organizational effort, as the object of commitment, and as the source of constructive motivation and self-control in the organization itself." ([33], p. 2:30)

Further, they focus on strategic planning of institutions.

Strategic planning of institutions involves a series of major decisions which do not occur in a definite sequence but, rather, overlap. The planning is not necessarily formal and systematic; in general practice, even in progressive business firms, it consists of both predetermined lines of action and a series of ad hoc decisions. In fact, one of the major issues in planning is the appropriate degree of predetermination as opposed to maintenance of flexibility to meet changing and unforeseeable situations. ([33], p. 2:3)

Subsequently, these authors identify a series of key elements in the strategic planning of institutions, which is too lengthy to present here.

Finally, Garth Jones discusses both strategies and tactics.

In general terms strategy refers to the planning and directing of operations; while tactics relates to the maneuvering of forces into positions of advantage. Both aspects involve manipulation and should be treated somewhat together. Manipulation is the substitution of judgement in such a way that those influenced are not aware that it is happening. Although this process may be known later, it is not known while the manipulation process is taking place. Manipulation is accomplished by a controlled distortion of the appearance of reality as it is seen by those affected. The actions of those influenced are based on their own judgement of what they perceive, but they are permitted to see only those things that are calculated to call out the kind of judgement desired by the control agent.

5.1 *Strategies*. These deal with the main forces of planned organizational change; they determine the general direction along which the change movement should be directed with a view to achieving the best results with the developing correlation of forces.

5.2 *Tactics*. These are part of strategy (or strategies), subordinate to it and serving it. They are methods used to achieve the directive of strategy. As such, they demand a constant appraisal of existing social potentialities and must be adjusted according to the rise and decline of social forces. The implementer of change must devise tactics best able to promote the overall objectives of the fundamental strategy. It is never really possible to say where tactics leave off and strategy begins, but the distinction does exist between day-to-day operations and broad policy directives. ([251], p. 202)

MISCELLANEOUS CONCEPTS AND DEFINITIONS

In addition to the concepts discussed above, there are numerous other terms that must be specifically defined in order to thoroughly understand individual contributions to the institution building literature. A number of the important terms are presented below, although this is not an all-inclusive list.

1. *Change agent:* "One who deliberately works toward inducing change through creative thinking and innovations." (Bruce Anderson and others, [116], Appendix A)

2. *Client system:* "This major class heading refers to the specific system, community, organization or group that requests help by an agent of change and desires change in order to achieve improved performance." (Garth Jones, [251], p. 197)

3. *Gemeinschaft-like:* "This is defined as a social system in which the individual member is the end purpose or *raison d'être* of the system, i.e., providing for his social and material needs." (Garth Jones, [251], p. 190)

4. *Gesellschaft-like:* "This is defined as a social system in which the individual member is only a means to the end, i.e., increased production of commodities and services for the enterprise." (Garth Jones, [251], p. 190)

5. *Innovations:* "New technologies, new patterns of behavior, or changes in relationships among individuals or groups." (Milton Esman, [116], Appendix A)

6. *Normative:* "Relationships with organizations that share an interest in social purposes." (Woods Thomas and Judith Fender, [34], p. 23)

7. *Openness:* "The belief that change is desirable and possible. Willingness and readiness to accept outside help. Willingness and readiness to listen to needs of others and to give help. Social climate favorable to change." (Ronald Havelock, [238], Summary)

8. *Structure:* "The degree of Systematic Organization and Coordination:
   a) of the resource system
   b) of the user system
   c) of the dissemination-utilization strategy." (Havelock, [238], Summary)

9. *Synergy:* "The number, variety, frequency, and persistance of forces that can be mobilized to produce a knowledge utilization effect." (Havelock, [238], Summary)

10. *Variables:* "The various ingredients or elements that identify each institution in varying degrees are referred to as *institution variables,* which are essentially concerned with the organization itself, and the *linkage variables,* which are mainly concerned with external relations." (R. W. Roskelley, [116], Appendix A)

PART III
Relationships Among Concepts

Guide to Part III

Like chapters 1 and 2, this part of the book is focused on micro- and macro-oriented interrelationships in the literature on institution building. In the process of identifying these interrelationships quotations are used to demonstrate (1) the underlying potential for integrating many concepts in the literature, and (2) different perspectives with regard to other concepts. This part is designed to demonstrate significant relationships, where possible, among the previously defined concepts.

6

Micro and Macro Aspects of Institution Building Prior to 1973

The nature of much of the literature on institution building facilitates categorization in one way or another. In discussing relationships among concepts found in the literature, a division between micro and macro aspects is convenient. This same division was observed at a symposium planned by the Foundation for Research on Human Behavior, for which proceedings were published. The editor, Hollis Peter, states:

> Another recurrent theme in the meeting revolved around the interactive linkages between micro and macro systems. The smallest unit in social science is a man, while the largest units discussed in relation to social change were nation states. To understand the individual as a "system" requires probing the myriad micro systems of which he is composed, and their complex inter-relationships, which make up the human being as an entity. In discussing social change, however, man and the small groups of which he is inevitably a part comprise the micro systems, whereas larger groups, organizations, communities, regions and nations approach the macro systems. ([115], pp. 5–6)

One other manuscript written by an interdisciplinary team is noteworthy in setting the tone for this chapter. The six authors of the manuscript, each representing a different discipline, were members of the Modernization Workshop at Cornell University. Their major aim was to understand a particular form of change— the modernization of low-income countries in the twentieth century. Chandler Morse provides an overview of this work.

> In the end it turned out that a common methodological conviction, two leading questions, and an emergent agreement came to influence our

work, largely determining the form and content of the essays produced. The conviction was that, in order to be successful, the study of modernization had eventually to proceed at both microanalytic and macroanalytic levels, and in a language that permitted one to move freely between the two poles, as in economic theory. . . .

The first of the two questions related to the differences between premodern and modern societies, regarded as definably different modal types. To determine and state the crucial distinguishing characteristics of each type thus came to be one of our ambitions. The second and related question, which concerned the manner in which premodern societies were transformed into modern, defined another focus for our intellectual curiosity. . . .

With our interests thus convergent, it soon became apparent that the phenomenon we wanted to examine was different in important respects from that which had given rise to modern, industrialized, high-income countries in the first instance. We found ourselves coming to early agreement that the main difference between the two phenomena (which ought to affect the analysis of modernization far more than it has) was in their origins and modes of evolution. The processes of social change that steadily increased the wealth-creating powers of the North Atlantic nations from the early Middle Ages to the nineteenth century took place in a series of small steps, the cumulative effects of which were not apparent to their initiators. Increasingly complex and formal organizational structures emerged as the cumulative consequence of activities at the grass roots. . . . The countries that have undergone modernization since the last quarter of the nineteenth century, on the other hand, beginning with Japan (and even Germany), have seen quite clearly the need to initiate indigenous processes of growth and development under forced political draft in order to close in on the early modernizers. Their efforts have been highly organized. . . .these late modernizers have had to start by creating complex, formal institutional structures *de novo*, employing or adapting blueprints derived from Western experience. Modernization in the twentieth century, therefore, is "by design," typically following . . . an "inverse model". . . .

A second common thread concerned various dimensions of the difference between modern and premodern institutions. We came to believe that an operational understanding of the many dissimilarities and their implications is more important than is generally recognized. . . . the creation of formal organizations and structures leaves many nonformal features of the institutional framework untouched and out of touch with the new formal structures. As a result, the new organizational structures in the emergent modern sector find it necessary, though far from easy, to come to terms with the residual elements of the surrounding context. Related to this . . . is the dual social-psychological problem of building into the processes of developmental intervention a constructive dynamic that will lead to increasingly cooperative interaction, and of preventing such intervention from developing a degenerative dynamic, moving toward conflict. A dilemma of similar content . . . is that politically induced modernization generates various contradictions. The question . . . concerns the extent to which the resulting difficulties can be overcome or must be regarded as setting limits on the feasible scope and speed of modernization by design.

A third thread running through the essays relates to the practical implications of the analyses for the making of policy. . . .

When one looks closely at the low-income countries (or sectors) in the world of today, the limitations of traditional economic explanations and prescriptions and the need for a broader, more flexible approach are even more apparent than before. Economists in increasing numbers, therefore, are looking for an alternative. . . . They are coming to realize that in order to deal with institutionalized poverty wherever it may exist, but especially in the Third World, a somewhat distinctive theory and method, synthesizing the orthodox and less orthodox insights of diverse social analysts, will be needed. The final essay . . . does endeavor to indicate some of the points at which economic and other forms of social analysis intersect and interact. ([36], pp. x–xv)

This chapter will initially consider the macro aspects of institutions—that is, it will identify forces in a society that bring about institutional change and subsequent economic development. In the second portion of the chapter, the specific micro aspects of organizational-institutional change will be considered.

MACRO CONCEPTS AND RELATIONSHIPS

John Powelson uses Walt Rostow's term *takeoff* to identify the period of initial change in a society. Takeoff is a period in which growth-sensitive groups form and obtain power.

This power is not only political (i.e., in government), but also in business, the family, clubs, and informal social functions. Early-forming growth-sensitive groups may be those that have been "put upon" . . . entrepreneurial types who develop a need for achievement . . . persons who have migrated . . . persons subject to the demonstration effect because they have traveled abroad or met foreign visitors in their own country, persons subject to the exhortation of demagogues, persons persuaded through education of the virtues of growth, government functionaries hired for planning ministries or development corporations whose jobs depend on successful growth, and the like. The formation of some growth-sensitive groups gives rise to others dependent on the first, such as politicians who represent them, suppliers who sell to them, and professors who teach them. We do not believe there is a single, universal cause of the formation of growth-sensitive groups. Clearly, however, they interact, and they try to persuade other groups of the virtues of growth. It is only as these groups grow proportionately within a society that consensus on growth as a dominant goal is achieved. ([35], pp. 10-11)

A number of authors discuss the forces which trigger formation of new institutions and significant reformation of old ones. W. E. Bjur lists three generic causes of the initiation of change forces.

a) The differentiation of social functions, inherent in the development process, creates a vacuum in which the institution is born and perhaps grows to fill;

b) Pressing problems are identified and their solutions seem to require the establishment of a remedial institution or institutions;

c) New physical and social technologies are deemed desirable, perhaps for more efficient and effective performance of existing services or as a part of other changes taking place. ([93], pp. 212–13)

Hollis Peter notes that "Lerner shows how global communication, seen as the main instrument of socialization, influences people in traditional societies, creating higher expectations and readiness even before modernizing activities take place" ([115], p. 2).

In some cases, e.g., at the University of Nigeria [28] or the academy of Comilla, Pakistan [61], the key may be the charisma of a leader, but Bjur notes that this frequently is short-lived.

Weber observed that "routinization of charisma" is inevitable, that with the passage of time other elements must necessarily be substituted for charisma's magic, for the immediate followers constituting the internal organization of the entity, as well as for the larger society. In the case of an organization sponsored for the purposes of introducing technical innovation, it is inevitable that first stage charisma be gradually replaced by professional competence *vis-à-vis* the functions which the new organization is created to carry out. The long-term ability to acquire resources for its operations is related to its degree of excellence in performing some functional service to its environment, so that as far as the environment is concerned, functional competence is indispensable. ([93], p. 266)

Regardless of the cause of the formation of growth-sensitive groups, Powelson questions their selection of institutions.

> The basic principle in the selection of an institution is one of benefits and costs. An institution is chosen if its benefits exceed its costs, both being subjectively judged (and not necessarily measured) by members of the power groups capable of forming it. These groups . . . may be politicians or appointed officials in a position to establish new government agencies; or they may be labor leaders who organize unions; or they may be heads of families who influence the design of the family system; or revolutionaries able to seize power; or other.
>
> If these groups are growth-sensitive, any potential institution will, consciously or not, be judged by its capacity to achieve growth. We theorize that effectiveness measured by the three criteria (identification, rules, and consensus) then constitutes effectiveness in achieving growth, though the relationship need not be linear or continuous. If other benefits than effectiveness are perceived, we will treat these as negative costs, which make it "easier" (less costly) to accept one institution than another.
>
> The cost of an institution consists of the pain felt by the power group in forming it. This may include sacrifice of resources, prestige, values, or even life (in a revolution). Cost also includes the effort to overcome the resistance of others, by either coercion or persuasion. Such cost may include the attempt to increase the cost to others of maintaining archaic institutions that conflict with the ones the power groups wish to establish. ([35], pp. 20–21)

T. W. Schultz provides valuable insights by viewing institutions as suppliers of services. Changes in these services and, hence, indirectly through them in institutions that produce them, may constitute the prime targets of growth-sensitive power groups. Schultz states:

> The institution is treated as a supplier of a service which has an economic value. It is assumed that the process of growth alters the demand for the service and that this alteration in the demand brings about a disequilibrium between the demand and supply measured in terms of long-run costs and returns. ([37], p. 1117)

Subsequently, Powelson amplifies the concept of cost.

> Each value sacrifice thus involves both cost and benefit. Values that are more cherished are more costly. They will be sacrificed only if the benefit is great. Less cherished values are easy to give up, but they may or may not yield much increment in product.

... Ideology lies among the values difficult (hence costly) to change. Since institutions conforming to divergent ideologies may be equally effective, it is sometimes not necessary to sacrifice an ideology; rather, the institution conforming more closely to it is selected. ...

... Where two institutions are not perfectly substitutable for each other, the one with the greater marginal output in proportion to its costs will be selected. ([35], pp. 137–38)

Since many growth-sensitive groups are active during takeoff, Powelson contends:

The takeoff period is one of tension, as growth-sensitive groups vie with growth-resistant groups for support. The danger of violence lies in the fact that social institutions have not been formed to cope with this type of conflict. Sometimes growth-sensitive groups select coercive instruments in order to eliminate an opponent who would otherwise not join in the consensus. If he is eliminated completely (e.g., executed or permanently exiled), this ploy may be successful. The principal problem of violent revolution, however, is that it is impossible to eliminate *all* opponents completely. Revolution often divides people more than it unites them, making their absorption into the consensus even more difficult later. ([35], p. 11)

He further describes the takeoff period as

... further complicated by conflicts among growth-sensitive groups, principally over how political power and increments of national product will be shared. Inability to resolve or manage these conflicts lengthens the takeoff period, preventing or delaying the formation of post-takeoff values and institutions. ([35], p. 11)

Based on his own historical analysis, S. N. Eisenstadt substantiates this point.

Thus we conclude that the institutionalization of a system creates the possibility that "anti-systems," or groups with negative orientations toward its premises, will develop within it. While the nature and strength of such anti-systems may vary, as between different institutional (i.e., religious, political) systems and between different types within each, and while they may often remain latent for very long periods of time, they also constitute important foci of change, under propitious conditions.

The existence of such contradictions or conflicts among the different institutional spheres and among different groups does not, of course, preclude the possibility that the system will maintain its boundaries more or less continuously, through a hierarchy of norms and accommodation or partial insulation of different subsystems, and that a definite order and stable relations among the system's parts will persist. But the possibility of conflict and potential change is always present, rooted in the very process of institutionalization, and the direction and occurrence of change depend heavily on the nature of this process.

Just as the predilection for change is necessarily built into any institutional system, so the direction and scope of change are not random but depend, as we have shown in discussing the processes of change in the Empires and in the great religions, on the nature of the system generating the change, on its values, norms and organizations, on the various internal forces operating within it and on the external forces to which it is especially sensitive because of its systemic properties. These various forces naturally differ between religious and political institutions and among different societies, but sensitivity to these forces and the tendency to change are inherent in all of them. ([144], p. 247)

Fredrick T. Bent identifies some of the administrative difficulties.

. . . as administrative policies take on increasingly secular tones, government agencies lose the legitimacy they once enjoyed. Deprived of traditional support, yet more developed than the other modernizing institutions, agencies do not easily achieve synoptic relations with the masses of people. In contrast to modern states, the decline of the class basis of the bureaucracy reduces its prestige and therefore its effectiveness to gain the respect of those adversely affected by modernization and most in need of help to adjust to a changed social order. ([36], p. 226)

John W. Lewis discusses the action of revolutionary elites in a similar vein.

Two priorities of the revolutionary elites typically affect their strategies. These have been implied in the foregoing discussion, but now must be made explicit. First, revolutionary elites seek to induce radical and rapid social development with a principal, if not an exclusive, emphasis on technological change; and, second, they desire to maintain or strengthen their current positions of power irrespective of the changes wrought in their societies. The first priority causes them to reject accommodation with the premodern elites who usually oppose any fundamental social changes in the direction of modernization. The second leads them to obstruct the rising power of the more technically trained successor sub-elites. The particular social groups and classes included in the three elites may vary, but the significant general patterns usually reflect the modes of competition among these three types of elites.

> ... Each elite places the cloak of nationalism around its pronounce-
> ments and its image of the requirements for social welfare and national
> unification. ... Technology constitutes an important means for the
> revolutionary elite to maintain its power and realize its dominant
> political goals. The revolutionary elite also joins the successor sub-elite,
> which it oversees and fosters, in assuming that the essence of modern-
> ization is technological development. But, for the successor sub-elites,
> technological advancement signifies the broadening of social wealth and
> the increased opportunities for acquiring power. The competition be-
> tween the revolutionary elites and the successor sub-elites thus centers
> in that part of the political system that controls the economy. Both of
> these elite groups seek to diminish the residual power held by the
> premodern elites. In virtually every case, socioeconomic development
> constitutes a complex struggle for power. ([36], pp. 10–12)

The chain reaction set off by growth-sensitive power groups
is suggested by several authors. Schultz illustrates the process.

> When agriculture acquires a growth momentum, ... the dynamics of
> that growth will induce farmers in these parts of Asia to demand
> institutional adjustment. They will demand a larger supply of credit,
> with stress on its timeliness and terms, and they will organize coopera-
> tives should these be necessary for this purpose. They will demand
> more flexibility in tenancy contracts. They will join with neighbors to
> acquire tube wells and to undertake minor investments to improve the
> supply of water. Both tenants and landowners will also use whatever
> political influence they have to induce the government to provide more
> and better large-scale irrigation and drainage facilities. ([37], p. 1118)

Also using an agricultural illustration, Ira Baldwin points out
that a system or network of institutions exists within a sector of
an economy. This network, with its component forward and
backward linkages, makes possible the developmental leverage
afforded institutions as strategic catalysts of the development
process. Baldwin states:

> At the start, in most less developed nations, little attention was given to
> the development of a *system* of services. Rather, almost total energy
> was devoted to the development of a series of services, and only
> minimum attention was given to the need for the development of a
> functioning system with adequate linkages between the various newly
> created institutions. Those responsible for developing an institution to
> provide a new service often have little understanding of other services
> which are being introduced, and each group tends to confine itself to its
> assigned task. Only recently has research on institution building and
> agricultural development revealed the importance of building "a system
> of services to support agricultural development." ([114], p. 22)

Another author indicates the consequences of taking a narrow rather than a sector-system view. According to Melvin Blase,

> Technical assistance and indigenous personnel alike are often frustrated when the development of one institution—designed to remedy a constraint within an economy—does little more than provide an opportunity for another poorly developed institution to substitute as the effective constraint. Consequently, the layering of institutional constraints often misleads individuals who feel the elimination of one institutional barrier represents a panacea for transforming traditional agriculture. ([44], p. 11)

An empirical methodology for identifying networks of linked institutions and the power positions of such institutions within a system is provided by Robert Anderson, who applied it in the United States. He describes his approach to forming an institutional sociogram as follows:

> Despite our recognition of the interdependency of organizations, it is rare to find sociological research that penetrates inter-organizational phenomena. Our primary objective, therefore, was to develop a methodological approach for use in the study of the inter-organizational relationships of a society. We did so within a developmental context. . . .
>
> Two specific methodologies heavily influenced the design of this sociometric approach. The first was Hunter's nomination-reputational method of social analysis. Using a modified version of this technique, we produced an organizational inventory profile of the perceived organized structure of Michigan's Upper Peninsula. The universe of organizations to be included in the sociometric analysis was drawn from this inventory. Secondly, Weiss and Jacobson's set of structured concepts and methodology demonstrated the feasibility of using sociometric analysis in the study of complex structures. While Weiss and Jacobson [113] have done more than anyone else to develop and promote the use of the sociometric approach in the analysis of complex organizations, they do not extend such use beyond intra-organizational activity. The success of sociometric techniques in small group research and Weiss and Jacobson's imaginative use of them in analyzing the structure of complex organizations led us to believe that sociometric techniques would provide a useful means of gaining information at the inter-organizational level. ([123], pp. 1–3)

Another dimension of the catalytic nature of institutional change is stressed by Eugene Jacobson.

> A new institution in a developing country with an explicit program for selection, training and placement of staff, will, in many instances, be a

unique resource for providing new cadres of leadership throughout the society. ([29], p. 18)

Powelson identifies repetitive changes of individual institutions as another source of impetus for the chain reaction catalyzed by growth-sensitive groups.

> . . . an institution in takeoff need not conform exactly to existing values. Since the conflict to which it is addressed is new, the institution is bound to strain values in order to encompass it at all. There are, however, psychological limitations on the amount of strain a society can accept. Even after a violent revolution the forms of new institutions are influenced by the previous value framework. However, after the institution has lived for awhile and come to be accepted in the community, then values have changed, and a new institution similar to it (according to the institutional dimensions) can be created. Indeed, the new institution can strain values further, and ultimately even the pace of strain may be accelerated. When a society becomes accustomed to having its values strained—that is, becomes change-oriented—then the strain involved in change may itself become a value. ([35], p. 24)

William H. Friedland identifies the source of some of the strain during this process.

> While late modernizers experience advantages because of the existence of external models, transfer of these models creates strain. Transfer can never take place without some distortion or change. Out of the complex of behaviors in a transferred model, only a limited number can be selected by the donors for emphasis. Similarly, out of the large number of elements suggested by a model, not all will be understood or accepted without change by the receiver. The organizational reality, as it takes form in the modernizing country, represents a version that is different from the original model.

> Another source of variation during transfer results from the fact that institutions develop within a cultural framework and reflect the preoccupations of that culture. While a bureaucracy may be a bureaucracy, the manner in which it works will be conditioned by the culture of the bureaucrats. . . . In transferring institutions, a process of modification can be expected to take place as institutional elements filter through the culture of the receivers. Because the interrelationships between roles in transferred institutions are required to develop rapidly, yet cannot do so, considerable problems are experienced; roles are found to articulate badly. New interrelations between the roles are worked out in time but vary from the original model, and strain is experienced until the new relationships are institutionalized. ([36], pp. 81–82)

C. W. de Kiewiet documents this with the experiences of African universities.

> That the universities have not moved easily and painlessly from their foundation in response to criticism and challenge is true. But they moved, not uniformly, not at the same time, and not with equal willingness. There was progress in achieving balance between cultural and functional objectives. The university as a place for academic specialization, for an undirected pursuit of knowledge and its unchallenged expression, sought increasing room for a role and design directly and functionally related to jobs, the process of production and the generation of wealth.
>
> The universities have clearly begun to accept an explicit and intentional, as opposed to an implicit or incidental role in the immediate task of national development. There is a more sincere effort to do honor to the concept of relevance to an environment still greatly lacking in literacy, science, a distribution of modern skills, and habits that underlie productivity and accept innovation. Such charges bring pressure on the universities to modify the three forms of status to which they so readily succeeded—their position as an enclave within the limited modern sector, the recruitment of a student body increasingly favored by socio-economic forces, and the emphasis only upon standard fields of learning leading to the standard professions. Such effort measures also the progress of the universities toward assuming shapes and functions that are adequate and responsive to their own time and their own place, without concern for invidious comparisons or labels of secondariness. ([64], pp. 36–37)

In summarizing the process that he calls inverse modernization, John W. Lewis states:

> In sum, development affects the distribution of power in the society and opens up new channels of access to positions of power. The close relationship between development and the struggle for power frequently causes the revolutionary elites to impose ideological constraints on developmental activities as part of their efforts to sustain their position and contain divisive forces. These constraints tend to narrow the outlooks of the revolutionary elites, causing them to emphasize unanimity and conformity. This emphasis conflicts with the motivations fostered among the youth with respect to achievement and means-orientation. Ideological formulations may thus exaggerate the conflict and produce a generational split. Under some conditions, the desire to maintain ideological purity may so far outweigh that for rapid development that developmental goals are replaced by regulatory goals. This has been a typical way in which politically induced change has been

limited or diverted. In some cases, it has been the way in which such change has been completely subverted or negated. ([36], p. 17)

But this macro process can be successful. Powelson explains:

Successful completion of takeoff depends on two requisites. In the first place, growth-sensitive groups must gradually pervade society, either eliminating others or winning them over. Thus, consensus on growth as a dominant goal is achieved. In the second place, the groups must learn that the sum of their immediate goals exceeds the nation's capacity to accommodate them, but that no group's goals will be achieved until all groups' goals are partially met. *It is preferable to sacrifice one's immediate goals rather than permit continued conflict to violate the dominant goal of growth.* Thus groups must agree on priorities. At this point, society turns to the formation of a dominant set of conflict-resolving values on which to form consensus. ([35], pp. 11–12)

The limits of the process are identified by Chandler Morse.

Institutionalized institutional change is brought about by the innovative use of institutionalized power to resolve "social problems." Social problems occur as a consequence of "strain" . . . meaning a perceived inconsistency, or incongruence, in institutional arrangements. Strain thus reflects either the inadequacy of equilibrative mechanisms or emergent dissatisfaction with equilibrium itself. In the context of growth, strain is most likely to reflect the occurrence of diminishing returns in one of its many possible forms.

Strain means that a state of affairs perceived by some elements as unsatisfactory—poverty, ignorance, racism, corruption, for example—has been institutionalized because of the inability of equilibrative mechanisms to eliminate the causes of the dissatisfaction. Hence institutional change, innovation, is required to eliminate strain. But innovation, unlike equilibration, is not and cannot be subject completely to an institutionalized frame of reference. By definition, standards to guide it and limits to check it are both missing in greater or lesser degree. The moral order, to be sure, provides certain standards for, and sets certain limits on, the possibilities of pragmatic innovation, and vice versa, but the applicability of the standards and limits is seldom clear and precise. That is one reason why innovation is never perfectly institutionalized, never wholly predetermined. A more important reason is that the processes of institutionalized change operate on the initiative and at the direction of the power structure or with its tacit approval. ([36], pp. 281-82)

Regardless, Powelson contends that there is a path of successive institution formation. He states:

Now, economic growth generates *new* conflicts, which continuously call for *new* institutions. In a static model, the choice of optimal institution-types depends entirely on existing values. But institutions so chosen are likely to be ineffective (apparent solution lines far below physical), since the values to which they conform were not evolved with the new conflicts in mind. Contestants will be vaguely aware that a physical solution line lies "somewhere out there," and they will seek more effective institutions. . . .

In seeking more effective institutions (an outward shift of optimality as values change), power groups ordinarily choose among many directions, for there is no unique path to effectiveness. Normally they select those institutions that yield the greatest marginal economic growth per marginal unit of sacrifice (to the power groups themselves) as they push out on the dimensional continua. . . .

Successive institution formation leads to selection of an ideology because each choice makes easier a subsequent choice of the same kind of institution. To justify all choices, a nation is led into an ideology. By direct pursuit, on the other hand, power groups select an ideology and form economic and political theories to support it. Since it is difficult for a nation to form consensus on ideology until it has had experience with other types of consensus, and since popular nationalism is a relatively low-cost object on which to form consensus and one that fits in closely with ideology, takeoff countries usually expend great sums on the promotion of nationalism. Some of these sums represent resource sacrifices that physically retard economic growth (as, for example, the rejection of foreign investment). These sacrifices, which puzzle foreign intellectuals of other ideologies, may nevertheless constitute the least costly path to maximum *net* economic growth. ([35], pp. 180, 189-90)

Powelson discusses the period following takeoff as follows:

Post-takeoff norms and institutions have a different character from those of the pre-takeoff stage in that they depend *for their survival* on continued growth. Once the social system learns *how* to manage the conflicts of growth, it discovers that it can manage them *only* if there is continued growth. More and more, conflicts become positive-sum games. The question is not one of who will win and who will lose, but of how much each will win. More effective institutions lead to efficiency in conflict management, and more and more solutions become Paretian-optimal (the point at which all positive-sum moves are exhausted). "Exile for the loser" gives way to "loyal opposition." ([35], p. 12)

MICRO CONCEPTS AND RELATIONSHIPS

What are the implications for individual institutions as a consequence of the changes that occur during a nation's takeoff? Insofar as each institution represents a component of a larger institutional system or network, it is obvious that there will be some implications. Clearly, for those institutions which employ as inputs some of the outputs of other changed institutions in the network, this development is one of the inevitable disequilibrating forces. Similarly, changes demanded in the outputs of traditional institutions as a consequence of changes that have occurred in other using entities in the process of modernization have implications for the output mix of the traditional institution. Identifying the ramifications of some of these disequilibrating forces on the organizational-institutional dimensions of individual institutions is the object of this section.

In addressing the question of output mix Melvin Blase states:

> Two considerations are noteworthy in dealing with this question. The first is that there is a decision to be made with regard to the combination of outputs, i.e., the production of one output may be competitive with the production of another. The other point is that analytical techniques are available for aiding in the determination of the desired output mix.

> Frequently, foreign observers view institutions in traditional societies critically due to the lack of progress in building the institution as a force for development. All too often these critics fail to recognize that except for very narrow ranges of complementarity there is direct competition for resources between the production of current services and institutional reinvestment outputs. Tradeoffs must be made. In traditional societies, where future output is discounted very heavily, emphasis on the production of a large amount of current services is entirely realistic. Frequently, some exogenous force must be brought to bear on the system in order to alter this output mix. These disturbances can range from the availability of technical assistance teams to natural disasters, e.g., drought.

> In the private sector market-oriented firms conceptually have relatively little difficulty in determining their combination of outputs. . . . However, in the public sector institutions do not exchange their outputs in price oriented markets. Nevertheless, an exchange is made and the institution markets its products. The relevant consideration at this point is not a set of prices (which merely reflect the preferences of

consumers for one good relative to other alternative goods) but rather the preferences of key decision makers in the society reflected by their indifference curves formulated with regard to alternative system out-puts . . . . [and] the possible consequence of shifting indifference curves on combinations of output. This can result from exerting influence on key decision makers in the larger society with regard to their prefer-ences concerning combinations of system outputs. Frequently, this takes the form of providing new information to key decision makers with regard to what is being done in similar institutions elsewhere. Identification of key decision makers and providing them with addi-tional information may represent a crucial initial element in an institu-tion building strategy. ([120], pp. 22–25)

Not only are changes in traditional institutions triggered by changing output demands, but also by modernizing elites within individual institutions who see the institution as a potential means of influencing the larger environment. Hans Blaise comments on both of these sources of change.

The genesis of institution building is in the minds of a man or group of men. The beginning of the social change process is always the same. It is either the response to a distortion in the social system created by the uncoordinated changes of its elements, or it begins with a vision of a state of affairs preferred to the existing reality. In the developing countries today—engaged as they are in a process of rapid transforma-tion to catch up with the modern industrialized parts of the world— both situations can be found in abundance. Modernizing elites, moti-vated by a sense of urgency to improve the standard and quality of life in their countries and by drawing on values, experience, and techno-logies of the advanced countries, develop a vision of the preferred state of their society or an aspect thereof. They construct, as Wallace puts it, "a new utopian image of socio-cultural organization." They develop new values or conceive new forms of social and physical organization and technology to be introduced into their society. Once these new values are accepted in the society or in segments of the society, once new programs of action and new social and physical technologies have been implemented, new conditions have been created which may result in further changes.

The new or reconstituted organizations in which and through which the innovative leadership embodies, fosters and protects the new values, norms, and technologies, are the vehicles of change. The institutions forged by the agents of change are the instruments of innovation. Whereas the origin of innovation is a reconfiguration of values, objec-tives, and means taking place in the minds of the change agents, the institutions which they create are the operational expressions of this reconfiguration. In the structure, process, and functions of the institution they translate their ideas into reality. The immediate target of the change agents, then, is the organization into which they introduce their innovations. Seldom, however, is the organization—or can it be—the only or ultimate target. It is an intermediate target system. By the activities and output of the organization the innovators attempt to have an impact on the environment. The organization becomes in this manner an instrument and an extension of the individual or group of individuals who constitute the innovative leadership. They create in the organization a stable reference point, intended to represent the values, action and behavior patterns which become normative in the environment.

The ultimate target system of the innovators is the task environment. This task environment consists of those organizations which enable an institution to carry out its operations, those which are complementary to its operations, and those which embody and protect values and norms relevant to the operation of the institution. Only when a task environment has been created which supports the values of the institution, which is complementary to it, and when the norms of the institution are shared by the task environment, can an institution effectively carry out its functions and services.

The three elements of our analysis, then, are (1) the change agents or leadership group which creates or innovates the organization; (2) the organization as the intermediate target system in which and through which new values and technologies are introduced; and (3) the task environment as the ultimate target to which new norms and values are spread to create a compatible and complementary environment for the institution to perform its functions and services. ([27], pp. 185–86)

Blaise's emphasis on the importance of change agents or leadership groups is supported by a number of empirical analyses. In reflecting on the results of the first four empirical analyses completed under the IRPIB program, Milton Esman states:

These cases thus confirmed the salient character of the leadership function, the prospects for success associated with competent and committed leadership, and the costs likely to be exacted by inept, uncommitted, and weak leadership. Little guidance was being given on the tactics available to innovators to compensate for inadequate institutional leadership. Yet at the early stages of institution building there appears to be no substitute, no effective way of circumventing inadequate leadership, and the likelihood is that the venture will stall, be reduced to ineffectiveness, or even fail unless adequate leadership is forthcoming. ([17], pp. 11–12)

Although the importance of leadership seems to be agreed upon in many of the empirical studies, the importance of the other institutional variables in the framework formulated by Esman et al. seems to vary from institution to institution. In two of the four institutions initially studied in the IRPIB program, doctrine appeared to be significant, in one case with positive and in the other with negative consequences.

In the case where doctrine was an element of success, the analyst, John Hanson, states:

> It was the function of doctrine to establish normative linkages between the old and the new, between establishment and innovators, such as would legitimize innovations which came with the new organization. Doctrine itself could not perform this function; yet it could provide connections which made organizational innovations appear less new, less threatening, and correspondingly more legitimate. It could tip the balance. At the same time that it might perform this function with those publics who would ultimately either institutionalize or reject innovations, it could also provide University leaders with norms or standards which could guide them in projecting programs, establishing priorities, and assessing accomplishments. It could provide a sense of solidarity and progress so important to morale. These latter functions would be served only to the extent that there was genuine commitment to the doctrine by these leaders. . . .

> In this consideration of total University doctrine three factors stand out. First, the major doctrinal elements of the total University were matters of firm faith with the top Nigerian leaders in the College of Education. . . . Second, there was considerable agreement between leaders of the University and its most numerous school-related publics as to what the major innovations of the University were. . . . Third, . . . students and graduates not only identified these doctrinal elements but in large part identified with them. They had, in fact, internalized the doctrine and were enthusiastic in viewing themselves as examplars of the type of education which had been worked out to realize this doctrine. ([28], pp. 99, 136)

In the other instance the lack of a clear doctrine apparently contributed materially to the lack of institutionalization. Guthrie Birkhead comments:

> So much can be explained about the Public Administration Institute for Turkey and the Middle East in terms of the confused, ill-defined doctrinal goals that were assigned to it. The leadership and the staff to this day have not succeeded in making them operational to any signifi-

cant extent. The obvious connections between doctrine and leadership also seemed to become clearer in this study. Possibly, if they had possessed stronger resources of a personal or intellectual nature, the leaders in this Turkish enterprise might have been able to operate better in the absence of clear-cut doctrine. That is a point for speculation. In this case, however: 1) doctrine was ambiguous; 2) it was not understood by Turks in the key positions; 3) none of them took the time or opportunity (perhaps even had the capacity) to make it better understood; 4) doctrine was never clearly related to any specific needs of administration; 5) it was never made clear how to identify such needs and thus how doctrine might be adjusted to potential needs or new doctrine evolved. ([89], Appendix, p. xi)

The importance of combinations of institutional variables is underscored by Norman Uphoff and Warren Ilchman.

This is to say then that the importance of leadership is a function of the scarcity of resources to achieve collective objectives. To some extent, the two—resources and leadership—are substitutable. Leadership involves the skillful use of resources. The more plentiful they are, the less important is leadership to achieving a given goal. A corollary is that with a given amount of resources, the more quickly a goal is to be achieved, the more important is the contribution of leadership in formulating productive strategies. . . .

The scarcer are available resources and/or the shorter the time in which ends are to be achieved, the more important is the role of doctrine in Institution Building. Doctrine can make the process more efficient and effective by clearly specifying ends and presenting appropriate and productive means. But when resources are scarce or time short, then the more ambiguous are doctrine's ends or the less reliable its means, the less it can contribute to Institution Building. ([24], pp. 11–12, 14)

In still another study, the importance of internal structures is underscored. Ramon Hermano reports:

From the study, two organizational elements seem to stand out as critical factors: (1) the leadership style and political viability; and (2) the manipulation of structure as a tactical element to build up strong linkages with the environment. ([79], p. iii)

The interrelationship between doctrine and program is identified by John Hanson.

Categories which have a certain analytic cleanness do not necessarily reveal the same cleanness when applied as schemes for organizing action. When the scholar becomes educational leader, he is seldom concerned with doctrine *per se;* he is concerned with the interpretation and implementation of doctrine, and in his hands and in this context the distinction between *doctrine* and *program* loses significance. When this occurs, the search for a distinction is often like trying to locate a shadow line: at times it seems neat and clean, at other times blurred. Such a line has the further unsettling characteristic of being constantly on the move; what today is expressed purely as doctrine has tomorrow been given programmatic interpretation, and allegiance has spread from the slogan to the program which has been attached to it. Conversely, what has been introduced on the action level finds need for rationalization, and from this rationalization a new increment is added to doctrine.

When operations have begun, a further difficulty develops. On the one hand, doctrine without programmatic interpretation has a hollow ring; one questions if it has real content or meaning. On the other hand, once programmatic interpretation has been worked out, this interpretation begins to usurp the place of original doctrine. ([28], pp. 113–14)

On the subject of linkages, Thomas Hill, Warren Haynes, and Howard Baumgartel state:

The most important functional linkages are with the institution's customers. In an institution heavily dependent upon markets, the enabling linkages tend to merge with the functional linkages, but we shall here treat them as conceptually separate. The mere fact that a market demand has been identified is insufficient to guarantee that the institution's services will in fact be sought. The normal techniques of advertising and sales promotion are only a partial answer to the marketing problem. The expression "functional linkage" is an apt one, since it suggests that the problem is one of identifying a mutuality between the institution and its potential clientele, that they may serve one another and become increasingly dependent on each other. ([33], p. 2:13)

In discussing enabling linkages Esman reflects on the Thai and Turkish studies in the initial group of four undertaken in the IRPIB program.

The Thailand case demonstrated the overwhelming sensitivity of the institution's leadership, within that authoritarian social structure, to insure support from higher status political and bureaucratic sources, i.e., from enabling linkages of the I.P.A. Any felt need to cultivate functional linkages or to identify demands from elsewhere in the environment, or to build linkages with prospective clientele groups, were quite subordinate to the cultivation and strengthening of enabling linkages. Indeed the leadership, as long as it could sustain favorable enabling linkages, had little inducement to build functional linkages or supports in other groups in the society. Thus the problem of managing its environment was not perceived as requiring any real effort from the institutional leadership. It was necessary to keep the institution out of trouble, to avoid threatening any interest which might create problems in its relationship with its enabling linkages, and this it could do by offering a low key program which provided useful unthreatening services but made little direct effort at establishing and manipulating relationship within the environment that would make innovational transfer a real possibility. To an even greater extent, the Turkish case involved a minimal sense of dependence on establishing useful transaction patterns with external linkages. Indeed the survival strategy adopted by its leadership precluded this search for linkages for fear, paradoxically, that such linkages with the rapidly changing bureaucratic clienteles in Turkey might generate pressures to initiate programs which were more innovative than the Institute's passive leadership was prepared to sponsor or to handle. The effect was to protect itself from being perceived as a threat to any other organization or to have to respond to environmental pressures, and to allow it to vegetate, bothering and being bothered by no one, but drawing funds sufficient to supplement the incomes of its part-time staff. ([17], pp. 33–34)

The interdependence between enabling and functional linkages is stressed by Richard Duncan and William Pooler.

If successful institution building takes place, functional linkages with other recipient institutions provide a positive alternative to enabling linkages by creating a pattern of legitimate interdependencies and giving the organization a needed measure of autonomy. ([26], pp. 68–69)

Duncan and Pooler also report the following results of their cross-sectional analysis of normative and diffuse linkages:

As regards normative and diffuse linkages, the recipient society seems to make more consistent efforts than technical assistance. This was the case for mass media support where the percentages were 30 and 40 respectively. Also, consistent mass media support by the recipient resulted in a somewhat higher percentage of successful projects than did technical assistance encouragement although both were high. Again, one can tentatively conclude that when considering those linkage relationships that come to prominence at the end of the life cycle of the institution building process, the recipient society effort is more effective and vital when compared to technical assistance. Probably technical assistance effort is needed in certain situations, but the specifications of these situational contexts is not possible given the quality of the data and analytical tools now available.

There are some other tentative conclusions that are worth mentioning. For instance, where consistent effort is expended by either technical assistance or the recipient society in building a favorable image for the organization, the project *always* proved successful. One could hazard a guess that this type of activity is not undertaken unless many favorable indications of success for a project are already evident and it is recognized that the creation of a favorable image of the project in the recipient society will further insure success. This linkage relationship occurs at the end of the life cycle process. Hence, it is possible that image building is a function of having personnel and resources free because of the successful conclusion of other activities related to the total enterprise. ([26], pp. 63–64)

In a number of instances authors encountered difficulty placing type of linkages into the four categories in the framework formulated by Esman et al. Prior to quoting Esman, who reaches a similar conclusion, David Derge et al. state:

IRPIB and Indiana University researchers both encountered difficulty operationalizing the categorization of linkages which is formally presented in the IRPIB working papers. Clear or meaningful distinction between linkage categories was frequently impossible. Not only did points of contact between the institution and the environment defy categorization, but the same linkage relationship could serve different purposes at different times and many were multifunctional at any given time. Although the classification of linkages was not meant to be rigid, a research strategy designed to evaluate institution building may be more effective if it focuses upon transactional relationships rather than the linkage matrix per se. ([31], p. 126)

They suggest that a new definition of *institutionality* is needed.

It is only when relevant publics, instrumental accounting, and transactional accommodation cease to be pivotal concerns of organization-institution leadership and the pressure for survival ceases to be the preponderant factor in decision-making that the essence of Esman's approach to institution building becomes relevant as an operational model. For it is then that one meaningfully speaks of intrinsic valuation of the institution. If the society is characterized by a low level of social mobilization, intrinsic valuation is very much secondary to transactional accommodations, instrumental accounting, and utility maximization of relevant publics and clients in general as an index of institutionality. ([31], p. 132)

Finally, other limitations of the framework formulated by Esman et al. that have been articulated by several authors are worthy of note. Aluizio Pinto states:

The first limitation, significant because of its overall importance, relates to the rationale of the field of institution building itself. It stems from the bias that institutionalization is a positive process which is closely related to societal innovation. No matter how intentional this orientation may have been, it seems improper to equate institution building entirely with innovation and positive change. This restriction could, among other things draw attention away from the dysfunctional aspects of the process of institutionalization which have been the object of attention in the literature of the social sciences in general and in the modern organization theory, in particular. ([72], p. 36)

Subsequently, he identifies another limitation that is due to

... the tendency of the model to view the process of institution building largely from the perspective of the institution under study, and from the omission of the role of individuals as linkages in the process of organizational institutionalization. The former view could lead to the impression that institutionalization is a onesided process that depends entirely upon the organization being institutionalized. While organizations tend to devise ways of controlling their environment, total environmental control is never within their power. The process of institutionalization of an organization may be enhanced by the decision of another organization with needs for complementary services. . . .

Individuals play other important roles as linkages in the process of institutionalization at least in two additional ways: namely, as "prestigious personalities" and as "carriers of institutional values." Organizations in the United States, for example, follow the general policy of hiring retired admirals, generals, and congressmen, for example, for their board of directors. Universities do likewise for their board of trustees, and often a president or a chancellor may be chosen because of his prominence in the community and his ability to raise funds when needed. The presence of these outstanding individuals in a given institution constitutes a very important element of attraction of support from other social units. ([72], pp. 38–40)

Ilchman and Uphoff suggest a modification of the institution building concept in order to incorporate a temporal dimension.

The goal of institution builders is not simply social change. Some change in social, economic and political relationships is likely to occur over time with or without their efforts. The aim of institution builders might better be described as social control. By building institutions, persons should be better able to control the course of change and to accomplish certain desired changes within a shorter period of time than would otherwise be possible. Once established, institutions commonly permit persons to control in some degree the demands for change which arise over time. Thus, institutions may be seen as giving their members some control over time itself. What social scientists seeking to assist in institution building need to formulate and verify are models of social change and social control. ([24], pp. 1–2)

After attempting to apply the institution building framework developed by Esman et al., Ward Morehouse concludes:

In sum, then, the institution-building model provides a helpful way of looking at complex phenomena but thus far has demonstrated limited relevance to policy makers because of its limited predictive power (save in special circumstances such as decisions regarding external aid). It is limited in predictive power not so much because the model is faulty but because we have not yet developed sufficiently sharp analytical tools to find answers to what policy makers need to know and to provide comparability in data between different organizational entities. In short, the institution-building model, at its present stage of refinement, is more analytically elegant than relevant to the real world of public policy in India. ([78], p. 90)

7
Revision and Refinement of Micro and Macro Aspects of Institution Building, 1973– 1983

In the immediate post–World War II period, during the early phases of technical assistance efforts, little literature on institution building existed. Only after a number of obvious mistakes had been made did a realization evolve that a body of knowledge about how institutions were developed was needed. Hence, in the late 1950s and early 1960s, research was initiated and literature began to flow. This period can be characterized as the conceptualization phase. Most of the literature developed during this period was focused on individual institutions, i.e., it was micro in focus. Not until the late 1960s did a systematic, scholarly approach of some of the sector-wide or macro considerations appear.

The application phase began in the late 1960s and extended until the late 1970s. This period was marked by attempts to apply institution building concepts in general, and those developed by Esman et al. in particular. Hence, authors turned their attention to such things as indicators of institutionalization and strategies for modifying institutions. Most of these efforts also concerned individual institutions and, therefore, were micro in orientation. However, macro considerations began to attract attention during this period also. Work by Baldwin et al. [98], Schultz [37], and Powelson [35], in particular, was concerned with questions related to networks of institutions, impetus for our institutional change, and methods of transforming a traditional set of institutions into one supportive of the development process.

During the late 1970s, literature began to appear that caused the present period to be referred to as one of revision and refinement. Serious attempts were made by several authors to develop quantitative indices to assist in the measurement of the status of and progress toward goals of change of selected institutions. Another facet of revision of some of the earlier institution building concepts took the form of gaining more precise insight into the importance of the previously identified variables in the institution building (I.B.) model developed by Esman et al. Although various authors have attached differing degrees of import to individual variables found in the earlier literature, such as leadership and linkage, no consensus has evolved with regard to discarding any of the variables.

Although none of the components of the I.B. model earlier conceptualized have been discarded, the entire approach has been questioned by some authors. Two forces have been responsible. First, the reorientation of assistance programs toward the poorest of the poor, especially by USAID, made the focus on institutions less obvious than had been the case previously. Second, the paternalistic image of programs planned and administered "from the top down," i.e., the centralized approach to development, increasingly came under question during the period. The location-specific nature of many components of agricultural sectors where many of the technical assistance programs were concentrated made planning and organizing self-sustaining development efforts for entire nations very difficult. Suffice it to say, during this period, many authors have shifted their attention to a participative approach to development. They have placed special emphasis on widespread local participation in the formulation and operation of relevant institutions. Unfortunately, some of the recent literature suggests a polarization, with an elitist, social engineering approach to institutions on the one hand and a participative, pragmatic approach to institution building on the other. A method of dealing with this dilemma will be discussed later in this chapter.

While much of the revision and refinement work currently underway, having been initiated in the late 1970s, has focused on the micro aspects of institution building, there have been some noteworthy additions to the literature in the macro area also. Most noteworthy in this regard is work by Ruttan [323]. His conceptualization of the induced innovation hypothesis represents further development in an area of thought originally associated with Schultz [37]. Ruttan's use of the hypothesis to interpret institutional change in three countries has lent further credence to this approach.

Much of the literature that was forthcoming in the conceptualization stage and the early parts of the application phase has been discussed in the preceding chapter. Attention here will be given to the latter phase of the application phase and the current period, which are characterized by literature designed to refine older concepts and revise entire perspectives.

ORGANIZATION OF CHAPTER

As indicated above, several efforts have been made to quantify some aspects of institution building so that the concepts could be more easily operationalized. Initially, this chapter will consider several approaches to quantification and, in general, efforts to operationalize some of the institutional building concepts. Subsequently, a perspective in regard to the macro oriented literature will be the focus of attention. Next, interrelationships will be examined among concepts in the more voluminous aspects of the literature—that is, the literature in the macro area. The chapter will close with a consideration of methods of relating some of the schools of thought so that a more effective approach to institutional development can emerge.

THE QUANTIFICATION QUESTION

As indicated above, the bulk of the literature in this area has had a micro focus. Attempts to operationalize the institution building concepts have caused a number of authors to turn their attention to methods of quantifying the characteristics of an institution at any one point in time as well as quantifiable changes in it between two different points in time. Before turning to these, however, the historical setting will be developed into which this literature was introduced.

Early Attempts at Measurement

A prerequisite for measurement is the formulation of a precise definition concerning what the concepts mean. Hence, much of the early literature concerned itself with attempts to improve this precision. The effort made by Thorsen [25] to develop institutional profiles represented an early attempt to come to grips with measurement problems. Attention will be turned to improving the precision of definitions before considering attempts at measurement.

Toward Precision in Definitions

Clearly one of the most usable attempts to elucidate and clarify the principal concepts in the I.B. approach by Esman et al. was published by Duncan in 1975. His summary statements bear repeating.

> Leadership delivers resources – Leadership promotes the doctrine internally and externally – Leadership keeps the internal structure functioning – Leadership mobilizes the organization to accomplish the program – Leadership establishes and cements linkages with external groups – Leadership is alert to opportunities to incorporate new groups for support, output and acceptance. ([3] p. 57)

> Doctrine dramatizes the new idea, as well as innovation and change – Doctrine helps to sell a program and the organization with it – Doctrine defines the goals – Doctrine can generate support – Doctrine helps to define and limit internal and external conflict – Doctrine absorbs ideas and needs and combines them with the new ones to make the organization acceptable in the society. ([3] p. 60)

> Program provides impact in the environment – Program provides visibility – Program provides vital contact with the environment – Program is the ultimate testing ground for output – Program promotes support by the environment of the organization – Program provides a specific focus for change-oriented activities – Program provides an identity for clientele and staff and ultimately for the society. ([3] p. 63)

> Resource mobilization involves using old and new sources – Resource mobilization involves a wide variety of elements, money, people, technology, etc. – Resources hold the organization together until it can become accepted – Resources provide internal strength and cohesion in the organization – Resources contribute to autonomy. ([3] p. 66)

> Internal structure is a key to converting resources to program – Internal structure is a base for organization mobilization – Internal structure is a device for demonstrating innovative capacity – Internal structure provides a means for resolving internal conflict – Internal structure is a means for reflecting goals and doctrine. ([3] p. 68)

> Enabling linkages provide power to act – Enabling linkages provide

protection – Enabling linkages provide initial resources – Enabling linkages support a new public image. ([3] p. 71)

Normative linkages show what values must be observed – Normative linkages can provide support in making new ideas fit present values – Normative linkages define relationships with other organizations – Normative linkages can help legitimize activities – Normative linkages provide the framework for defining objectives in the national institutional structure. ([3] p. 73)

Functional linkages provide inputs the organization needs to function – Functional linkages promote the use of what the organization does – Functional linkages help define program boundaries – Functional linkages provide opportunities for mutually beneficial support in the environment – Functional linkages reinforce the effect on organizational clientele. ([3] p. 75)

Diffuse linkages broaden the base of support – Diffuse linkages strengthen the public image of the organization – Diffuse linkages provide alliances with other change-oriented groups – Diffuse linkages promote an understanding in the society of the goals of the organization – Diffuse linkages help reinforce acceptance by the society. ([3] p. 77).

Although other authors have made similar attempts to elaborate on concepts, this work by Duncan is the most succinct published thus far.

Institution Building Profile Approach

Although published several years earlier than the Duncan work, the effort by Thorsen was also an attempt to become more specific and to enhance the operationalization of the I.B. approach by Esman et al. As indicated in Chapter 2, Thorsen developed a matrix for formulating an I.B. profile. In order to better judge the institution under study, Thorsen further developed the six major categories of the I.B. model into thirty-seven subcategories. This enabled subjective ratings to be made to facilitate the intertemporal comparisons of a given institution. In this pioneering work, Thorsen suggested that comparative profiles be made of an institution every two years in order to assess the trend in its development. The work by Thorsen served as a forerunner of some of the subsequent efforts to refine and quantify the I.B. model.

Recent Introduction of Measurement Alternatives

Recent contributions to the literature involving measurement of institutionalization and component parts of the I.B. model include work by Bjur [12], who has been doing research involving institution building for two decades. Like Thorsen, his index is designed to make possible comparison of a given institution between points of time. In contrast, the work by Barnett and Engel [11] provides a guide for project designers rather than for expert evaluation of an institution. Rather than being strictly quantitative in nature, the guide is in the form of a checklist that has narrative weightings of factors much the same as they could be weighted numerically. Finally, Practical Concepts Incorporated [13] has developed the PCI model, which is useful for accessing organizational viability. In reality, three approaches to the viability of an institution are presented by Practical Concepts Incorporated. One, the balance sheet approach, is recommended by the authors. It, as well as the approach by Bjur and that by Barnett and Engel, warrants further elaboration.

The Institutionalization Quotion Index

Part of Bjur's institutionalization quotion (I.Q.) index is the following equation:

$$Q(y) = (L + K + P + R + V)$$
$$\text{and } IQ(y) = Q/M$$

when L = legal legitimacy status
      K = charisma; leadership characteristics
      P = program autonomy and success
      R = resources and resource autonomy
      V = valuedness, internal and external
      Y = years-in-function of the organization
      M = mean of Q-scores of similar institutions

By applying this equation to an institution at two points in time, an analyst can obtain an easily understood index number indicating the relative level of institutionalization at any given age. Hence, one can determine the degree of institutionalization for the subject institution compared to that of similar institutions of a comparable age.

The premise upon which the I.Q. index rests is that in the early and middle stages of an institution's life cycle institutionalization is analogous to social legitimization. An organization's legitimacy improves as a function of the length of time that it performs its function, i.e., is accepted in its identity role. Further, legitimacy is viewed as being cumulative in that the more role-legitimating qualities possessed by the organization, the more legitimate or institutionalized it is viewed as being.

The use of the index in analyzing four institutions, three of which were outside the United States, suggests that the approach is easily applied and has considerable utility.

A Guide for Project Designers

The I.B. model has limited value if it can only be used for ex post analyses. Analysts and practitioners alike need an analytical capability for preparing strategies for institutional development and predicting the consequences of these approaches. Improving the utility of the institution building approach in this vein was the objective of Barnett and Engel.

Based upon a rather exhaustive examination of AID evaluations and audits, they formulated a checklist for project designers. Although not as detailed with regard to the subject institution as the Bjur index, the checklist encompasses both micro and macro factors that need to be considered, especially by those concerned with AID programming procedures. By incorporating terms such as *stress* and *avoid* in the checklist, in narrative form the authors provide weights on various elements much the same as a mathematically derived list.

Clearly, the guide for project designers is oriented toward AID procedures. Hence, its utility for other donors is somewhat limited. Nevertheless, the work is noteworthy as an example of the efforts being made to come to grips definitively with the elements of the institution building process.

The P/C/I Model

Actually, the P/C/I model consists of three alternatives. Practical Concepts Incorporated developed three approaches to the measurement of organizational viability. The recommended one, the balance sheet approach, is given more attention here than the effect/feedback model or the approach of examining individual transactions engaged in by the organization, i.e., the transaction analysis approach. Regardless, the P/C/I model is based on the premise that an organization's three most basic assets are purchasables, connotation, and image. Purchasables are defined as having a monetary common denominator. On the other hand, connotation reflects the attitudinal assessment of individuals within and outside an organization. Likewise, in contrast to things that have a monetary common denominator, image represents the cognitive dimension of what people think an institution is and does and its reasons to exist.

In turn, these categories of resources or assets of institutions can be assessed in various ways. Of the three presented, the balance sheet approach deserves further consideration.

An organization's balance sheet can be viewed as consisting of elements of internal asset value and external asset value. Important within the former is doctrine and its closely related concept of staff morale. The latter is the perception of an institution's clients, sponsors, competitors, and others, relatively speaking, within their value systems. Quantitative estimaters can be developed with regard to image strength, connotation strength, and endurance of purchasables by using prescribed techniques for identification of these dimensions of an institution.

One final comment is in order regarding the utility of the P/C/I model. The authors strike an analogy with biological phenomena in explaining aspects of institutions. The biological analogy to doctrine is that of genetic coding. In both instances there is something internal to the organism that limits, constrains, and defines what it does. This is helpful in making doctrine measurable rather than simply an abstract concept as it has tended to be in previous literature. The biological analogy in the case of program is the adaptiveness that an organism has in accommodating itself to its environment within the limits prescribed by its genetic coding. Likewise, an institution's program must be changeable in order to accommodate the needs of its environment but must do so within the limits prescribed by its doctrine. Finally, the author suggests a number of proxies that can be used to quantitatively assess some of the important dimensions of an institution, e.g., the distances patients travel to obtain treatment reflect their connotation of a medical institution. This type of quantification enables an institutional analyst to put some of the more abstract dimensions of an institution on a quantitatively comparable basis with the monetary resources which it commands.

A Summary Note

Suffice it to say, efforts are being made to quantitatively and precisely assess dimensions of institutions which will permit both their more precise planning and more objective evaluation. While the literature thus far has been impressive, it is far from being exhaustive with regard to the potential that exists. Historians may well record that these efforts made in the revision and refinement stage of the institutional building literature were only first attempts. Regardless of whether that will be the case, they constitute important additions to the literature.

THE MACRO PERSPECTIVES

The role of institutions in societies, in general, and in their development processes, in particular, has not received the amount of attention in the literature in the current revision and refinement phase as have the more micro-oriented concerns. Nevertheless, some significant insights have appeared with regard to how institutional change within a market-oriented society occurs. Prior to discussing these contributions, however, the stage needs to be set with regard to the effect of the orientation of donors and the early insights provided by previous writers.

The Poorest of the Poor: Do Institutions Have a Role?

Within the donor community USAID has been perhaps the most explicit in focusing on those in the low end of the income distribution in developing countries. This so-called "New Direction" has significantly influenced the programming of USAID resources in the last decade. However, the United States has not been alone in tilting its programs in this direction. Clearly, program initiatives in the International Bank for Reconstruction Development (World Bank) have been more conscious of this target audience during the past decade than previously.

This orientation of important members of the donor community is relevant in that questions have been raised concerning the role of institutions in donor efforts to reach the poor. Unfortunately, because a level of education and sophistication is required in order to develop and direct institutions, some have contended that institutions are elitist in nature and, hence, are irrelevant when programs are focused toward the poorest of the poor. This contention begs the question of how any continuity and indigenous self-sustaining capacity can be developed within the host countries with regard to dealing with the problems of the poor. Although it has been highly unfortunate, this cleavage in the literature must be recognized. What remains to be said emphatically is that the development of both institutions and programs to serve those on the low end of the income distribution scale in developing countries is not mutually exclusive. In fact, institutions are indispensable as a means of permanently moving the poorest of the poor to a higher income level if something other than the conversion of the donor community into a welfare community is to occur. Also obvious from the literature is the fact that the focus of donor programs on those at the low end of the income spectrum has obvious implications for linkages, programs, and doctrine of the institutions that are needed in order to generate the capability for dealing with these problems of the times.

Early Insights: Institutions as Components of Systems

As mentioned in the previous chapter, early work by Ira Baldwin [98], Theodore Schultz [37], and John Powelson [35] has provided a base to which literature has been added in the last decade. As a backdrop for discussing these additions to the literature, the contributions of these three will be briefly summarized.

Although focused on the agricultural sector, much of what Baldwin developed with regard to the concept of an institutional infrastructure need for agricultural development applies to other sectors as well. His central thesis is that a system of services is needed in order to support agricultural development. Given the decentralized nature of agriculture, the individual farmer is dependent upon a number of agencies for goods and services so that his production process can proceed. If that production is to proceed at an expanded rate consistent with agricultural development, then obviously the flow of goods and services from these supporting agencies will have to likewise grow. Over time, the agencies may or may not become institutionalized. If, however, a dynamic commercial agriculture is to evolve, that institutionalization process must occur so that an entire institutional infrastructure exists and supplies the necessary inputs for the agricultural production process.

In the first Fellows Lecture given to the American Agricultural Economics Association, Schultz argues that institutions are variables within the economic domain that respond to the dynamics of economic growth. Schultz reviews institutions as providers of goods and services within an economic system. In addition, he contends that the demand for these changes over time as a function of the development process. The momentum of growth generates changes in the farmers' demands for services from institutions such as credit agencies and educational institutions. A key factor is the economic value of human agents, which increases as a consequence of growth. The demands for services of many agricultural institutions change as the consequences of this growth process. Hence, the Schultz perspective essentially argues that an economic view of institutions in the sense both that there is a demand for their output and that they are suppliers of output is useful in understanding how institutions function in response to the growth process.

Powelson's multidisciplinary theory of institutions represented a significant addition to the development literature. In it he envisions that the power groups capable of forming or commanding an institution or its services may, if they are growth sensitive, represent a significant force for development. These growth sensitive power groups seek consensus in the society with regard to ideology. That consensus can be formulated either via numerous media or indirectly by first creating the type of institution desired and then using it as a model for fashioning other institutions. Hence, Powelson views the growth process as being one in which an individual institution serving the needs of a growth sensitive group can serve a catalytic function in bringing about change in the entire institutional structure of the developing country.

In integrated form, the work by Baldwin [98], Schultz [37], and Powelson [35] provides a unified insight into the macro aspect of institutions with regard to their role in the development process. Clearly, an institutional infrastructure is needed for growth in most sectors, especially agriculture. Institutions come into being and are modified as a consequence of the changes in the demand for their services. Finally, growth sensitive groups can play key roles either as demanders of institutional services or as leaders within institutions that provide new, essential services for the development process in order to serve as an "engine" for development.

Induced Institutional Innovation

Ruttan [323] further develops the ideas originally articulated by Schultz in his induced institutional innovation hypothesis. Like Schultz, Ruttan views changes in institutions as a consequence of shifts in the demand for their services. More specifically he advances "a theory of institutional change in which shifts in demand for institutional change are induced by changes both in the relative price of factors and products and in the technology associated with economic growth, and in which the shifts in the supply of institutional change are induced by advances in knowledge in the social sciences" ([323] p. 34).

In applying the induced innovation approach to several case studies, insight is obtained into significant changes that occurred during the growth process. In the Philippines, increases in rice yields and population pressures brought about changes in the tenure institution. In particular, the increase in rice yields was due to the expansion of the national irrigation system and the introduction of high-yielding rice varieties. Even though they were illegal under the land reform code, the number of subtenancy arrangements increased dramatically as a consequence of the pressures due to increased rice yields and population growth. The second induced institutional change that occurred in the Philippines was the emergence of a new pattern of labor-employer relationships between farm operators and landless laborers. In this instance because of the increased rice yields, for the customary fraction of the crop which laborers customarily received for harvesting rice, farmers demanded that only those laborers who helped with the weeding operation during the rice growing season had a right to participate in the harvesting operation. Although not of an organizational form, this institution did result in changes as a consequence of the economic development that occurred in the society.

Ruttan's second illustration does involve an institution with organizational manifestations. In this case, the institution involved is agricultural research in Argentina. The lack of economic incentives for larger farmers to adopt yield-increasing technology acted as a stagnating force in that the demand did not shift for yield-increasing biological and chemical technologies which might have resulted from the development and expansion of agricultural research institutions. Further, he contends that the technology that was produced by the research institutions was oriented toward saving labor, a technology desired by the large land owners, rather than land-substituting biological and chemical technology which would have been more profitable on small rather than large farms.

Ruttan puts the theory of institutional innovation in perspective: "The public choice literature . . . has been concerned primarily with proving institutional performance through the design of more efficient institutions. The theory of institutional innovation complements this body of literature in that it is concerned with the forces which influence the direction of institutional innovation. It identifies changing resource endowments, interpreted through changing relative factor prices, as an important source directing both technical and institutional change" ([323] p. 267).

The final contribution in the macro area has been made by Blase [178]. He contends that the development of an institutional infrastructure is equally, if not more, important than the development of physical infrastructure in order for economic development to occur in a given economic sector of a developing country. Using agriculture as an illustration, he contends that the institutional infrastructure is only as strong as its weakest link. Hence, the productivity of any given institution within that institutional infrastructure is partially influenced by the relative productivities of the other institutions in the infrastructure.

Revisions and Refinements of Micro Concepts

A substantial revision in the micro approach has evolved in the school of thought lead by Korten et al. In addition to considering this new school of thought, refinements in the institution building approach associated with Esman et al., will be considered. Finally, the suggestion will be made that elements of both the new school of thought and the older school can be combined, resulting in a product that will be larger than the sum of the individual parts.

The New School of Thought: The Learning Process Approach

The leader of this school of thought, Korten, contends that relatively little attention has been given to the difficult problems of how to involve the poor in their own development. In fact, he questions whether planning using the "top down" approach is consistent with their needs. "The concepts and methods of the blueprint approach may be more of a hindrance than an aid in the programming of effective rural development action where the need is for an adaptive, bottom-up process of program and organizational development through which an adequate fit may be achieved between beneficiary needs, program outputs, and organizational competence" ([1] p. 502). After reviewing five successful programs in the area of rural development, Korten states, "These five programs were not designed and implemented—rather they emerged out of a learning process in which villagers and program personnel shared their knowledge and resources to create a program which achieved a fit between needs and capacities of the beneficiaries and those of the outsiders who were providing the assistance. Leadership and team work rather than blueprints were the key elements" ([1] p. 497).

Suffice it to say, the learning process approach is participative in nature and pragmatic in style. It emphasizes an evolutionary approach rather than grandiose strategy. The proponents of this school of thought see it as an alternative to the more traditional method of initiating projects, including their institutional manifestations.

Refinements in the Institution Building Approach

Numerous authors have viewed the institution building approach from different perspectives. As a consequence of applying the methodology, different views result concerning the most important of its component elements responsible for describing or explaining the evolution or the development of a host institution.

While leadership is frequently mentioned as the most important institution building variable, others are mentioned as crucial also. In *Bureaucracy and the Poor* [2], Korten and Alfonso illustrate how the internal structure of an institution can defeat the intentions of its leaders to refocus it. In addition to leadership, Esman and Uphoff found in their study of Asian institutions that linkages were of key significance [15]. Suffice it to say, the evidence is now clear that there is no one single institution building variable that spells the difference between life and death in the institutionalization process.

Toward Heterosis

In their anlaysis of Asian institutions Esman and Uphoff consider the extremes of the "top down" versus "bottom up" approaches to institutional development.

The following represent the two extremes with regard to the "top down," paternalistic approach and the "bottom up," populistic one:

> Two approaches appear to have dominated thinking about rural institutions, and both are unfortunately fallacious. The *paternalistic* approach assumes that rural people are passive and fatalistic, uninterested in improving their lives and incapable of initiative in making improvements. Consequently, everything must be done for them (or to them) in a top-down, bureaucratic manner.
>
> An opposing view is the *populistic* approach which assumes that rural people are vitally interested in change and completely capable of transforming their communities if only the politicians and bureaucrats would leave them alone. Both approaches derive from unreal stereotypes of rural people, who are neither as inert and ignorant as the first assumes, nor as virtuous and wise as assumed in the second. ([15], pp. xii–xiii)

In their analysis of Asian rural institutions, Esman and Uphoff identify participation as one of four behavioral factors making for more vital local organizations supporting rural development:

> *Participation*. In understanding the performance of local organizations, one key consideration is the opportunity they offer members for participation in decisions and programs that affect their interests. We do not mean "participation" in the *ex post facto* sense that some economists use the term, to describe the distribution of benefits from growth. Rather we refer to *ex ante*, before-the-fact involvement in the choices and efforts producing growth, which in fact has great influence on who will benefit from the fruits of growth. Local participation can bring useful, locally-based information and local interests into decision processes, and it can reveal and tap previously unrecognized managerial and leadership talents. The opportunity to participate, even when it is taken up by relatively few local people, enhances the legitimacy of local institutions and also of national government, provides a ready outlet

for the expression of grievances, and can generate local cooperative and self-help activities for development.

Like all good things, participation can be overdone and become unproductive for the welfare of most members of the community. Local organizations can become overpoliticized, immobilized by factionalism, with rural development objectives displaced by struggles for local power and control. Unfortunately, this extreme is often accepted stereotypically as the likely consequence of participation, especially by administrators who stand to benefit or at least have their lives made simpler by deprecating and eliminating any significant popular participation. Because of the possible outcome of wayward participation, there is utility in maintaining some central power of inspection and enforcement of standards, already mentioned above. There is an equally real danger, that inspection and controls will be used to throttle participation, as seen from the case study on panchayat raj in the Indian state of Andhra Pradesh. The challenge for central government is to encourage and tolerate, even promote, a significant range of participation at various levels of organization, without having it deflect effort from the urgent needs of rural development.

Our case studies reveal a considerable range of modes of local participation. At one extreme, participation may be manipulated by the central authorities and controlled within narrow regime-determined parameters, while at the other extreme, there can be freedom of farmers to determine how much they as individuals want to participate in the governance of local institutions and on what issues they should attempt to make their voices heard. There can indeed be much or little participation at either extreme, depending on people's response to the pressure, on one hand, or the opportunities, on the other. Observers must guard against culture-bound interpretations of participation which judge farmers' meeting for long hours in China or Korea simply as ritualistic or coerced because it is government-sponsored and even ordered, while regarding the same extent of participation in Sri Lanka or Israel as "real" because it corresponds more to Western ideas of "democratic" participation. We think it is important whether or not rural people can, by their own decisions, affect the course of government activity, local and/or central, and we consider such participation to be of great value to farmers and their families. But we also recognize the function of less empowered participation, where there can be considerable communication, venting of grievances, solicitation of suggestions, and winning of agreement on what is to be done. Rural China today seems alive and even sometimes adrift with participation, as often thousands of cadres from many communities meet for days on end; put up in schools and shops, using sleeping bags and open fires to sustain themselves, while issues, directives and evaluations are thrashed out. At the same time, we find Village Councils in Sri Lanka debating and passing resolutions on the Allende regime in Chile and on the international energy crisis, passing these up to the center, with every expectation that they will be considered seriously. In either case, the morale and enthusiasm of rural people can be heightened by such opportunities, however vicarious in substance and however effective or ineffective in outcome, for involvement in efforts beyond their own private sphere.

Our analysis of participation . . . showed an association, though not a perfect one, between participation in rural development. On the other hand, some success in rural development, as registered in Malaysia, can be achieved without much popular participation providing two conditions are met: (a) there is an effective administrative system capable of top-down action to influence rural areas, and (b) the center has sufficient resources not to need local contributions. These conditions are met in Malaysia, but very seldom are both satisfied elsewhere. Where administration is not so effective and where local resources must be mobilized for rural development, fairly extensive local participation becomes a requirement for effecting and maintaining change. ([15] pp. 81–84)

Again, with regard to the decentralization issue, Esman and Uphoff draw important conclusions from their analysis of a group of Asian institutions:

The more successful cases had engaged much more extensively in *decentralization* of operating decisions as well as local-level planning. Decentralization is usually more effective if it is *controlled* rather than complete. It is not an all-or-nothing proposition, but rather a matter of *kinds and degrees*. Decentralization is best seen and implemented in terms of specific functions, depending on the technologies involved and on the capacity of subordinate levels of administration and organization to perform the functions. Two patterns of decentralization should be distinguished: (a) *deconcentration* of authority for decisions and action within an administrative structure, and (b) *devolution*, which involves transferring functions and the resources to carry them out from agencies of the center to lower-level organizations not administratively controlled by the central government. ([15] p. xix)

Much of the early literature on institution building emphasized a social engineering, implied "top down" approach to institutional development. Recent literature, especially concerning rural institutions, by Korten and by Esman et al., indicates the need for much more emphasis on a participative, "bottom up" approach. The change in approach does not mean, however, that the need for institutionalization will disappear. On the contrary, such a change has profound implications for modifying the use of the institution building principles by those who build and implement strategies for the development of institutions and for the agencies that finance the development process. Both deserve elaboration.

Institution building practitioners will find that a more participative approach impacts especially on (1) "the rule makers at the center," (2) linkage formation, (3) leadership recruitment, (4) doctrine, and (5) strategy formulation. Each will be discussed briefly.

The need for rules formulated at the center is emphasized by Esman and Uphoff.

> On the whole, rural people are more capable and responsive than the paternalistic model of social change suggests, but less able to change their lives autonomously than the populistic model presumes. There is a deep-rooted contradiction in the paternalistic approach to rural development, which expects that passive "recipients" will become active cultivators and responsible citizens. On the other hand, the populistic approach neglects the common fact that entrenched local interests can dominate organizations at the community level unless there are some rules and even controls from higher levels. What should be developed is an institutionalized system which is neither just top-down nor bottom-up nor exclusively governmental. ([15] p. xiii)

The challenge for "the rules makers at the center" to formulate directives that will delegate the proper authority yet not enable local power brokers to dominate is a formidable one. In many developing countries where the distribution of wealth is highly skewed, clearly defined "rules of the game" and continuous monitoring from the center seem to be essential if the participative approach is to be truly that.

Linkage formation and management is stressed in the institution building literature. Indeed, some authorities contend that it is the most important contribution found in it. Some of the early writings infer that this should be given high priority as soon as the organization is in place. However, the more participative approach suggests reversing the order of these two events. Work with key existing institutions and their leaders in the environment should precede formation of the organization—even determine the type of organization put in place, if a more participative approach is followed. The implications for time required and order of events in an institution building strategy are substantial and will be discussed subsequently.

Leadership recruitment differs considerably under a participative as compared to the traditional institution building approach. Under the former, much of it could be expected in the preorganizational phase. If leaders did not emerge indigenously from the group, those recruited from the outside would likely need to be approved by the organizing group. Clearly, the emphasis on leadership in the literature warrants the early leadership cadre being approved by the organizing group, at minimum, and being selected by them, at maximum.

The implications may be greater for doctrine than for any other element in the institution building model. The participative approach has doctrinal implications in and of itself. The motivating function of doctrine should be strong for the organizing group if they feel they largely "own" the new institution from the outset. Likewise, the clarity of purpose and singleness of vision for an institution should be enhanced by a more participative approach. Clearly, the opportunity to "infuse the new institution with value," i.e., institutionalize it, should be expected to be greater for a participative approach than for a "top down" orientation.

Strategy formulation and content for a new institution under a participative approach will differ from the traditional one. Used in the sense of a series of predetermined, time-phased steps directed toward a specific goal, strategy with regard to formation will differ in terms of the actors who serve as its chief architects in the participative as compared to the traditional institution building approach. In the former, some of the chief architects could be expected to come from the organizing group. In the latter, these architects can be expected to be at the center. A change in the project designers will frequently result in a change in the design as well. Even more, the content of the strategy can be expected to be different. The time for preorganizing an institution building project in its environment will add considerably in most cases to the time allocated up front for a project. Advocates of the participative approach would be expected to justify this additional time by maintaining that it increases the probability of ultimately institutionalizing the effort. Early evidence in the literature tends to support that position.

Before turning to the implications for funding agencies, two comments are in order. The first is that the above discussion speaks to new organization situations rather than revitalization of an existing institution. While the implications for the latter are somewhat different, the basic thrust of grounding an institution as solidly as possible in its cliental groups in the environment is equally applicable for all institutions, regardless of where they are in their life cycles. The second is that the basic need is for institutionalization of development-oriented institutions. The difference is one of approach, not ultimate objective.

Funding agencies, especially external donors, have a limited number of alternative points of intervention available to them. Bernstein argues that institutions and government policies offer the greatest potential for influencing the direction of development ([34] pp. 5–6). In many instances, government policies are not accessible as points of intervention. Hence institutions take on increased importance for donors as well as being crucial to the host governments' development efforts. As a result, the potential to overwhelm, from the "top down," recipient host institutions is very great. There is a potential to be paternalistic in designing institution building strategies to accomplish the donor's objectives in as short a time as possible. Evidence in the literature suggests this is a formula for failure if the ultimate objective is a self-sustaining, auto-catalytic institution, one that truly is infused with value by the using society.

The role of a donor truly interested in fostering institutions that will serve as "engines" of the development process is a most challenging task. Hence, donors are well advised to read carefully the literature of lessons learned, especially in the last decade. Two of them are especially worthy of attention. First, the capital-assistance process format does not fit institution building situations well. The rush to obligate technical assistance funds results in, for example, technical assistance personnel arriving on the scene with counterpart personnel hardly knowing they are coming, much less agreeing to the objectives some high-level administrator in their institution agreed to. How can the clientele groups, which the institution is supposed to serve more effectively as a result of the technical assistance, feel they have an ownership interest in such a venture? Clearly, a shift to a more participative approach, especially at the outset of a project, has merit if the creation of truly viable institutions is the donor's ultimate objective.

The second lesson learned is that institution building is both an extremely complex and a time-consuming process. The complexity of the process is indicated by scholars, some of whom are in their third decade of studying institutional building, who say much remains to be researched. In fact, analysts are just learning to ask some of the right questions in complex areas of the process. The time-consuming nature of the process is evidenced by the apparent success of the learning process approach, which is likely to always require more time than the traditional approach. But this is not surprising. Careful reflection on what institutionalization is all about—*infusing an organization with value*—suggests that there are no quick, easy solutions.

Index of Authors